THE SUN & THE MOON
& THE ROLLING STONES

THE SUN & THE MOON & THE

ROLLING
STONES

SIDE 1

SG 9232

SPI
EG
EL&G
RAU

SPIEGEL & GRAU
NEW YORK

RICH COHEN

ISBN 978-0-8041-7923-2
ebook ISBN 978-0-8041-7924-9

Printed in the United States of America on acid-free paper

randomhousebooks.com
spiegelandgrau.com

2 4 6 8 9 7 5 3 1

FIRST EDITION

Book design by Simon M. Sullivan

To my wife, Jessica, for the lessons and the guitars

You tell me. I don't know. What's it like to live in a world where the Stones were always there? For you, there's always been the sun and the moon and the Rolling Stones.

—Keith Richards in conversation, 1994

CONTENTS

THE SUN & THE MOON
& THE ROLLING STONES

1

ROCK STARS TELLING JOKES

When it happens, it happens fast.

I was sitting on the stoop of my West Village apartment, waiting without knowing it. In the summer, the city smells like trash. The streets are desiccated, empty. It seems as if everyone has gone off to the mountains or the sea, leaving the ne'er-do-wells to haunt the red-brick alleys. Then, just like that, I was carried away by the Rolling Stones. It was akin to my childhood dream of running off with the circus. The midway. The strong man. The Ferris wheel revolving against the flat Kansas sky. In 1994, I was twenty-six years old and the Stones were crossing America. I'd been assigned to report on the tour for *Rolling Stone* magazine. I'd been bored, but I was not bored anymore.

In the next two weeks, I crossed half the continent. I stood in the corners of a dive bar as the Stones played their warm-up gig, got drunk in arenas open to the sky, dozed in hotel lobbies and dressing rooms, leaned against a speaker at the edge of the stage as the band played its encore, saw my country through rock star eyes, airports and towns becoming an insubstantial blur—only the next show was real. I sat beside Keith Richards on the Stones plane, goofed with Mick Jagger, who made fun of my hair when it was long and more fun of my hair when it was short, talked to Charlie Watts about New Orleans and the Civil War, then sat in his hotel room listening to jazz. I drank whiskey with Ron Wood and Bobby Keys when they got word that their friend and colleague, the pianist Nicky Hopkins, had died in Nashville. Keys grimaced, then tossed back four fingers of Jack Daniel's, eyes filled with tears.

In New York, we stayed fifty blocks from my apartment but a hundred miles from my old life. It had been summer. Now it was fall, glittery Manhattan, the endless avenues. I spent one long day at Radio City, watching the Stones rehearse for the *MTV Video Music Awards*. The appearance was to goose sales of their new album, *Voodoo Lounge*, but for the musicians it was just a quick hit between somewhere and somewhere else just like it. I didn't even go by my apartment, nor see friends. The circus had stopped in my town, but I was different, having been remade by proximity to the greatest sword swallowers, high-wire artists, and sideshow freaks in the world.

I hung out with the band instead, lingering backstage as Keith Richards and Ron Wood traded acoustic licks on Hank Williams tunes, sat in the empty theater as Mick Jagger snaked down the aisle, playing the sinewy harmonica intro to the single "Love Is Strong." On the way back to the dressing rooms, I had an encounter greater even than my childhood encounter with Joe DiMaggio before an old-timers game—the Yankee Clipper shouted at reporters, "Can't you sons-of-bitches see I'm naked?" Behind the curtain, Jagger and I bumped into Bruce Springsteen, who regarded us warily. It was a look I'd seen in high school on the faces of rival linebackers. There was a mumbled exchange, a comparing of notes. Mick introduced me as his "good friend." As we went away, Jagger shrugged, playground-style, whispering something like, "Well, you know, Bruce, he gives a very long concert."

That night, after the show, Virgin Records threw a party for the Stones at the Four Seasons hotel on Fifty-seventh Street. Empty at midnight, it was packed by two, crowded with rock stars who'd once filled posters on my bedroom wall. There was music, leather, eye shadow, Spanish heels, gin. Mick's publicist told Mick that Steven Tyler wanted to have a picture taken—"just the two of you."

"What do you think?" asked Jagger.

"Give it a miss," said the publicist. "Tyler wants people to think Aerosmith is up with the Stones, whereas, in fact, I mean, come on, Mick!"

The publicist talked about a *New York Post* article on the band's recourse to body waxing. It had been written by a reporter who'd covered the Stones for years. "She's enjoyed life on the inside," said the publicist. "Let's see how she likes life on the outside."

One of the Stones' people pushed me against a wall and asked me to "come upstairs and blow a joint."

Slipping away, I found myself in a circle of rock-'n'-roll masters: Steve Winwood of Traffic; Jim Capaldi, the band's drummer; Ron Wood; and Keith Richards. Though each had his own identity, they seemed to share a single face. Creased and beaten, aged like leather, pounded by abuse into a kind of beauty. An old guy getting a close look at Jagger once said, "You have more wrinkles than I do!" "They're laugh lines," said Mick. The guy guffawed: "Nothing's ever been that funny." But the guy was wrong—there has been something that funny, mainly, the joke that this generation of rock stars played on fate, which had them marked for lives of quiet desperation in factories and insurance firms but instead set them up like medieval princes in frock coats and buckles—a life that for centuries had been the sole entitlement of the debauched nobility.

Each man in that circle had electric energy and strung-out glory— drank too much, stayed out too late, brain fried and fingers gnarled, but my God, could they play. These were the last of the great rock stars, a species that's going the way of the snow leopard. Those who survive are precious and strange, relics of an ancient dispensation, that era when the music mattered above all else—when you believed the next album would clarify everything. The men in that circle were human expressions of that belief, heroes who established the revolution, then followed it to the end. They stood laughing and drinking, telling dirty jokes. "Did you guys hear the one about the pianist who was playing songs for his producer?" Capaldi asked. "He plays two beautiful songs, saying, 'The first is called "My Dick Is Long" and the next is called "My Penis Is Huge."' Then he goes to the bathroom. When he returns, the producer says, 'Do you know your fly is open and your dick's hanging out?'

"'Know it?' says the pianist. 'I wrote it!'"

Richards leaned back and roared. "'Know it? I wrote it!'"

As the men laughed, it hit me. I'd always sensed there were people somewhere having more fun than me. I'd always believed there was a better party. And there was! And I'd found it! No need to check my messages, look over someone's shoulder, wonder where to go next. I

was at the center of the best party in the world. For the first time in my life, I was exactly where I wanted to be.

"What about you?" Capaldi said. "Do you have a joke?"

I told him I did not, that I was, in many ways, humorless.

Steve Winwood looked at me, really looked at me, for the first time. A legend of British rock, author of "Back in the High Life Again" and "Higher Love," and before that a driving force behind the Spencer Davis Group, Blind Faith, and Traffic, Winwood was forty-six with tousled hair and a needle-sharp face. When I told him I worked for *Rolling Stone*, his sharp eyes became accusatory. "You know, you're a bastard," he said, suddenly. "A nasty bastard. I've been waiting years to tell you that, and there it is! You nasty bastard!"

"Hey, Stevie, do you know this kid?" asked Ron Wood, surprised.

"Hell, yes, this bastard has trashed every solo album I've ever released. You think there's no life after Traffic?" Winwood went on. "What was I supposed to do, lay down and die when the band broke up? Well, I won't die for you. No, I won't die for you."

There was an awkward silence, then everyone cracked up. It got an even bigger laugh than "Know it? I wrote it!" Taking my arm, Keith said, "You're crazy, Stevie. You're talking about fucking nineteen seventy-four. This kid was six years old! What does he know about Traffic?"

"You do know *Rolling Stone* is a magazine, not a person," Wood added.

Just then, I had my second epiphany. Time would always separate me from these guys, from this generation. I'd missed everything: 1964, 1969, 1972—those were the years that mattered. I'd been born too late. Whatever happened had happened already. I'd spent my entire life trying to reach this party. By the time I got there, everyone was old. Belatedness: it's the condition of little brothers and sisters, the sons and daughters of old parents, third children who showed up just in time to see a cigarette floating in the last cocktail of the night. It defines my generation. We're pinched. Above us, the baby boomers, who consumed every resource and every kind of fun. Below us, the millennials, the children of the baby boomers, who've remade the world into something virtual and cold. The boomers consumed their childhood, then, in a sense, consumed our childhoods, too. They overimbibed, lived to such excess there's nothing left for us but to tell the story.

Time distanced me from the Stones, but it gave me something, too. Perspective. Coming at the end means being able to comprehend the entire story. Rock 'n' roll was more than just a million garage bands; more than just Top Forty radio; more than just A&R men and record companies. It was an attitude and an age. The Stones were the greatest band of that age, and in a way the only band that mattered, because, in them, you had both the ultimate and the ur, a group that can stand for all the others. If you tell their story, you tell *the* story. But you need perspective to do it. You have to know the end to understand the beginning. Evening light. Venus in the east. The story of the boomers told by Generation X. The Stones are a train rolling across a valley. I can see every car, the first and the last, the engine and the caboose, which gets smaller as it goes away.

I would travel with the band on various tours, first as a writer for *Rolling Stone,* then as the screenwriting partner of Mick Jagger. We were working with Martin Scorsese on a script about a fictional record executive, whose rise and fall would encapsulate the era. I got stories firsthand and was able to test ideas with the world's greatest front man, though Jagger tends to diminish his own role. He abhors the temptation to turn singers into gods, the fate of John Lennon seemingly never far from his mind. Yet it's clear the Stones were, for a time, the avant-garde, which is one reason Jagger keeps his mouth shut. If you live audaciously, don't brag. Over time, it became obvious to me that what began with a magazine story was turning into something more—an epic and an obsession, a saga in which a handful of musicians stand for the longings of a society.

I began to seek out witnesses who could fill in the gaps, explain puzzles, add color. I tracked down colleagues and friends of the band; competitors; pioneers; precursors; producers and engineers; drug buddies and assistants; record men; girlfriends of the one-night variety and those more akin to common-law wives. I read memoirs, biographies. There've been dozens, perhaps hundreds of books. For people involved with the Stones, no matter how briefly, the experience tends to be the most vivid of their lives. I watched documentaries and listened to the records again and again. I looked at pictures. The Stones were among the most photographed people of the twentieth century. I went to places that loom large in their story: houses where Mick and Keith grew up in Dartford, England; the pub where they first performed; the apartment where they lived in squalor one cold winter; the club in Richmond where they became a sensation; the swank flats and estates they purchased when they'd made it; Olympic Studios in Barnes; Chess Records in Chicago; the Altamont Speedway; Joshua Tree National Park; the mansion in France where they recorded their greatest album; the clinic in Switzerland where Keith Richards kicked heroin. I kept a handful of questions in mind: Why was this music important? Why do the soap-opera adventures of the Stones still fascinate? Can rock save your soul? Is it a religion? If so, why did it go the way of Zoroastrianism? Should we worship the life or the message? Is there a graceful way to get old?

That night at the party in 1994, the Stones struck me as decadent. They were an oldies act, which is less about biological age than about spirit. The Stones had become predictable. Invention had given way to repetition. They were doing what they did because it's what they'd always done. At the beginning, they imitated black blues musicians. At the end, they imitated themselves. And yet, even at the most tired shows, before the most jaded crowds, you could still, now and then, just for a moment, catch a glimpse of what they had been: a revolution with ten hands, four chords, and a groove.

2

THE COWBELL AND THE POSTER

When I was ten years old, my brother ascended to heaven. He did it by moving from the second floor of our house to the attic, which, with its shag carpet and cedar walls, was the frontier. No curfew. No law. Though not allowed up, I now and then stood at the bottom step, listening to the music that cascaded down from the speakers, woofers and tweeters, amp and subamp, turntable. Once, tagging after my father, who'd gone up to let my brother know he was not in fact beyond all authority, I was able to get a good look at the stereo.

When did that bastard get a Nakamichi tape deck?

The other time I saw the equipment, and it hardly counts, was at the stereo store in the mall. There was an outer room filled with downmarket brands and Mickey Mouse doodads; then, behind glass, an inner sanctum with the sort of intricate equipment favored by people who had understanding as well as knowledge. Inside *that* room, inside the inside, was still another room, an oblong enclosure known as "the listening egg," where, squeezed between walls of speakers, a customer could have a dramatic last listen before making the purchase. One afternoon, just before the deal was done, I got to recline in the egg as my brother's soon-to-be speakers blasted a song the salesman considered perfectly suited to "demo the gear": "Life's Been Good" by Joe Walsh, cranked to the max, the druggy guitar solo wandering through me like the flu.

Otherwise, I had to enjoy my brother's stereo from a distance, usually picking up just the rumble of the bass or the scream of a rock god kicking a power ballad into gear. But one day, a strange rhythm touched something inside me, something I did not even know existed. I was lying in bed when I heard the cowbell and twangy guitar. I got up, walked over, and stood at the bottom of the stairs. Opening the door, I crept up and quietly took in the scene: a coffee table covered with empty beer bottles, a record on the turntable, the stereo aglow. My brother was in a chair, head back, eyes closed. A poster was tacked up behind him. Somehow I knew the people in that poster were responsible for this song, "Honky Tonk Women." For a moment, it seemed as if they were actually playing it, as if the music was coming from the band in the picture, which looked exactly like a band should. The Stones in Paris circa 1976. Jagger in front, leading his commandos on a nighttime raid. In concert, he darts like a hummingbird, impossible to study. In the poster, he'd been pinned like a specimen to a board. He was grotesque yet handsome, with the outsized features of an adolescent, a man who never grew into his face. Richards stood beside him, in striped pants and a gauzy shirt undone to the fourth button. He looked down as he played, eyelashes long and black. Bill Wyman, the bassist, stood beside the drummer, Charlie Watts, who grinned mischievously. All the musicians were jammed into a small space—the belts and crankshafts of a compact engine. It was a real band. That's what got me. Not the sold-out arenas or the hit records, but five guys playing together, like a family or a gang. I could imagine no better fate. School at bay, parents at bay, adulthood at bay. A group of buddies who started as kids and kept on forever. My brother suddenly loomed above, ordering me to leave, but it was too late. The arrow had stuck fast.

Before this, music had played a background role in my life. It was wallpaper. If it was peopled by clowns, I'd look. Otherwise, I didn't notice. It was usually just my father blasting Frank Sinatra in the Sedan de Ville. "Nice 'n' Easy," "Come Fly with Me." Until I was eight,

I believed "My Way" was the national anthem, as that's what Sinatra says on his record *The Main Event*. "Ladies and gentlemen, I will now sing the national anthem, though you needn't rise." "Rhinestone Cowboy" was the first song I loved. I heard Glen Campbell sing it on WLS, then saved up to buy the single. The defiant self-pity, the cheap sound of dime-store finery. When treated wrongly, I closed my bedroom door and convened another session of rhinestone therapy. "I've been walkin' these streets so long, singin' the same old song, I know every crack in these dirty sidewalks of Broadway . . ."

Like everyone else, I soon found my way to the Beatles. This was 1977 or 1978, years after the group had split. You could listen to them with confidence. You did not have to worry about the Beatles making a bad record. It was all out there, finished and done. I remember my father dismissing "Here Comes the Sun." "If the sun really did come," he said, "we'd all burn up in about a second." But there was something annoyingly safe about the Beatles. They represented granny glasses and peace signs. By then, I'd already made my first forays to the local record store, a mom-and-pop shop run by Wally King, a cantankerous old man who'd opened his place in the sheet music days. For years, Wally offered a promotion: for any purchase over seven dollars, he'd throw in a mouth harp, that brassy instrument held between the teeth and plucked. In the 1970s, parts of my Illinois town resembled Appalachia, the kids on their haunches, dead-eyed and twanging.

My first solo trip to the store was a baptism by fire. For months, I'd been pleading with my brother to take me into his musical confidence. I wanted to sit with the big kids, listen, pontificate, theorize. One day, he gave me a kind of test. Shoving a ten-dollar bill into my hand, he said, "Go to Wally King's and get the new Kansas album, the one with 'Dust in the Wind.' We'll listen to it in the attic."

I searched the racks for twenty minutes, then went to the old man for help. He took a fat book from under the counter, flipped it open, scanned. He found a listing for the Kansas record with a picture of the cover: a waterfall, a boat going over. "We're out of this record," said

Wally, "but let me show you something." He got a different record from the stacks, held it beside the Kansas cover. "This album also has a waterfall on it," Wally told me. "See for yourself. Almost exactly alike. Your brother will have a hard time telling the difference."

"Who made it?"

"A fella called Slim Whitman," said Wally. "He's been all over the world, singing over his own guitar, playing beautiful country songs. Which, if you think about it, is a wonderful life for a singer. The only life. And, in truth, in all those travels he most assuredly visited Kansas, probably dozens of times. So you see, the story of that other band, the 'Dust in the Wind' boys, is, in a way, included in the story of the great Slim Whitman. Like I said, your brother will have a hard time telling the difference."

When I gave the record to my brother, he looked it over and sighed. If my brother had been my father, he'd have called me a schmuck. As it was, he merely handed it back, saying, "You owe me five bucks." It was my first lesson in the difference between the right music and the wrong music, the perfect song, which is like the sky ten minutes before sunset, and a song that chills like a rainy Tuesday afternoon.

I did my research after that, reading the literature, making my way into this new consumerist world with terrific deliberation. The first authentic album I purchased was Jimi Hendrix's *Smash Hits*, which I placed atop my pile of kiddie records like a C-note on a stack of one-dollar bills. For a time, I lingered between two worlds: childhood and adolescence. But all that changed when I heard "Honky Tonk Women." The cowbell that opens the song was like a muezzin call, ushering me in to a new life. I became a rock-'n'-roll monotheist. For years, there was just one band, the Rolling Stones. Their music suggested a dangerous world of drugs and liquor and all manner of sin that I looked forward to trying myself.

My collection began with *England's Newest Hit Makers*, the first record the Stones released in the United States. The cover is stark. Five faces: Mick, Keith, Charlie, Bill, and beautiful blond Brian Jones.

If you see a towhead amid brunets, pray for him, as he's marked for destruction. This was early Stones; most of the songs were covers. "Not Fade Away," "I Just Want to Make Love to You," "I'm a King Bee." Its distinction was voice, energy. The electric guitar lines of Brian Jones, the driving rhythm of Keith Richards. The best songs hum like an engine, a machine on a black night. "Honest I Do," "Little by Little," "Carol." They made me feel grown up, mean. And sent me out for more records. It became a routine: save five bucks, go to Wally King's, buy a Stones album.

When I'd exhausted Wally's inventory, I expanded my search, seeking out stores up and down the North Shore of Chicago, eventually finding my way into the city. As I entered the second year of junior high, my internal map was riddled with record stores. Record City in Skokie. Vintage Vinyl in Evanston. On red-letter days, I'd tell my parents I was going to my friend Mark's house, then make my way into the city. From a window in the back of the bus, I watched the suburban lawns give way to concrete. In Evanston, I'd transfer to the "L," which wandered beside asphalt roofs and apartment buildings beneath a sky so blue it hurt. I got off across from Loyola University, walked a block, went up a flight of stairs, through a door, unmarked in the way of a speakeasy, and into Round Records. Having burned through the legitimate catalog, I had come to that part of my life dedicated to the hunting of bootlegs, illegal recordings of Stones concerts. Some were elaborate productions, complete with cover art and liner notes, but most were amateurish—a tape made by a guy in the fifteenth row. You could hear people talking between numbers. Such recordings were usually worthless. But now and then, when you came across a song the band hardly ever played, an oddity or a gem, the feeling of triumph was akin to that of a big game hunter. The more unlikely the find, the greater the satisfaction—it was a quest made obsolete by Napster, YouTube, Google, and Sonos, where everything is right here, right now. Those poor millennials! They'll never know the glory of stumbling across a recording of the Stones playing Eel

Pie Island in 1964, or the lost art of the mix tape, all those blissful hours spent assembling the perfect sequence of songs.

When you really get into the Stones, listening is not enough. You want to embody the music, live the life. Depending on temperament, you will be Mick, Charlie, Keith, or Bill. You will move like Jagger down the middle school hall or shrug off preteen miseries with the nonchalance of Richards. For me, this resulted in junior high talent shows. In 1981 and 1982, we dressed as the Stones, then played in the auditorium, having learned just enough technique to get through a song a year. I walked into the crowd dressed as Keith in my sister's studded shirt. I lit a cigarette in the aisle, took a drag, and flicked it into a crowd of sixth graders.

I got to see the Stones in concert that year at the Rosemont Horizon, an arena out by O'Hare Airport. It was my first real concert, and what a way to begin! They were promoting *Tattoo You*. I remember waiting for them to come on, the cheer that went up whenever a roadie crossed the dark stage, the smoke that hung above us like a cloud. For me, these were like the atmospherics before the Battle of Austerlitz. I'll never forget them. Bill Wyman played the bass riff that opens "Under My Thumb." Keith took after him with a crisp lick. Mick danced out in football pants and jersey. "Let's Spend the Night Together." "Shattered." "Start Me Up." They played it all. At one point, Mick rode a cherry picker over the crowd, hands reaching up to him like the tentacles of a sea anemone. There is nothing quite like Jagger on the move, stalking his turf, shimmying in that dangerous space between male and female. If you are an adolescent boy, it can touch you in a place that makes you excited, confused, and a little ashamed. I danced, thrilling in the fact that Mick and Keith and Charlie and Bill and Woody were right there in front of me, in all dimensions, sharing the same space, grooving and real. Going from the record and the fantasy to the arena and the reality—it was one of the best moments of life. Just like that, you morph from a kid in a bedroom, alone and lonely, to a body in a crowd, lost in the communal energy of the great band. There was a beautiful dirtiness to the familiar songs played live, the way the band screwed up but smiled and kept going, missed chords, the most practiced material giving way to unexpected tangents. It was the familiar toy taken out of its protective wrapping. It came as a revelation—perfect ain't perfect; rock 'n' roll is chaos. I liked it best when Jagger stood at the microphone, the Stones arranged as they'd been in the poster in my brother's room. Not a band—a gang, a pack of junkyard dogs.

Like most great groups, the Rolling Stones begin and end with friendship.

3

THE 8:28 TO LONDON

It's a founding episode in rock 'n' roll.

October 17, 1961. Mick Jagger was on the city-bound platform of the Dartford train station in suburban London, waiting for the 8:28 into the city. An eighteen-year-old student at the London School of Economics, he was late for a lecture in financial history. Keith Richards, a student at Sidcup Art College, does not remember where he was going. He'd known Mick when they were kids in Dartford— a gritty town famous for insane asylums and a fireworks factory that exploded—but they'd lost touch. Keith recognized Mick first. He had a businessman's glaze, but he was carrying records. It was unusual to see a kid with one album, let alone a stack. Keith went over: "Whatcha got?" He later said it was the first time he'd ever seen a Muddy Waters record. Before that, the bluesman had been a kind of legend, spoken of as the Indians once spoke of a great river beyond the horizon. Mick also had records by Little Walter and Chuck Berry. All were on the same label: Chess Records. The name resonated of far-off Chicago, that strange city where Mississippi farmers plugged into an urban current. When the train came, Keith and Mick sat side by side and talked all the way into the city.

Because it's a legend, details vary. In one telling, Keith wears a scarf, Mick wears a blazer. In another, Keith wears a trench coat that sweeps along the platform. In still another, he carries a guitar. Mick's inventory changes, too. Sometimes it's Chuck Berry's *Rockin' at the Hops* and *Muddy Waters at Newport*. Sometimes it's *The Best of Muddy Waters* and Chuck's *One Dozen Berrys*. But the crucial details remain the same. It's always Chess Records—because Chess pressed the sort of electric blues Mick and Keith loved. (Jagger had begun sending away to the label a few months before.) It's always the train platform, city-bound side, which can be read literally—Mick was late for class—or metaphorically, as a preacher reads the Bible. Though they did not know it, Jagger and Richards were headed for the city—that is, the big time. And they were going together. It's perfect that they met on a train platform, as the train has always been of great symbolic importance to the blues. The train is escape—it carries the Delta farmer from slave country to the metropolis. The train is freedom, power. That's why, when you listen to the great old blues songs, you almost always hear steel wheels in the rhythm.

In every version, Mick is the one with the records, whereas Keith has only a guitar. Because records equal wealth. Mick had it. Keith did not. Keith played rock 'n' roll for the same reasons as Chuck Berry—because he loved it and because there was nothing else he could do. But Mick had choices, was on his way to a comfortable life when he ran into Keith. Which is why Keith would always question Mick's commitment. Mick loved the blues in the way of a rich kid: like a hobby. Keith loved it as a sick man loves penicillin. It was his best hope.

It was a golden moment in rock 'n' roll—some think it never got better. Elvis had remade the world in 1956 with the release of "Heartbreak Hotel." Just about every important British rock musician of the sixties and seventies remembers lying in bed listening to Armed Forces Radio when the King lit up the night. It was style as much as anything: the stripped-down production, the tremble in the vocal, the tinny guitar. The emptiness between notes brought the country roads of the New World to life. English showbiz impresarios cashed in with knockoffs: Tommy Steele, Adam Faith. British Presleys riding a craze for everything American, not just the music but the clothes, the lingo. It raises the big question: Why? Why did American trash music, poor-boy music, so idiosyncratic and unique to the American experience, a music that came out of the forbidden mix of white and black, mulatto and octoroon, a music that combined the oldest country traditions with the deepest Delta blues, a music that tells the history of the nation—from slave ships to civil war to the Great Migration to factories in the smoky Midwest—find such fertile ground in England?

If you ask people who lived through that period, who were ten or fifteen when Elvis broke, they paint the same picture: England after the Second World War, supposedly victorious but experiencing a kind of ruin. Bombed-out blocks and rubble, muck in the passageways. The country was broke, the empire being dismantled. Goodbye, India. Goodbye, Mandalay Bay. Just this bleak island, where it began, where it will end. Wartime rationing continued into the mid-1950s. During the Beatles' first U.S. tour, a reporter asked George Harrison if he'd had a record player growing up. "A record player?" Harrison said, incredulous. "We didn't have sugar!" Keith later spoke about scoffing at the Germans during an early gig in Munich: "It's 'cause of you we got bad teeth—no oranges!"

Filth, rot, dissipation, gray shadows on broken walls. Brits who came of age after the war liken their youth to a black-and-white film. No vibrancy, no warmth. The coming of rock 'n' roll was Technicolor. Bubblegum pink! Eggshell blue! No one ever cared more about music than that first generation, for whom it was brilliance and life, a chance for fun, an escape from history—America as only a sad kid could dream it. "There'd been a tremendous war," Ethan Russell, an official Stones photographer in the sixties, told me. "Western civilization was in shambles. England was a wreck. Keith Richards was a kid, living in a shitty house on a bombed-out street in Dartford. But he was listening to Chuck Berry. One of my favorite pictures is Keith doing Chuck Berry's duck walk on that street! He's fourteen years old, but he's already out of there!"

Rock 'n' roll's first flush had played out by the time Keith accosted Mick on the railroad platform. Part of it was just the normal cycle. "It's a five-year progression," Neil Sedaka told me. "The Everly Brothers had five years of hits. Connie Francis, five years. Fats Domino and Brenda Lee, five years. All those artists who broke in the 1950s were done by the time the Beatles and Stones came of age." Part of it was a cascade of mishaps and disasters. Elvis went into the Army in 1958. He'd come out in 1960 but would never be the same—the service bridled him, snuffed out that blue electricity. Jerry Lee Lewis married his thirteen-year-old cousin, which took him out of the game. Chuck Berry was arrested for violating the Mann Act. Little Richard, the most foppish and over-the-top of the early stars, had a vision that convinced him he was in danger of losing eternal life. "If you want to live with the Lord, you can't rock 'n' roll," he explained. "God doesn't like it." It happened on a flight in Australia. An engine flamed out, the plane shuddered. Little Richard got on his knees—and his purple pants did not wrinkle, nor his pink handkerchief crease—and pleaded with God, promising that if his life were spared, he would devote himself to gospel. He threw his rings into Sydney Harbor a few days later, returned to Alabama, and entered the Seventh Day Adventist Church.

By 1963, the pop charts were littered with bubblegum. "Hey Paula" by Paul & Paula. "I'm Leaving It Up to You" by Dale & Grace. That's when many Brits found their way to the blues. It was a refuge, a place to escape the deprivations of radio. The blues was real. Kids like Jagger and Richards got into the blues for the same reason kids of my generation got into Public Enemy and NWA. It was about authenticity. At the beginning, they listened to whatever they could find. Over time, the pole stars emerged. Muddy Waters. Chuck Berry. Jimmy Reed. The Delta blues became an obsession indistinguishable from faith. For the Stones, it was religion. In this, they've been fortunate. An artist needs a belief. It does not matter whether that belief is Rastafarianism or Communism. It's the structure of belief that matters—it gives their work coherence, shape. It's there even when you don't know it. Of course, the Stones have made some terrible records, but the blues always saved them in the end.

4

COLLECTORS

Jagger and Richards started as geeks. "Record hounds and record collectors," Mick explained. "We'd go from store to store, from house to house, listening. Then we'd go to other people's houses and listen to their records. It's that time in life when you're like a stamp collector. The records were interesting in themselves, but collecting was the real point. We were getting to know this music, the labels and the business, learning the songs inside out."

"We must've spent a year before the Stones got together just collecting," said Richards.

When I asked Ian McLagan of the Faces—a keyboardist who later toured with the Stones—how he'd started in music, he said, "By going around buying records, which was close to impossible. Because there were no good records for sale in England in the late fifties and early sixties. I lived in a suburb called Hounslow, near Heathrow Airport. I walked into the local store one day and said, 'I want *Muddy Waters at Newport*.' And the guy behind the counter said, 'There's nobody called Muddy Waters.' I said, 'I also want Thelonious Monk.' He said, 'You've made it up.' But he looked in the guide and sure enough! It took weeks and weeks for my records to arrive. The boom was all about availability, or lack of. That's my theory. The music wasn't available in England, which made us crazy. When you heard it, you'd go,

'What the fuck? I've got to have it.' It was a small bunch of us doing this. We all knew each other. It was like a secret club."

If Jagger and Richards couldn't find a particular song, they'd teach themselves to play it. That's really how the Stones began. Even then, Mick was out front, carrying shy, whispery Keith. It was a perfect role for Mick, who was raised in the bottom rung of show business. His father was a gym teacher, in sweatsuit with stopwatch and whistle, who ascended to the level of small-time guru. In 1959, he hosted the BBC show *Seeing Sport*. In one clip, Mick lingers as his father says, "Here's Michael wearing a pair of ordinary gym shoes."

Mick was precocious. Several people told me the same astonishing fact: Jagger was the first kid in Dartford to discover rock 'n' roll. It was the summer of '55, *before* Elvis. By high school, he was singing at parties—always the same song, "La Bamba" by Ritchie Valens. After all, you couldn't mess up the lyrics. He teamed up with classmate Dick Taylor, a Dartford kid who followed the same trajectory. One night, when Mick was fifteen, they borrowed a car, lied to their parents, and drove to Manchester to see Buddy Holly and the Crickets, who'd just released their second album, which included several classics. It was Jagger's first real concert. "After that, it was only rock 'n' roll for Mick," Taylor told me. "Nothing else stood a chance. All the way home, he couldn't stop talking."

Jagger formed his first band a few days later. That's what happens when you see Buddy Holly. They rehearsed at Taylor's house. Dick played guitar. Mick sang because he had no shame and could, without feeling self-conscious, mimic the intonation, phrasing, and mojo of black Americans. "We rehearsed for goodness knows how long but never thought of doing a gig," Taylor said. "We just played. It was me, Mick, my friend Rupert Beckwith. Now and then, my mother would look in and smile."

"Me and my friends used to sit in the next room and crease up with laughter," Taylor's mom said. "It was lovely, but so loud. I always heard more of Mick than I saw of him. I didn't dream they were seri-ous."

When I asked Taylor what kind of music they played, he said, "La Bamba."

When I asked Taylor about Mick's voice, he told me a story: One day, Mick collided with a kid on the basketball court and bit deep into his tongue. On doctor's orders, he didn't speak for a week. Taylor fig-ured, *That's it, time to find a new singer.* But Mick turned up at rehearsal and insisted on performing. When he opened his mouth, he sounded different, guttural, strange. It was akin to the moment when Marlon Brando, wrestling with stagehands, busted his nose. Too pretty before, a sensation after. Imperfection made him interesting. It was the same with Jagger: his voice was formed by a happy accident. I don't know what it sounded like before, but it was sly and dirty after, instantly rec-ognizable. Good voices are a dime a dozen; what a front man needs is distinction. "Mick's voice sounded so weird after that," Taylor told me. "How it sounds now, actually. That crash-up changed it completely."

Mick Jagger's voice is a perfect vehicle for the blues. Not just the tenor, but how he employs it. Phrasing is an instinctual art. It can't be taught. Phil May, who, along with Taylor, later formed the band the Pretty Things, used to play with the boys in Dartford. "They were all very amateurish at this stage of the game," May once said, "but Mick was unique even then. He could get inside a blues lyric and give it expression. He acted out a lyric instead of just performing it."

Jagger's talent began in mimicry. He could imitate any sound, be-come any person, which often meant a nineteen-year-old kid howling like a black bluesman. At times, he parodied to the point of min-strelsy, but he usually got it right. "Even when the rest of us could barely play," Taylor said, "Mick was spot-on."

Richards joined the band in a roundabout way. Though he'd been hanging out with Jagger, it was Taylor who recruited him. Taylor was

at Sidcup Art College with Richards. They'd hang out in the boys'
club, where would-be bohemians smoked cigarettes, talked philosophy, and jammed. "Keith wanted more than anything to sound like
Elvis's guitarist, Scotty Moore, while everyone else was playing folk or
jazz," Taylor told me. "Keith knew I was in a band but never asked to
come along. I never thought to ask him. Then he had that famous
meeting with Mick at the Dartford station. That's how he came in.
There was suddenly a mutual friend. So Keith got on the bus with me
one day, and we started rehearsing. He had a little arch-top
Höfner"—an acoustic guitar—"and we put a pickup on it. At that
point, we had a surplus of guitarists, so I said, all right, I'll play drums."

"I think one night we all just went round to Dick's house and had
a jam," Keith said. "That was the first time we got into playing. Kids'
backroom stuff, just for ourselves. . . . We started doing things like
Billy Boy Arnold's 'Eldorado Cadillac,' Eddie Taylor, Jimmy Reed.
Didn't attempt any Muddy Waters yet, or Bo Diddley."

"Keith was limited," Taylor explained, "but what he played, he played good. It was two Scotty Moore songs at first, some Billy Boy Arnold. But he developed quickly. Very soon he was getting off those Chuck Berry licks. It didn't take Keith long to turn into Keith in his playing."

In the summer of 1962, the boys performed at the Dartford church hall, their first show. A few weeks later, they played the Odeon theater in Woolwich. By then, Taylor had decided to make a demo—four songs, roughly played: "I Ain't Got You," "Shop Berries," "Around and Around," and "La Bamba." When I asked Taylor if the band on the demo sounded like the Stones, he said, "Sort of. In a way. Not completely. A bit. Kind of. You can tell. Not really. But yeah, why not?"

Taylor planned to send the tape to Alexis Korner, who fronted the best blues band in England, but first he needed to name the group. "I have a horrible feeling it was Mick who thought of Little Boy Blue and the Blue Boys," Taylor told me. "Because what sort of name is that? I often fantasized about what would've happened if, when we met Brian Jones, instead of calling ourselves the Rolling Stones, we'd said, 'There's more of us than you; we're going to stick with Little Boy Blue and the Blue Boys.'

"I recorded the demo on my tape machine," Taylor went on. "We must've made a copy, so I suppose we had two tape machines. I sent one to Alexis, kept the other. In 1965, I went on tour to New Zealand, and when I came back I discovered that some idiot had recorded over my Little Boy Blue and the Blue Boys demo. Even then, I realized it was a foolish thing to do. The Stones were already huge. Then, about fifteen years ago, I got a call from a big auction house, Sotheby's, I think. And they said, 'We have this tape we'd like you to authenticate.' I leapt in the air; maybe the demo didn't get taped over! But it turned out that a friend had taped one of our rehearsals. Mick bought it for fifty grand."

At those first gigs, Keith kept to the shadows, watching his fingers as he played. He was like a character out of Dickens, an urchin, a dodger emerging from tenement shadows, skinny and fast. The guitar was his revenge and only chance. Otherwise, he'd be the hack that picks you up at Heathrow and talks all the way into London. His persona has been exaggerated over the years, but the outline was plain from the start. The outlaw, the pirate. "[He] used to dress in a cowboy outfit, with holsters and a hat, and he had these big ears that stuck out," said Jagger, who met Keith when they were six years old. "I asked him what he wanted to do when he grew up. He said he wanted to be like Roy Rogers and play guitar."

Richards grew up in an apartment on the wrong side of Dartford, amid coal fires and men in shirtsleeves staring out second-story windows. His father was named Bert and had side-whiskers and smoked a curved pipe. He'd been in the first wave at Normandy on D-day. The English rockers had that big thing behind them: the war and the poverty that followed. Bert Richards was a printer and later a foreman for General Electric. For a time, he worked in a lightbulb factory, where he met Keith's mother, an office girl named Doris. Keith was born December 18, 1943, an only child. He was funny looking, a gutter rat with dark circles around his eyes. They called him Monkey because of his ears. He was a loner and was bullied. He learned to linger in his own mind, he learned to run—a perfect childhood for rock 'n' roll, shared by a thousand runts who found solace in a symphony of power chords.

He attended Wentworth Primary with Jagger. Choir was the only thing he liked, an angel with a dirty face hitting the high notes. He was chosen for an ensemble that performed for the Queen at her coronation. Westminster Abbey. Royal Guards. Handel's *Messiah*. He was removed from chorus when his voice changed—the first blow. Then he tanked the eleven-plus, the British exam that determined a kid's fate—the second blow. Mick, having passed, was sent to Dartford Grammar, where he'd be prepared to enter the middle class. Keith, having failed, was sent to Dartford Technical. He was one of those kids who vanish, then turn up years later behind a pneumatic drill. When poor attendance proved him ill-suited for even the trades, he was given a spot at Sidcup—his final chance. "A lot of music goes on in art schools," he said later. "That's where I got hung up on guitar, because there were a lot of guitar players around, playing anything from Big Bill Broonzy to Woody Guthrie." Keith spent many afternoons in the record section of the Dartford Woolworth's. He later described the listening booths, with their turntables, glass walls, and kids always banging to get in, as his classroom.

Music was a family business. Keith's maternal grandfather, Gus Dupree, led a dance band in the thirties and another dance band, Gus Dupree and His Boys, in the fifties. Gus played saxophone, but he could tease a song from any instrument. Even when semiretired, he still performed on weekends. Though Keith plays a different kind of music, he credits his grandfather as a key inspiration. (No Gus Dupree, no "Satisfaction.") For years, Keith stared longingly at a guitar set atop his grandfather's upright piano. When he asked if he could hold it, Gus said, "Someday, when you're ready." "I can't remember when it was that he took the guitar down and said, 'Here you go,'" Keith writes in his memoir, *Life*. "Maybe I was nine or ten, so I started pretty late." Gus insisted Keith learn just one song, the faux-traditional Cuban ballad "Malagueña." If you can play that, Gus told him, you can play anything.

Keith got his first real guitar when he was fifteen, a Rosetti "professional style" acoustic. It was a gift from his mother. Perhaps this is when Keith started referring to guitars in the feminine. *A beautiful lady! A lovely girl!* Over the years, Keith remade himself in the shape of a guitar, took guitars to bed, held them tenderly as he slept. Steel guitars and hollow-bodies, resonators and twelve-strings, Fenders and Gibsons, Starlites and Stratocasters, a cataract of wah-wah pedals and pickups, cherrywood gleaming. If you look at pictures of the Stones in the sixties and seventies, you'll always see Keith in the background with his guitar. *The cops are searching the flat?* Keith is on the bed, strumming his beautiful lady. *The customs agent is cutting open the luggage?* Keith is on the bench, plucking his lovely girl.

5

UNBROKEN

Mick Jagger had already changed. Imagine it happening in a series of time-lapse photos, the good manners and careful training, the inhibitions and breeding of a thousand years of civilization fading away. His hair grew long, his shirts came undone, his mouth went slack, his limbs languid. The music had gotten underneath, the funk, rhythm and beat, the nasty sentiment and vulgar verse. It turned the inside out, exposed what had been hidden. Lust and appetite. A teacher at the London School of Economics named Walter Stern, who witnessed the transformation, was horrified to see this "scrupulously polite boy from the provinces [turn] to a Ted, who lounged around and smoked his way through our appointments."

The parents of the 1960s were right to fear rock 'n' roll. It turned their children against them. Over time, it undid everything. Imagine winning the World Wars only to watch the power abdicated in the London dives. An eighteen-year-old at the Marquee Club in 1962 would have been twelve when Elvis broke. Having been blown away by the King, he would be an entirely different creature than his parents had been at the same age. He would be a rock 'n' roll native in the way kids who grew up with the Internet are said to be natives of cyberspace. He would have been the product of scarcity and hunger. He would have two parents: Churchill and Presley. "A certain kind of guy came out of England at the end of the Second World War," Sam Cut-

ler, who later worked for the Stones as a kind of stage manager, told me. "The country was hard in the late forties and fifties. If you look at all the English rock 'n' rollers that survived it, from Pete Townshend to what's his name, you find tough, lean guys with bad teeth because we didn't get to eat properly; they came through a fire, which made for a unique group."

Eighteen-year-old boys had been drafted into the British military since time out of mind. Conscription filled the ranks, but, more important, it broke the rowdies, crushed their spirit, and remade them for the machine. ("Your whole life you'd heard, 'When you're eighteen, you'll be in the service, and that will sort you out,'" McLagan told me.) But after the war, England could not afford to maintain a large standing army. The country was busted, the Empire, that vast archipelago of subservience, painstakingly dismantled. Instead of being sent to patrol in distant lands, the young men of working-class England were cut loose, set free. In this manner, a generation slipped away, undrilled and unbroken. In England, their energy became an important factor. In the past, it would have been spent in Burma, Egypt, India. These boys went off to the blues clubs instead. England lost the Empire but got rock 'n' roll—yet another unintended consequence of war.

As all Russian literature is said to have come out from under Gogol's "Overcoat," all British blues can be said to have come out of Chris Barber's trombone. "When people talk about the British blues boom, they don't go back far enough," Paul Jones, the British blues legend who fronted Manfred Mann, told me. "They only go back to John Mayall. As if everything comes from John Mayall. But it really started in the fifties with Chris Barber and his band."

Chris Barber is gray: gray face, gray fedora, gray eyes, trembling gray fingers. You'd never pick him out of a crowd and say, "There's the guy who started it!" He's the last pioneer still out there performing. A slide trombone solo executed by a man in his eighties is something to admire. I met him in London, where we spent a day talking. He told me about his life. He grew up in the English countryside, where the only escape was the albums that turned up in the general store like birds blown off course. Sidney Bechet was his favorite. The melodic runs of the clarinetist. Songs that break your heart. Songs that make you wish you were outcast so your heart could be properly broken.

He listened, then taught himself to play. He performed in small combos, then big combos. By the early 1950s, he was leading the most popular jazz band in Britain. It took him to America, where he saw Muddy Waters play on the South Side of Chicago. Ripple and rotgut. The blues master on his knees. Barber raised money to bring Muddy and other American musicians to England. Big Bill Broonzy, Sister Rosetta Tharpe, Sonny Terry, Brownie McGhee. It was these shows that gave Barber the idea for the blues break. During intermissions, when his band knocked off to smoke or whatever, a few players would remain onstage—a band within a band—to perform a primitive variety of blues known as skiffle. It lacked sophistication—the instruments were often homemade—but it reeked of emotion. Though Barber meant the break as a novelty, it began to get a bigger response than his regular set. The breakthrough came when he recorded a handful of skiffle songs: "John Henry," "Wabash Cannonball," "Nobody's Child." Cyril Davies on harmonica, Alexis Korner on guitar, Barber on bass, Lonnie Donegan sang. "Rock Island Line" was the standout. Released in 1955, it launched a craze. "Everyone started a skiffle group," Peter Asher, who became famous with Peter & Gordon, told me. "It was easy to play and you had everything you needed to make the instruments in your house. You'd get a wooden tea chest and strap a broom handle to it and string it. You'd have multiple guitars playing three chords. You could take any American folk song and skiffle it up."

With its low bar of entry, skiffle was the perfect musical gateway drug, the schoolyard joint that leads to the heroin of rock 'n' roll. The pantheon is filled with artists who came into the fold via the skiffle of the Chris Barber blues break: Van Morrison, Paul McCartney, Cliff Richard, Eric Clapton, Brian Jones, Chas Hodges, Bill Wyman.

According to Chas McDevitt, a skiffle star and the author of *Skiffle: The Definitive Inside Story*, thirty thousand to fifty thousand skiffle groups were started in the United Kingdom in the wake of "Rock Island Line." The names have the flavor of the old East Side street gangs: Terry Kari and the Cruisers, Derry and the Seniors, Cass and the Casanovas, Rory Storm and the Hurricanes, Kingsize Taylor and the Dominoes, Gerry and the Pacemakers, the Silhouettes, the Four Jays, the Bluegenes. The Beatles began as a skiffle group, first called the Blackjacks, then called the Quarrymen. A typical Quarrymen set included skiffled-up versions of "Cumberland Gap," "Wabash Cannonball," "Midnight Special," and "Rock Island Line."

When I asked Chas Hodges—he's had numerous hits as part of Chas & Dave—to describe skiffle, he asked if I'd ever listened to the Traveling Wilburys, the supergroup that included George Harrison,

Bob Dylan, Roy Orbison, and Tom Petty. "Because the Wilburys were basically a skiffle group," he told me. "The way they gathered together, a band with a hundred guitars, each guy shouting a verse for a laugh. You go from there right back to Chris Barber, who, really, I mean, has any man ever been so screwed out of proper credit?

"The musicians of my era—Albert Lee, Eric Clapton, I can't name them all—started out in skiffle," Hodges continued. "The ones who found they could play went on to rock 'n' roll. I was in the Horseshoe skiffle group. I bought a banjo at a rummage sale for a shilling. I strung it with fishing wire. I was twelve, and in the window of the local paint shop was an advert for a guitar or banjo player for a skiffle group. And my mum said, 'Go audition for it.' I said, 'Mum, I'm not good enough.' 'Yes, you are,' she said. I auditioned and was the best guy in the band. I floated out. I said to me mum, 'They want me.' And she said, 'Of course they do.'"

For Barber, the success of "Rock Island Line" was disorienting. In its aftermath, there was a tidal pull in that direction. But the trombonist stuck to jazz, which created a rift with his guitar player, Alexis Korner, who was tired of patiently waiting, night after night, for the blues break. There was an argument: Dixieland or skiffle. To jazzmen, the blues presented a threat. Qualities that had always been treasured—ability to read music, proficiency—lost value. The blues is not about skill, it's about attitude. "It was rather disconcerting to young jazz players when rock 'n' roll came on the scene," Stones manager Andrew Loog Oldham writes in his memoir *Stoned*. "It put a lot of guys off, because there they were studying their instruments and all of a sudden a music came on the scene where, if you were game enough to learn two or three chords on a guitar and dye your hair blond, you could stand up on the stage and earn a lot of money."

After quitting the Chris Barber Band, Alexis Korner, along with the harp player Cyril Davies, formed Blues Incorporated, a loose outfit fleshed out on any given night by whoever felt like getting up to play. "It was always in a state of flux," Paul Jones told me. "For a while Alexis had Jack Bruce [who later played in Cream] on bass. He had Spike Heatley. At different times, he had Ginger Baker [who later played in Cream and Blind Faith] and Charlie Watts, who was very young and a step ahead of everyone, on drums."

"That was the first electric blues band in England," Dick Taylor explained. "It was pretty much our version of the Muddy Waters band. There was nothing else like it here. You'd hear them play and think, 'My God . . .'"

"Alexis came out of the Chris Barber Band on a mission," Paul Jones told me. "Like Eddie Condon and a bunch of other leaders, he tended to recruit people better than himself. His major talent was not as a guitar player or as a singer, but as a bandleader and a scout. He had amazing ears. He didn't have to hear much of somebody to know, 'I want him.'"

"I played with [Alexis] in a coffee bar, the Troubadour in Earls Court," Charlie Watts said later. "There was a crowd of us who used to play in a band that was a straight nick of the Thelonious Monk group, and Alexis used to sit in. Six months later, I was in Denmark working in advertising and I got a call from Alexis saying he wanted me to come back and start this band."

Blues Incorporated began by playing music from the blues break: skiffled-up versions of American folk. They had a residence in a Soho club called the Roundhouse. The early crowds were small, but word spread and soon the place was packed. It got so loud the music was lost, at which point Korner made a decision once made by Muddy Waters, for the same reason. He'd plugged in to be heard. But you can't dabble in electricity. Once you're wired, noise becomes the point. In this way, the music got louder and louder until Blues Incorporated was evicted from the Roundhouse. Korner found a new home for the band across from the Ealing tube station in West London. Between numbers, you could hear the rumble of feet, a million nine-to-fivers unaware of the revolution being hatched below. The entrance was easy to miss. For many musicians, going down the steps was like slipping through the wardrobe into Narnia. It was a rectangular cellar, with a bar in back and a tiny stage. Water dripped from exposed pipes and pooled on the floor; concrete walls echoed everything into rockabilly. As Lake Itasca is the headwaters of the Mississippi River, this cave in West London was the headwaters of the British blues.

A few days before the club opened, an ad ran in the *New Musical Express*, a sort of bible for the trade that began publishing in 1952:

ALEXIS KORNER'S
BLUES INCORPORATED
THE MOST EXCITING EVENT OF THE YEAR

G CLUB
Ealing Broadway Station.
Turn left, cross at Zebra and go down steps
between ABC Teashop and Jewellers.
Saturday at 7:30 pm.

Early in the twentieth century, when the blues pioneer Buddy Bolden wanted to gather a band in New Orleans, he'd stick his cornet out his window and blow three to five bars. He described it as "calling my children home." Korner's ad had a similar effect. It was underlined and clipped in towns all over England, little places where Korner never dreamed the blues had penetrated. It was as if, in every province, kids suffering the same malaise had found the same cure.

Jagger and Richards traveled from Dartford for the opening. Charlie Watts was there. Ditto Ginger Baker, Eric Clapton, Long John Baldry, Ray and Dave Davies. "There [were] only about a hundred people in London that were into the blues," Korner said, "and all of them showed up at the club that first night." Alexis Korner was not just playing music; he was building a movement. He'd audition musicians at the bar, then invite the most talented up to play. Jagger made his first appearance a few weeks after the club opened. He sang Chuck

Berry's "Around and Around" and Muddy Waters's "Got My Mojo Working," a doe-eyed nineteen-year-old in a cable-knit sweater. "In general terms, Mick wasn't a good singer then, just as he isn't a good singer now," Korner said. "[But he] had this tremendous personal charisma—which is what the blues is about, more than technique."

Jagger became something of a regular at the Ealing, doing the same two or three songs every week. In the spring of 1962, a newspaper identified him as "Blues Incorporated's 2nd string singer." Mick's first press clipping alarmed his parents. "I remember his mother ringing me up one night and saying, 'We've always felt that Mick was the least talented member of the family, do you really think he has a career in music?'" said Korner. "I told her I didn't think he could possibly fail."

Mick Jagger, Keith Richards, and Dick Taylor went to Ealing one night in April 1962, two or three weeks after the club opened. They slouched and smoked in doorways, but it was a pose. Mick and Keith still lived at home and kissed their mothers good night. You grow your hair and neither shower nor shave, letting dirt accumulate, or roll in the mud in search of character, but scratch away that top layer and it's clean underneath. They stood through the first set but were bored and ready to leave when Korner stepped to the microphone: "And now, folks, a very fine bottleneck guitar player who has come all the way from Cheltenham to play here for you tonight . . ."

The incongruity will be lost on Americans. Bottleneck guitar meant black Mississippi, cotton fields, the river on a rank afternoon— "bottleneck" being a utilitarian term, derived from the skinny end of the pop bottle that musicians broke off and fitted over a finger— often the ring finger—and used as a slide; moved along the guitar strings, it slurs and distends each note, rendering even a simple tune spooky and strange. Cheltenham meant resort life, antiques shops, and tree-lined streets. A bluesman from Cheltenham was like a rapper from Amagansett. It didn't work. Of course, the intro was a setup, a bit of misdirection, because, hearing "a bottleneck guitar player . . . from Cheltenham," you expect a lightweight. He did look like a wannabe, small and blond and impossibly young, a guitar positioned high on his chest. His shoulders were broad, but his waist was narrow and his legs were short and his hands were small, as if the architect designed big but the contractor ran out of materials. But when he played, you forgot all that. "He was absolutely incredible," Taylor told me. "No one else in England knew fuck-all about slide guitar. We loved the sound but could never think of making it. It was otherworldly, mysterious. And then here's this strange little guy from Cheltenham—fuckin' *Cheltenham!*—who'd actually mastered the thing."

Brian Jones had not been introduced as Brian Jones, but as Elmo Lewis, a stage name meant to evoke his hero, the great Chicago bluesman Elmore James, who recorded the definitive version of "Dust My Broom," the first song Brian played that night. Like most traditional songs, the origins of "Dust My Broom" are unknown. The harder you look, the older it gets. Robert Johnson recorded it in 1936, but he'd taken the lyric and melody from earlier songs, some incredibly dirty. The version Elmore James recorded in 1951—the old tune remade by electricity, engorged with voltage—is defined by an opening lick as recognizable as the sound of a freight train at night, a two-chord scream that echoes through rock 'n' roll. You hear it on the Beatles' "Revolution" and on Bob Dylan's "Crash on the Levee." That lick took hold of Brian Jones like a demonic possession. He taught himself to play the slide to exorcise it.

Brian Jones was tiny, maybe five foot six and a shade over 120 pounds in boots. He had a porcelain quality. He was beautiful, but you imagined him shattering. He was bathed in light at the Ealing club, slurring chords as if his guitar were drunk. To Mick and Keith, he seemed untouchable, beyond real. "[Brian] picked up this Elmore James guitar thing, which knocked me out when I first heard him," Jagger once said. "I'd never heard anyone play it live before—I'd only heard it on records. And it was really good. He really had that down and he was very exciting. The sound was right. The glissandos were all right. There was a really good gut feeling when he played it in the pub. . . . It's all to do with getting the right tone out of the guitar. . . . He was good at that, he definitely was."

After his set, Brian put down his stick like a gunslinger and walked to the bar, where he was swarmed. Mick and Keith worked their way into his presence, then peppered him with questions. Though only a few months older, Brian was light-years ahead. "He was already out of school," Keith explained, "he'd been kicked out of university and had a variety of jobs. He was already into living on his own and trying to fund a pad for his old lady. Whereas Mick and I were just kicking around in back rooms, still living at home.

"When I first met Brian he was like a little Welsh bull," Keith added. "He was broad, and he seemed to me very tough."

6

"VICAR APPALLED"

A few months ago, I went for a walk in Soho, London. I wanted to look into some of the places where the Stones got started. I stopped by the building that once housed Regent Sound, where the band cut its first sides, a slapdash establishment that once teemed with life. I stood before the Marquee Club and the Roundhouse, then wandered through London's Tin Pan Alley, where, in the fifties and sixties, the coffee bars were jammed with songsmiths. In an alley off Denmark Street, I studied a bulletin board plastered with wanted ads and audition notices.

A few caught my eye, especially this one:

BASSIST AND GUITARIST
Looking for
Singer and Drummer
to Start a
Stoner Rock/Grunge Band
We're two young guys (20–22) looking for a
rough **filthy pissed off** singer/songwriter with
a negative approach to life and a drummer with a
powerful approach to the drums **that hits hard**
as a beast, between 19 & 23 years old, to start a
full-time kickass project.
Our influences are bands like Kyuss, Nirvana,
QOTSA, early Incubus, Snakepit, Korn, Snot and
RATM and RHCP as well
NO assholes, No excessively religious, NO moralists
Dirty hair required

It hit me, this notice, because yes and wow, but also because it expressed a truth about the Einsteinian nature of rock 'n' roll. Simply put, there is no time. Rock 'n' roll is quantum. The beginning is tangled up with the end, the exits are entrances, every moment is present in every other moment and it's always now. How else can you explain the Rolling Stones filling stadiums decades after all the important stuff happened? Or the records released by long-dead stars? There is no progress—it never really got better than Elvis in 1956. Every band has to rediscover what's already been discovered and forgotten. It's a cycle: Elvis to Sedaka; Stones to Bee Gees; innocence to decadence.

Which accounts for the similarity between the notice above and the notice Brian Jones put in *Jazz News* in 1962, his call for musicians to form a rhythm-and-blues band. He'd already recruited Geoff Bradford to play guitar and Brian Knight to play harmonica. Brian asked Paul Jones to sing, but Paul Jones said no, which, over time, turned him into the man who could have been Jagger. "I had two reasons for saying no," he told me, "the main reason being that I thought it ridiculously optimistic to think we could make a living playing blues. The other is that I had a good job with a dance band, singing the hits of the day. It was a mistake, but life is nothing but a series of mistakes. At least mine have been colorful."

Auditions were held in the Bricklayers Arms, a pub off Wardour Street. Arriving early, Keith stood in the doorway watching a young man play boogie-woogie piano. This was Ian Stewart, a Scottish truck driver who rattled the keys like Professor Longhair on a swampy Delta night. He was barrel-chested and lantern-jawed, with big arms and bulging eyes. His lips were twisted, a lock of hair swung across his face. He looked less like a bluesman than a stevedore. From 1963 till his death in 1985, Ian Stewart—Stu!—was a crucial part of the band, the so-called sixth Stone, yet, for reasons that will become clear, he remains largely unknown. A shadowy figure, a forgotten man.

Keith entered the room quietly, strapped on his guitar, began to play. Stu looked up, smiling. Jagger turned up a short time later. "Jones said he didn't think Jagger was a particularly good singer but had something," Norman Jopling, a journalist who covered the scene for *New Musical Express,* told me. "And he did. Jagger could always front."

Brian asked Mick to join the group. Mick said he'd come in only if Keith was included. The other members didn't want Keith because Keith was a devotee of Chuck Berry, whom aficionados dismissed as pop, near beer. There was an argument. Geoff Bradford and Brian Knight stormed out, exiting history. As the band was now under-staffed, Mick asked if he could also bring in Dick Taylor. "When I met Brian, he asked, 'Can you play bass?'" Taylor told me. "I told him maybe, but I didn't have a bass. He said, 'Fix that.' So I went out and bought a bass guitar, then learned by doing it."

The musicians rehearsed all summer. Brian ran these sessions, set-ting the schedule, choosing the songs. It was his project, a second family to ease his loneliness. In the early days, the Stones were driven less by Mick's ambition or Keith's love than by Brian's need. His life was a sickness that he believed could be cured by the blues.

Jones was born in February 1942, one of the worst months of the Second World War. His father, Lewis, was an aeronautical engineer at Dowty Rotol, an aircraft parts manufacturer in Cheltenham, a spa town on the edge of the Cotswolds. Lewis looked like Brian faded by worry, obligation. The life you lead is dependent on when you're born. Being fifteen when Hitler becomes a Nazi makes you Lewis Jones. Being the same age when Elvis releases "Heartbreak Hotel" makes you Brian Jones. He had two sisters, including a baby that died before age three, a tragedy never sufficiently explained. Brian came away thinking the child had been sent away for transgressions unknown.

The family was musical. Brian's father played organ at church. His mother taught piano. Brian started piano at six, but switched to clar-inet when he heard jazz. He was restless, jumping from instrument to instrument.

Girls loved him in a way that made him the enemy of boys. He was pretty, with blond hair and long lashes, but it was the neediness they found irresistible.

So what fucked him up?

The blues, of course, the Delta funk heard on the radio late one night. Like Mick and Keith, he began to haunt the dime stores in search of obscure sides. His mother bought him a guitar for his seventeenth birthday. It became an obsession. Listen and play. Listen and play. He formed a skiffle group, but also played jazz. He fronted combos: the Cheltone Six, the Ramrods. He began drinking in pubs after the shows in search of sex, excitement. He bragged about his disdain for condoms. The old jokes. Raincoat in a shower, etc. When he was sixteen, he got a fifteen-year-old girl pregnant. It caused a scandal, first locally, then nationally. The story appeared in the London *Times* under the headline VICAR APPALLED. Brian was not allowed to see the baby. He became a pariah, shunned by friends, denounced by family. Forced to leave school, he went wandering. Thus began the period of exile that turned him into a legend. He'd been the suburban son of an engineer. He became just the sort of girl-ruining rapscallion who populates the ballads. As if he'd planned it. He spent months in Europe—Sweden, mostly. He raved about the local girls, worked part-time, dined and ditched, lit out of hotels without paying. According to Bill Wyman, Brian's vagabond early life, by approximating that of the blues greats, gave the Stones authenticity. Brian lived it so Mick and Keith could write about it.

Jones returned to Cheltenham in 1960, where he frequented clubs with names that flicker in neon: the Aztec, the Waikiki. When not playing, he worked odd jobs. An unreliable employee, he slacked off, turned up late. On occasion, he stole. His second illegitimate child was born before he was twenty. A nickname preceded him ever after, reaching rooms before his arrival: "the Cheltenham Shagger."

Looking through the newspaper one day, Brian's girlfriend noticed that England's only authentic electric blues band, Blues Incorporated, was scheduled to play at Cheltenham's town hall. Brian got a seat in back, then worked his way up front. He hung on each note of each song: "Got My Mojo Working," "I'm a King Bee," "Walking Blues." He went backstage to meet Korner but was told he'd gone to the bar across the street. Brian followed in the way of Johnny B. Goode— with a guitar in his hand. He bought Korner drinks, then started asking questions, sharing opinions and schemes. Korner described Brian as a "pent-up ball of obsessive energy, talking away in an incredibly intense manner."

Korner told Brian to "take out the stick and play me something." Brian set his guitar case on a chair and opened it with a cascade of buckles. Korner sat back as Brian played, considering him in the way of a radar-gun-wielding scout in the bleachers of a Dominican ballpark. It's not control that matters, it's power. Brian had it from the beginning, that raw thing. Korner wrote his address on a napkin: If you're ever in London . . . Five days later, Jones knocked on Korner's door.

There's a moment when your real life starts, when you realize that what came before was prelude. Old friends and mentors—you shed them like baby teeth and you're free. Jones became a regular presence at Korner's apartment. He'd been taken under the wing—to be trained in the dark arts. Alexis escorted him to clubs, introduced him around, jammed with him. In the wee hours, Brian, who slept on the couch, worked his way through Korner's encyclopedic record collection. The big moment came when he happened across Elmore James's "The Sky Is Crying," a song driven by a single-string guitar solo that fades into a slide. It blew him away, as it will blow you away if you come across it on a night when you are feeling sorry for yourself. It's haunting, strange. It's like the cry of a killer on his lonesome getaway, the lament of a man who's blown his last chance. It's not just music you hear—it's the studio where it was recorded, Chicago, the elevated trains and tenements, the factories, the migrants who ascend to heaven each night and return to hell each morning. It was a new sound for Brian, a new tone. It was like discovering a color he never knew existed. When he got back to Cheltenham, he told his girl-friend, "Elmore James is the most important discovery I've ever made in my life."

Brian taught himself to play the slide guitar with the neck of an old Coke bottle, then with a knife. As neither approximated Elmore's sound, he switched to a length of steel tubing he found in a scrap heap on the outskirts. It was the last thing Cheltenham gave Brian, who quit the town soon after. He moved to London in 1961 and lived with Korner until he found a place. He got a job and a new girlfriend, whom he soon impregnated. Child number three. He played in blues bands at night, including Thunder Odin's Big Secret, with Paul Jones. When Mick and Keith saw Brian at the Ealing Club, he was already an established figure, the Cheltenham Shagger, a rising star on the scene. But the pace quickened when he got together the new band. They rehearsed four or five times a week. Brian was the best musician. He taught the others how to play. Keith had a handful of licks down cold but was otherwise green. He now describes his work with Ron Wood as an "ancient form of weaving," two guitar lines turning around each other like strands in a double helix, but that began with Brian Jones demonstrating, explaining: you're the rhythm; you establish the floor, the beat beneath the song; I'm the lead; I carry the melody in the way of a singer—for what is the guitar if not a human voice? Brian instructed Jagger, too. "I'd just met Brian at the [Ealing] club," drummer Ginger Baker said later. "He'd just got together with Mick Jagger and they were going to play the interval. Alexis asked Jack Bruce, Johnny Parker, and myself if we could help them out. I didn't like Jagger, but we agreed. It was really quite amusing. Jack and I got into some pretty complicated time patterns with the evil intent of throwing Jagger. And it worked! Then, to my surprise, Brian went over and stood beside Mick and shouted, 'One, two, three, four,' show-ing Mick where the beat was!"

On another occasion, when Jagger was struggling with the harp, Jones "pulled his harmonica out of his pocket and said, 'Mick, I think you should play it this way,'" Pat Andrews, Brian's girlfriend at the time, said. "I'll never forget the look on Mick's face. It was like, 'Oh, shit. What else can this guy do?'"

Brian was the band's spirit. It was his vision, his dream: a blues engine—two guitars, a backbeat, amplified harp, a singer on his knees. They played their first show July 12, 1962, at the Marquee in Soho—a last-minute fill-in for Blues Incorporated, who had to skip their regular Thursday night gig to appear on the BBC. The notice appeared in *Jazz News* on July 11. "R&B Vocalist" Mick Jagger will perform at the Marquee Club with his band—"Keith Richards and Elmo Lewis (guitars), Dick Taylor (bass), Ian Stewart (piano) and Mick Avory (drums) . . . the Rollin' Stones."

Jones had come up with the name when the reporter asked, "What do you call your band?" Panicked, he looked here and there till his eyes fixed on the back of an LP, *The Best of Muddy Waters*. Side one, song five: "Rollin' Stone," Muddy's version of "Catfish Blues." Though coined on the fly, the lyric did express the swagger Brian had in mind for his group: "I got a boy child's comin'/ He's gonna be, he's gonna be a rollin' stone."

As for the personnel at that first show, there's disagreement. Brian, Mick, Keith, Ian Stewart, and Dick Taylor—that much is agreed. But who was on drums? *Jazz News* said it was Mick Avory, later of the Kinks, but Avory says he never played with the Stones. "It's a big mystery," Dick Taylor told me. "Stones fans obsess over it. Who the hell was drumming at the very first gig? I always thought it was Charlie Watts. Then it got around, 'No, it wasn't Charlie Watts, it was Mick Avory.' Only trouble is, Mick Avory denies it. So in the last few years it's been like, *who, who?* No one seems to know. Upon reflection, I think it might well have been Mick Avory. I speak from experience about memory. There's whole years I can't remember."

Ian Stewart wrote the set list in his diary. It reads like code. It tells you who the Stones loved, what they wanted to be. They opened with "Kansas City," a Leiber and Stoller song that had been a number one hit for Wilbert Harrison in 1959. Leiber and Stoller, the composers of "Hound Dog" and "Poison Ivy," were brilliant white mimics of the black sound. From the first song at the first show, the Stones were therefore neither black nor white—they were black *and* white, a mash-up, covering the hit of a black artist composed by white writers who'd been imitating still other black artists. The band went on to play a score of tunes, including "Honey What's Wrong," "Hush, Hush," "Ride 'Em Down," "Up All Night," "Bad Boy," "Tell Me That You Love Me," "I Want to Love You," and Chuck Berry's "Back in the USA." They closed with the Elmore James number "Happy Home." *Melody Maker* dismissed the show as consisting of little more than "well-meaning but interminable songs about share croppers." "If I had known Jagger and company were going to play R&B the way they did," Harry Pendleton, who owned the Marquee, said later, "I would never have booked them."

7

CHARLIE AND BILL

When Blues Incorporated's BBC gig became a regular thing, the Stones took over the Thursday night slot at the Marquee. It set the band apart from other would-be bluesmen: a regular gig meant playing time and exposure, which was everything. Harry Pendleton booked the Stones against his better judgment, then kept them on because they began to draw. Whereas four hundred people might show up for Blues Incorporated, many more were soon coming out for the Stones—kids wanted to see other kids, not mustachioed men in their thirties. Pendleton resented the teenage crowds, the stink and noise, an irritation expressed in snide remarks, put-downs. One afternoon, having had enough, Keith Richards took a swing at Harry Pendleton. Witnesses disagree. In some versions, Keith does not connect. In others, Pendleton is sent sprawling. Either way, that was the end of the gig.

It was also the last straw for Dick Taylor, who'd been thinking about going back to school. As Paul Jones said, "I thought it ridiculously optimistic to think we could make a living playing blues." The fear for a young musician was staying on the circuit a season too long, only to realize that all your friends had gotten degrees and careers while you were in the exact place you'd been at eighteen, only you weren't eighteen anymore. It was an autumnal mood, the way you feel when you wake from an afternoon nap and the house is empty. "When we lost the Marquee, I thought, well, there goes our best chance," Taylor told me. "I decided to take a hard look at myself and really think through my situation. I wasn't getting any younger. I suddenly realized what I had to do: quit the Stones and try to get into Royal Art College. I told Brian. He was nice about it. He said, 'You're the best rhythm and blues bass player in England,' which was strange because I was the only rhythm and blues bass player in England. I got into college, and almost as soon as I started, the Stones became the biggest stars in the whole fuckin' world! But I guess I cleared the way for Bill and Charlie. Without me quitting, who knows what would've happened."

The Stones began auditioning bassists and drummers in late 1962. Bill Perks showed up at the Bricklayers Arms on December 7. He'd prepared by listening to the sort of music favored by the band, which he described as "slow blues." When Bill came in, the Stones were at the bar smoking and laughing, a mean little circle. Jagger said hello, but Brian and Keith hung back, snickering. In whispered asides, they called Bill an "Ernie," their term for the uncool who populated the outside world. Perks combed his hair in the fifties pompadour style. He wore sport coats, pressed pants, and sensible shoes. He was abbreviated, with narrow shoulders and a big head, dark eyes, and his hands . . . how can you play guitar with such small hands? The others were slapdash in comparison, with long, greasy hair and wrinkled, loose-fitting clothes. Having come from a bandstand world of neat jackets and shiny shoes, Bill was appalled by the Stones.

Bill Perks was of an earlier pop generation, five years older, but a decade back in time. Born October 24, 1936, he could recall World War II. The Battle of Britain, the air-raid shelters. In an early memory, he's "standing in the street, looking up to a sky completely filled with formations of German bombers." He grew up in South London, a runt, a tadpole. His father was a bricklayer, which is perfect, for what is a bassist if not a man who establishes the foundation? Like Muddy Waters, he lived in a house without plumbing or electric heat, thus came to the blues honestly, one cold walk to the outhouse at a time. At fifteen, he was apprenticed to a mason, but he'd already found rock 'n' roll. He took up guitar but was troubled by his tiny hands. One night, he went to see a group called the Barron Knights perform in an old movie theater. "The sound of their bass guitar hit me straight in the balls," he said later. "Staggered by its impact and the foundation it gave to the sound, I realized immediately what was missing in [my band]. From that moment, I wanted to play bass." He removed the top strings from his guitar and restrung the bottom with bass strings. When he'd saved enough money, he bought a proper instrument. He loved bass because it matched his personality—the way he hung back, heard but rarely seen, the bricklayer, shy but crucially important.

After a hitch in the air force, he worked on the Royal Victoria Dock, married, became a father. On weekends, he played in bands. His key acquisitions came in the way of infrastructure. "I decided that if music was worth taking seriously, I'd better get good equipment," he explained. Bill Perks was a classic type: the small man made large by rock 'n' roll. In any other era, he would've been content with his wife, job, television, and beer, but he was instead pumped to monstrous proportions. He was twenty-six years old at the time of the audition, a fact later obscured. (In press materials, his birth year was changed from 1936 to 1941.) He jammed with the Stones, but it was listless, dispirited. "The big turning point came when I got my equipment in from the car and set it up," he writes. "Their eyes opened wide on seeing my Vox AC30."

When Bill Perks made his first appearance with the Stones, he was asked how he wanted to be introduced. It's the great thing about rock 'n' roll. You can reinvent yourself, assume any identity you want. Michael Jagger becomes Mick Jagger. Brian Jones becomes Elmo Lewis. Bill Perks recalled a kid he'd known in the Royal Air Force, a greaser, took what he wanted, never apologized. His name was Lee Wyman. It sounded nastier than Perks, tougher. Perks is a guy you ask for a loan. Wyman is a guy who parties from can till can't. In this way, Bill Perks became Bill Wyman. In this way, Bill Wyman was born.

Ginger Baker took Brian Jones aside one night. He said the Stones were good but needed a decent drummer. He suggested Charlie Watts, which wasn't a surprise. Watts was considered the best drummer on the scene. At one time or another, he'd played with just about everyone in the Stones, including Brian and Mick, but he resisted their entreaties. He did not need the gig, nor much care for their music. "You've got to understand something," he told me years later, in his room, on the road, as we drank tea. "I'm not a rocker. Never have been.

"You couldn't hold me up as an example of a rock-and-roll person at all," he went on. "I was never like the lovely Keith Moon. My personality isn't like Keith Moon's. I liked him an awful lot as a person. He was lovely, but I was never like that. I am not an Aerosmith drummer, never have done. A TV producer, if he wanted a rock 'n' roll band in a nightclub, would give you an Aerosmith clone, or the drummer in Pearl Jam. That look. Do you know what I mean? I'm not being offensive to them, I don't mean to be if I sound it. I'm just saying I don't look like that. I just play the drums. I happen to play in the Rolling Stones. I've done that for a long time. It started and continued. It's a blues band. You can call it rock 'n' roll but it's blues. Chuck Berry is a blues player, but he virtually invented rock 'n' roll."

Charlie Watts was born on June 2, 1941. He grew up in Islington, north of London. His mother worked in a factory. His father was a driver for British Rail. Meanwhile, Charlie was listening to Duke Ellington on the BBC. He loved bebop. After graduating from Harrow Art School, while working as a designer in a London advertising firm, he put together a graphic biography of the trumpeter Charlie Parker:

Ode to a Highflying Bird. For Charlie Watts, Elvis '56 was Earl Bostic '52, an alto sax player who fronted a Harlem combo that hit the charts with "Flamingo," a jump blues. Charlie studied that song. It was the first time he became aware of any drummer, in this case Lionel Hampton, who played percussion as well as vibraphone. The beauty of the drumming, how it held everything together. It was a fascination that grew into an obsession with America, not the rock-'n'-roll energy, but cool blue jazz, the horn solo, the snare when it's as faint as the heartbeat of a junk addict. "I used to listen to the records and dream of going to the Savoy Ballroom to see Chick Webb," Watts said. "I'd love to have seen Ellington at the Cotton Club. I would have dressed beautifully for the occasion. I'd love to have seen Charlie Parker at the Royal Roost and Louis Armstrong at the Roseland Ballroom with a big band behind him . . ."

When Watts was fourteen, he heard "Walking Shoes" by the Gerry Mulligan Quartet. The drumming—Chico Hamilton playing with

brushes—spurred him to action. He tore the strings off an old banjo and taught himself to play the snare. To fill out the sound, he banged pots and pans. His parents bought him a drum set that Christmas. He learned by listening to records, copying not just the sound but the style of his heroes. Cool eyes, impassive calm, the half smile that suggests the brain is not aware of what the hands are doing. And the clothes—my God, the clothes! More colorful shirts than Jay Gatsby, finer tweeds than Lucky Luciano. He's handsome in an unusual way, with high cheekbones and eyes so wide-set he resembles a tropical fish. He strikes me as particularly British. The demeanor, the elegance, the bemusement. Half listening, never missing a thing, an oddball in the grungy world of rock 'n' roll, humor so dry it can be detected only in trace amounts. "I give the impression of being bored," he once said, "but I'm not bored. I've just a boring face."

He began playing jazz in London with older musicians. He hung around Ronnie Scott's club in Soho, jumping into combos that found themselves down a player. In this way, he was spotted by Korner, who mentored Watts as he'd mentored many others. Watts later spoke of his first visit to Korner's flat as magical, an introduction to a new life: "The walls were full of records. The hip thing was to have them on the floor as well. All the records had been sent by record companies and I thought it was the hippest thing in the world. The whole Alexis setup was very glamorous to me, something I wanted to be a part of." Korner urged Watts to join the Stones, who represented one of the best chances to carry the music forward. They lacked only a proper pulse. He finally took the plunge on January 14, 1963, when he debuted with the Stones at the Flamingo Club.

Charlie's presence pulled together the loose ends, audio and visual. Perhaps because of his jazz training, his style is unique in rock 'n' roll. In most bands, the drummer establishes the beat and the others fall into step. In the Stones, the rhythm guitarist establishes the beat, which the drummer picks up and follows. It gives the Stones' sound a characteristic drag, a kind of musical drawl. You notice it even if you can't explain why. It's just the Stones, that idiosyncratic murmur. It's one reason cover bands can never quite duplicate the sound: they lack the abnormality.

I saw it myself one night, watching the Stones rehearse. On song after song, it was Keith who got things going, as Charlie watched, waited, then, in the manner of a surfer catching a wave, grabbed and delineated the beat. In one extreme instance, Keith started the riff while Charlie was across the room drinking tea. When Charlie finished, he carefully disposed of his trash, adjusted his shirt, crossed the floor, sat down at the drums, twirled his sticks like Shane twirling his pistols, grinned at me, nodded at Keith, took a breath, then jumped in. "The Stones always had a very unique style built around a kind of delay," Ron Wood said. "Keith plays something on the guitar, Charlie follows on the drums, and Bill is slightly behind Charlie with the bass. When Brian was playing with them he'd be somewhere in the middle. It combined to create a kind of chugging effect."

When I asked Darryl Jones, who replaced Bill Wyman as the Stones bassist in 1994, what this felt like for a musician, he laughed. "When I first started with the Stones, it was like, these guys are chaos," he said. "And there is a certain amount of chaos! It's like a wheel spinning on its edge. But there's got to be a little of that or it sounds too conceived. It's been an important part of rock 'n' roll from the beginning—from Elvis and those guys. Perfect just ain't perfect, you know?"

It was not just Charlie's drumming that completed the picture. It was his persona, stoic and unflappable. For the Stones, who, as Darryl Jones said, seem forever on the verge of spinning apart, Watts serves as an anchor, as ballast in the belly of the tossing ship. Cool as a jazz drummer who's stumbled into the wrong party, signed on for a deviant gig, collar undone, tie undone. With Watts situated beside Wyman, the Stones had an implacable second line.

8

EDITH GROVE

In the late 1980s, I lived with a half-dozen friends in a house on a side street near Tulane University in New Orleans. Most of my housemates had dropped out of school. A few had come for the orientation but never enrolled. They'd gone to the French Quarter, turned around twice, and were lost forever. Everyone had a guitar. They'd sit on the porch playing Lefty Frizzell songs as the streetcar went by. In the morning, you could smell the Mississippi River, the unprocessed bile, the innards of America vomiting into the Gulf. It must've once been a beautiful house, but, like us, had been allowed to dilapidate. There were rotten dormers and eaves, a weedy carport glistening in the tropical rain. Rats scampered along the power lines and the trash cans overflowed with empties. A thin narcotic haze hung over everything. I saw a kid named Travis, attempting to get off a couch, punch a hole in it with his elbow, then puke into the hole. I saw a cockroach nailed to a wall under the words "He died for your sins."

In the mornings, we spoke in the mock-heroic way of characters in John Steinbeck's *Tortilla Flat*. At night, we went to hear music. The jazz band at Preservation Hall. Walter Wolfman Washington at the Maple Leaf. Jerry Jeff Walker at Tipitina's. A friend of mine knocked on Charles Neville's door and asked if he could interview him for a school paper on Mardi Gras Indians. The musician sighed and said, "Yes, but first we smoke-um peace pipe."

Though there were arguments and rivalries, we considered ourselves brothers, a gathering of Huck Finns who'd broken from the
bourgeois path and were making our own way, though most of us
were in fact proceeding in a rather orderly fashion toward prescribed
destinies. We spoke in a secret language made of terms picked up in
French Quarter bars, from the most degenerate of the regulars, from
movies and songs, or invented from scratch. Rotgut alcohol was "blue
ruin." An especially reckless spree was a "death tango." If you were
clueless we'd call you a Melvin or a Marty. If you were in possession of
that kind of understanding that seemed like the key to everything,
we'd call you *keek*.

Then we left—some to Texas, some to California, some to New
York. I never spoke to any of them again. It was as if we'd been con-
spirators in a crime. Or just forgot. At the time, it seemed like nothing
more than a party. It's what you'd do if you did not have to wake up,
pay bills, or be anywhere. Only later did I realize that we'd actually
been doing something important in that house—shifting from the
lives our parents made for us to those we'd make for ourselves. I'm not
a Masai warrior. I never went on a night ramble or a sacred hunt. Nor
am I a Sioux from the Black Hills. No sweat lodge for me, no vision
quest. I'm an American born in Illinois after World War II and before
the Internet: my rite of passage was my sojourn on Cromwell Place in
New Orleans, getting hammered, making vows, debauching my way
to transcendence. Search the past of many Americans and you'll find
a version of that house, a place where they let themselves go, sought
justice, and made promises they could never keep. I mention it only
to draw attention to the flat where Mick, Keith, and Brian lived from
the fall of 1962 to the summer of 1963, where they drank, listened,
played, vomited, argued, and became the Rolling Stones.

Number 302 Edith Grove is a three-story townhouse on the edge of
Chelsea in London. The Stones lived on the second floor: two par-

lors, a kitchen, a bedroom in back. It cost seventeen pounds a month, most of it paid by Jagger, who was receiving a college stipend. He split time between classes, the flat, and his parents' house in Dartford, where he'd retreat to wash clothes and recover. Keith had left home. Brian had been kicked out by his girlfriend—not the one who'd given birth to his third child, but yet another woman. He moved into Edith Grove soon after. There was a shared bathroom, but no central heat. Decades later Mick and Keith were still talking about how cold they'd been at Edith Grove—coats and blankets, newspaper shoved between long johns and trousers for insulation, the blue flame of the kerosene burner. The boys snuggled for warmth, sharing a bed like the aunts and uncles in *Willie Wonka*. Filth and stench—a scene familiar to anyone who's ever been in a fraternity house. Boys without parents. No law, no rules. Garbage in the hallways, puke in the sinks, trash out the windows. Now and then, they came home to find the landlord in the entry, shaking his head.

At some point, they decided they needed a roommate to help shoulder the costs. Mick made an announcement during a show. Later, as the Stones were putting away their gear, a shy young man appeared before them. Mick explained the situation, gave the address. James Phelge turned up with his suitcase a few days later. He has since become a myth. Having neither the talent nor desire to succeed as a musician, he made his name by grotesque outrage. It was Phelge who went through the rooms naked, peed down the stairs, spat on the walls. A stand-in for fans, an eyewitness to the band in its first home, which he chronicled in his memoir *Nankering with the Rolling Stones: The Untold Story of the Early Days*. "Nankering" was their term for making faces—faces of a particular kind, lower lip thrust over teeth, eyes bugged out. If you look at old pictures of the band, you'll see many in which the Stones are nankering. When they began to write music, the songs composed in the studio by the entire group were credited to James Phelge. When they formed a corporation, they called it Nanker Phelge, after the civilian who represented the crude spirit of the band in infancy.

According to Phelge, the Stones' principal pastime in those months was hanging around, keeping alive. They slept late, then spent the day searching for warmth, sustenance. They lived on potatoes and beer. They stole food from stores and scavenged parties for empty bottles, which they returned for the deposit. That's how they made the rent. "Mick, Keith, and Brian were starving," Ian Stewart said. "Bill and I were buying them food with what little money was left out of our wages. I used to go there straight from work at about six, and they'd still be in bed. When Bill and I arrived we would take them around to the Wimpy Bar for something to eat."

"Keith and I had grown into the habit of going to bed at around midnight," Phelge writes. "We would stick a pile of singles on the record player and lay there listening to them and making comments. It was always the same selection of records . . . 'Donna' by Ritchie Valens, Jerry Lee's 'Ballad of Billy Joe,' Ketty Lester's 'Love Letters,' Arthur Alexander's 'You Better Move On' and Jimmy Reed's 'Goin' by the River.'"

Life at the house was about listening to music and learning to play together. Brian and Keith would keep at it for hours. Bewitched by the Everly Brothers—"Wake Up Little Susie," "Love Is Strange"— they'd spend weeks perfecting a single song. Every few days, a new record would arrive by mail: Chuck Berry, Bo Diddley. The Stones passed it around, carefully examining the cover, the liner notes. Eventually, they'd put it on the turntable. If a song moved them, they'd add it to their show.

The tensions that would trouble the band later were already evident. Jones was moody. Jagger was aloof. His insistence on continuing at school raised doubts. The way he sneaked off to class each morning as Jones and Richards slept suggested a certain craftiness. He was hedging, keeping both paths open. Jagger did not quit school till the fall of 1963, by which time the Stones were on their way. And even then, he took a leave of absence, just in case. It irritated Richards, who's a rock 'n' roll Cortés: *Burn the boats!* "Keith is a man of belief, and Mick is a man of fear . . . 'What if I fuck up?'" Alexis Korner said. "It's a lot easier to be like Keith than it is to be like Mick."

The Stones lived at Edith Grove for less than a year, but the experience resonates. Because it was the cradle, because we all had a place like that. If you go there today, you'll see the same house, the same stoop, the same faded rooms, but it feels diminished, like a body without a soul.

Meanwhile, the Stones were playing almost every night. Eel Pie Island. The Flamingo. The Railway Club in Harrow. A cover band of the most brilliant variety: it was not their musicianship you trusted, but their taste. When I complimented Charlie Watts on the band's creativity, he frowned and asked, "Where are you from?"

"Chicago."

He laughed.

"What's so funny?"

"Well, I'll tell you. All we've ever done is play a version of Chicago music. It's all we wanted to do. In other words, you have had to travel, musically speaking, all the way to England just to hear your own music. I find that funny."

But even in the beginning, the Stones were doing more than cover and copy. That's indeed what they intended to do, but it's not what they accomplished. In attempting to mimic the Chicago blues, they created something distinct, unique to them, in the way that no matter what Frank Sinatra sings, it becomes a Frank Sinatra song. When the Stones played Chuck Berry, it sounded like the Stones. In trying to imitate their heroes, they infused the songs with their own experiences and personalities and invented something new.

. . .

The Stones first heard the Beatles in the winter of 1962, while living at Edith Grove. Phelge called them into the parlor to listen to the BBC, which was playing "Love Me Do," the Beatles' debut single, released on Parlophone, where the Beatles had signed after being rejected by Decca. According to Phelge, Brian and Mick panicked. The lyrics were bubblegum, but the music hit like a hammer. It was everything the Stones were working for.

Jones: "Oh, no. Listen to that. They're doing it!"

Richards: "Hang on, let's hear the guitar."

Jones: "They've got harmonies, too! It's just what we didn't want."

Phelge: "What's the problem?"

Richards: "Can't you hear? They're using a harmonica—they've beaten us to it."

Jones: "They're into the same blues thing as us."

Keith later said that "Love Me Do" caused him physical pain. The shock was less musical than philosophical; it was Robinson Crusoe discovering footprints in the sand. "We thought we were totally unique animals," Jagger said in 1988, while inducting the Beatles into the Rock and Roll Hall of Fame. "Then we heard there was a group from Liverpool ... this group ... they had long hair, scruffy clothes, but they [also] had a record contract and a record in the charts with a bluesy harmonica on it called 'Love Me Do.' When I heard the combination of all these things, I was almost sick."

Every band in London was unmoored by "Love Me Do" and the string of Beatles hits that followed: "From Me to You," "She Loves You," "I Want to Hold Your Hand." Here were the Stones, the Kinks, and the Yardbirds paying their dues in the capital, when, out of nowhere, they're beaten to the prize by provincials—Liverpool being to London what Pittsburgh is to New York City. It presented dozens of musicians with the same question: Is there room for another British blues band, or have the Beatles done it?

It would have been easier if the Beatles had been popular but not good, like so many Top Forty acts. But the Beatles were popular and great. Every aspect of their sound was polished, perfect . . . it was intimidating. Some people were convinced they must've had help. When I spoke to Paul Jones, he talked about this while explaining the seismic shock registered by the first Parlophone sides. "John Lennon was much better on the harp than people realize," he told me. "He was so good, in fact, that I suspect that it wasn't him on that first record. I even have a theory. Delbert McClinton was in [England] in 1962. He'd come for a short tour and one of the gigs was at the Adelphi Theatre in Slough, a town where I happened to be playing with a dance band. I was a fan of Little Walter, Sonny Boy Williamson, and a bunch of other guys. But when I heard Delbert play harmonica I thought he was as good as any of them. Now, it's a known fact that the Beatles *also* went to see Delbert McClinton. So, when I heard 'Love Me Do,' I thought, 'You've sneaked Delbert McClinton into the studio! You know you have, you little buggers!'"

In the end, the success of the Beatles would prove a boon for all British bands, even those who resented them. It was the Beatles who showed the record executives that the kids in the clubs were something more than the detritus of an evening tide.

9

GIORGIO!

And here comes Giorgio Gomelsky! In a floor-length black coat and skinny jazz tie, goatee, handlebar mustache, leather boots and suspenders, cigarettes and a cackling Middle European laugh! Tall and skinny, gaunt, with cavernous eyes. He bounds into this book as he bounded through London, spreading fantastic stories of faraway places, tyrants and czars, Nazis and opium dens. He chats, befriends, listens, hugs, and hums, shuffling to an internal beat that's driven him across the Continent in search of an authentic sound, a music that will finally flush out the last memory of war. If you followed him around a room, you'd see people light up in his wake. He made everyone feel included, a citizen of his special nation. His smile changed the weather. And his voice? Well, once, years ago, when I asked the talk show host Larry King how, though being a froggish man, he'd been able to romance so many beautiful women, he said, "Never underestimate the power of the voice." Giorgio Gomelsky had a voice like that, syrupy, yet punctuated with the percussive consonants of the Warsaw Pact.

When he turned twenty-eight in 1962, he was at peak energy, on a mission from God. He wanted to spread the music he loved, the sound of black America, which, when he was living under a military curfew in France as a boy, breached the walls via American Armed Forces Radio—a pure expression of freedom. He'd been born in Tbi-

lisi, Georgia (the country, that is, which at that time was part of the
Soviet Union), but the family drifted. Syria. Egypt. Italy. Switzerland.
He began subscribing to British music newspapers after the war, following the scene at a distance. He moved to London in 1955. Harry
Pendleton hired him to make a film about Chris Barber in 1962, but
Giorgio became convinced the future lay not with the aficionados but
with the kids who made Pendleton want to puke. He rented a room
in back of the Station Hotel in Richmond, a swank London neighborhood, and began putting on shows every Sunday.

One night, because of a tremendous snowfall, Giorgio's house
band, an early version of the Kinks called the Dave Hunt R&B Band,
had to cancel. As he scrambled for a replacement, Giorgio called Ian
Stewart—Brian Jones had been hounding him for a gig. An hour
later, the Stones were setting up onstage. The snow was still coming
down, the streets deserted. No more than a handful of people turned
out. Gomelsky puts the number at three. When Brian asked, "What
should we do?" Giorgio said, "What do you mean? Play!" You don't
punish the people who showed up for the sins of those who stayed
home.

Afterward, Giorgio asked each member of the audience to return
the following Sunday with two friends. Which they did. This process
was repeated until, a few months later, the shows were packed. By
then, the Stones had taken over as house band. "At first, most of this
new audience was boys, blues fans, and collectors," Gomelsky said
later. "Some were budding musicians. Like the soon-to-be Yardbirds
and Eric Clapton, who often showed up with hard-to-find albums
under their arms, [but] word of mouth worked like a dream. The
place got so popular people had to stand in line from two o'clock in
the afternoon to get into the place five hours later." In this way, Giorgio's club became a landmark, as important to rock 'n' roll as Café
Wha? or Max's Kansas City in New York. As the Cavern Club gave
us the Beatles, the Station Hotel would give us the Rolling Stones. "At
Richmond we became a cult in a way," Charlie Watts said. "Not be-

cause of us—it just happened. We followed the audience, then the audience followed us."

The room was licensed for a hundred people but Giorgio crammed in three or four times that many. "One night, when the band was really giving out, I signaled my friend and assistant Hamish Grimes to get up on a table so everyone would see him, and start waving his arms over his head," Giorgio said. "Within seconds the whole crowd was undulating. This was perhaps the single most important event in the development of the Stones' ability to build a link between stage and floor, to connect and become joined to an audience, to bring about something resembling a tribal ritual, not 'unlike a revivalist meeting in the deep South,' [as a journalist said]." Black-and-white film of this dance is often shown in documentaries about Swinging London, as if it alone tells the story. Because the dance was usually performed during the Stones' cover of Bo Diddley's "Crawdad," it came to be known as the Crawdad, as did the room itself.

The Crawdaddy was a furnace in which the Stones cooked to perfection. Everyone who saw them there remembers it vividly. "There was a very low stage, a foot or two high," Ian McLagan told me. "You could stand in front, watching their hands, studying how they did it. Brian played that slide guitar. *Oh my God!* I'd never heard anything like it. We were astounded. Keith? We never looked at him. He was over there. Bill was stationary. You couldn't hear [Ian Stewart]. It was Brian and Mick. Mick, who would lean over the crowd and tease us and get us going. Nobody else was playing that sort of music in England. Not like that. Chuck Berry, fuckin' Jimmy Reed.... The whole place used to throb. I'd get drunk on two pints and wait for them to play 'Route 66.' They wouldn't play it till the end. It was fuckin' amazing. Watching them, we were all thinking the same thing: 'Maybe I can do that.'"

If you love music, you probably had a night like that, a place like that, a bar and a band that blew you away. For me, it was Dash Rip Rock at Carrollton Station in New Orleans in 1988. Dash, who played a variety of music they called "cowpunk," descended, in a roundabout way, from the Stones, though I did not know it at the time. All I cared about was the energy of the musicians and the crowd, the communion. It was transcendent, being packed in, swaying together, greeting each song with recognition, drunk but clear, the music working as the prayers never did. I especially liked Dash's rockabilly version of the Hank Williams gospel song "I Saw the Light." I'd been at Jazz Fest all day, cooking in the sun. I was angry at my girlfriend, or she was angry at me. I'd driven her BMW along the streetcar tracks into a tree. I was wearing a shirt that said I DRINK, THEREFORE I AM. But I forgot all that when they played that song, which burned into me like a brand. If you're lucky enough to see a show like that when you're nineteen, you'll never be the same.

10

MEET THE BEATLES

In April 1963, *The Richmond & Twickenham Times* published an article about the hysteria at the Station Hotel. The reporter wrote about the mood in the club, the pounding rhythm, the ecstasy of free-range rock 'n' roll, kids in the darkness, musicians wailing away on-stage, Jones playing off Jagger, who summoned the demons.

Brian carried the clip in his wallet for years. It was a triumph, confirmation his father had been wrong. Brian would become more successful, but never more satisfied. Thousands of others read the story, too, including the Beatles, who happened to be in London. Giorgio Gomelsky tracked John Lennon down at the Ken Colyer Jazz Club and invited him to the Crawdaddy.

The Beatles showed up halfway through the set. John, Paul, George, Ringo—they stood in the middle of the room, smiling. "They were dressed identically in long leather overcoats," writes Bill Wyman. "I became very nervous and said to myself, 'Shit, that's the Beatles!'"

"Brian beamed over the top of his guitar, and Keith's face seemed to light up for a moment, too," James Phelge writes. "The Beatles were then invited up onto the stage. As cheers and applause greeted them, John Lennon waved back, and then the other Beatles took their hands from their pockets and waved, too."

Members of the Stones often dismiss the Beatles as an influence or a facilitator of their success. Keith has damned them with faint praise:

necessary but not always great. "They were perfect for opening doors," he said, "but somewhere along the line they got heavy." But artists tend to obscure their most important benefactors. By turning up at the Station Hotel, by dancing and waving from the stage, the Beatles anointed the Stones, touched them with Beatlemania. Over time, this gift would also prove a curse, raising up but limiting the Stones, consigning them to second place—the Beatles and the Stones, never the Stones and the Beatles. There's tremendous power in being first. In birth order, in the mysterious circle of fame. Being first means being free to invent and go it alone. Being in any place but first means riding the wake. It means being defined in comparison. It means being the next Beatles, the anti-Beatles, the new Beatles, or the shitty Beatles. No matter how successful the Stones became, they could never entirely get over arriving on the scene when John, Paul, George, and Ringo were already stars.

The Beatles followed the Stones back to Edith Grove. Eisenhower and Khrushchev, a rock 'n' roll summit, the key players comparing notes at the dawn of the era. Lennon and McCartney were shocked by the squalor of the flat. Mick Jagger and Brian Jones were middle-class boys playing at being working class; they'd let themselves go in a special way known only to rich kids. The Beatles really were working class, sons and grandsons of the proletariat. It was a weird irony—how the Beatles were cleaned up and sold as respectful middle-class boys, while the Stones, raised to be all those things, were remade into just the sort of raffish characters the Beatles had been born to play.

John Lennon and Brian Jones stood over the turntable, drinking wine and listening to music. Taste is more important than knowledge. Anyone can learn; only a few can *know*. On some things they agreed (Chuck, Muddy), on others they did not. When Jagger played Jimmy Reed's "I'll Change My Style," Lennon listened for a moment, then said, "It's crap." The Beatles stayed till four in the morning. On their way out, they invited the Stones to their show at the Royal Albert Hall. It was a painful contrast: Royal Albert Hall versus the Crawdaddy. Just like that, you remember you're akin but not alike. Lennon told the Stones they didn't need tickets: just go to the loading bay, grab a guitar out of the van, and walk in like you're crew. When Brian, with his long hair and velvet coat, got to Royal Albert Hall and picked up an instrument, he was mobbed by girls. They mistook him for a Beatle. He was disheveled when he got inside, but happy. He suddenly knew exactly what he wanted to be—a rock star.

11

TEENAGE TYCOON SHIT

When you work on a book like this, you listen to rock 'n' roll, and, when you listen to rock 'n' roll, you expect youth—from yourself and from those who wrote, performed, recorded, publicized, and discovered it. But Norman Jopling, like everyone else I interviewed about the Stones, is old. I sat in a hotel in Knightsbridge, watching as he made his way across the lobby. At seventy, he's retired, tall and stooped, with an angular face, eyes magnified by thick lenses. He may wear an overcoat and carry a briefcase, but his inner switch is still set to rock 'n' roll. He drank coffee and talked about his childhood.

He loved the blues. He didn't have the chops but did have the ears, his taste just as keen as that of Brian or Keith. He became a record collector, then a writer. His first article was published in the *Record Mirror* when he was seventeen. To the editor, he was a godsend, a teen correspondent to report on the Youthquake. "I had the first British interview with Little Richard," he told me. "They sent me to his hotel room, tiny with two single beds. Billy Preston was asleep on one, Richard was on the other. I had no idea he was gay until he stroked my face and said, 'You've got such soft cheeks, but the man with the softest cheeks of all is Elvis. That boy is a peach.'"

Jopling's boss asked him to check out the scene at the Station Hotel, which he'd learned about from Gomelsky, who was always pitching. As a rule, the *Record Mirror* covered only artists with a record to sell, but the buzz around the Stones was intense. Jopling disparaged the assignment. "White people simply can't make that kind of music," he explained. What Jopling loved about R&B was neither the fine musicianship, for it wasn't fine, nor the polished showmanship, for it was crude, but the authenticity, the sense that you were getting the truth of another man's life, the groove fashioned from suffering. But this would be impossible for a band like the Rollin' Stones, who hadn't suffered. What makes a work of art authentic? Why is an original painting more valuable than a perfect forgery? It's the purpose that motivated the artist. Muddy Waters was motivated by the pain of his history—he turned misery into music; the Stones were motivated by Muddy Waters. No matter how good their music, it would always be secondhand, a fantasy of someone else's existence. When Jagger crooned, "I'm gonna retire on the Delta, layin' out there in the fallin' rain," he was encased in many layers of make-believe. "To sing that sort of music, I thought you'd have to know a lot of things Jagger and company could never know and, at the same time, not know a lot of things they could never forget," Jopling explained. "It did not seem like that sort of sound could possibly be made by the British middle classes. They hadn't the life for it."

But when the editor of the *Record Mirror* threatened to write the story himself, Jopling put on his overcoat, picked up his girlfriend, and went to Richmond. "There was a big crowd outside," he told me. "Giorgio was waiting out front. He took my hand and dragged me through the crush. Then I saw it: the Stones onstage tearing it up. And it hit me immediately, the way it hit everyone lucky enough to see them at the Station Hotel: 'We can do it!' By which I meant white people, British kids. We can play R&B. Because it was not just about the music. It was about the whole feel. I hadn't experienced anything like that from any white band. It's what all those English groups had been missing. You have to feel it. And you could feel it with the Stones. It came off them like heat."

Jopling placed a copy of his article, which ran on May 11, 1963, between us:

The Rollin' Stones: Genuine R&B!

The Station Hotel, Kew Road, in Richmond, just on the outskirts of London. There, on Sunday evenings, the hip kids throw themselves about to the new "jungle music" like they never did in the more stinted days of trad . . . maybe you've never heard of [the Rollin' Stones]—if you live far away from London the odds are you haven't. But by gad you will! The Rollin' Stones are probably destined to be the biggest group in the R&B scene if it continues to flourish. And by the looks of the Station Hotel, Richmond, flourish is merely an understatement considering that three months ago only fifty people turned up to see the group. Now club promoter, bearded Giorgio Gomelsky has to close the doors at an early hour—over four hundred R&B fans crowd the hall.

A few days after Jopling filed his story, but before it was published, the editor of the *Record Mirror*, Peter Jones, ran into a young PR hack named Andrew Loog Oldham. Jones told Oldham about the article. It was unprecedented to run a major feature on a band before they'd even made a record, let alone scored a hit.

Every prophet needs a handler, a guru who can package the message for sale to the masses. Jesus had Paul. Elvis had the Colonel. The Stones had Andrew Loog Oldham, the boy genius who would turn the Rollin' Stones into the Rolling Stones and Mick Jagger into a rock 'n' roll Lucifer.

Andrew Oldham was a skinny eighteen-year-old waif, a full year younger than Jagger and Richards. He was blond with high cheekbones and dazzling blue eyes. He could play masculine and tough or feminine and coquettish. He was emblematic—the baby boom in the

form of a boy, the good and bad, the inventiveness, energy, and ambition, but also the narcissism and need.

Jazz, radio, theaters, balconies, crystal chandeliers, red convertibles, and cash . . . that's what he loved. He wanted to melt his particulars into a fantasy of America, New York in the 1950s, Walter Winchell and Humphrey Bogart, the Royal Roost and the Five Spot, sharpies in fedoras pounding the pavement in search of the big score. Though he attended elite English schools, he said he was raised by Hollywood. His first record, purchased in 1955, was "Cherry Pink and Apple Blossom White" by Pérez Prado. He quit school and went to work for Mary Quant, the fashion designer who invented the miniskirt. But he was impulsive. When he'd gotten enough of an experience, he'd take off. One morning, he called Quant and told her he'd be late.

Where are you calling from, Andrew?

Paris.

He was also working at Ronnie Scott's Jazz Club. He manned the cloakroom and waited tables. His ambition was the second thing you noticed. Asked what he wanted to be, he'd grin and say, "A teenage tycoon shit." He began hanging around the Stratford Palace Court Hotel, where American musicians stayed. He approached them in the lobby, pitched them in the elevator. He promised to get their names into the gossips and trades. He'd help sell records. He soon had a handful of clients including Brian Hyland ("Sealed with a Kiss") and Little Eva ("The Loco-Motion"). On his nineteenth birthday, while escorting an act to the TV show *Thank Your Lucky Stars*, he saw the Beatles for the first time. He went up to John Lennon in the green room and said, "Who represents you?" Lennon pointed to Brian Epstein, the scion of the NEMS music store fortune who'd discovered the band on his lunch break in Liverpool. Oldham was lucky in that he met Epstein when Epstein was still trying to break the Beatles. Epstein complained about Parlophone—they were not doing enough promotion. By offering his services as a London press agent, Oldham attached himself to the Beatles a moment before they exploded.

According to Richards, Epstein fired Oldham after "some bitch fight." In the lore, Oldham recruited and remade the Stones as his instrument of revenge: the Stones as Beatle killers. In fact, Oldham never intended to stay with the Beatles. He was always going to star in his own movie. He'd be with them only until he found some Beatles of his own.

In telling the story of his first trip to the Crawdaddy, Oldham lingers on the atmospherics, how he fell into the band's orbit as you fall into a dream. He checked out the crowd in front of the hotel, then went for a walk. In the alley off Kew Road, he came across a boy and a girl arguing. He hunched his shoulders, not wanting to intrude, but couldn't stop looking. Ugly in every particular, the boy was beautiful in sum. Indolent, languid. The girl was a model, Chrissie Shrimpton, Mick Jagger's first serious girlfriend, the inspiration behind many of those early tunes. "[The boy] gave me a look that asked me everything about myself in one moment," Oldham writes. "He was thin, waistless, giving him the human form of a puma with a gender of its own."

A few minutes later, Oldham was in front of the stage, listening to the boy sing. "I was already standing up but what I saw, heard and felt stood me up again, as the remaining air left the room from the whoosh of hundreds of waving hands, dancing feet and heaving bodies, having sheer, sheer pleasure."

Andrew Oldham lost his mind at the Crawdaddy. After the show, he stood in the street, dumbstruck. He could not bring himself to approach the band. He had to go somewhere, collect himself, think. He called Brian Epstein and told him what he'd seen, then met with Eric Easton, an experienced show business manager. Oldham told Easton about the Stones and asked if he wanted to go in as partners. Oldham was only nineteen; he needed an established figure to give his operation credibility.

Oldham and Easton returned to the Station Hotel the following Sunday. They buttonholed Charlie Watts after the show and asked who led the band. Watts pointed out Brian, who then stood at the bar as Oldham proclaimed: *We can make you stars!* After describing himself as a crucial part of the Beatles apparatus, Oldham said he wanted to take the Stones into the studio to cut a demo. "Andrew was even younger than we were," said Richards. "He had nobody on his books, but he was an incredible bullshitter, a fantastic hustler, and he'd also worked on the early Beatles publicity." The details were finalized at Easton's office on Regent Street.

Where was Giorgio Gomelsky?

It was Giorgio who'd made the key moves, stirred the crowds, and set the craze in motion, gotten the Beatles and the newspaper reporter to the Crawdaddy Club. Giorgio, who considered himself the Stones' manager, had even helped the band cut an early demo. Yet it's Giorgio who, at his father's funeral in France when Oldham showed up at the Station Hotel, is about to exit these pages. "I thought we had a verbal understanding and felt tremendously let down when they left me," he said later. "Brian was so determined to be a star at any price."

Youth is the quality that needs to be stressed. Jagger was a kid. Richards was a kid. Jones was a kid, as was Oldham. How young were they? When it came time to sign that first management contract, Jagger and Oldham needed their parents to cosign. It flavored the moment, gave everything the aura of revolt. *Vogue* editor Diana Vreeland called it the Youthquake: kids in charge of kids, building an entertainment machine for still other kids; kids on the stage and kids in the crowd; kids in the wings, with clipboards and checkbooks—the only authority being Andrew, the teenage tycoon shit with his sunglasses, pronouncements, and ironic pose. "Andrew was fascinating back then because he was a baby but he was absolutely assured," Marianne Faithfull told me. "I'd never met anyone like that—a boy who wore makeup, and the way he talked! 'Baby, I'm gonna make you a star.' I'd watched *Sweet Smell of Success* and seen all the Laurence Harvey films, so I understood where he got his persona, but it was still incredibly persuasive."

Because he did not know what he did not know, Oldham was fearless. He made big changes fast, with the instinct of a somnambulist. His first move was painful. It had to do with the band's presentation, which troubled Oldham, who was modeling the Beatles. "I was convinced that six members in a group was at least one too many," he writes. "The public would not be able to remember, much less care, who the individual members of a six-piece band were."

Sitting with Jagger and Jones, Oldham spoke softly—"Look, from the first time I saw you, I've felt . . . I can only see . . . five Rolling Stones"—then made the case that Ian Stewart, the boogie-woogie pianist and driver of the van, had to go. "I compounded the cruelty," Oldham later explained, "adding that [Stu] was ugly and spoiled the 'look' of the group."

It didn't take a genius. One look at early photos of the band and you know Ian Stewart is the odd man out. Whereas the other five have the starved look of urchins, Stu is beefy and square with, according to Oldham, "a Popeye torso, a William Bendix jawline and a bad Ray Danton haircut." A calcium deficiency caused by a case of childhood measles had left him with a lantern jaw. He might be a wonderful musician, Oldham explained, but his face ruins the fantasy. Oldham said it was okay for Stewart to record with the band, but he could not appear with them in photos or on television.

Jones broke the news at rehearsal. *You understand, don't ya, Stu? And don't worry, as long as the band exists, you'll get a full share. And you can still drive the van!*

To me, the moment the Stones dumped Ian Stewart is the moment they fell from grace. They had torn open their chests and shown each other their craven hearts. No sacrifice would be too great, no member too important. Jones would later complain that the Stones sold out when they went pop, betrayed the blues for fame, but it was Jones himself who made the deal when he told Stu he could drive the rig but not be seen in public.

Stu took it well . . . that's what they all said, for years and years. It's what they still say now. (Keith: "Stu took it better than I would have.") He continued to travel with the band, didn't he? Play on records, sit around the hotels, and patch up the fights? "The Sixth Stone." The most important unimportant man. Should've been a rock star but wasn't. Which doesn't mean he didn't burn inside. "Whatever Stu or anybody else said, he *did* care about being relegated," Stewart's wife, Cynthia, said later. "He had enough to worry about because he was so painfully shy. But the bottom line for Andrew was that Stu's face didn't fit. Andrew loved the pretty, thin, long-haired boys. Stu felt bitter, not because he was not up there onstage, but about the savage way he was kicked to the side."

The moves that followed were trivial in comparison, orthographic in nature. Hoping to play off the fame of pop singer Cliff Richard, Andrew persuaded Keith to shorten his surname, a change that Keith later unmade. The shift from Richards to Richard to Richards is Stones history at its most subtle. While Richards had one too many letters, Oldham believed the group had one too few. The Rollin' Stones? "How can you expect people to take you seriously when you can't even be bothered to spell your name properly?" Thus the Rollin' Stones became the Rolling Stones.

Oldham then took the band to Carnaby Street for clothes. In a movie, the shopping excursion would be shown in a montage, the boys going in and out of dressing rooms, now in long coats and boots, now in furs, now in velvet, falling together giggling. Oldham still had the Beatles in mind. Cute, clean, melodic, fun. The manager dressed his charges in houndstooth and turtlenecks, but the Stones were not the Beatles. They were nasty from the start, anarchic, delinquent. The coats were lost, the turtlenecks reduced to tatters. "There are photographs of us in dog-tooth checked suits with the black velvet collars," Richards said. "Everybody's got black pants, a tie, and a shirt. For a month on the first tour we said, 'All right. We'll do it. You know the game.' But then the Stones thing started taking over. Charlie'd leave his jacket in some dressing room and when I'd pull mine out there'd be whiskey stains all over it or chocolate pudding."

And the interviews . . . no matter how well the Stones dressed or behaved, they came off like hoodlums. It was their scowls, their faces. Realization came to Oldham when he took the band to the Thames for publicity shots. "I put the Stones . . . against a grim-looking wall," Oldham wrote later. "That look, that 'just out of bed and fuck you' look—the river, the bricks, the industrial location—was the beginning of the image that would define and divine them. Word got out: the results of the Embankment photo session were 'disgusting.' The Stones were unkempt, dirty and rude. I loved the photos, got the picture, the penny dropped."

The manager suddenly knew what he had: not the Beatles but their antipode, candy cover torn away, dark soul revealed. "By the time we came along, the Beatles were wearing the white hats," Richards told me. "So what does that leave us?"

"[John Lennon] believed the Stones had hijacked the Beatles' original image," Chris Hutchins, an editor at *New Musical Express*, said later. "Brian Epstein made [the Beatles] behave, conform, perform, wear suits, be polite, made them do Royal Variety Shows. That left the field open for Andrew to say, 'Fuck that, the Stones don't do that.'"

"[Andrew] deliberately set us up," Richards said. "Stunts. You know if you go to the Savoy Hotel without a tie you're going to get thrown out. So he'd send us, and, as predicted, we'd get thrown out, and the picture of us being escorted away would run in the newspapers. It was a game. It was a laugh."

Oldham had stumbled on a simple truth: kids most fiercely embrace that which their parents most fiercely hate. To make the Stones loved, he would make the Stones hated, a strategy capped the following year when he coined a famous tagline: *Would You Let Your Daughter Marry a Rolling Stone?* "The Beatles want to hold your hand," Tom Wolfe wrote at the time, "but the Stones want to burn down your town."

In 1963, Andrew Oldham met with Dick Rowe, the top A&R man at Decca Records. Rowe was a buzz-cut forty-one-year-old product of the big band era. But Oldham was less interested in his ears—he'd signed Tommy Steele, Tom Jones, and Engelbert Humperdinck—than in his psyche. Rowe was "the idiot who'd turned down the Beatles," a judgment that stuck to him like paint. (When he died in 1986, it was in the first line of his obituary.) In other words, Dick Rowe was primed. Oldham didn't even have to play a demo. He just had to say, "These guys are gonna be the next Beatles." In this way, the Stones were shaped in the space opened by their biggest competitor. Not a copy, nor a tangent, but a product of the moment. Brian Epstein cut the Beatles out of a swatch of fabric, then walked away. Oldham used what remained of that fabric to stitch together the Stones.

They signed with Decca in May 1963, then went into Regent Sound on Denmark Street to cut a record. In their prime, the Stones would laze around the studio for weeks, riffing and getting high till the moment was right, but that first session was *bang, bang,* a handful of songs that struck Oldham as potential hits cranked out in a single afternoon. Though he knew little about the art of recording, Oldham had hired himself to produce. This meant pacing behind the glass and shouting at the sound engineer, who was surprised when Oldham suddenly left, the work half finished.

"Aren't you gonna mix the songs?"

"Nah," said Oldham. "You do it."

Though Decca redid everything, the tracks were still terrible. The energy that made the band electric onstage, the chaos and violence—none of it was captured. This was not the Stones as they'd later exist in the studio, nor the band from the Crawdaddy. It was neither and nothing. The patient had died on the table. Oldham picked the first single, "Come On," a tarted-up version of a Chuck Berry song. It's awful. Too fast, wobbly, unconvincing. Whatever had been dangerous about the tune is watered down, tamed. It's super white and grasping, which is probably why Oldham chose it. When looking for that all-important first hit—because most bands only get one shot—he'd naturally gone for the song most like songs he'd already heard on the radio. It was the audio equivalent of dressing the boys in houndstooth. The Stones hated it as much as they hated the jackets. The Beatles were perfect from the start, but the Stones' ascent was drunken.

When I was a boy, my father, who wrote a book called *You Can Negotiate Anything* and was in fact an expert at treating everything like a game, told me that life is 99 percent marketing. "You're better off with a great salesman and a mediocre product," he said, "than with a masterpiece and a moron to sell it." Though "Come On" stank, Oldham figured out just what to do. There were only about 450 record stores in England that reported to the charts. He sent members of the Stones fan club—teenage girls—into those stores to buy out the single on Saturday. On Monday, another wave was sent only to discover that the stores had "sold out." When the managers called Decca to reorder on Tuesday, word burned through the industry—the Rolling Stones have a hit record.

12

PICTURES FROM THE ROAD

That September the Stones set off on their first tour. It was a season of goodbyes. The last rehearsal at the Bricklayers Arms, the last nights at Edith Grove. Years later, in a private jet with the band's logo painted on the fuselage, musicians sleeping all around him in the dark, Keith told me that this leave-taking was the key moment, though he did not realize it at the time. When the Stones quit the local dives, they lost their first audience and completed their first mission, which was to play the blues for aficionados. On the road, they would perform for crowds of screaming girls who had neither the interest nor knowledge. "That's when I made my deal with the devil, right there, when I left the little scene and went after big fame," he said softly. "You do it because it's logical, it's the next step. You do it without knowing what you're doing. But once it's done, and you've become—stupid term—a rock star, there's no way back."

The band toured as part of a package, playing with their heroes, the Everly Brothers and Bo Diddley, whose songs made up no small part of the Crawdaddy show. "It won't be a case of the pupils competing with the master," Brian Jones said at the time, "as we'll be dropping all Bo Diddley numbers from our set." For the Stones, the gig became a kind of graduate seminar, a chance to learn the tricks of the trade from the pioneers. Each night, they stood in the front row or the wings, studying.

The tour was scheduled for five weeks, but in a sense, once the band went on the road, they never left it. Southend-on-Sea. Guild-ford. Watford. Cardiff. The theater in Cheltenham, which was a tri-umph for Brian. Derby and Doncaster. The Cavern in Liverpool. Manchester. Glasgow. Sheffield. Birmingham. A wash of faces, gray and black, the crowd roaring. "Between then and 1966—for three years—we played virtually every night, or every day, sometimes two gigs a day," Richards said. "We played well over a thousand gigs, al-most back to back, barely a break."

Pictures of life on tour: the van ghosting over the midnight moors; a bandshell by the sea; ballrooms and bowls; autumn closing in; Mick staring sleepy-eyed through the slats of a drawn blind; Keith stum-bling through a hotel lobby, eyes like asterisks; gas stations on the outskirts; pubs where the boys ask for the sort of amphetamines that keep the truck drivers going all night; the Stones crowded onto a small stage in the sticks, the drums pounding as Charlie looks away; Brian playing in a pool of light, lost in a melodic dream.

These were lightning raids. Three or four tunes, thirty minutes, done. The Stones began as understudies, but the interest built until the crowds wanted only Brian and Mick. It had less to do with their playing than their identity: teenagers, no different from the audience—what you might be if you keep practicing.

Brian Jones wrote a column about life on the road:

Standing in the wings, waiting for the curtains to part, you get your first real glimpse of all the excitement. Stagehands frantically beat off girls who are trying to wrench back the drapes. The atmosphere is more than electric by now—it's something tangible, like a vast elastic band, ready to snap at any moment. And then we're off. The curtains slowly part, Keith roars into "Talkin' About You." As our music gains momentum, the kids sway like palm trees in a hurricane. A huge roar swamps our amplifiers. We feel as if we're really in there with the fans. As the excitement mounts, the girls surge down to the footlights and start showering us with gifts—sweets, peanuts, and

cuddly toys. We're feeling very good. Suddenly it's all over. The curtain closes quickly, shutting off the faces behind the ear-splitting
roar. Back in the dressing-room, we swallow Cokes to get the sand-
paper taste out of our throats. We start to unwind as we wait for the
police to arrange our getaway. We always feel a little sad driving away
through the surging throng.

The shows became increasingly chaotic, even violent, as the Stones
gained fame. The band was tapping the energy that had driven rock
'n' roll from the start. According to the critic Robert Palmer, the first
rock riot predated Elvis. It happened March 21, 1952, at Moondog
Coronation Ball, hosted by disc jockey Alan Freed in Cleveland.
When the box office ran out of tickets, the teenagers went wild, as if
the beat released the mania. It's what Frank Sinatra meant when he
described rock 'n' roll—"played and written by cretinous goons"—as
"the martial music of every sideburned delinquent on the face of the
earth." Beatles fans tended to behave, but the Stones summoned the
dark angels. On many nights, they got through only half a tune before hooligans started rushing the stage. According to those who
lived through it, Jones sparked the riots. "When Brian was onstage,
playing, he was inciting every male in the room to hit him," Ian Stewart said. "Really and truly. That was the feeling one got. At the start,
Brian was the image of aggression in the Stones much more than
Mick."

"He would deliberately play at someone's chick," Alexis Korner explained, "and when the bloke got stroppy, he'd slap a tambourine in his
face."

In a moment, the Stones had gone from small clubs packed with
blues fanatics, almost all of them male, to big theaters jammed with
teenage girls who yelled till there seemed no point in playing. It's what
Keith meant when he talked about bargaining with the devil: you
gain money and notoriety, and in return you lose connection with the
audience and the music itself. "There was a time in the early sixties

when we wondered what the hell we were doing," he told me. "We'd do shows for ten or fifteen minutes; then there's either a riot or we're dragged offstage by the cops. You never knew. The audience—louder than us. Coming out of the clubs, suddenly we're pop stars playing to twelve-, thirteen-, fourteen-year-old girls, screaming and throwing their shabby underwear. But that was the audience. Same for the Beatles. It's disheartening 'cause you try to get your gig down but we could be playing anything—they wouldn't hear it.

"I couldn't get laid a month before and suddenly they're throwing themselves at me," Keith went on. "Picture in the paper and—who knows? I don't know about that shit. The thing is that most rock and rollers—if they don't get a bit of that at the start, then they ain't never really gonna get started. If you get to go through it, and actually survive it, you get to part two. But you don't know that at the time . . . at the time, you think it's going to be nothing but a girl riot forever. Later, if you survive, you can rest on what you really do. But first you've got to get the audience tamed."

In a movie, a director might show people dancing a waltz. As they turn around the floor, the world—without the dancers' realizing it, because the dance is everything—changes. Nations rise and fall. Wars are fought. The land settles into an uneasy peace. It was like that with the Stones, who, sealed in the hermetic bubble of the tour, only half realized they'd become nearly as famous as the Beatles. "You can feel this energy building up as you go around the country," Richards told *Rolling Stone* in 1971. "You feel it winding tighter and tighter, until one day you get out there halfway through the first number, the stage is just full of chicks screaming, 'Nyeehhh!'"

When I asked Charlie about that first tour, he was quiet for a long time, then laughed. "For me, it's a bit like the morning after you've gotten drunk in a bar," he said. "You think and think, but you just can't remember how you got home."

. . .

The Stones couldn't agree on a single to follow "Come On." Gathered in Studio 51, the Soho club where they were rehearsing, Jagger, Richards, and Jones fooled with half a dozen blues covers as Oldham watched nervously, but none seemed right. Exasperated, Oldham put on his coat and left, emerging like a shot, the flashiest figure in Swinging London. There's nothing so entertaining as a dandy storming through the streets. A taxi rolled up, two men got out, John Lennon and Paul McCartney. They'd come from a ceremony where they won a music writing award and were a little tipsy. Lennon told Oldham he looked upset. Oldham explained. McCartney said, "Let's go see the Stones." A few minutes later, they were all gathered in the basement gloom. Lennon told the boys he and McCartney had been working on a song—not right for the Beatles, but perfect for the Stones. Picking up guitars, they quickly finished "I Wanna Be Your Man," a blues tune as ersatz as a cubic zirconium. The lyric hints at sacred touchstones: "I Just Want to Make Love to You" by Muddy Waters; "Let's Get Together" by Jimmy Reed. You can still hear the trademark Beatles sound—the harmonies falsettoing toward woo-woos!—but Lennon and McCartney had retooled it. They knew what fans wanted from the Stones before the Stones knew it themselves: love from the Beatles, sex from the Stones; hope from the Beatles, sin from the Stones. Jagger and Richards were too close to understand, but Lennon and McCartney could see it from the outside. Underline it and put it in bold. It took John Lennon and Paul McCartney to write the first Rolling Stones song.

"I Wanna Be Your Man" reached number twelve on the UK charts as the Stones experienced their first moment of pop stardom. New clothes, new cars. They'd given up Edith Grove, gone out the door as it collapsed behind them. Because they had money now, and who wants to live like that? It was one of those moves the import of which becomes clear only later, when you realize it was less a place than a time. Clubs, parties, gigs, a perfect world of London streets, hit records and money, blue days and black nights that seemed as if they'd

continue forever until . . . one day . . . you turn on the television . . .
"I saw it on a little black-and-white TV," Dick Taylor told me. "I was
at a girl's flat and I remember because at the same time the cat was
sick. I don't think it was connected. It was just like, 'Oh, the cat's very
sick, and President Kennedy's been shot.'"

"I had a record going up the charts, 'Misty,'" Lloyd Price, who wrote
what is arguably the first rock song, "Lawdy Miss Clawdy," told me.
"I'd remade myself as leader of a big band, and had recorded that slow
tune, 'cause a slow tune is a signature. It was eighteen with a bullet.
Then the president got killed. November twenty-second, nineteen
sixty-three. I was in a barbershop in New York looking at the television while getting my hair done. What they called 'process' at that
time. Burning my brains out. I couldn't believe the president got
killed. The record business just died. It was turn the page, party's
over."

Melancholy washed across America. No one wanted to hear anything, go anywhere. The streets were quiet, the taverns empty. Every
now and then, a nation experiences a caesura, a pause between eras.
To those who recognize such things, it's an opportunity. Because a
death is a birth and an exit is an entrance. Because you can only weep
for so long. Because after tears you need laughter. As America emerged
from its nightmare, Americans wanted something untainted with
tragedy, fresh and new. It's no coincidence that the Beatles landed in
the United States less than three months after the assassination.

13

NO LOVE IN A DOME

In the fall of 1989, a friend gave me a ticket to see the Rolling Stones. I was a senior in college, living in New Orleans. I went to class during the day and went to see music at night. The Replacements. The Pogues. Dash Rip Rock. The Long Ryders. Lone Justice. The Wild Tchoupitoulas chanting, "Me got fire, can't put it out . . ." Or wandering from Dumaine to Rampart Street behind a jazz funeral, the horns playing "Nearer My God to Thee" on the way to the grounds because death is awesome and "Didn't He Ramble" on the way back because life is more awesome still. Music was more than music; it was belief. It spoke to the nature of my condition. Certain dives were holy: the Christmas Club Lounge on Oak Street, a shanty right out of the French Antilles; Benny's on Camp Street, a house with a tin awning where musicians played after all the other places shut down. But Tipitina's was Mecca, a storied establishment named after the song by Professor Longhair. There was a bust of Longhair up front and we used to joke that, in the way of a religious miracle, we'd seen the stainless steel Afro grow. I heard just about every band I cared about at Tip's: the Neville Brothers, Clifton Chenier, the Radiators, Snooks Eaglin, Jerry Jeff Walker, Big Audio Dynamite, Marcia Ball. One afternoon, I stopped by for a T-shirt, the famous one with the banana. The club was closed but the manager let me in. As I paid, I listened to a band doing a sound check. The guitar was intricate and clean. The bass and drum formed a web. This was Oingo Boingo, a group I had not cared about until that very minute. It made me realize how good you have to be just to be okay.

The god of the Hebrews is wrath. The god of the Christians is forgiveness. The god of rock 'n' roll is energy. The enemy of that god is arena rock, which looks and feels like real rock but is in truth an abomination. Which brings me to that ticket I'd been given. This was 1989, and the Stones, in the midst of their Steel Wheels tour, were playing at the Superdome. I'd already quit them. It was not the boys—it was me. I'd become a fan too early. I was the sixth-grader singing "19th Nervous Breakdown." I knew the words before I understood their meaning. But later, when everyone caught up, my love for the Stones, which had been precocious and cool, became commonplace. So I moved on to ever more obscure music, thickets of vinyl where no one could follow me. And yet even then the Stones remained my foundation. They were the model, the ur-group. Because of the Stones, a band should have five members. Because of the Stones, a rock star should be addicted to something. Because of the Stones, every guitar lick should have a hint of Chuck Berry, as every martini should have a hint of vermouth. I felt about the Stones as you might feel about the girlfriend you did everything with first. Yes, we fought. Yes, we split up. But always, and forever, and who knows?

When I went to see them in 1989, I was hoping to recapture that old magic, but Mick and Keith were old, Brian was dead, and the Superdome was monstrously impersonal, cavernous and cold. My seat was in the top row of the upper tier, as high as you could get. The band opened with "Start Me Up," or "Satisfaction," or "Jumpin' Jack Flash." Who remembers? Who cares? All the songs were the same in the way all the food at McDonald's is the same. Even from that distance, there was something embarrassing about Jagger's dancing. There was no blood in it, no life. He was going through the motions, doing it because it had been exciting when he'd done it long ago. What a drag! To see a band you'd worshiped, emulated, and loved reduced to a Fabian-like oldies routine. Do you have to be young to rock 'n' roll? Does early success leave grooves so deep you can't get unstuck?

That summer, I got a job at *The New Yorker*. I was a messenger. I carried galleys around Manhattan, standing in the first car of the subway, watching the sepia tracks unspool. I sat in the apartments of writers who asked me to wait while they made corrections. Back on the train, I might read a story Alastair Reid had marked up with pencil, replacing the phrase "tiny little" with the phrase "little tiny," or changing the color of a Dominican beach from "white" to "blonde." You might think seeing into the nitty-gritty would cure me of wanting to be a writer, but the opposite happened. The fanaticism for the exact detail struck me as akin to Keith Richards's returning to the studio again and again in search of the perfect tone for the opening lick of "Honky Tonk Women."

I'd wanted to be a writer since I was small. I think it had to do with the library in our house. From the beginning—before records, before guitars—it seemed clear to me there was nothing more important than a book. When God wanted to tell his story, he did not make a movie. I read every book in our house. It was less the subject that I cared about than the sound of the words. I began freelancing at *Rolling Stone* in 1993. The magazine was perfect for me, as the sensibility of its founder, Jann Wenner, mirrored my own. Gonzo plus rock 'n' roll. After my second or third story, an editor called and said Jann wanted to meet me right away.

"I think he's going to offer you a full-time job."

I was staying in a townhouse on the Upper East Side. *Rolling Stone* is at Fifty-second Street and Sixth Avenue. I thought about Jann as I walked across Central Park. I knew him as a background character in Hunter S. Thompson's books. I'd also seen him, not long before, being interviewed. He was out west, in cowboy boots, boyish and nasal. I admired his story. He'd quit Berkeley when he was nineteen, borrowed money from friends and family, and started the magazine, which began in San Francisco. He wanted *Rolling Stone* to be about music but also about the culture being made by that music. His subject was the world; his lens was rock 'n' roll.

We sat at the round desk in Jann's office. He put his feet up and leaned back. Through big windows behind him, I could see Sixth Avenue. He asked about my childhood, college experience, hometown. He told me about the first years of the magazine, dealing with Hunter Thompson, the great pieces he'd published. I would come to know Jann well. When he wanted to report on a friend—Clive Davis, Lorne Michaels—he'd often send me. I wondered why but never inquired. "If Jann likes you," an editor told me before the interview, "he'll ask what band you want to write about. Don't tell the truth. Any band you name, he'll never give you that assignment." In other words, I was prepared. Because I wanted to interview the Stones, I told Jann, "Well, if it could be anyone, I guess I'd choose Bruce Springsteen."

In my first months at *Rolling Stone*, I was assigned stories of the oddball variety. I wrote about a mountain biker named Insane Wayne, about Jennifer Lopez and Rosie Perez and the Fly Girls, about the underground deejay Junior Vasquez. I road-tripped through Maine with the prop comic Carrot Top, who came out of a bathroom in Bangor with toilet paper streaming from his pants. But over time, Jann moved me closer to the central concern of the magazine: music. I did stories on Naughty by Nature, Hootie & the Blowfish, Nas, the Mavericks. Then, in June 1994, I got the call from Sid Holt, the magazine's managing editor.

He asked what I would be doing that summer.

"No special plans. Why?"

"Jann needs you to fly to Toronto to watch the Rolling Stones rehearse for their tour."

"I'm pretty busy," I said. "When would you need me to go?"

"Tonight."

"Okay."

. . .

The Stones had just finished *Voodoo Lounge*, the second album since Jagger and Richards had reconciled their famous feud and gone back on the road—that was the tour I'd seen in New Orleans, Steel Wheels.

"We got through it," Keith told me. "We broke our bones but they've healed and we're never going to break them in that same place again."

My plane left LaGuardia at sunset. I looked calm on the outside, but my innards roared like a car in neutral with the gas pedal pressed to the floor. The plane took off to the north. The country was dark out the window, but you could tell it was summer. I went through Canadian customs like a shot, then got a taxi to the Harbour Castle hotel—where, a dozen years before, Richards had been busted by the Mounties and charged with heroin trafficking. I got a room on the same floor as the entourage and was unpacking when Keith's manager, Jane Rose, knocked. Sweet and pretty, Jane carried a tiny dog. (I have a picture of me and that dog in my desk.) It was late and I was not expecting to hear from anyone till morning, forgetting we were now on rock 'n' roll time. "They just started rehearsing," Jane told me. "Let's go check it out."

We drove beneath a crescent moon, past houses with yellow porch lights, TVs glowing in blue living rooms. We were on a mission, rendezvousing with rebel leaders in the outskirts. The car parked in front of an elementary school and we went in. It was a typical arrangement of trophy cases and pegboards, halls achingly quiet. No place is spookier than a primary school at night. Then I heard it. "Brown Sugar"! That unmistakable riff. It went through me like a bullet. Jane led me along corridors, past classrooms, and finally down stairs. I pushed open a swinging door and stood on the threshold, staring. The drums and the guitars. The microphones and sound board. The Stones, their faces as grotesque as gargoyles'. Familiar yet strange.

Giant heads on tiny bodies. Keith caught Jane's eye and smiled, a wicked grin. Seeing the Stones in a gym so much like the gym where I'd been made to run laps for being a smartass was perfect. It meant I'd come full circle, returned to the habitat of junior high tyrants with crew cuts, aphorisms, and whistles now repurposed for rock 'n' roll. Over the mountain, through the looking glass, inside the chocolate factory, down the rabbit hole, into Narnia.

At midnight Jane left. For the next several hours, it was just me, an engineer, and the band. I sat on a bench and watched them put together a show. Because I was a kid focused on doing a good job, the strangeness of the situation did not occur to me till later. Hour after hour, they jammed for an audience of exactly one. Between numbers, they stood around, tossing out song suggestions from the catalog and talking them over. "It's all very well in rehearsal," Jagger told me, "but what if you get onstage in front of all those people and it goes down like shit? What if they get bored? It's not a good feeling." Once everyone had agreed on a number, the engineer flipped through a stack of CDs, then cued up the original cut. Keith fingered his guitar as it played, considering. Ron Wood, often tasked with replicating the work of Brian Jones or the later Stones guitarist Mick Taylor, identified chords and jotted them down on a pad. Mick bounced. In fact, he never stopped moving. "You remember the songs one way but when you go back and listen you realize that it was different," he told me. "For us, with so many songs and so many shows in our past, listening to the old recording is a way to remember how we did something, to find the groove."

Describing the rehearsal in *Rolling Stone*, I wrote: "Jagger calls out a title, a technician cues up the track, and the Stones, like kids tracing an image from a comic book, play right over the original. Then there's a second, leisurely run-through, this time without aid of the record. By the third time out, the band comes on with a full-blown rendition. At the end of all this, if the song has retained some of its original power, Wood crosses the gym floor and scribbles the title on a chart from which the band will eventually create a set list."

"Not Fade Away," "Connection," "Rip This Joint," "Doo Doo Doo Doo Doo (Heartbreaker)," "Far Away Eyes." The band worked through ten or twelve Stones songs that night. There were also covers: "Mr. Pitiful" and "I Can't Turn You Loose" by Otis Redding; "I Can't Get Next to You," a Temptations song that Jagger said he wanted to "do the way Al Green does it." In the early morning, Jagger and Richards stood at electric keyboards at opposite ends of the gym, singing together on "Memory Motel," a melancholy ballad about a beachside affair in Montauk, Long Island. Watching them, hearing their voices intermingle, reminded me what I've always loved about the Stones—the ups and downs of Mick and Keith, which embody friendship in general.

Now and then, one of the Stones would look at me and smile. Keith said, "How we doin', kid?" Mick winked. On his way to the lounge, he whispered, "It's more fun than it looks." I tried to fade into the background as I wrote song titles and bits of dialogue in my notebook. At one point, Charlie called me a spy. I flushed but later realized this was Charlie's sense of humor. If he mocks you, he approves. Otherwise, silence. During breaks, the Stones talked about the World Cup, the O. J. Simpson trial, or the oddness of returning to Toronto, the site of Keith's infamous drug arrest. "If I held a grudge against every town where I've ever been busted," he told me, "there'd be nowhere left to go."

Assistants began turning up with town cars around five in the morning. "We're all staying in houses about fifteen minutes apart," Ron Wood told me. "Except Charlie, who's in the hotel. He needs to have his little room where he can place his little things out neatly. Drummers are like that."

I rode with Charlie back to the Harbour Castle. He'd been playing all night, but still seemed fresh in chinos and the sort of T-shirt you realize only when you get close is made of something finer than cotton. His gray hair was close-cropped. He spoke softly. In a band filled with members whose old clothes are on permanent display at the Rock and Roll Hall of Fame, the drummer is the most stylish. And it's not even close. Suits and ties, silk scarves and bowler hats— Charlie is at once in the heat of the action and at a remove, detached, ethereal, cool. When I told him I used to drink at the Checkerboard, Buddy Guy's place in Chicago, he smiled. We talked about Chess Records and the South Side, the lake in the summer and the lake when it's carrying ice, Muddy Waters and Howlin' Wolf. He said there were only five Americans who had made a difference in modern music, then named three: Charlie Parker, George Gershwin, and Duke Ellington. "It's not that I like them the best," he explained. "For example, I like Count Basie better than Duke Ellington. I just think Duke Ellington's influence on American music was much greater." We talked about Charlie's collection of Civil War artifacts, which seems connected, in an unstated way, with the American music that is his passion. As we pulled up, I asked why he stays at the hotel, away from his bandmates. "You don't need to live together, as the

Beatles had done," he told me. "We were never that way. I like being around Keith but it doesn't mean I have to be around him all the time."

The next night, we drove out to the school around eight o'clock, which would give me time to talk to the Stones before rehearsal. Ron Wood and Keith Richards were playing snooker in a room down the hall from the gym—a snooker table is set up wherever they make camp. Keith wore jeans, boots, a T-shirt, and a leopard-skin coat. He looked tired, glassy. Ronnie wore a shirt probably swiped from his wife— lacy and black. I got a warm greeting because Charlie had told every- one I was okay. Ronnie offered me a swig from his bottle of Jack. Which I took, grimacing. Keith was sorting through the old-fashioned doctor's bag he carried everywhere. His face was stoic and frighten- ingly sane, hair hanging over glittering black eyes. I noticed his earring and the skull-shaped band on his ring finger. I noticed his teeth and gnarled fingers. He looked exactly the way Keith is supposed to look, handsome in a way that will never be replicated, as tested as Monk Eastman, king of the East Side gangs.

Jagger and Richards were fifty-one years old. As I'm writing this, I am forty-six. But I feel the same as I've always felt, whereas they seemed as old as a person can possibly get. The newspapers were filled with cracks about their creeping senility. One headline referred to them as "the Strolling Bones." When I asked Keith about it, he scoffed. "On any given night, we're still a damn good band," he told me, "and on some nights, maybe even the best band in the world. So screw the press and their slagging about the Geritol Tour. You assholes. Wait until you get our age and see how you run. I got news for you, we're still a bunch of tough bastards. String us up and we still won't die."

After I'd hung out with everyone else, Tony King took me to see Mick Jagger. Tony, then serving as something like Mick's personal as- sistant, has been part of the scene from the beginning; he was at

Decca *before* the Stones signed. He's tall, funny, slightly wicked, and ridiculously handsome. There is nothing he does not know.

Mick kept apart from the others, in a trailer behind the school. Tony led me to him as a petitioner or peasant is led to the queen. We stood outside until Tony got the signal. There was a pause, the moment expanded, we went in. It was a kind of mobile home. I sat on the couch. Jagger was on the phone, talking venues, prices. He did not register my presence. I was not there. He leaned his forehead against his palm, sighed. His movements were fluid. He sat up quickly, crossing his legs. His face was ordinary and gray, just another Englishman playing the markets. Then, as he finished up the call, he turned to me, smiled, and became Mick Jagger. The transformation was astonishing. It was as if a light had gone on inside him. We spoke for thirty or forty minutes. He asked about my favorite music, about O.J. and American football, made fun of my hair, which had grown, while I wasn't paying attention, into something stupid. Tony tapped my shoulder. Time to go. He ushered me out, but I never got over it: how this exhausted businessman had thrown a switch and turned into a rock star.

I spent a week in Toronto. Every day was the same. I woke at noon, hung out till eight, then went to the school to watch the Stones rehearse. I interviewed the musicians and the members of the entourage, roadies and engineers and tour executives. We talked during breaks or back at the hotel or while walking in the city or drinking at the bar or having a meal. I sat with Jagger in his trailer, then again at dinner. He leaned close as we spoke, dropped a hand on my arm. In public, he's usually accompanied by a bodyguard. There was a time when people expected Mick's assassination, as they expected Keith's overdose death. These men must now believe themselves years past the danger zone, but the old fear never goes completely away. Mick walks through airports and hotel lobbies with a stride I call fast casual—as quickly as he can, while drawing as little attention as possible. I recognized panic in his eyes one night at dinner when a drunk fan sat suddenly beside him, pinning Mick in a booth and talking boisterously about a Stones show he'd seen in 1972: the rush of the crowd, the encores. The bodyguard froze, and I could see Mick calculating the odds, wondering if this was the night.

We talked about the new record and the band's new label, the arithmetic of concerts and whether it's against type for a rocker to be involved in the business of the tour. "But to me, that's not *business* business," said Jagger. "I think people get it kind of wrong when they say, 'Mick's interested in the business.' Business is looking at the dollars and cents and how much you're getting and how much you're spending. I'm not interested in that. What I find interesting is making the whole thing work."

When you interview Mick Jagger, you become aware of a strange phenomenon. I suppose it has to do with the magnitude of his fame, his presence and persona, which make his most mundane utterance seem profound. As he talks, you look at your tape recorder and think, "I'm a fisherman catching wonderful things in my nets." Every turn of phrase feels like a scoop summoned by your own trusting presence. But later, when those interviews are transcribed, you realize your nets are empty. Once again, the mythical beast has slipped away. The unknowability of Mick Jagger, who is not understood because he does not want to be understood; who gives only what needs to be given; who has mastered the pro athlete's trick of answering everything while saying nothing. Mystery is power. Distance is charisma. You want to peg him and walk away but can't, so keep listening forever. It's a paradox. Mick Jagger is overexposed and yet remains hidden. He's among the most famous people in the world, but who is he really? Does anyone know? Does even he know? Is he Mercury—a solid planet—or is he Neptune—a ball of gas orbiting the sun? How has he survived? How has he gone from tragedy to tragedy seemingly untouched? Here is the rock star in platonic form. Even his given name sounds like a pseudonym, as menacingly unreal as stage names invented by lesser performers: David Bowie, Sid Vicious, Joe Strummer, Johnny Rotten.

"Do you remember that show?" I asked later.

"What show?"

"The one that drunk guy was talking about—1972."

Mick laughed. "No, I'm sure I don't."

"Do you remember any of the old shows?"

Mick thought a moment, then said, "More than you'd think. I'm pretty good about that. Sometimes people come up to me on the street and say, 'Oh, I saw you in Heidelberg in 1976.' I say, I don't remember. Then they say, 'Do you remember the guy that ran out and jumped off the stage?' And I say, 'Yeah, *that* I do remember!' For some reason, these things stay with you for years. Especially audiences—it's quite amazing how much you do remember."

I asked Mick if he missed performing when he was off the road.

"I don't miss it that much, no," he said. "I'm not one of those people. There are some people, they talk about getting back on the road all the time. I'm very lucky I'm not like that. I do get a bit miserable and depressed sometimes, and need to perform. But I don't have that lust for it some people do. It's a sort of addiction."

I asked the question every reporter asks: Did you imagine, when you were young, that you'd still be doing this at fifty? Of course, when they ask it now, it's not fifty but seventy—seventy years old and singing "Satisfaction." Mick once said he'd rather be dead than singing "Satisfaction" at forty-five. It was a general sentiment. The Who were screaming "I hope I die before I get old." But it was not playing rock 'n' roll in middle age that was unimaginable—it was middle age itself. Everyone was twenty-four. Then everyone was forty-nine. "I didn't think about the future at all when I was twenty," Jagger told me. "One or two friends thought about it and they were boring. I don't care about the past or the future much. Just now. Whatever makes you kick now is what counts."

. . .

I interviewed Ron Wood at the school. I have a picture taken just as I'm sitting down. I'm wearing a Stones all-access pass and holding my tape recorder. I look very young and very serious. Woody looks like a rock star straight from the box. Black lace, eye shadow, and hair that mysterious shade of Elvis black. He joined the Stones in 1975—after Brian Jones died and his replacement, Mick Taylor, quit. He told me that he was still referred to as "the new kid." He's probably the easiest band member to caricature. Mug, beak nose, black eyes, jagged teeth. Ugly in a vintage British way. His talk is pure Spinal Tap. "What came along in my lifetime which is horrible for the youngsters is AIDS," he told me. "That's why [my wife] knows I would never ... Of course, boys will be boys. In the old days, if somebody said, 'Hey, you could come off with me ...' All right, you know, yeah! And I really do miss the old groupies 'cause there used to be some great characters. But they're not as good-looking as they used to be and there's always that element of catching the old full-blown."

When I asked Wood if *he* remembered the old shows, he laughed. "I remember it all," he said. "I remember Anaheim when Mick said 'Give me your shoes,' and onto the stage came a hail of shoes and one cowboy boot, and after the show we went out and looked for the other boot and could not find it, and it was a great comic mystery. And I remember Barcelona, where we played in the bullring and the red dust rising and the people."

I talked to Charlie Watts in his hotel room. He sat in a chair with his back to the window. He looked frail, refined. From the moment he joined the Stones, he's been a crucial element, emotionally as well as musically. He remained sober when the others got high. He stayed humble when the others believed in their greatness. He never dropped LSD, never went for flower power. He's been the balance, stoic and unperturbed, the buffer between Jagger and Richards, as necessary as the cartilage that keeps the bones in your knee from grinding each other to dust.

I asked Charlie what he thought of hip-hop.

"What, rap?" said Watts. "I love it! I've always loved jive language from Slim Gaillard, his last poems, and a guy called Scott-Heron. Fantastic. It's like jazz talk. But I don't really like it now. It's got sort of predictably monotonous. But that's what happens with popular things. It's like cha-cha-cha. The first two times they played a cha-cha, a lovely little thing. 'Cherry Pink and Apple Blossom White.' Kind of nice. But by the time you got down two years later it was crap. Rock 'n' roll was like that, too. It roars out of the gate, then dissipates."

We talked about clothes. Charlie has tremendous style. It's not something you can pull off just because you can afford to. It's like an ear for music. You have it or you don't.

"What are you getting at?" Charlie asked.

"Your sense of style," I said.

"If you want to see my clothes, why not just ask?"

"May I see your clothes?"

Charlie crossed the room and opened the closet. I stood beside him and looked. Checkered coats and gabardine suits, cashmere scarves and ties, shirts arranged by color from parrot primaries to candy yellow. Charlie came to his wardrobe the same way as Gatsby. It's aspirational. Gatsby wanted to dress like the Manhattan swells. Charlie wanted to dress like Dexter Gordon and Miles Davis, jazz greats with a dandyish sense of nightclub picturesque. Charlie's look, which has always been visual ballast for the band, is the resolution of opposites: the staid Fleet Street financier bleeding into the Beale Street sharpie. "Age doesn't give you talent, but it does give you character," he told me. "Old players like Ben Webster and Lester Young had a hell of a lot of character. They *were* characters and had it in their playing. I don't mean to say Louis Armstrong when he was sixty was playing better than Louis Armstrong when he was twenty. I don't think he was, necessarily. But he did get Louis Armstrong off better, if you know what I mean."

Interviewing Keith is the opposite of interviewing Mick. Mick is crystal clear, Keith is hard to understand. Mick's sentences are concise, Keith's are circuitous. Now and then he laughs for no apparent reason, as if the humor of his life suddenly occurred to him, and that laugh often gives way to a coughing fit. He seems to proceed by free association, from non sequitur to non sequitur. When recording Keith, you worry you're getting nothing in your nets but catfish and perhaps a tire. But when *those* tapes are transcribed, you realize you've hauled in a bounty. Whereas Mick's answers, clear and precise, revealed little, Keith's mumbled responses were candid, sharp, and surprising.

When I asked Keith about his feud with Jagger, he said, "You make it personal, but from this distance it seems the main thing bugging Mick and myself, without us realizing, was knowing that we couldn't keep doing what we'd been doing forever. The band. We had to do something else if we wanted to take it further down the line; we had to be something else. We'd reached a plateau. At that point, after we'd gone off and made solo records, the band either breaks up or it weathers the storm. I never doubted it. Not really. But there was always that chance. All that infighting. We were trying to break out of the vacuum of being exclusively the Rolling Stones. There was something missing."

Keith sat in a velvet chair when we spoke, red with ornate wooden arms, like a king in a fairy tale. A Telecaster is his scepter, a skull ring his signet. Here's a monarch who's been too long at the banquet, getting tipsy on mead. His face was riddled but handsome, romantic. Marianne Faithfull once described him as a tortured Byronic soul. Dark and wasted, stripped to the struts, as disillusioned as an existentialist who knows that the only truth is that which you create with your guitar. "You're talking to the madman," he told me, laughing, "the original fuckin' lunatic."

Keith was off heroin, but there was still booze, cigarettes, pills. Now and then, you need to dement the senses. There's a kind of reassurance in talking with Keith. There's nothing you've done he's not overdone—nothing you've suffered he's not survived. You confess to him as you confess to a whiskey priest. Keith is Methuselah, perhaps not infinitely wise but infinitely experienced.

Because I could not think of what to say, I asked about his lifestyle.

"My lifestyle?"

"Yeah, your lifestyle."

He laughed.

"I haven't got a lifestyle," he said. "I'm just me. I do what I do. What's my lifestyle? I don't know. I drag it on a chain behind me. Junkie and madman, should be dead, mythical genius. It depends where you come from and how you look at me."

I asked what he hoped to accomplish with yet another tour. "Don't you ever say to yourself: 'We've done it'?"

"Nobody's taken a rock-and-roll band this far. So why quit?" he said. "Why not find out exactly how long we can keep it going? The boys are playing well. And what I really know is the music of this band, and if one of them felt they weren't cutting it or couldn't do it or didn't want to, it wouldn't happen. The only reason this is happening is because we want it to. And you don't really need any reason other than that."

"Has performing changed over the years?"

"The feeling of doing it has always been the same," he said. "You can be feeling like dogshit with five minutes to go—you might have a fever or maybe you drank the wrong water—but the minute you hear 'Ladies and gentlemen, the Rolling Stones'—you're cured. When you come off, you feel great. It's a cure for everything. I recommend it for everybody."

When the Beatles quit touring in the late sixties, John Lennon said, "We've gone as far as we can on the road," but according to Keith, there is no end to the road. Rock 'n' roll only lives in front of a crowd. "We can't exist by ourselves," he told me. "We might sound fantastic in the rehearsal and who even knows? Only the band. We need the final ingredient, which, for the Rolling Stones, is the audience. It's that give and take: we take energy from them, then give it back. It's a two-way street. Onstage you're three seconds ahead of life. With a bit of luck, you're sometimes five, ten seconds ahead. You know what's going down just before it does. There must be a fortune-teller up there when it's going well because you're looking at your fingers, thinking, 'I can't do that. I can't do what I'm doing.' That's what the audience does for a band.

"I'm always amazed," Keith added, "when I look around the room just before we go onstage—there's Mick, there's Charlie, here's me—and realize, that's it. That's all it is and that's all it ever was. Just mates that met way back and we've known each other since before rock and roll."

I asked Keith if he could explain the Stones' continued success.

"I don't examine it too closely," he told me, "but by some mysterious ingredients this band is interesting to people. I like to think that it's because we're a good band. And it's as simple as that. But I'm not sure that really covers the whole ground. There's something about the chemistry between these guys. The good times and bad times, too."

"How long do you think the Stones will keep playing?"

"I don't know: how long am I going to live? I was number one on the death list for years, so I'm not into predictions."

He took a swig of something, grimaced, smiled, cleared his throat, then started asking me questions: what did I think of the new record, the rehearsals, hanging out? When I tried to explain what the Stones have meant in my life—the poster in my brother's room, that first record, the junior high talent shows—he interrupted me, "What year were you born?"

"Nineteen sixty-eight."

"I can't imagine that," he said, smiling. "It's weird. You should be answering questions for me. You tell me. I don't know. What's it like to live in a world where the Stones were always there? For you, there's always been the sun and the moon and the Rolling Stones."

Keith laughed quietly—dull wheeze, muted hack—grabbed his doctor's bag, stood. Time to rehearse. But before he left, he paid me a compliment that's carried me through many hardships: "I'll tell you what. Charlie likes you. He really likes you, which is very unusual. It's not every decade Charlie will do an interview and say, 'I like him. That is an interesting fellow.' That's very rare. You've got the gold medal for that, boy."

One afternoon, the Stones gathered in the lunchroom of the school, which had been filled with cameras and green screens, to film a video for "Love Is Strong." This was 1994, when MTV was MTV. David Fincher was directing. The scenario was cool—the Stones, blown up to mammoth proportions, stalking through Manhattan like Godzillas—but the way Jagger and Richards leaned together, whispering, interested me more. It was the first time I'd seen them hanging out. The Stones split in the 1980s and reunited in the 1990s, but Mick and Keith never really got back together. What they'd had the first time was love; what came later was an arrangement. But watching them work on the video, you could imagine what life was like before everything went wrong.

14

FIRST LICKS

George Gershwin wrote his early melodies at the family piano on the West Side of Manhattan. Jack Kerouac banged out *On the Road* at his mother's house in New Jersey. Mick Jagger and Keith Richards did their first composing in their London flat—33 Mapesbury Road, Chelsea—where Andrew Oldham had locked them in with the admonition: "Don't come out without a song."

Oldham did not understand the absurdity. "I was not a songwriter," Keith told me. "I played guitar. I stood on the stage. But Andrew didn't know that." Mick and Keith were performers, not composers. They played traditional numbers that developed by accretion, in the way of a rubber-band ball, new material added to old material until it became impressive and strange. A song like "Stagger Lee" does not belong to anyone. It's a found object. It washed up on the shore. Writing an original blues song would therefore be a forgery—a new work made to sound old. A fake.

Why did Oldham insist?

It really had to do with the blues catalog, that pool of numbers the Stones could draw on for their records. Oldham believed the band had already used most of the songs that could cross over as pop hits. That's why he'd had to wrangle that second single from Lennon and McCartney. What's more, creating originals, owning the publishing, was the obvious next step. The Beatles had changed the rules: a band had to write songs. Bob Dylan made it even more important. It was about authenticity. A singer singing his own words is an artist; a singer covering someone else's words is an actor.

Why did Oldham tap Mick and Keith to write that first song, a decision that would upset the dynamic of the band? There were five Stones, after all, six if you included Ian Stewart. Mick and Keith were not even the logical choice. It was Brian who had started the group, spoke to the press, had the burning sense of mission. Oldham later said it was because he'd seen Mick and Keith arranging in the studio, thus knew they could write. But you should also consider proximity. In 1964, Oldham had moved in with Jagger and Richards. When he decided to order up an original tune, Mick and Keith were close at hand. Geography is destiny. Besides, Brian was too pure. His staunch defense of traditional blues made him less willing to write the kind of material needed. What would be a challenge for Mick and Keith would reek of sellout to Jones. There was also the matter of talent. According to Oldham, Brian just didn't have it. He prospered when musicianship was everything, but struggled when writing became paramount.

Jagger and Richards were not natural writers in the way of Lennon and McCartney, who would've been composers in any era. Having come to it as a result of a demand, they made their way by trial and error. Their early songs tended to be ballads—"It Should Be You," "That Girl Belongs to Yesterday"—entirely inappropriate for the image Oldham had crafted for the Stones. Oldham farmed these early compositions out to other clients. The first Jagger/Richards tune to break the Top Ten was "As Tears Go By" by Marianne Faithfull. It took Mick and Keith months to figure out how to write for their own group. The breakthrough came not from imitating the blues but from emulating the approach of the blues musicians, whose lyrics achieved power by including the particulars of their lives. Whereas pop writers tended to linger on the universal—love and heartache—the bluesmen named names, clubs and taverns, certain women in certain towns. When Robert Nighthawk sings, "I went down to Eli's, to get my pistol out of pawn," you can see the blood that will flow on Maxwell Street. It was only when Mick and Keith began plugging in their rock star particulars that their sound emerged.

They were reluctant to bring one of their own tunes into the studio. "It was not like fooling somebody in Tin Pan Alley and letting them add a nice arrangement," Keith said later. "We had to lay this song on the Stones. We hoped Charlie wasn't going to kick us out of the room and that we'd get a smile of approval rather than a slight frown or that look of confusion that is even worse than an outright 'No way.'"

"Tell Me" was the first Stones original, brought to the others eight months after Oldham had reportedly locked Mick and Keith in the kitchen on Mapesbury Road. Keith opens the song on a twelve-string guitar. Then Charlie on the big drum. Then Mick, that lazy drawl:

> You said we were through before
> You walked out on me before

You want to read personal details into it, Mick and Keith, the unprecedented lives of young rock stars, but it's not the lyric that you remember. It's the purple menace behind the words, Keith and Brian singing in the background, the guitars, the cacophony of a great bar band. The production is rudimentary, homemade—as if ruffians had broken into the studio—which gives the single the sort of power the Sex Pistols and the Clash would achieve a decade later. Released in February 1964, "Tell Me" was the first Stones song to break into the American *Billboard* Hot 100.

The Jagger/Richards process was already in place. A Stones song usually begins with a riff, a three- or four-note sequence that Richards cooks up on guitar. "Jumpin' Jack Flash." "Beast of Burden." "Start Me Up." Keith's ability to devise a seemingly infinite number of indelible licks has been one of the miracles of rock 'n' roll. He'd goof with it for weeks or months, add chords, and record it on his portable tape machine. "I can't write a note of music," he explained, "but neither could most of the best songwriters of the last fifty years." After appending a characteristic phrase—say, "Goodbye, Ruby Tuesday"— he'd hand it off to Jagger, who filled in the rest: lyrics, bridge, everything.

It's impossible to name a single Keith Richards antecedent, but certain precursors stand out. It was Chuck Berry who established the pop electric-guitar tune. In a sense, every Stones riff is just a play on Berry's greatest songs: "Sweet Little Sixteen," "Carol," "Brown Eyed Handsome Man.""Even his leads are rhythm," Richards told *Interview* in 1988. "It's all two-string stuff, beautiful. . . . Chuck Berry's solos take off as an extension of his rhythm work without losing the drive or point of the song." Of course, Chuck Berry did not invent his style from scratch. His tricks were elaborations on other artists, instruments, genres. In him, you hear the saxophone solos of Louis Jordan and the playful fills of his own pianist, Otis Spann, as well as the guitarist T-Bone Walker, who learned to play on the streets of Dallas, Texas, early in the twentieth century from Blind Lemon Jefferson, who might well have invented country blues. You feel all this history in the best of the Stones: the peripatetic lives, the juke joints, the riverbank where the blind man sings beside the boy. "Everybody passes it on," said Richards. "If Chuck passed it to me, for instance, who turned Chuck on? Louis Jordan and Nat King Cole. Who turned Nat King Cole on? . . . It goes back and back and back, probably to Adam and Eve."

As Mick and Keith's songwriting proficiency increased, Brian's confidence decreased. Bill Wyman said the band's power structure began to change as soon as Jagger and Richards brought that first song into the studio. When Brian tried to respond with songs of his own, they were dismissed. Oldham had decided: Jagger and Richards were the writers.

"They won't even listen to anything of mine," Jones told James Phelge.

According to Oldham, Brian's songs were just not good enough. That is, he did not fail because he was rejected; he was rejected because he failed. Oldham even brought in an American singer and composer who'd had hits in the 1950s to work with Brian. But it didn't help. Brian Jones simply could not write a pop tune.

Richards considers "The Last Time," recorded in the spring of 1965, the first real Stones song. It has all the elements that would become characteristic: the opening riff, the groove, and the subject matter, which is lowdown and particular. Yet if "The Last Time" is not a cover, it's as close as you can get without ending up in court, closely mimicking the Staple Singers' version of the gospel song "This May Be the Last Time." Keith reworked it, adding steel and speed. In this way, the Stones broke through via cover, tracing so far outside the lines that an old song became new. But the signature movement remains the same, the decrescendo, the lament of the vocal declining from verse to chorus: "This could be the last time, this could be the last time, maybe the last time, I don't know." The biggest change was lyrical, an adjustment that replicated a broader shift from church music to rock 'n' roll. A hymn about Jesus and Judgment Day had become a pop song about girls and teenage comeuppance. It's why preachers assigned this music to a special circle of hell. Hammond organs and hand claps, call-and-response—defining tics of rock 'n' roll had been swiped from the house of God, dragged from the altar into the street.

15

AMERICA

The tour bus sped through Pennsylvania coal country, each town hemmed in by bituminous hills. Bill Wyman was up front with the driver. The rest of the band was in back, staring out the windows. They were traveling from Harrisburg's Farm Show Arena, a gig booked by a manager with a map but little sense of scale. Three hundred people had turned up in a venue meant for twice that many. Outside New York and L.A., no one had heard of the Rolling Stones. But for the musicians, being in America—the land of Disney and Elvis—was enough. A storm rolled in, an Appalachian tempest, sudden and drenching, the valley filling like a bowl. Keith pressed his face to the glass, amazed by the clouds, the canyons of heaven. The mountains turned black. Big raindrops landed with a splash, popcorning the fields. Small raindrops fell inside big raindrops. The lightning was far away, then it was right above the van. A bolt crawled down the sky like two walking fingers. It hit a farmhouse—crash!—which burst into flame. It's fitting that the Stones' first U.S. tour began with an apocalyptic image.

They'd landed at JFK airport on June 1, 1964. When the Beatles had crossed the same tarmac the previous February, they were met by crowds of screaming girls, reporters, experience collectors. The Stones, having yet to score a significant American hit, were greeted by weeds and wind, men in cheap suits, a handful of girls hired by the record label. The drive from the airport was along junkyards and lots, brick porches and aluminum awnings, empty streets, factories. Manhattan appeared in the distance, the towers rising like a vision. New York in 1964 was closer to the city of Legs Diamond than to the Starbucks and West Elm city of today. Robert Wagner was mayor. Joe Bonanno controlled the rackets. Mickey Mantle dominated Yankee Stadium. Frank Sinatra was getting loaded with Jackie Gleason at Toots Shor's. The Stones arrived as if from the future, puffed up like socialites with beauty parlor hair and manicured fingernails.

Their first American LP—*England's Newest Hit Makers*—had recently been released. It was really just an excuse to cross the ocean in hope of replicating the success of the Beatles, who'd plugged in to the longing that followed the Kennedy assassination. For many Americans, the Beatles and Stones were their first experience of the blues, a native sound unknown to most natives. If you were white, listening to black music meant crossing lines, both physical and symbolic. It meant desegregation, miscegenation. First you dance with 'em... Taking a train from the North Side of Chicago to the South Side joints therefore required courage. Listening to this same music in England took no courage at all. In Liverpool, the blues could be enjoyed without reference to cultural order. In Dartford, you could love race music without taking a position on race. That's why it required Brits to introduce white kids to black music. Whereas in America, the blues was a history of intolerance and pain, in England it was a groove. Musicians like John Lennon and Keith Richards removed that groove and those lyrics from context and copied them. In the process of copying, they returned the music to the place of origin.

The Stones stayed at the Hotel Astor in Times Square, a fading landmark. In old photos, it's a pink behemoth beneath a mansard roof. By 1964, it was dust motes and mildew. The band took four rooms on the third floor, doubling up for economic reasons as well as companionship. Once upon a time, being in a rock group meant never being alone. Brian bunked with Bill. Mick bunked with Keith. Charlie Watts bunked with Andrew Oldham. Ian Stewart bunked with Eric Easton. Each had his own itinerary, hot spots. "We went to the Apollo Theater the first time over," Richards said. "Joe Tex and Wilson Pickett and the complete James Brown Revue. Could never get over the fact that they were into the soul bag in sixty-four." Watts sought out his long-imagined jazz joints, red velvet and blue light. "In those days, the only way to get to New York was in a band or on a cruise ship," he said. "I was lucky to get there before Birdland closed. I saw Charlie Mingus with a thirteen-piece band."

Murray "the K" Kaufman had been hired to usher the Stones around town. Let's pause to remember that lost breed of high-intensity A.M. disc jockey, their caffeinated voices filling the bedrooms of America. Murray, with his suspiciously youthful hair and faddish catchphrases, was king of the record spinners. His tag—"It's what's happening, baby!"—could break an artist.

> Murray the K: What's happening, baby?
> Ringo Starr: You're what's happening, baby.
> Murray the K: You're what's happening, too, baby!
> Ringo Starr: Okay, we're both what's happening, baby.

Though not able to help the Stones as he was said to have helped the Beatles, Murray did give them a song. He played it for them at his station: "It's All Over Now," co-written by the black singer Bobby Womack, is less R&B than country. Murray had recognized a melancholy in the Stones, that place where the blues touched B-minor hillbilly twang. Recorded ten days later, it was the Stones' first foray into country and their first number one hit. "Bobby Womack was outraged that a white group from Britain copied his song," Norman Jopling told me. "Then he got the royalty check: it was more money than Bobby Womack had seen in his entire life."

. . .

The Stones flew to Los Angeles on June 5, 1964. L.A. in the early sixties was America at its most American. It never got better. They were humiliated on Dean Martin's variety show, *The Hollywood Palace.* Goofy, mischievous Martin should've appreciated the Stones, but he mocked them instead.

It's a fascinating encounter: here you have an avatar of Eisenhower-era cool—there was no one more hip than Dino singing with glass in hand—reacting to the avatar of the new generation in the old-school way. If you recognize your successor, step on his neck. But in the long run, all that mattered was the performance. The Stones played "Not Fade Away," "I Just Wanna Make Love to You," and "Tell Me." Look it up on YouTube. It's incredible. Footage of bands from that era—the Beach Boys, Jan & Dean—is usually tame, dated. But the Stones look as fresh and raw as they must have looked that afternoon. Jagger explodes from the screen. In a moment, Dino had been relegated to pop history.

The western swing of the tour opened rapturously in San Bernardino, then went downhill fast. Thirteen shows, nine cities. Empty halls, desolate towns. Jukebox light in country taverns. Back roads in the moonlight. Charlie Watts began sketching his hotel rooms, every bed captured in a few strokes. A way to anchor experience, nail each day into place—otherwise the hours slipped by as in a dream. "I've heard stories from the boys about when they first came here in the old Beatles fanatic days, before the Stones were known," Ron Wood said. "They played huge outdoor arenas, massive attendances were expected, but no one came. They did a show in Omaha for five thousand people in a fifty-thousand-seat stadium. Those were the hard pioneer times."

"The early tours were fantastically strange," Gered Mankowitz, the band's photographer in the sixties, told me. "Remember, these boys had been educated by American TV. Cowboys and Indians were their lifeblood. Hopalong Cassidy, the Lone Ranger, Gene Autry, Roy Rogers. And the comics. And the music, blues and R&B. America was the place they'd all dreamed of, but it wasn't anything like they'd imagined, especially at the beginning."

The Stones were stunned by the South. Nineteen sixty-four was Freedom Summer, when volunteers traveled en masse to register black voters in Mississippi. There was tension in the towns, hatred in the air. On June 21, three civil rights workers, Andrew Goodman, Michael Schwerner, and James Chaney, vanished near Philadelphia, Mississippi. In August their bodies were found; they'd been shot and buried in a shallow grave. "New York was wonderful [in 1964]," Jagger said. "L.A. was kind of interesting. But outside that . . . we found it the most repressive society. Very prejudiced. In every way there was still segregation. And the attitudes were fantastically old-fashioned. Americans shocked me by their behavior and narrow-mindedness."

But Chicago was a thrill. As a reward for the band, Andrew Oldham arranged studio time at Chess Records, a label that did not usually let outsiders use its facilities. The lounge and smoke-filled passageways, the cozy-as-a-coffin studio with its mikes and stench—"funk," a Chess veteran told me, "guys playin' and sweatin' in the summer"—the sound board and sidemen, the storied producer Ron Malo—it was all reserved for Chess. But, as was often the case in those years, Andrew Oldham got lucky. When he told his mentor, the producer Phil Spector, what he had in mind, Spector called the label, and instead of getting Leonard Chess, the macher who ran the business, on the phone, he got Leonard's son, Marshall. Leonard did not understand British blues, nor did he believe music inspired by Muddy Waters and Howlin' Wolf could find a middle-class white audience, but Marshall understood the hunger of his contemporaries. He'd been a pre-Beatlemania consumer of British blues, hipped by request forms that streamed in from England. He remembered filling orders for Michael Jagger of Dartford, England. Thus, the request, related via Spector, came as an instance of blowback, an echo, the Chess sound bounced off the moon. "I was in love with those groups from the beginning," Marshall explained. "The early Yardbirds, the Kinks, the Stones. It was our first experience of getting redone by people. Over time, it was the way our message went wide, the way the records we cut on South Michigan Avenue helped change the consciousness of the planet. We'd never let outside people use our studios, but I knew who the Stones were. I had their record. It seemed like something special."

Marshall served as the band's guide in Chicago. He remembers driving down State Street in a convertible with Brian, long hair blowing as people in other cars honked and pointed and screamed every variation of "faggot." He showed them around the studio, making introductions. When I asked Marshall to describe Chess in those days, he said, "It used to get so hot. Muddy Waters, he'd be in one of those sleeveless T-shirts. And Willie Dixon, he was there, plugging songs. Willie used to say the best woman is a wino woman, you take 'em in an alley and fuck 'em, you don't have to see 'em after. Buddy Guy brought me a real mojo"—a magic amulet cooked up by voodoo doctors in New Orleans, which, according to the geography of Muddy Waters, is behind the sun. "I wore it, this little fucking bag," Marshall went on. "I pinned it on my T-shirt. It had bristles sticking out. If you put that on, you'd be able to get laid. That's what he told me."

The Stones arrived at Chess on June 10, 1964. Wednesday. Unseasonably hot, equatorial, the midnineties by noon. The studio was located at 2120 South Michigan, the center of Record Row. The building was nothing special—you see dozens like it all over the city. Two stories, deeper than tall, an awning over the door. "We walked into Chess Studios, and there's this guy in black overalls painting the ceiling," Keith wrote. "And it's Muddy Waters, and he's got whitewash streaming down his face and he's on top of a ladder."

Marshall denies this vehemently. No way. Never happened. But even if it's not literally true, it's symbolically true. The fact is, the artists who worked for Chess often believed they were shortchanged. Not paid what they should've been paid, given a car instead of royalties, tricked out of publishing rights, and so on. Among themselves, they sometimes referred to the label as Plantation Chess. If Keith did *imagine* the scene, how interesting that he put his hero in whiteface.

The Stones worked in Studio A. It was nerve-racking, playing on this hallowed ground as Chess regulars, including Willie Dixon and Chuck Berry, watched. According to witnesses, Jagger sang the first numbers with his back turned. He couldn't face all those eyes. But the old-timers loved the Stones, *especially* Jagger. Because he was doing something unique. In trying to imitate the masters, he'd filled the songs with his own experience and personality, the result being a new music, familiar yet strange. "You are sounding most well, if I may say so," Chuck Berry told them. Then, before he left, Berry added a coda: "Swing on, gentlemen."

Jagger says he does not remember visiting Chess. It's hard to believe, as the band spent several days there, cutting their second album. But Mick wants to come from nowhere, which means throwing dirt on his footprints. Keith is the opposite. He wants to ground himself in tradition—in this way, he gets to choose his own parents. He still speaks of those hours at Chess with excitement, awe: "There was a guy called Big Red, or something, playing in the B studio, storming blues stuff, a big, big albino black guy, with a Gibson that looked like a mandolin in his hands. Mick, Charlie, Stu, and I went in to listen to him; it was a powerhouse band, but we didn't even think of asking the Chess artists to sit in with us. We were just happy to be in the room."

For years, Keith had lain in bed listening to these musicians, imagining this studio, which seemed both insubstantial and like the most important place in the world. More than a record label, Chess was every artist who'd ever worked there, every song ever put on vinyl. It was the city and the sound. It was a perfect groove that appeared, as if from nowhere, on a handful of Delta farms at the start of the twentieth century.

The band leader W. C. Handy later spoke of seeing him play one night on a train platform in Tutwiler, Mississippi. Having dozed off, Handy was awoken by a guitar drunk on moonshine, slurring and haunted, moaning like a prisoner. That was 1903. Handy found himself staring into the eyes of "a lean, loose-jointed Negro . . . As he played, he pressed a knife on the strings of the guitar in a manner popularized by Hawaiian guitarists who used steel bars. The singer repeated a line three times—'Going where the Southern cross the Dog'—accompanying himself with the weirdest music I had ever heard." By referencing the place where the Southern Railroad crossed

the Yazoo & Mississippi Valley Railroad, aka the Yellow Dog, the progenitor had already staked out the key obsessions: the train and its promise, speed and escape.

The Delta blues began as a country cousin to sophisticated New Orleans jazz. From the start, it was characterized by guitar and harmonica, the preferred instruments of the poor—because they were cheap, but also because they came closest to approximating the human voice. This was especially true of the slide guitar, which wails like a man on the rack. "There wasn't a first guy who put it all together," David Evans, author of *Big Road Blues: Tradition and Creativity in the Folk Blues*, told me. "It was likely a gradual process we don't really understand. In the early stage it was probably as Handy describes it: snatches of songs, phrases, short fragmentary pieces with a lot of repetition. And then, over a fairly rapid period, people started to give the music shape. People who were more sophisticated musically, professional entertainers, would have created things like the twelve-bar form that emerged at the end of the first decade of the century."

"It's all got to do with bringing cats over from Africa and forcin' them to live here and work in the fields, in slavery," Keith Richards told the journalist Stanley Booth. "It's got to do with the crosscurrents of music, and of all the weird things that nobody thinks of when they need a bit of cheap labor. And they've never realized the ramifications, and the effects—all they want is now, now, now, money, money, money, cheap, cheap, cheap. Then you get a few hundred years down the line, and pressure forces you to free these cats. Meanwhile they've learnt all your shit."

At some point, everyone who loves Delta blues must grapple with Robert Johnson. Born May 8, 1911, he built his first instrument— a diddley bow—with wires and nails. At around fifteen, he began showing up at Funk's Corner Store in Robinsonville, Mississippi, mesmerized by the men who played guitars on the porch, especially Son House. Now and then, Johnson joined in on harmonica. He wanted to play guitar but was terrible. "Robert, don't do that," Son House would tell him, "you'll drive the people home."

Johnson's parents forbade him to follow the bluesmen to the joints, which is probably why he ran away. Some say he went north to work in the lumber camps, others say he went to the Carolina islands. He was gone six months, a year. Then, one night in 1931, he walked into a joint where Son House was performing with Willie Brown. Johnson had a guitar over his shoulder. "I said, 'Bill, Bill . . . Look who's coming in the door!'" House said. "Robert wiggled through the crowd, until he got over to where we was. And I said, 'Boy, now where you going with that guitar?'

"'I'll tell you what, too,' said Johnson. 'This your rest time?'

"'We can make it our rest time,'" I said. "'What you want to do, annoy the folks?'

"'Just give me a try.'

"So me and Willie got up, and I gave him my seat," House went on. "He set down. And that boy got started off playing. He had an extra string he'd put on, a six-string guitar made into a seven-string, he put it on hisself. Something I'd never saw before, none of us had. And when that boy started playing, all our mouths were standing open."

People who heard Johnson say he was the greatest guitar player in the world. Muddy Waters saw him on a street in Mississippi. He said it was like listening to a band. "The things he was doing was things that I'd never heard nobody else do," said bluesman Johnny Shines, who traveled with Johnson. "His guitar seemed to talk—repeat and say words. . . . His sound affected most women in a way I could never understand. One time in St. Louis we were playing one of the songs that Robert would like to play, 'Come On in My Kitchen.' He was playing very slow and passionately, and when he quit, I noticed no one was saying anything. Then I realized they were crying—both women and men."

The mystery endures: Robert Johnson leaves Robinsonville, Mississippi, an enthusiastic young fool and returns six months later a master. There were rumors, fantastic tales. Some said he'd made a deal with the devil, traded his soul for wicked ability. Not just for proficiency but for the music itself, the otherworldly rhythms that flowed from him like blood. Why was it so powerful? Why did it make women cry? Because it's the devil. The mechanics were described: how Johnson took his guitar to the intersection of Highway 49 and Highway 61, a crossroads at midnight, the fields going away. A man walked up, tall, with a long overcoat. Robert picked out a tune, then handed his guitar to the stranger, whose hair was white and eyes were blue, and he played a song of his own, then handed it back. And that was it—the deal was done.

When I asked David Evans, who described this story as an old African tale meant to explain creation, how it came to be associated with Johnson, he said, "It's all over his lyrics. He was obsessed with spiritual themes, the supernatural, God, the devil, voodoo, victimization, decisions that can't be unmade. He doesn't explicitly say he made a pact with the devil but he comes close and hints he was in the devil's clutches."

As far as I'm concerned, this is more than a story. It's a big truth behind the blues and rock 'n' roll. Robert Johnson bargained with the devil not just for his ability but for the music itself, church music fallen from heaven, God's music remade in sin. Everyone who followed in Johnson's footsteps inherited the terms, stood at the same crossroads, signed on the same line. The tenor of the deal echoes through the best of the Stones, Zeppelin, the Allman Brothers. Eric Clapton said he was shattered by his first encounter with Johnson. "It came as something of a shock that there could be anything that powerful," he explained. "At first it was too painful, but about six months after I started listening, I didn't want to listen to anything else. Up until I was twenty-five, if you didn't know who Robert Johnson was I wouldn't talk to you. . . . It was as if I had been prepared to receive Robert Johnson, almost like a religious experience that started out with hearing Chuck Berry."

The most vivid thing about Johnson, other than his music, is his death. He had a regular gig near Greenwood, Mississippi, in 1938. One night, when he asked for whiskey, the proprietor, ridden by jealousy—his wife had taken a liking to the musician—laced the drink with poison. Johnson was stumbling by two A.M., behaving like a man possessed. His last waking moment was spent on hands and knees, barking like a dog. He fell into a coma and died. He was twenty-seven years old.

A few years later, the archivist Alan Lomax, commissioned by the Library of Congress to record the Negro blues, went looking for Johnson. He searched the juke joints and bars but was always sent on to the next town with a wave of the hand. He got the news in Mississippi. *Yes, Robert was here. And his skin was alabaster and his teeth were ivory. But he's dead.* Lomax was told there was, however, another young man with a similar sound, the same demonic spark. He lived on Stovall Plantation near Clarksdale. His name was McKinley Morganfield, but everyone called him Muddy Waters.

Lomax took a picture of Muddy behind his shack. It's the earliest image we have of him. He looks as dapper as a Gap model in a long-sleeved T-shirt, chinos, and white shoes, his fingers resting on the strings of a Sears, Roebuck and Co. guitar, the latest version of a cheap model the store had been shipping since the 1890s. For many great players, this was their first real instrument. It came in the mail with instructions for playing a single song, "Spanish Fandango," which, as a result, is among the most stealthily influential songs in history.

Lomax interviewed Waters, who gave his name and story, then played. Lomax eventually recorded fifteen of Muddy's songs, including "Country Blues," "I Be's Troubled," "You Gonna Miss Me"—the same songs he'd later record for Chess. They sound the same, too, only different. They're like pictures from the old country: your grandma in Bielsk instead of Miami Beach. Stripped, basic, beautiful, weird. For Muddy, recording was less important than playback. It was the first time he'd ever heard himself. In the 1940s, a person might go an entire lifetime without hearing his or her own voice. Muddy was thrilled. The men he'd listened to on records and the radio always sounded perfect. Hearing himself, Muddy realized he was just as good as any of them. "Later on [Lomax] sent me two copies of the

pressing and a check for twenty bucks," Waters said. "I carried that
record up to the corner and put it on the jukebox. Just played it and
played it and said, 'I can do it, I can do it.'"

Muddy Waters got on a train and went north. Dirt to steel. Fields
to towns. The outskirts of Chicago. Factories, smokestacks, flames.
Endless streets. Neighborhoods. Politicians, mobsters. Coal yards,
packing plants. Muddy was part of an exodus, the Great Migration,
which, between the world wars, drew hundreds of thousands of
Southern blacks to the Midwest and North in search of work, freedom. In Chicago, they settled mostly on the South Side.

Muddy got a job driving a truck. He went home at the end of the
day, showered, put on his good clothes, and hit the joints. By 1945, the
greatest bluesmen were in Chicago. Elmore James. Howlin' Wolf.
Johnny Shines. Honeyboy Edwards. Pinetop Perkins. They played in
taverns and at house parties and on Maxwell Street. Everyone had
just arrived. Everyone wanted to be Robert Johnson. Everyone
dreamed of the music Robert Johnson would have made had he lived
long enough to see Chicago after the war.

Muddy performed in little clubs. At first, when he played—
a moaning voice accompanied by acoustic guitar—he could not be
heard over the chattering crowd, the trucks in the street, the trains
rumbling past. When Bob Dylan went electric, it was to confound his
audience. When Muddy Waters went electric, it was to be understood. He put pickups on his guitar and plugged it into a speaker
behind the stage. He quickly realized the result was not his old instrument plus electricity, but a new instrument altogether. The mechanics were the same, but the effect was novel. Those who fought
this novelty—tried to play electric as they'd played acoustic—failed.
Those who accepted it as a new medium started a revolution.

In this way, Delta blues took on the sound of the city—the hum of
the Steel Belt, the rattle of the elevated, Cadillacs and Fords throbbing in the early-morning rush, steam hammer and factory whistle.
The perfect symbol of this transformation—country blues to R&B—

was Muddy's slide. In Mississippi, he used the neck of a Coke bottle, the sort found in the right-of-way along the railroad track, country trash. He swapped it on the South Side for a steel tube picked up in the factory where he worked part-time. It gave his guitar a precise, metallic ring.

Many years ago, I had a moment of clarity. I was at the Melkweg Café in Amsterdam and had just eaten a gigantic brownie. I was sitting with my legs stretched beneath the table, skinny and twenty, in touch with every bone in my perishable body. Music had been playing all night, but I did not notice it till the deejay put on "Mannish Boy" by Muddy Waters. The song fanned out like a poker hand—all face cards. Queens and jokers. The king with a knife to his head. The one-eyed jack. I'd heard it a million times but this was the first time I understood the music, how it evolved, where it came from. I could see Muddy playing for Alan Lomax behind his shack in Mississippi. I could see the train carrying him north, the music picking up the steel of the cities as it went. I could see the South Side musicians, each adding a particular sound. It was Robert Johnson turning into the Rolling Stones.

In Chicago, Muddy Waters found a perfect collaborator in Polish-born Leonard Chess. After stints in junk and liquor, Chess started a record label because he recognized a market where others had seen only a mass—the Mississippi emigrants who filled the ghetto. Leonard's initial intention was to sell party records. Over time, his vision evolved. In the first sessions with Muddy, Leonard recorded him in the most basic way: alone with acoustic guitar. But at Muddy's urging, he soon brought in Muddy's electric band, resulting in a string of classics that form the bedrock beneath my feet: "Rollin' Stone," "I've Got My Mojo Working," "I'm a King Bee." Leonard never imagined this music would last. It was detritus, the remains of a Saturday night. Its ability to transcend escaped him entirely. In essence, he remained a junk dealer. He was like the hunter who went for venison and returned with cougar. He did not understand the nature of his kill. But the records he made changed the world. They had a small impact in America, but a large impact in England, where they were free of racial implication. Which is why it took the likes of Jagger, Richards, and Jones to hear the music for what it was—music.

On their first day at Chess, the Stones recorded five songs, including "It's All Over Now" and "Time Is on My Side." They cut eleven more on day two, including "Around and Around." It was not just product they were after. It was atmosphere, the moodiness of the famous blues sides, the rawness and the reverb, the laughter between takes. Until then, the Stones' performances had towered above their studio work. In Chicago, they finally captured the energy of the live show. "Under the Boardwalk," "Congratulations," "Susie Q," "2120 South Michigan Avenue"—the band's second album, 12 X 5, is a dream of Chess Records.

16

SATISFACTION

"You can get very blasé about a song like 'Satisfaction.' It's been around forever, was written and recorded so long ago, has been played on so many radios so many millions of times, it vanishes. You don't think about it, maybe get tired of talking about it. But it was not inevitable. It did not have to happen. If it had not been written and recorded when it was, who knows? It prevented us from being just another good band with a nice run. That big early hit is essential. You might have a lot of success without it, sell a lot of records, but you won't get over. 'Satisfaction' did that for us. You absolutely need that one song."

This was Mick Jagger talking circa 1998. I was trailing him, taking in every word and gesture in a vain attempt to unlock the mystery. I revered him as you revere a master atop the mountain. He smiled and offered wisdom. He seemed to love me and I loved me because he loved me. He was the king and everything he touched glowed.

Of course, it was not always thus. . . .

Jagger returned from his first trip to America deflated. The tour was seen as a terrific failure. Whereas the Beatles had made a fortune in the USA, the Stones made nothing but the echo of a band playing an empty arena. The Buddha asks: *What is the sound of one man booing?* But the second tour was better, and the third better still. By late 1964, the Stones had begun to stake their position as the antipode of the Beatles. The turning point was probably their appearance on *The*

Ed Sullivan Show—the first dunk into the broad mainstream. They played "Time Is on My Side," Jagger, lank and suggestive, talking to the crowd like a fallen preacher. People who'd been shocked by Elvis and soothed by the Beatles were shocked all over again. "They put the touch on me," singer Patti Smith, eighteen years old and watching with her father, wrote later. "I was blushing jelly. This was no mama's boy music. It was alchemical. I couldn't fathom the recipe but I was ready. Blind love for my father was the first thing I sacrificed to Mick Jagger."

Success meant more gigs, more towns. Hard drugs had not yet come in, nor big money. "That was the best time," Gered Mankowitz told me, "because they were still a gang. We didn't have luxury or so-phistication. We didn't have backup bands. We didn't have sound checks or lighting. We just had each other. It was primitive, and it was fantastic. One night, we camped out on the Apache reservation out-side Phoenix. It was like something out of *The Lone Ranger*. We slept under the stars, cooked on a fire. Keith bought us all guns and Stet-sons."

In Los Angeles, Joe Smith, co-head of Warner/Reprise, invited Andrew Oldham and Keith Richards to a Frank Sinatra recording session. In the storied studio on Sunset, "[Frank] sat down, adjusted himself into the stool, put a headphone on one ear, indicated he wanted the playback via the headphones and speakers," Oldham writes in his follow-up memoir, *2Stoned*. "He snapped his fingers to feel the air in the room, agreed with the shine on his shoes, and sig-naled to the booth to roll the tape. . . . Keith and I sat a wee bit gob-smacked at the pro-ease we were seeing and hearing. In the next forty-five minutes, Frank Sinatra recorded two or three takes each on three songs. When satisfied with his handling of a song . . . he didn't stop . . . or ask to listen to what he had just done. He knew what he had done and just said, 'Next one,' and perhaps, 'please.'"

Between takes, Sinatra and Richards stood in a corner of the con-trol room, laughing together like pontiffs from different eras. Keith was a scruffy, scrawny, snaggletoothed urchin. Frank was plump with middle age, beautifully groomed and Barbasoled, in silk and leather, but they were, in a sense, the same person, living varieties of the same existence. Both grew up on the music of their time, which they re-fashioned into a sound that touched generations. Both surfed the zeitgeist. Both stole from and emulated the black musical genius of America. Both were chased by bobby-soxers. Both had careers that went on and on, a feat only the savviest entertainers manage. Both craved live performance, the shimmer of front-row heat. Both were wild and dangerous when young, stately and sage when old. Both had to learn, in middle age, how to do what they'd once done by instinct. Both had a broken heart and expressed that heartbreak in song. Both had ups and downs, binges and cold turkeys. Both devoured yet re-mained hungry. Both were role models, expressions of a certain kind of manhood. Both inspired how-to books. On my shelf, beside *The Way You Wear Your Hat: Frank Sinatra and the Lost Art of Livin'* by Bill Zehme, is *What Would Keith Richards Do? Daily Affirmations from a Rock 'n' Roll Survivor* by Jessica Pallington West. Both elicited, from male Americans, the same response I got from my college friend Ricky Heroes when I asked his opinion of the wrestler Jerry Lawler: "That sonofabitch is a man!" Both stared into the darkness wonder-ing, *Why, baby, why?*

Oldham and Richards gossiped with Smith after Sinatra left. "We ambled into the hall and were chatting about life in general, or slag-ging other acts, when I turned and looked down the long hall, through the glass studio doors out onto Sunset," Oldham goes on. "There, black-straw-hatted, black silk or mohair slub-suited, in a black open Lincoln Continental, waiting for the lights to be green, sat Sinatra at the wheel. There was no entourage, bodyguards, Rat Pack or clan. Just a man, content, alone, the day's work done, joining the rest of the early L.A. evening traffic, going home."

. . .

Jagger and Richards were under tremendous pressure on the road. Between shows, they were expected to write the hits that kept everything going. "We traveled at night," Gered Mankowitz told me. "They'd come off the stage, go into the limo and straight to the airport. We'd fly until two, three, four A.M., check in to some dump. Nobody to welcome us. Nothing open. No food. Deadsville. The bulk of the tour was like that. You do the show, you're gone. And in all the between times, Mick and Keith were working. They had orders to come up with material. And struggled because the schedule wasn't conducive. But they pushed through, taking down the ideas whenever they came. You'd see them all the time, jotting little notes throughout the tour."

When it wasn't working, it was pain. When it was working, it was pleasure. Prizing a song from the void. Summoning a melody from nonexistence. If a Stones song begins as a riff, where does the riff come from? It's a mystery. In the case of "Satisfaction," it happened while Keith was asleep. Reports have placed the dreamer, variously, at a hotel in America, a house in Chelsea, or the London Hilton. In *Life*, Keith says he was at his flat on Carlton Hill, in St. John's Wood.

I sleep with an inhaler and a glass of water at my side. My son sleeps with a stuffed seal named Sealy. Keith sleeps with an acoustic guitar and a Philips tape recorder. One morning, in 1965, he noticed the guitar had been moved, the recorder turned on. Examining more closely, he saw that someone had recorded over the entire tape. When he rewound and pressed PLAY, he heard his own guitar being picked up and played. Five notes: second fret on the A string played twice slowly, once quickly, followed by the fourth and fifth fret on the A string. Baa-Baa Ba-Ba-Ba . . . The guitar was set down, a body hit the sheets.

Keith put the tape in an envelope marked "Can't Get No Satisfaction." He's never explained the origin of that phrase. Years later, in an interview I worked on with Jann Wenner at *Rolling Stone*, Jagger said Richards was probably influenced by Chuck Berry's "Thirty Days," which includes the lyric, "If I don't get no satisfaction from the judge."

"Keith might have heard it back then, because it's not any way an English person would express it," Jagger explained. "I'm not saying he purposely nicked anything, but we played those records a lot."

The riff seems part Chuck Berry, part something else. The four- or five-note progression, that dirty garage band sound, was in the wind. When I listen to "Satisfaction," it's less "Maybellene" I hear than "I Can't Explain" by the Who or "Where Have All the Good Times Gone" by the Kinks. To me, these tunes play like elaborations on a theme. It's the mood of the moment translated into guitar. As Keith himself has said, you operate, on the best days, less as composer than as medium. The fact that he received the riff in his sleep only emphasizes the point.

Jagger and Richards did not take up the song until several weeks later, by which time they were back on the road. Mick filled in the missing pieces: chords, chorus, bridge. One afternoon, they sat poolside at the Fort Harrison Hotel in Clearwater, Florida, working. The hotel had been built in 1926 and managed by Ransom Olds, the namesake of the Oldsmobile. To mark its opening, the daredevil Henry Roland had climbed the exterior in a blindfold. It's since become a Scientology headquarters. Shortly after the Stones checked in, Jones and Wyman hooked up with groupies, the sort that haunt astronaut bars and speedways. Brian's girl showed up black-eyed by the pool in the morning. Paranoid and increasingly jealous of the Mick/Keith writing partnership, Jones spent his rage on women. The keener his paranoia, the more violent the outburst. As Keith has said, "He was not a good man." As Charlie has said, "He was a little prick." Mike Dorsey, a British actor who drove and protected the Stones, told Brian off, then punched him out. In addition to the moral offense, it was just stupid to beat up a local girl in the Bible Belt.

Meanwhile, Jagger and Richards were finishing "Satisfaction." If the riff was all Keith, the lyric was all Mick. You know the plot: a young man, a lot like Jagger, big but about to become much bigger, decrying the pressures and people and commercial concerns closing in from every side. It's a pose as much as a song, Jagger's way of carrying himself in the world. It plugged into the cynicism of a generation beset by advertising. "When I'm watchin' my TV / And a man comes on to tell me / How white my shirts can be." In a few lines, you have the disdain for parents and received wisdom, as well as the omnipresence of "the man," who represents authority and discipline, and who, according to that seminal film *School of Rock*, it's our primary task to confront. It's one of Mick Jagger's talents: this freakish ability to capture the zeitgeist in a phrase. He's a social historian working from the inside, observing the moment as he remakes it.

When I asked Jagger about this—Where do the songs come from? How do you capture the moment?—he paused, then said, "It's about being a social animal. We're all in an anthill. We've all got these antennas."

The other Stones first heard "Satisfaction" in one of the hotel rooms. Keith played acoustic guitar as Mick mumbled the lyric. At the beginning, it sounded less like an anthem than a dirge. It bitched and complained. "Neither Mick nor Keith saw it as a potential single, and certainly not a hit," Wyman writes. "Keith's instinct must have told him it was worth some effort, because he kept working on it." The biggest influence on the lyric was probably Bob Dylan, whose album *Bringing It All Back Home* had been released that year. There's actually a picture of Jagger, poolside in Clearwater, studying the back of the record cover. Dylan was rewriting the rules, giving composers permission to write about their own lives in a personal language that, like a private joke, could never be fully understood by an outsider. It's a trick Dylan borrowed from the Beats—a modernist trick that obscures a song toward enigma. By withholding, the writer invites repeat listening. What's more compelling than the half-heard table talk of a rock star, the story you have to complete yourself?

. . .

On May 9, 1965, the Stones played the Arie Crown Theater in Chi-cago. The next afternoon, they returned to Chess Records, where they cut "Try Me," "That's How Strong My Love Is," "The Under As-sistant West Coast Promotion Man," and "Mercy, Mercy." At the end of the nine-hour session, they recorded "Satisfaction." Oldham later described this early version as "acoustic, wayward, harmonica-laden: [It] just would not do ... the hook registered as marginal to nowt." Jagger and Richards were ready to ditch the song, but Oldham urged them to keep after it. *Because of that riff!* It was buried, but there, toll-ing like a bell: B–B–B–C#–D.

The band flew to Los Angeles the next day, where, at RCA Studios in Hollywood, they hooked up with sound engineer David Hassinger and producer and musician Jack Nitzsche, who'd prove essential. Nitzsche, who deserves a book of his own, urged the band through each iteration of "Satisfaction." He played piano on the sessions. Though his track was later removed, it was, according to Oldham, essential in delineating and holding together the groove. In other words, even though you can't hear him on the record, he's there.

Jagger nailed the vocal, but the rest of the song had to evolve. The first RCA take was weak. Oldham compared it to "Walk Right In" by the Rooftop Singers—"[It] called for striped shirts, Brylcreem, bas-ketball slacks and a time-out." The grit was missing. In the early morning of May 12, at the end of a fourteen-hour session, Charlie Watts switched tempo and everything else began to fall into place. When Keith listened to the new version, he knew what was missing. *The riff!* He had to crank it up. The next morning, Ian Stewart came back from the music store with a Gibson Maestro fuzz box, a new gizmo that distorted guitar, junked it up. The sound was akin to the lead on the Kinks' "You Really Got Me," which, according to legend, resulted from a fight between Dave Davies and Ray Davies. One of the brothers cut an amp speaker with a razor blade, causing the same sort of snarled line Keith achieved with the fuzz pedal. It's exactly what was needed to emphasize the lick that opens "Satisfaction." "It was a miracle," Richards told *Guitar Player* magazine. "I was screaming for more distortion. 'This riff's really gotta hang hard and long.' We burnt the amps up and turned the shit up, and it still wasn't right. And then Ian Stewart went around the corner to Wallach's Music City or something and came around with a distortion box: 'Try this.' It was as offhand as that. It was just from nowhere. I never really got into the thing after that, either. It had a very limited use, but it was just right for that song."

Oldham took a vote: Should "Satisfaction" be the next single? According to Bill Wyman, it was close, with Charlie, Bill, and Brian voting yes, while Mick and Keith opposed. Brian's vote is the most surprising, as he later claimed to hate that song. *Fleur du mal*—an evil flower that signified ruin. Keith did not consider the song a hit. Mick does not remember voting. Andrew says no vote was necessary as everyone realized "Satisfaction" was going to be a monster. And yet Keith says he was surprised when it was released, only learning of it when the song came on the radio as the band drove through Minnesota in June. "We didn't even know Andrew had put the fucking thing out!" he explained. "At first, I was mortified. As far as I was concerned, that was just the dub."

But it's that raw, unfinished quality that gives the single its power. Of course, you can't understand it in isolation. You have to consider the context. If you want to appreciate Marlon Brando in 1954, compare him to Gary Cooper. If you want to appreciate Elvis Presley in 1956, compare him to Perry Como. If you want to understand "Satisfaction" in 1965, compare it to "The Birds and the Bees" by Jewel Akens or "This Diamond Ring" by Gary Lewis and the Playboys. Beside them, "Satisfaction" is raffish and strange, a kid wearing motorcycle boots at a prep school. It went up the charts like a projectile, surpassing "Help" (the Beatles), surpassing "Crying in the Chapel" (Elvis). It hung like a crescent moon, the Stones' first number one in America, the sound of summer in 1965, blasting from every transistor radio. It was ten times bigger than anything the Stones had experienced— a quantum leap that resolved all doubts. In the commercial world, there are generally two of everything. It's either/or, the dialectic of consumerism. Pepsi or Coke, Marlboro or Kool. It was not going be the Kinks, nor the Who, nor the Dave Clark Five. From the release of "Satisfaction" to the entrance of Yoko Ono, rock 'n' roll was going to be either the Beatles or the Rolling Stones.

Success on a grand scale can be isolating, dangerous. It separated the Stones from mentors and friends. It made them suspect by members of the older generation who considered pop stardom an offense against the blues, apostasy. When I asked Chris Barber about the Stones, he replied in the way of Obi-Wan Kenobi discussing Darth Vader, the failed Jedi knight. "It's not real," he said of Mick and Keith's music. "And the sad thing is, they were capable of the real thing. But they found something else which is not real but makes them an awful lot of money. And everybody else makes a lot of money on it, too. So everybody likes it. But it's not real, and, if you are a serious musician, you know it's not real. Just look at Brian Jones. He was serious, very serious. He was Alexis Korner's prodigy. But he couldn't stop it. Because they were tempted, terribly tempted, right from the start, and could not resist. But Brian never felt right about it. It was clear to anyone who knew him."

Brian Jones was the first casualty of "Satisfaction." The song was a gun pointed at his head. It blew him away. It was the transgression, the way it converted some of the most beloved tics of the Delta into teenage pop. The success—the magnitude of it—that was toughest of all. It estranged Brian from Mick and Keith, who, with "Satisfaction," took control of the band. When the song hit number one, it was over and out for Brian. He'd never lead again, or hold center stage. He'd been relegated to the background. And hated it. And rebelled.

His real problems began that summer. He acted out, got drunk, violent, and mean, stumbled around, hair falling in his eyes, snarled or vanished. As the rest of band played "Satisfaction," he vamped the theme to *Popeye the Sailor*.

"In the first photo sessions I did with the Stones at the start of sixty-five, Brian had the glamour, the charisma," Gered Mankowitz told me. "He was the most polished. He was the star. Mick and Keith were still rough at the edges. And, I'd say, studenty. But Brian's difficult and odd personality issues came to the fore quite quickly. By the time we were on tour in mid-sixty-five, he was becoming quite erratic and unreliable. He would disappear, he would play very badly. He was like a child. For instance, I remember stopping for a hamburger between Fort Worth and Dallas. Brian said he didn't want anything, he'd stay in the limo. And so we went into this place and had our hamburgers, and as we got back into the limo, Brian decided he did want something and went into the café. It was stupid stuff like that. Andrew didn't let him get away with it—he was dragged out."

Andrew Oldham was the second casualty of "Satisfaction." It was less a direct hit than a ricochet. It started with Oldham's realization that the size of the score put the Stones in another league, which put him in over his head. Oldham was a visionary, a PR man, a teenage tycoon shit; this called for a professional. Allen Klein was a music business accountant known for record label audits that netted clients like Sam Cooke hundreds of thousands of dollars in unpaid royalties (of which Klein kept half). By the mid-1960s, Klein, who dreamed of cornering the market in British pop, had management deals with the Dave Clark Five, the Animals, and Herman's Hermits, among others. Oldham met him at a Miami record convention. And was impressed. In the summer of '65, Oldham broke with partner Eric Easton and brought in Klein to negotiate a new Stones deal with Decca, put the operation on a sound financial footing, and co-manage the Stones.

Allen Klein! The legend! The menace! His picture hangs in the rogues' gallery of rock 'n' roll, the shyster who rolled the Stones like a drunk in an alley. He spent much of his childhood in a New Jersey orphanage, went to school on the GI Bill, drank whiskey from the bottle, carried money in a roll—the rare CPA who's packing. Behind him stands a legion of record men, street-corner ganefs who worked their way up from nothing. Syd Nathan. Morris Levy. Hy Weiss. They cruised the pristine waters like reef sharks, understood the small print and trapdoor and figured, *Why take 20 percent when I can have it all?* For the Stones, Klein was the dark side of the dream. You want to live like the blues legends? Well, what's more characteristic of those lives than getting taken by the likes of Allen Klein?

It was the tough guy persona that attracted Oldham. He figured the bullet-headed Jersey accountant would be a perfect weapon in the coming negotiations with Decca. "Andrew liked having me portrayed as this shadowy American who could take care of anything," Klein said. "That was Andrew, he just created it, that I was like a gangster. He said, 'They'll love it in England.' No one would ever talk to me about it. That's what the British think of all Americans who might be Italians."

"Was he vilified? Absolutely," Ronnie Schneider, Klein's nephew and a Stones tour manager, told me, "but vilification works two ways. Saddam Hussein used vilification to keep himself safe for many years."

The Stones are a Russian novel. Open to any page, you find a dramatic incident. On this one, they play "La Bamba" in a Dartford basement. On that one, they get busted for peeing against a gas station wall in London. "We'll piss anywhere," Jagger shouts. On this one, Keith stands in the foyer of Chess Records watching Muddy Waters paint the ceiling. On that one, the Stones, in sunglasses and dark suits, stand behind Allen Klein as he talks terms with Decca president and founder Edward Lewis. "He had us dress like hired goons, a gang of mafia," Charlie Watts said. "He told us exactly what to say, which was nothing." If Lewis is quiet, Klein explained, we're going to be quieter. Let him fill the silence with his own demons. Whoever talks first loses.

It was a famous showdown, the new guard prying the coin from the fist of the dying king. The Stones came away with the most lucrative recording deal in history. They were advanced a million pounds in cash for their next album. Citing Britain's punitive taxes—the top marginal rate was well above 90 percent—Klein advised the Stones to incorporate in the United States. It was a decision they'd regret.

17

REPORTING

My first story about the Stones appeared in *Rolling Stone* on August 25, 1994. That cover and the surrounding hoopla seem like relics of rock's last golden moment, the last time everyone cared and there was nothing more important. The Stones display a kind of confidence in the photos that no band will ever display again. The tether that ran from Elvis Presley through Mick Jagger was cut when Kurt Cobain put the gun to his head. I remember Jann Wenner coming out of his office one afternoon, irritated by a run of recent covers: Green Day, Hootie & the Blowfish, the Lemonheads. *Who'd want to fuck Evan Dando?*

At the time, it struck me as the raving of a baby boomer. But looking back, I think he was right. The fire that lit early rock 'n' roll and passed like a torch from Buddy Holly to the Beatles, from the Stones to the Clash, had gone out by the late 1990s. I suppose it had to do with the Internet, computers, and video games, all those immaterial worlds. The energy that powered music scenes in Chicago and Detroit and Alabama and London has moved to Silicon Valley.

Music is still being made, of course. The best bands are as proficient as ever. The best songs still rock. But the underlying belief is gone. No one thinks music will change the world, or wants it to. It's like a lot of religion. People fill the churches, though less out of fear and trembling than out of habit. We do it because our parents did it.

We do it because it's what we've always done. As we still stand in bars listening to bands. Because it's fun, not because we believe in it or think it will give meaning to our lives.

To me, that Stones cover is a memory from another time, a snapshot from a country that was my home. Where rock 'n' roll was king. Where stars guided us. Where you waited for the next record as people once waited for the next pamphlet by Voltaire. Where a song could change a season and the right tune at the right time could mean transcendence. As it fades toward sepia, my childhood, which ran from the midseventies to the late nineties, seems closer in spirit to the 1950s of Gene Vincent and His Blue Caps than to Taylor Swift.

A few days before the story hit the stands, the Stones invited Jann Wenner, me, and my editor, David Fricke, to a pretour warm-up show in Toronto. It was to be a tiny private gig, with the band performing in a Canadian bar. I took the number 9 subway to midtown Manhattan, swaying in the dim light as I stared at my reflection in the window. I was young, but I'd been younger. I was not old, but I was getting older. You're twenty-two. Then you're twenty-four. When you turn twenty-six, you realize you'll never turn twenty-five again. This train travels in one direction only. At the amusement park, they put you in the car and you believe you are steering until you lift your hands and understand you've been on a track the entire time. It does not matter what you do. The friends you have, the music you love, the schools that made a difference—all of it because your parents chose this town instead of that town, this street instead of that street.

At *Rolling Stone*, there is a hallway lined with covers. You go through it the way you go through the Tunnel of Love, the entire history unfolding. Not just the singers and comedians, not just Bowie and Belushi, but the editors and correspondents, all that reporting and writing and rewriting. As I walked along, I told myself, "I am a writer and I work for *Rolling Stone* and I have written a cover story about the Rolling Stones." In *Fast Times at Ridgemont High*, Spicoli imagines himself on TV talking about hanging out with Mick and Keith. Well, I had just done that. For real! And was about to do more of it. For real! I've never been part of a tradition, nor felt like I'd made it into the club or gang. I'd been a Chicagoan, a Bears fans, a Trevian, a Tulanian, but none of it fit securely, none of it accepted me completely. But for a moment, in that hall, my cover linked in that long chain of covers, I felt that I belonged.

I went to David Fricke's office and dropped into a chair across from his desk. He looked less like an editor than a rocker—not just any rocker, but a rocker from the Lower East Side circa 1977. Tall and wan, with long dark hair, in a motorcycle jacket, jeans, and sneakers. On the street, you might take him for a Ramone. He greeted me in his usual way: "Hey, man." We talked a little, then went down to the street. A car was waiting. It took us to Teterboro Airport in New Jersey, where we got on Jann's private jet. I believe it was a Gulfstream, perhaps a G-II. The interior was fitted with lounge chairs and screens. We took off to the west, then banked over Manhattan, the glass towers rising and falling like notes on a musical staff.

Brooklyn and Queens, Nassau and Suffolk, the south shore of Long Island unspooling far below, subdivisions giving way to barrier islands, beach roads. I paged through Jann's guest book. Paul McCartney's handwriting jumped out: *Thanks for the plane!* Knowing that the Beatle had occupied this same seat turned everything rock-star blue. We landed at East Hampton Airport, where Jann got on, grumbling. He's stocky, with a big smile that turns his eyes into dots. He looked out the window at another plane as we taxied, a G-IV. It put Jann's plane in the shade. He cursed the owner of that other plane, whoever it happened to be. We rolled to the end of the runway, turned, and took off. The plane ascended steeply, in concert with my soul. An hour later, we were in Toronto. We spent the day mingling with rock stars. When I called the magazine and spoke to my friend Bob Love, he asked, "How's it going?"

I said, "Good, but I've been smiling so much my head is killing me." He said, "I'm familiar with that headache."

That night, we went to El Mocambo, a club where the Stones had done warm-up gigs in the past. The bar was packed with music industry heavies, as well as a handful of lucky locals. The Stones came on at nine. The stage was tiny, the band crowded close together. Jagger shouted something. Richards played the opening riff of "Honky Tonk Women." The room exploded. I've seen the Stones in theaters, stadiums, a dome. I've even seen them in a school gym. But in that smoky club the Stones put on the best rock show I've ever seen. They played rough and dirty, more like a garage band than a group of old pros. For a moment, it put me back in my friend Jamie Drew's room, shotgunning a Mickey's Big Mouth and pontificating. It's a shame most fans will never experience the band this way, on a small stage, in a small room, arranged like parts of an engine. In a stadium, the energy dissipates, but at the Mocambo the boys played off and amplified one another. Mick and Keith. Charlie and Woody. The interactions were chemical. A group of friends having fun. A gang. The Stones have grown beyond their ideal proportions, become too big for the good of their music. I was seeing them in their natural habitat—a bar packed with fanatical drunks. It was like seeing Elvis at the Eagle's Nest in Memphis, or the Beatles at the Cavern in Liverpool, or Springsteen at the Stone Pony in Asbury Park, or the Ramones at CBGB on the Bowery. To people who tell me they don't get the Stones, who say, "I went to the Meadowlands show and liked some of the stuff, but ..." I say, "You've never seen the Stones. That band exists only in a bar after you've had three drinks, and Charlie has gotten loose, and Keith has found the groove, and Mick has remembered who he really is."

I met up with the band in North Carolina a few weeks later. I had a press pass, a place on the bus, and a seat on the plane. I was reporting a follow-up to the cover story, a letter from the road. I watched one song from the sound board, another from the wings. On one occasion, I sat behind Ron Wood's amp, right beside Charlie Watts, who, now and then, in the middle of a number, turned and smiled. That is, I watched not from the seats nor from the wings but from the stage itself, as if I were a Rolling Stone. Best was "the guitar room," where Richards and Wood warmed up before each concert. It was replicated in every arena, so that if you were a rock star moving in a haze, you might believe you'd never moved at all. In fact, everything was disassembled and reassembled, turning each town into the same town. The layout of rooms, the sheets on the beds, the books in the shelves— none of it changed. There was a snooker table in the "guitar room," couches, coffee tables, ashtrays, and of course guitars: acoustics and electrics, lap and pedal steel, Martins and Fenders.

I'd find a chair in the corner and fade into the pillows, just another part of the bric-a-brac, watching Keith and Ronnie jam toward readiness. They'd smoke and drink, laugh and tell jokes, but mostly just play, alone and together, trading rhythm and lead, country songs, Hank Williams, George Jones, Ernest Tubb. Richards hunched over his guitar, cigarette glued to his lip, grinning as he bent his way through "We Had It All" or "You Win Again." Ron Wood might comment on a tune, say something unintelligible, then pick up a hollow-body electric to demonstrate a point. This was the inner sanctum, the back room where the cardinals prepare for communion.

About twenty minutes before the show, Mick Jagger would start singing through the scales with a voice coach. You could hear him, in the distance, in his trailer. Richards would look up, scowl. In addition to a voice coach, Mick toured with a choreographer and a physical trainer. Keith toured with a doctor's bag, guitars, and bottles of booze. "What can he do in there that we can't do out here?" he asked, grinning. Dropping to the floor, Keith did five push-ups, good ones, the tip of his cigarette burning a hole in the carpet, a rock 'n' roll signature.

Richards and Wood took a short break between the guitar room jam and the concert itself. Standing beside the trailers like freaks on the midway, they breathed the warm evening air as the announcer made the introduction: *Ladies and gentlemen...!* The show itself went by in a moment. As the Stones played the encore, the crew waited in a line of vans, with police cars at either end, lights flashing, for the rush to the airport. I was in the second vehicle as the Stones finished "Jumpin' Jack Flash." Fireworks filled the sky, walkie-talkies burst to life. A moment later, the band emerged from the arena at a half jog. Jagger got into the first van, where he rode with his body-guard and assistant; everyone else got into the second van. I slid to the window, notebook in lap, making room. Charlie sat in front of me, as serene as ever. Wood sat behind me, arms folded. Keith sat beside me, a mess. He does not seem to move much onstage. The occasional Chuck Berry flourish: a duck walk, strum hand flying away for em-phasis, legs in a power stance. Otherwise, his demeanor is cool. As if he's just woken from a nap, swallowed a handful of blues. Even when he sings, it's as if he's doing it from the back porch on a summer after-noon. But he's drenched by the last number, shirt soaked. He couldn't catch his breath in the van, hunched over, wheezing. The other Stones didn't seem to notice, but I was concerned. When his wheezing be-came ragged, I offered him my inhaler. "I'll be fine in twenty minutes," he said. "I leave every bit of me onstage." A moment later, he sat up and grinned through his fatigue, a wry, Bogartian grin, then channel-ing the boxer Jake LaMotta after taking a pummeling in *Raging Bull*: "'Put my robe on right! Hey, put on my robe!'"

When the article ran on November 3, 1994, I got a firsthand glimpse of the rivalry that almost destroyed the Stones. Jagger's pub-licist called me in a fury. "You've misnamed this article, haven't you," he snapped in a clipped British accent. "You have called it 'On the Road with the Rolling Stones,' but that's not right. You should have called it 'I Love Keith Richards and Want to Have His Baby.'"

Of course, he was right. I do love Keith. He stands for survival. He can teach you how to remain dignified in a fallen age. Mick? Who can be Mick? Mick is Elvis in a gold lamé jacket. Mick is Michael Jackson moonwalking across time. One in a million, a freak of nature. Can't be copied, can only be enjoyed. But Keith? If you live long enough, and maintain an even strain, and focus all your passion, then, maybe, at the very end . . . I suppose, in a sense, I really do want to have his baby.

When I think back on that tour, it's not the plane I remember, or the shows, or the hotels. It's Keith's doctor's bag, an old-fashioned leather case covered with buckles. He patted it knowingly, looked into it lovingly. Snake oil and elixirs. In my mind, something inside it glows, bathing his face in a chemical light—the face of a benevolent pirate, dark eyes and pale skin, the tresses hanging down. Here's a man who's sailed every sea, touched every isle, stormed every city; who's walked the plank and lived; who's busted through the noose at the end of the yardarm and swum to freedom as bullets peppered the river. He looked up as he poked through the bag, saying, "Tell me what's wrong. In here, I got a cure for whatever ails ya."

From a certain perspective, the story of the Stones is drugs. It started during that first tour of England. Amphetamines and diet pills, speed—the sort favored by truckers. You took them to get through the shows with no sleep. Keith remembers copping in diners and at gas stations, the pills handed over in an envelope, the famous reds downed by anyone on the night shift, from Beat poets to beat cops. By day five, your vision bleeds white and your heart races. In 1965, Johnny Cash was arrested with 688 capsules at the Mexican border. "I'd talk to the demons and they'd talk back," Cash said. "They'd say, 'Go on, John, take twenty more milligrams of Dexedrine, you'll be all right.'"

In the beginning, drug use was seen as practical, even sensible, just another tool in the kit of the road warrior. Later, when the Stones became famous and the last semblance of normal life had slipped away, it was a means of escape, a hallway to a quiet room at the center of the mind. Later still, it was a path to enlightenment, a way to remove the doors from the hinges, the hinges from the jambs. "We were actually trying to do something by taking a few chemicals," Keith explained. "Everybody at that point was prepared to use himself as a sort of laboratory, to find some way out of this mess. It was very idealistic and very destructive at the same time."

This is where my generation, Generation X, parts company with the baby boomers. They ruined drugs, as they ruined Frye boots and bell-bottoms. We never shared their dream of opening the doors of perception, or touching the face of God. Because of them, enlightenment seemed like bullshit. All that remained was the high. With their embarrassing enthusiasm, they turned everything into a joke. They ate the fruit and left the peel, smoked the pot and left the resin, swallowed the epiphanies and left the reality. When it was our time, they scolded us, saying it was too dangerous—you'd have to be a moron to try it. About their own youthful behavior, they'd say, *We didn't know then what we know now*. By the time we came along, everything was banned, feared, and covered in protective foam, but can you imagine how much fun LSD must have been in 1964 when it was legal?

I asked Marianne Faithfull what drugs were like in the sixties.

"Fantastic!"

"What did you learn from LSD?"

"Everything. It was a holy and important experience for me, Mick, Keith, for all of us. It changed us and made us into better people. It was a wonderful, wonderful time. I never had a bad trip, but of course I was taking incredibly good acid. But I wouldn't recommend it to anyone today, because it's not good anymore, not pure, it's cut with shit, so don't bother, it's over."

18

ACID

If LSD wasn't invented by accident, it might as well have been. Albert Hofmann, a chemist at the Sandoz Company in Switzerland, searching for a treatment for poor circulation, had fruitlessly experimented with lysergic acid in the 1930s. In 1943, while examining his old work, he came across his twenty-fifth mixture—LSD 25. He took the first trip inadvertently when some of it got on his finger. Intrigued, he intentionally dosed three days later. It kicked in as he bicycled through Basel. "I had great difficulty in speaking coherently," Hofmann wrote in his journal. "My field of vision swayed before me and was distorted like reflections in an amusement park mirror." He did not record tangerine trees or marmalade skies, but he did speak of a loss of ego.

News of the drug spread—scientists told friends, who told other scientists and their friends, until an army of evangelists formed. It began with CIA agents and government types who believed LSD was either truth serum, a way to dispel fears of death, or the key to understanding the universe. Aldous Huxley, the British novelist and dystopian who'd written the paean to hallucinogens, *The Doors of Perception*, believed that the mind is a filter. It gives the illusion of individuality but blocks ninety percent of what's out there. LSD tears out the sieve, letting you experience the fantastic plethora of creation. The self dissolves. You taste music and hear colors and realize you've never been alone. On his first trip, Huxley said he had seen "what Adam had seen on the morning of his creation."

When rock stars began experimenting with the drug, the result was a new kind of music, a new kind of song. Bob Dylan pioneered it, the Beatles perfected it. As for Dylan, no one is sure when he took his first dose. Some date it to April 1964, by which time the singer had fallen under the spell of the French Symbolist poets, especially Arthur Rimbaud, who described the artistic process as a kind of derangement: "The poet makes himself a seer by a long, prodigious, and rational disordering of all the senses." In this way, the acid freaks were really just a modern version of the old absinthe drinkers. Questioned directly, Dylan said, "[I'm] pro-chemistry." Phil Ochs described him as "LSD on the stage." It explains the leap he made from faux-naïf folk ballads to Ezekiel visions of the fiery wheel. *Bringing It All Back Home*, released on March 22, 1965, is forty-five minutes of delirium. "Mr. Tambourine Man," "Gates of Eden," "It's Alright, Ma (I'm Only Bleeding)." The songs caused a sensation among musicians. It made them all want to hallucinate.

By the midsixties, LSD had remade everything. There were the clothes, the godawful drapey parrot-colored shirts and coats, which, being studded with beads, made a terrific racket in the dryer. There were the cars, Kandy-Kolored, riding in first gear along the Sunset Strip. There were the movies—*The Trip* with Peter Fonda, *Easy Rider*, the chopper blazing down the roads of small-minded America. There were the novels and festivals and be-ins and dreams of a new age—Aquarius—when people would wander as freely as the lilies of the field, how they grow, though they toil not, neither do they spin. There were the spiritual quests: the Beatles following the Maharishi, Jimmy Page studying Aleister Crowley's satanism. There was the language, the repurposed adjectives and verbs that might well stand as the era's most enduring legacy: bummer, burnout, bad trip, crash, dose.

And there was the music. Acid rock. Psychedelia. The first such songs, apparently recorded by a Texas band called the 13th Floor Elevators, opened the age of the endless jam, laser show, and parking lot concessions. You go to the bathroom and return twenty minutes later to find the guitarist trapped in the same never-ending riff. The Animals had a hit with "A Girl Named Sandoz." The Byrds had a hit with "Eight Miles High."

What makes an LSD song?

The lyric, of course, but also the minutiae, weird effects cooked up in the studio, Eastern instruments, trippy bells, pennywhistles, bouncing balls, and bits of code written for the whacked-out close listener perfectly prepared to play the record in reverse. The main action is between musician and chemistry. It sounds terrific when you're high, but it ages like a blacklight poster. One does well to consider Keith Richards's distinction between "druggy songs" and "songs about drugs." The Beatles wrote druggy songs. The Stones wrote songs about drugs. "Tomorrow Never Knows," from *Revolver*, 1966, is the Beatles' "LSD masterpiece." John Lennon said it was inspired by *The Tibetan Book of the Dead*. I defy anyone to listen to it while jogging, or writing a book. It's less song than relic, proof of a strange mood that overtook millions.

Psychedelia was a closed loop. It led only back to itself. John Lennon said he dropped more than a thousand hits of LSD, quitting only when his body became immune. He said acid had destroyed his creativity. For years, convinced of his unpersonhood, he couldn't write. For what is a more audacious expression of ego than imposing your will upon language? He was one of a legion of trippers who did not make it all the way back. When I asked Paul Jones about LSD, he talked about the ruins, all the damaged kids who, as if at the end of a blaze, stood gutted and hollow.

The Stones came to the party late. The first time most of them remember seeing a joint was backstage in 1964, when they were on the same bill as Bo Diddley. Some hanger-on was leaning in a corner, smoking a bomber. It caused a panic among the boys, who, imagining headlines and perp walks, kicked out the offender. This was akin to a Jew asking Elijah to leave the Passover table. For here was the liberating ganja—in ten years, Keith and Peter Tosh would smoke until the walls melted into Jah. According to Bill Wyman, Charlie Watts was the only Rolling Stone who knew anyone who indulged, because Charlie hung out with jazz musicians, and you know what they're like.

Linda Keith, whom I tracked down in New Orleans, told me Richards was an unbelievable drug prude. The fashion model and wild child who broke Richards's heart, Linda turns up in a handful of Stones songs, notably "Ruby Tuesday." When she started dropping acid in the midsixties, Richards had no clue. She scattered wine bottles around the apartment so he'd assume she was drunk. "I was a year or two ahead of him, but back then it might as well have been a century," she told me. "I was going through things that scared him, things he could not yet understand."

That changed quickly. Keith said the Stones returned from their third American tour with pockets full of acid. Brian did it first, which is important. It's not just what you do, but when you do it. There are three tenses: too late, too early, and just right. Brian was always too early. Fast to live, fast to impregnate, fast to get famous, fast to disorder his senses. In a way, he was just another acid casualty. His mind opened too wide, to the bad as well as the good. According to Tony Sanchez, the band's drug dealer and author of *Up and Down with the Rolling Stones*, Brian began to deteriorate soon after his first acid trip.

(Can you imagine your story as written by the guy who sells you dope?)

In a moment, the bluesy guitarist gave way to the freaked-out, baggy-eyed, Kandy-Kolored wastoid.

Richards dosed next. "The first time Brian and I took acid we thought it was like smoking a joint," he said. "We went to bed. Suddenly we looked around and all these Hieronymus Bosch things were flashing around. That was in 1965."

Bill and Charlie avoided the scene altogether. It cast them as bystanders, looking on from the back row. "Regretfully, I never took acid," Watts said later. "I say regretfully because I've been terrified of the fuckin' stuff and I wish I'd taken it to know about it. I think I was the only rock star never to wear a pair of beads. I wished I could have done, but it never looked right on me."

Mick Jagger was the last to go. He'd always been prudent, calculating. One foot in the London School of Economics, another in Edith Grove. One foot in the boardroom, another on the stage. He finally succumbed because it was the sixties and if you were a pop star and a leader you had to do it. For a dangerous moment, he flirted with the fecund language of the hippie aristocrat. "When I'm on stage I sense that the teenagers are trying to communicate to me, like by telepathy, a message of some urgency," he told *The Daily Mirror* at the time, "not about me or about our music, but about the world and the way we live." I could fill pages with trippy Jagger quotes, but I won't because I recall things I said in my twenties that still make me burn with shame.

Each Stone reacted to the drug in his own way. Whereas Mick became a hippie king, Keith entered the cloud where, in a sense, he'd spend the rest of his life. Look at pictures of Richards taken before 1966. His eyes are clear and sharp, his face is drawn in simple lines. Now look at pictures of him taken in '69, '75, '97. It's the same guy, but the look is foggy and unfocused. Something has been lost, but, weirdly, something has been gained. By the seventies, he is wizened, tolerant. The Buddha pre- and postenlightenment. He dropped acid under the bodhi tree. He levitated as he meditated on Muddy and Wolf. In short, drugs are bad for everyone but Keith Richards, whom they almost killed but enriched instead.

What was the Stones' first drug song?

Some name "Satisfaction" ("He can't be a man 'cause he doesn't smoke the same cigarettes as me"). Others posit "Mother's Little

Helper" or "19th Nervous Breakdown." Over time, it became one of the band's great themes: getting high, coming down, and the weightless moments in between. To my mind, the Stones composed the best drug songs of the era. Unlike most examples, the Stones' songs can still be listened to without nostalgia or irony. Like literature, the best of them have stayed new. You think less of titles than of particular phrases. "Drop your reds, drop your greens and blues." "There will always be a space in my parking lot, when you need a little coke and sympathy."

These songs survive while so many others—I'm looking at you, "White Rabbit," "White Room," and "Lucy in the Sky with Diamonds"—have curdled because the blues put bedrock beneath them. While Beatles drug songs seem untethered—a spirited attempt to recreate an acid trip—the Stones still chug like Chicago. They are less like missives from inside the hippie than reports from the back room where the hippie is slumped in a chair. With two exceptions, the Stones never gave in to the sixties, or sat at the foot of the Maharishi, never became besotted by abstract notions of peace or thought themselves bigger than Muddy Waters. While the Beatles ran hot, the Stones kept cool, writing about drugs in the gritty way of old cowboy singers. Dick Justice, say, who recorded the first hillbilly version of "Cocaine" in 1929, or Tommy Duncan, whose 1937 "I'm a Ding Dong Daddy from Dumas" includes the line "I can sell you morphine, coke, or snow," or the Texas Rhythm Boys, who in 1948 sang, "Throw away your Ovaltine / Buy yourself some Benzedrine / and roll, roll, roll on down the line."

Aftermath, the first Stones album composed entirely by Jagger and Richards, was released in America in June 1966. Brian, frozen out of the songwriting, sought to distinguish himself elsewhere. When you hear a strange instrument on that record, it's Jones: the sitar on "Paint It Black," the dulcimer on "Lady Jane" and "I Am Waiting," the xylophone on "Under My Thumb." *Between the Buttons*, released a year later, includes a handful of obvious drug songs, including "Connec-

tion" and "Something Happened to Me Yesterday." Though it's considered a great album, it's the cover people remember: the Stones in
overcoats on a cold day. Charlie is out front and sharp as an injury, but
the picture blurs at the edges—an effect Gered Mankowitz achieved
by smearing Vaseline on his camera lens. Keith is fuzzed like the pope
in the painting by Francis Bacon. It spoke in code of acid, of general
distortion. Brian grins maniacally, in the way of a warlock or wizard.

When I asked Gered Mankowitz about the photo session, he
spoke mostly about Brian, who was increasingly becoming a problem.
"They were recording at Olympic," Mankowitz told me. "In those
days, they used to start at about ten, eleven at night and go on until
six or seven in the morning. I often spent the night with them, hanging around, taking pictures. One morning as we tumbled into the
dawn, I turned around and looked at them and I thought, 'Jesus, they
look just like the Rolling Stones.' Everything that we thought about
the Rolling Stones was embodied in this sort of blur. They were out
of focus, if you know what I mean. And I said to [Oldham], 'I think
it would be great to do a session right now.' I suggested Primrose Hill,
which was on the other side of London, but in those days and at that
hour it only took about twenty-five minutes to drive there. I wanted
early light, sky and trees. It would only last twenty minutes or so because we were tired, stoned, and cold. So it had to be fast. I got angry
because I thought Brian was fucking the shoot up, burying himself in
the collar of his coat, or reading a newspaper, or turning his back to
me. I told Andrew, 'I'm worried about Brian, what can I do?' And
Andrew said, 'Don't worry about what he does, because we're at a
point with the band that it doesn't matter. He can't take away from
the Stones. He can only contribute.' It was brilliant direction because
it freed me completely. I just stopped worrying about Brian. And fun-
nily enough, he's fantastic in every shot. But it was because Andrew
recognized it didn't matter. He had a band where if you couldn't see
all five of them equally or smilingly or looking into the camera, it
didn't matter. It just made them more intriguing."

Mankowitz photographed the Beatles as well as the Stones, so I asked which band was more interesting to work with.

"The Beatles had their moments visually," he said, "and there were two or three fabulous covers right at the beginning. *Rubber Soul* is fantastic. But the Stones had something magical. They didn't appear to play any game. The Beatles—at the beginning, at least—were always very willing to smile, grin, pose. Shirts and ties, for Chrissake! They looked clean. Your granny liked the Beatles. It was terrible. But the Stones? They'd piss anywhere, man."

19

THE BUST

One day, Brian Jones went into Blaises Club in Kensington, a bear cave of a rock star haunt. Twenty-four years old and already on the other side of everything, he sat at the bar cadging drinks. The stranger who took the stool beside him was in fact a reporter for *News of the World* who'd been tipped by a patron: "A Rolling Stone is in here." The tabloid had been publishing a series on the drug scene, with special emphasis on rock 'n' roll. The reporter bought Brian a cocktail, then started asking questions. There's a Sonny Boy Williamson lyric: "Don't start me talking, I'll tell everything I know." Jones went into particulars that night: his first use of narcotics, timid experiment and mean habit, the challenge of finding good stuff, the beauty of the perfect buzz, riding the midnight train. Standing outside, he showed the reporter a block of hashish and asked if he wanted to "come back to my flat for a smoke."

When the *News of the World* article ran on February 5, 1967—POP STARS AND DRUGS: THE FACTS WILL SHOCK YOU—the musician drinking at the bar was identified not as Brian Jones but as Mick Jagger. "During the time we were at the Blaises Club in Kensington, London, Jagger took about six Benzedrine tablets. 'I just would not keep awake in places like this if I didn't have them,' he said."

Did the reporter simply misidentify his subject, or was he intentionally misled? Your answer depends on your opinion of Brian Jones.

Was he a wayward butterfly deserving of pity? Or was he, as Charlie Watts suggested, a little prick?

"I remember the morning Mick read the piece that set the whole thing off," writes Marianne Faithfull, who'd begun dating Jagger about a year before. "It was Sunday morning in early February of 1967 and we were in bed with coffee and croissants when the papers came. Mick is a newspaper junkie, he reads everything from the *Observer* to the *Sun*. We were very happily going through the papers and suddenly Mick came upon the article in the *News of the World*. He completely flipped out.

"'Fuckin' 'ell!' he raved, leaping out of bed.

"'What is it, darling?'

"'Listen to this: 'Jagger told us: 'I don't go much on it (LSD) now the cats (fans) have taken it up. It'll just get a dirty name.'"

Jagger was depicted as a deviant in the *News of the World* story, a disturbed youth. Bad luck, and unfair. Not only was this not Mick, it was not anything like Mick. He was not a heavy drug user. Or reckless. He did not confess to strangers. How could it have been an accident? Mick looked nothing like Brian, talked nothing like Brian. He was still angry that night when he appeared on the *Eamonn Andrews Show*, a popular British talk show. He wanted justice. He said he planned to sue. Because he was young, he did not know what gospel singers take for granted: You can't wash your hands in muddy water. To win in court, Mick would have to prove not only that he was misidentified, but that the article was untrue. *News of the World* would have only to verify the essential claim: Mick Jagger takes drugs.

Jagger decided to get away about a week later. He was tired of the scrutiny, the reporters and fans, the jimjams closing in. After an all-night session at Olympic Studios, he drove to Redlands, the estate Keith had purchased in the country. Mick was traveling with Marianne Faithfull, perhaps the most beautiful woman in the world. According to lore, Faithfull had emerged in March 1964 at a launch party for Adrienne Posta. Swinging London at its peak moment.

Paul McCartney was at the party, as were John Lennon, Peter Asher, Andrew Oldham, and several of the Stones. Marianne was a twenty-year-old convent boarding-school girl engaged to the artist John Dunbar. Willowy and blond, virginal and buxom, made more beautiful by being seemingly unaware of her beauty. Oldham described her as "an angel with big tits." "The moment she walked in, we all noticed her," Linda Keith told me, "and of course we all hated her."

Faithfull's father had been a British naval officer, a philologist, and a spy. Her mother was a Hungarian countess. She'd studied existentialism and jazz. Approaching Faithfull, Oldham murmured, "You have something, I want to meet you, and can you sing?"

"In another century you'd have set sail for her," Oldham explained later; "in 1964 you'd record her."

A few weeks later, having quit school, Faithfull was in a recording studio in London. "I had been preparing to go to university," she told me, "but then . . . well . . . I was discovered, for God's sake!" She recorded "As Tears Go By" in 1964, the first Jagger/Richards song to go Top Ten. Mick was crazy about her, but she was interested in Keith. "It was quite clear even then that he was a genius," she wrote. "He isn't a bit shy now, but when I first met him he was agonizingly shy and painfully introverted. He didn't talk at all."

Faithfull hooked up with Richards at the end of a long party. In her book she describes it as the greatest sex of her life. She was smitten with Keith, but Keith, in love with someone else, urged her on to Mick, saying, "Y'know who has it really bad for you, don't you?" Jagger followed up with letters, flowers, sweet talk.

According to Chrissie Shrimpton, who spoke about all this much later, Jagger and Faithfull first got together after a Stones concert in Bristol, England. Shrimpton and Jagger had been fighting. Chrissie overdosed on sleeping pills. She woke up in a hospital and later checked in to a mental-health clinic. Meanwhile, Jagger began dating Faithfull. They tried to keep it quiet—Faithfull was married and had a kid—but news leaked. A photo in the paper, gossip splashed across the society pages. By 1966, they'd become London's It couple. Marianne Faithfull, proto–hippie chick, barefoot, braless, freckled, and blond, clinging to the rock star in velvet and silk. Elizabeth Taylor and Richard Burton. Joe DiMaggio and Marilyn Monroe. Beautiful people, perfect lives—living the dream for the rest of us. Shrimpton fell apart.

It's Mick's romantic pattern—you spot it again and again. The courtship, the honeymoon—a yacht floating in the Mediterranean, a hotel in France—the marriage, sanctioned or not, followed by neglect and dissolution, abandonment, the cutting of ties. None of this much concerned Marianne, who was certain she and Mick would live happily and forever.

Keith Richards purchased Redlands in 1966. Built half a century before John Hancock signed the Declaration of Independence, it was called a cottage but was in fact a mansion, rich in the sort of features generally associated with storybooks. Dormers and gables, secret gardens and shady nooks, a caretaker, a moat, a gardener named Jack Dyer but called Jumpin' Jack. Keith refurbished the house until the interior resembled a tale from the *Arabian Nights:* pillow-covered couches, floor cushions, and muslin curtains that set each encounter in the half light of incense-sweetened air. A reporter who visited soon after Keith moved in itemized the books in the library: *The Great War, Dictionary of Slang. Great Sea Battles, Drawings of Rembrandt.*

Redlands, an hour south of London in Sussex, became a sanctuary. If Keith were Superman, it would be the Fortress of Solitude. If he were LBJ, it would be White House West, where he could punch ponies, roast weenies, and unwind. Only instead of ponies it was guitars and instead of weenies it was songs. American rock stars aspire to immortality. They want to be James Dean and die beautifully. British rock stars aspire to aristocracy. They want to acquire titles and houses with names. As the stars of the British blues boom became rich, the story shifted from city streets to vast estates, where many set themselves up like the Sun King at Versailles. Jagger bought Stargroves, a sixteenth-century manor in Hampshire. Charlie Watts bought a seventeenth-century horse farm in Devon, in the southwest corner of England. Ron Wood bought Sandymount House, an old Irish mansion where the Stones recorded *Voodoo Lounge*.

Jagger and Faithfull arrived at Redlands on February 11, 1967. A crowd of pop stars, enablers, and hangers-on had already assembled, including the dandified London art dealer Robert Fraser and the aristocrat Christopher Gibbs. Most of the guests planned to stay for the weekend. Others came and went. Charlie Watts. George Harrison and his girlfriend, Pattie Boyd. Brian Jones did not make it, nor did Bill Wyman, but Michael Cooper, who would replace Mankowitz as the Stones' photographer, turned up.

David Schneiderman brought the drugs. Mystery surrounds the so-called acid king. He wore dark glasses and a suit. His name is spelled differently in different accounts. He was said to have sold Jimi Hendrix the variety of LSD called Purple Haze, but no one knows who he really was, where he came from, or what he wanted. In some tellings, he's barely mentioned. In others, he's the center of everything, a high priest conducting sacred rites. Faithfull says he carried "an aluminum case stuffed with drugs. . . . Inside were the most suspicious-looking contents you have ever seen: incredibly lumpy packages of various sizes all wrapped in tinfoil. Almost the classic dealer's suitcase."

The weekend unfolded like a religious retreat. In the pop age, as traditional belief receded, chemical enlightenment flooded in. The friends woke up early Sunday and sat sleepy-eyed on the edge of their beds as the acid king went from room to room, administering his elixir: a variety of acid known as White Lightning served with tea.

If you went back to sleep, as many did, you woke up in a new world. Everything shimmered. Everything glowed. Everything tipped into darkness. The handles on the mugs turned into fingers. The trees whispered your secret name. The day expanded like a bubble. They wandered through it. Old things became new, understood for the first time. You discovered antecedents, returned to childhood, and realized you'd been there a thousand times before. You understood how the universe is ordered, how creation is underlaid by tunnels and connections, how you could fall into one of those tunnels at any moment and lose yourself but still remain the essential blinking thing that abides when the details of biography drain away. For the first time, you knew there was nothing to fear.

They set out in the afternoon, driving the dirt roads, standing on the beach. They headed toward the art collector Edward James's surrealist home, with its strange garden sculpture. Jagger and Richards clung together like Sancho and Quixote laughing as they crossed the Castilian plain. Faithfull says it was a decisive moment in the friendship. Mick and Keith became brothers that day. They shared a vision, dreamed the same dream. In it, they saw the next turn the band would make, the move from Chicago blues to something looser, jangles and horns. "Brown Sugar." "Jumpin' Jack Flash," a sound conceived on that strange afternoon.

Michael Cooper photographed Richards on the lawn at Redlands. He wears a puffy Afghan coat and sunglasses, a fur hood enclosing his face, his expression blissful and serene.

Everyone sat around the fireplace at sunset. Aftermath, reentry. Charlie Watts had left, as had George Harrison and Pattie Boyd. It was just the core. The drug had left them diminished, calm and happy. Marianne went to take a bath, then came down in a fur rug worn like a towel.

There was a knock on the door. No one reacted, or was sure they'd even heard it. Then it came again, louder. Keith got up and looked out. Was he still hallucinating? More than a dozen cops and another one struggling in the distance. He'd fallen into the moat. When Keith cracked open the door, a man introduced himself as Chief Inspector Gordon Dineley of the West Sussex police. He said he had a warrant to search the premises. Keith let him in, then retreated to the couch. He put Bob Dylan's *Blonde on Blonde* on the turntable, that thin mercury sound. "Rainy Day Women #12 & 35": "They'll stone ya when you're tryin' to go home . . ." Inspector Dineley asked Keith to turn it off. He refused, but said he would turn it down. (The temperate man always finds a middle way.) The cops went through shelves, jackets, drawers, everything. As they opened the acid king's metal suitcase, Schneiderman asked them to please be careful, as the packets contained film. Apparently believing this ruse, the officer closed the case and moved on, fueling suspicions—*Who did this acid king know? Who was he really working for?* A female officer asked Faithfull to accompany her upstairs to be searched. Faithfull stood, walked a few steps, turned, smiled, and dropped the rug—this became the tabloid focus: NUDE GIRL AT STONES PARTY. The police did not find much. Some resin. According to Bill Wyman it was found in a pipe bowl and on a table. Four pep pills in a green velvet coat purchased legally in Italy. Though they were probably Faithfull's, Jagger claimed them, gallantly taking the rap.

Unluckiest was the art dealer Robert Fraser, found in possession of twenty-four heroin jacks, which he claimed were for his diabetes.

The Redlands bust was one of the great set pieces of the hippie sixties. It had everything the scenario writer wants: drugs, rock stars, nudity. Almost as soon as the police left—Jagger, Richards, and Fraser would later appear in court—people began searching for the rat. It's a mystery that can occupy a certain kind of fan for hours. The obvious suspects were the bosses at *News of the World*, motivated by Jagger's planned lawsuit to prove that he was in fact a drug user. The editors had received a tip about the party, then contacted the police, then sent a reporter to cover the ensuing mayhem. "The paper was embarrassed at not recognizing Jagger from Jones, but they knew they had been right about their report in the first place," Trevor Kempson, the writer who got the assignment, told author Terry Rawlings. "They in turn had contacted me at the paper and told me what was what, that there was going to be a party some of the Stones were having down in Sussex at Redlands and we were tipped off to that. It was someone who worked closely with the band and he told us there was supposedly drugs being taken down there."

Someone who worked closely with the band.

For years, everyone assumed it was David Schneiderman. In the most outlandish scenario, the acid king had been working not for *News of the World*, but for the "establishment"—notice how the cops waited for beloved Beatle George Harrison to leave before closing in?—which had come to regard the Stones as a threat. It's a somewhat paranoid story line, given heft by the strange case of the acid king who arrived with the metal suitcase, dispensed the medicine, then vanished.

What happened to David Schneiderman?

I've searched for him for years, as have others. He played his role, then went away. Faithfull said she crossed paths with him in a restaurant in Beverly Hills. He was old and she was, too, but the fury still burned. But the rat was not Schneiderman after all. Schneiderman was just what he claimed to be: the acid king. Who carries visions in his sack. Whose suitcase is filled with silver foil. He was merely being clever when he directed the cop away from his stash by telling him it was film. Keith later wrote that it was his driver who tipped off *News of the World*—money beats loyalty—the titan undone by his own bodyguard.

Why does the bust resonate?

Because it was lurid. Because it epitomized sex, drugs, and rock 'n' roll. Because if you could choose one party in history to attend ... Because it was the last moment of the old order when rock stars lived among us. The story of the bust entered folklore immediately, where it was larded up with rumor. "The first time I heard about the Mars Bar was from Mick shortly after the trial," wrote Faithfull. "Mick said, 'You know what they're saying about us in Wormwood Scrubs, they're saying that when the cops arrived they caught me eatin' a Mars Bar out of your pussy.'"

"Redlands was my moment of truth," Faithfull told me. "That's when I realized I was in a situation I couldn't stand. I didn't want to be there, I didn't belong. It had been fun, and I guess we all made the same mistake, we believed nothing could touch us, completely forgetting about working-class and middle-class envy, how people would feel. It didn't even occur to me in my arrogance."

Me: Is that what drove the bust, you think? Working-class envy?
Her: Yeah. It was us having all that freedom and fun. It was driving them balmy.

The bust had the perverse effect of amplifying the Stones, blowing them up, making them huge. Before Redlands they were a great band. After Redlands, they were the dark lords of rock 'n' roll. "We scuttered on for quite a long time, trying to pretend it was okay and we could still have fun," Faithfull continued, "but I was beginning to feel bad

about myself. And then, you know, I got the usual sort of problems every woman gets with Mick Jagger. I simply couldn't stand it any longer, all the different women. And I got terrible hate letters. I'll never forget it. You have to remember I was only nineteen. I took it all to heart. I believed the horrible things they wrote about me. I got depressed and nobody thought of that, you know, 'she might need a bit of help here.' Mick and Keith, God bless 'em, went on to be bigger, better, stronger, brighter, more wicked, more naughty, and more powerful than ever. But the rules were different if you were a woman."

20

MOROCCO

A few days after the bust, Keith and Brian decided to blow town. The trial was set for summer, which gave Keith time to get away. He'd go to Morocco to drink and smoke and unwind far from the prying eyes of barristers, editors, fans. He flew to France, where he met Tom Keylock, who'd come by ferry with the car, a Bentley that Keith called Blue Lena in honor of Lena Horne. Keylock was Brian's driver, but Keith had a way of co-opting people. They picked up Jones and his girlfriend, Anita Pallenberg, in Paris, where they were also joined by their friend Deborah Dixon, who was dating the filmmaker Donald Cammell.

They drove into the provinces, the France of quiet roads and forests, woodsmoke and rain. You could slip into one of these towns, vanish into another life. Pallenberg, Jones, and Dixon rode in back, sprawled out, luxuriating. Richards stayed up front with the driver, T-shirt and jeans, crooked teeth, arms as wiry as pipe cleaners. Now and then, he looked in the rearview mirror, trying to catch a glimpse of Anita . . . *My God, was she gorgeous!* Tall and blond, like the other girls who hung around, but entirely unique. Her teeth were like fangs. Her eyes were like daggers. Her face was character-filled, with cruel intelligence, her accent hard to place. She was German but grew up in Italy. Everything about her suggested experience—she knew more than you could learn in a hundred lifetimes.

Now and then, Anita caught Keith looking and held his gaze. If this were a highway instead of a book, I'd post a sign here to warn of a dangerous intersection, a love triangle. Though not in the Stones, Pallenberg would have just about as much influence as any member. It was Anita who introduced the band to the artists and aristocrats who became their circle. It was Anita who introduced them to the devil worship of Aleister Crowley. It was Anita who hooked them up with the Lucifer-loving occult filmmaker Kenneth Anger. It was Anita who inspired them to take evil as a subject, which the Stones played with till they got burned. "I believe that Anita is, for want of a better word, a witch," Kenneth Anger said later. "I was going to film a version of *Lucifer Rising* with the Stones. All the roles were to be carefully cast, with Mick being Lucifer and Keith as Beelzebub.... The occult unit within the Stones was Keith and Anita and Brian. You see, Brian was a witch, too. He showed me his witch's tit. He had a supernumerary tit in a very sexy place on his inner thigh. He said, 'In another time they would have burned me.'"

"That's a bit I could've done without," Marianne Faithfull told me. "I don't want to put Kenneth down, poor old man, but I was an idiot to touch that with a ten-foot pole, even a twenty-foot pole. Black magic. I should never have done anything like that, don't know what I was thinking. I was fascinated by power, and in that sense I am not the first and I won't be the last."

Me: Do you believe that stuff is real?
Her: No, I really don't. But I was very young and silly, I sort of thought it might be.
Me: I've read that Brian Jones had a witch's tit.
Her: Yes, that's Kenneth Anger. So what? I don't believe it.
Me: Yeah, well, I don't even know what it is.
Her: It's something that comes from the Middle Ages, or the Dark Ages, in the time of the witch trials. If you look up Salem, you'll find it. It was supposed to be proof of being a witch. It was like an extra nipple on your breast, with which you fed your beast.

Anita went for Brian first. It was after a Stones concert in Munich, Germany. She was twenty-one but had the air of an older person. A model and actress, she would later appear in a handful of movies. *Barbarella. Dillinger Is Dead. Candy.* She was never the star, but she always stole the scene. Even if you forgot everything else, you remembered her. The curl of the lip, how she listened. If I seem to be going on about Anita Pallenberg, it's because she was important. For a time, she seemed to control the Stones, she was what Brian and Keith lusted after. It's this desire, sublimated, that you hear in some of their best songs. Though her name appears in no credits, she was often their inspiration. And yet the quality that drove men to her, the sex and charisma, can't be captured on a page. Not really. It's like a vampire. You take the picture, but later, when you develop the film, it's not there.

She talked her way into the dressing room in Munich, got herself among the Stones. She was drawn to the band as the barrel-riding daredevil is drawn to the Falls. "Satisfaction" was atop the charts. The group was experiencing its first flash of infamy. She asked if any of them wanted to do amyl nitrate. Poppers. She had 'em in her purse. *Bust it open, inhale: Whoosh.* Brian was the only one to say yes. It could be his motto: Brian said yes to everything. "I don't know who you are," he told Anita, "but I need you."

They went back to his hotel room but did not have sex—they held each other instead. Anita later said Brian cried all night. About Mick and Keith, something they had done, something mean. In other words, the relationship started with Brian clinging to Anita, which is how it would end, too. They became inseparable: Brian and Anita, Bonnie and Clyde. Everyone commented on how alike they looked. Same height, same weight: doppelgangers swapping jewelry, trading clothes. When Brian turned up in Anita's outfits, fashion changed. It was the beginning of glam rock, David Bowie and Alice Cooper. In 1966 they lived together at One Courtfield Road in South Kensington. The relationship had already turned stormy. Brian puffed with pride around Anita, but he experienced tremendous pain when she turned cold. It sent him into violent fits. "He was short but very strong, and his assaults were terrible," Pallenberg said later. "For days afterwards, I'd have lumps and bruises all over me. In his tantrums he would throw things at me, whatever he could pick up—lamps, clocks, chairs, a plate of food—then when the storm inside him died down he'd feel guilty and beg me to forgive him."

Keith began sleeping at One Courtfield Road. He said he needed a place to stay—Redlands was being refurbished—but everyone could tell it was more than that.

The trip to Morocco was Brian's idea. It was his place, where he felt most free. On previous visits, he'd fallen for the local music, the food, the debauchery. When I asked Jagger about the scene, he described it as decadent. That's all. One word. Decadent. Not as a side effect of some other condition but as a goal in itself. Brian was not physically built for such extravagance. He was weak, beset by conditions. Chest, legs, head. He began to suffer as the Blue Lena climbed toward Spain. One sentence turns up again and again: "Brian got sick in the mountains." He stretched out in the back of the car, wheezing. He ended up at a hospital in Toulouse. Tests were run. He had an enlarged heart; his lungs were filled with fluid. Maybe pneumonia. He was admitted and told to stay at least a few nights.

He suggested the others go on without him. Thus Keith moved from the front seat to the back, taking his place beside Anita as the car continued into Spain. They spent the night in a village, where there was trouble with the police. Deborah Dixon returned to Paris. Keith and Anita went on. It was not long before they were touching, then more than touching. The Blue Lena, with Keith and Anita in their first mad fumbling, flashes through the annals of rock 'n' roll as the horse-drawn carriage flashes through the provincial streets in *Madame Bovary:* "From time to time the coachman on his box cast despairing eyes at the public houses. He could not understand what furious desire for locomotion urged these individuals never to wish to stop."

"We got over the Pyrenees and within half an hour already it was spring and by the time we got to Valencia, it was summer," Keith writes in *Life.* "I still remember the smell of the orange trees in Valencia. When you get laid with Anita Pallenberg for the first time, you remember things."

They registered at the hotel as Count and Countess Zigenpuss. In Algeciras, they registered as Count and Countess Castiglione. They reached Morocco by ferry. Sea-foam and salt, the lights of the Arab towns along the bay. In Tangier, they checked into El Minzah, a grand old hotel. They took separate rooms but made frequent visits. ("For a week or so, it's boinky boinky boinky, down in the Kasbah, and we're randy as rabbits.") A crowd of expats and friends turned up by the pool: Mick and Marianne, Robert Fraser, Michael Cooper, William Burroughs and his confidant Brion Gysin. They went on to Marrakech. One evening, Cecil Beaton stopped by, a fey little man in straw hat and loose clothes, a socialite and fashion photographer. As a bohemian from an earlier era, Beaton was fascinated by Jagger. "I was intent not to give the impression that I was only interested in Mick, but it happened that we sat next to one another as he drank a Vodka Collins and smoked with pointed fingers held high," Beaton writes in his diary. "His skin is chicken breast white and of a fine quality. He has enormous inborn elegance. He talked of the native music."

That night, they went to a Moroccan restaurant where Mick showed Beaton how to eat in the local manner, with his fingers. Beaton asked Jagger about LSD. Mick advised the old man to try it, as it would be beneficial to any artist. It should be taken with friends, Jagger said, amid sunlight and flowers: "You'd have no bad effects. It's only people who hate themselves who suffer." Beaton accompanied Jagger back to his room, where they sat listening to records. Mick nodded off. Beaton watched him sleep. Mick woke at eight in the morning and got under the covers. At eleven, they met at the pool. "I took Mick through the trees to an open space to photograph him in the midday sun," Beaton writes, "thus giving his face the shadows it needs. He was a Tarzan of Piero di Cosimo. Lips of a fantastic roundness, body white and almost hairless. He is sexy, yet completely sexless. He could nearly be a eunuch."

Telegrams arrived from Brian. Anita ignored them at first but they turned insistent. Bill Wyman reprinted one of them in *Stone Alone*. In it, Brian talks about his recovery and his need to rejoin the others. He demands that Anita travel to France and retrieve him. Desperation flashes between the words like sun off a knife blade.

After several more days of boinky boinky boinky, Anita finally went back to France to collect Brian. "From the moment I arrived," she said, "he treated me horribly."

Brian was in a rage by the time he reached the hotel. Though he did not know about Anita and Keith, he did know. He sulked and insulted, made sly remarks, stormed out, slammed doors, got high, puked, slept it off, reappeared, stormed out, and puked again. His irritation was palpable. In a cartoon, he'd be surrounded by jagged lines. A tiny man in pink bell-bottoms and a floppy hat might look fantastic in a magazine but is absurd in the midst of a tantrum. At this precise moment, Michael Cooper took a picture that can be read like a hieroglyph. Keith, Anita, and Brian sit in a hotel garden in Marrakech. Anita in hat, scarf, and sweater, stylish in a way that only seems accidental. She holds a cigarette, bored. Brian is beside her, a twin in ludicrous clothes, long hair framing his eyes. He holds Anita's hand but she does not hold his. Keith sits across from them in the same Afghan coat he'd worn at Redlands.

One day, Anita came back to the room to find Brian in bed with two prostitutes, described in accounts as Berber whores, pierced and tattooed. Brian held back the covers and beckoned as market sounds drifted through the muslin curtains into the blue room. When Anita hesitated, Brian ordered her to get undressed. She refused. "Brian had a penchant for prostitutes and group sex," Bill Wyman writes. "When Anita refused to have sex with him and some women he had met in town, his violent streak emerged: she was beaten up so severely that she said later she was in fear of her life."

Forced to deal with a bad situation, Keith and the others did so by neither confrontation nor ultimatum, but by trickery. Someone took Brian aside, and, breaking through the drug haze, told him that reporters were en route to the hotel. Everyone must scatter. Brian Jones and Brion Gysin took off for the souk, where they spent hours wandering the stalls. Meanwhile, the others fled: Keith and Anita up the coast in Blue Lena, Mick and Marianne to Ireland. Jones realized what had happened when he got back. He called Gysin in tears: "Come quickly! They've all gone and left me. Cleared out. I don't know where they've gone. No message. The hotel won't tell me. I'm here all alone. Help me."

Jones turned up in Paris a few days later. "He called me from the airport," the filmmaker Donald Cammell said later. "I had absolutely no idea what was going on. Brian was always so fastidious about his clothes, but when he came up to my place he was filthy; he hadn't changed his shirt and was wearing bedraggled lace and tattered velvet."

21

THE TRIAL

Magistrates Court, Chichester, England. They dressed as conservatively as bankers, but their dishevelment and ease gave them away. Jagger had been charged with possession of illegal narcotics—those four amphetamine pills. Richards had been charged with allowing his home to be used for criminal acts—that resin. Mick's trial took place June 27, 1967. Keith went in the dock the following day. It was a circus, rock stars and groupies filling the street and gallery. At some point, just about every friend or associate of the band turned up to show support, with the exception of . . . *Where the fuck was Andrew?* Just when Mick and Keith needed him, just when they were truly scared, he took a powder, fearful of his own arrest.

Jagger and Richards were represented by Michael Havers, a famous British defense attorney. The case was presided over by Leslie Block, a sixty-one-year-old judge who handled the Stones as if with tongs. "He was so offensive, obviously trying to provoke me so he could do what he wanted," Keith remembered. "He called me, for having used my premises for the smoking of cannabis resin, 'scum' and 'filth'—and said people like me shouldn't be able to walk free."

Malcolm Morris, a "master of the bench" who'd famously handled the investigation of the suspected serial killer John Bodkin Adams, prosecuted the case. Morris, born in 1913, had experienced Europe before the deluge. World War I broke the old order into shards and

sent those shards flying, giving us Charlie Chaplin's Tramp, bebop, and eventually rock 'n' roll. In Malcom Morris you could catch a hint of the Victorian sensibility. He understood how quickly things fall apart. Which is why, though the case was lowly, he handled it himself. It was a kind of show trial in which two young men stood for a way of life that must not be tolerated.

In a famous exchange, Morris pressed Richards: "In the ordinary course of events, [wouldn't you] expect a young woman to be embarrassed if she had nothing on but a fur rug in the presence of eight men, two of whom were hangers-on and the third a Moroccan servant?"

"Not at all," said Keith.

"You regard that, do you, as quite normal?"

"We are not old men," said Keith. "We're not worried about petty morals."

Until that moment, "the Stones" had meant Mick and Brian. By expressing the sentiment of his generation—old versus young—Keith changed that. It was the bust and the trial that gave him his identity, the pirate scowl and burned-out patois. Redlands turned Keith into Keef, a stand-in for all the death-courting hipsters.

Jagger and Richards were found guilty, as was Robert Fraser—don't forget that poor bastard. Mick was sentenced to three months in prison. Keith got a year. Fraser got six months. The trip these men made from court to penitentiary is a rock 'n' roll Passion play, a triptych of the march to phony Calvary. In panel one, you see Jagger standing before the judge, dandified and scared. In panel two, you see him in back of a police car, shackled as the scenes of his city drift by. In panel three, he is being led through iron doors into Lewes Prison outside London. He was handed a sheet of paper and told to write home. *Dear Mum and Dad, do not believe what they say . . .* Then his clothes were taken. He was given prison garb. The doors clanged shut. The inmates hooted, their faces primitive and evil, the England of the Dark Ages, imps, hunchbacks, and goons. In that moment, did he regret it all? The drugs? The motorcades and teenage girls? The groupies, the liquor, the bonfires by the shore where the Beach Boys sang Bob Dylan?

Marianne Faithfull visited a few hours later. They sat in the cell, the movie gangster and his moll conferring in whispers. She brought cigarettes—"smokes," as they say in the joint. Mick was in bad shape, wringing his hands, whimpering. The fall from pop god to common prisoner stunned him—never in his worst imagining . . . He mumbled, "What am I gonna do? What am I gonna do?" He started to cry. Marianne snapped. "God, Mick, pull yourself together! What are these cops going to think of you when they see you falling apart like this? You're just confirming their worst images about you. They're going to think you're just a spineless, pampered pop star."

Was that the moment when the last soft thing in Mick Jagger died?

That night, he wrote the song "2000 Light Years from Home," the distance from Lewes Prison to the flat in Chelsea.

Keith was in Wormwood Scrubs, a nineteenth-century penitentiary in West London. The inmates reached out as he went by, calling his name. *Keef. Keef.* Having recognized Richards as one of their own, they showered him with stories and cigarettes.

Meanwhile, the backlash had begun. The decisive turn came on the editorial page of the conservative *Times* of London, where the editor, William Rees-Mogg, published a pop age "*J'Accuse*": WHO BREAKS A BUTTERFLY ON A WHEEL? "Mr. Jagger was charged with being in possession of four tablets containing amphetamine sulfate and methyl amphetamine hydrochloride," Rees-Mogg wrote. "These tablets had been bought, perfectly legally, in Italy. . . . If after his visit to the Pope the Archbishop of Canterbury had bought proprietary airsickness pills on Rome airport, and imported the unused tablets into Britain on his return, he would have risked committing precisely the same offence."

Jagger and Richards spent one night in prison; they were released as their cases went through the courts. At the end of July, Mick's sentence was suspended; Keith's was quashed. (Malcolm Morris said orders to drop the cases had come "from above.") Mick acted as if the whole thing had been no big deal, another snafu handled with the cool of Chuck Yeager. "There's not much difference between a [prison] cell and a hotel room in Minnesota," he explained, "and I do my best thinking in places without distractions." In truth, the bust and trial had a tremendous impact on the Stones. These events closed them off, separated them from their audience. There would be no more hangers-on at parties, no more mysterious acid kings. From then on, they moved through crowds quickly, amid a phalanx of bodyguards and fixers. Their subject matter would increasingly come less from the greater world than from their own isolated rock star lives.

And Robert Fraser?

"I was shocked that poor Robert had to stay in prison," Faithfull told me, "but that's 'cause they found heroin on him. And he almost got away with it. I'll never forget that. I was right next to him and he had a stammer and was saying to the copper, 'Well, actually, officer, these are pills for my diabetes.' And the cop nearly gave it back to him, then didn't. When he got out, he wasn't the same. About fifteen years later, he died of AIDS."

. . .

That fall, the Stones released *Their Satanic Majesties Request*. It was terrible, a disastrous by-product of an overripe era: LSD, Redlands, too much of everything. Blame it partly on the prosecution, which distracted the band, and partly on the Beatles. This was a peak moment of the concept album, when a handful of bands pushed one another to ever-greater flights of studio-enhanced fancy: the Beatles' *Rubber Soul* led to the Beach Boys' *Pet Sounds*, which led to the Beatles' *Revolver*, which led to the Beach Boys' single "Good Vibrations," which took seven months and cost around forty thousand dollars to produce. On June 1, 1967, the Beatles completed this cycle with the release of their pop masterpiece *Sgt. Pepper's Lonely Hearts Club Band*.

How far was it from old-time rock 'n' roll?

Just as far as Wormwood Scrubs from the Station Hotel.

What had once been built on the model of the Muddy Waters band—two guitars, bass, drum—had become an orchestra, a soundscape, bells and horns, clocks, pennywhistles, and narrative arcs, songs about LSD, songs about death, songs about other songs. "Good Morning Good Morning," "A Day in the Life," "With a Little Help from My Friends." It struck its moment dead-solid perfect. The political prankster Abbie Hoffman said *Sgt. Pepper* expressed "our view of the world." (The John Birch Society damned it as a weapon in the Manichean war: the Beatles deploying hypnotism—all those whistles and bells—as part of a Communist plot.) In basement rec rooms across the land, kids smoked Thai stick, listened, decoded, and transcended.

Sgt. Pepper was number one on the U.S. charts for fifteen weeks—the entire summer of 1967. It took four Grammy awards, including Album of the Year. Yet it's strange. In art, you have a choice, though you probably won't realize it at the time. Posterity or right now. With *Sgt. Pepper* the Beatles rode a tidal wave of right now, pop music punked by hallucinogens, gone goofy in tie-dye. It had none of the sloppy energy that made rock 'n' roll a teenage medium. Each lick had been worked to perfection, each vocal polished to spit shine. It was trash culture at its most baroque.

Fans turned the album's cover into a fetish. It showed the bearded Beatles, in Day-Glo marching band uniforms, amid a sea of famous people. Dorm rats tediously identified each face, then tried to puzzle out what the Beatles meant by including it. Bob Dylan because Bob Dylan is the font of wisdom. Marlon Brando because Marlon Brando is always rebelling. Marilyn Monroe because she slept with both Kennedys before ascending to heaven. Sonny Liston because he was the baddest man in the world. Adolf Hitler because, though not as bad as Sonny Liston, he was infinitely more evil.

What about Elvis Presley?

"Elvis was too important and too far above the rest even to mention," Paul McCartney said. "He was more than a pop singer. He was Elvis the King."

For pop musicians, *Sgt. Pepper* presented a problem. How do you follow it? How do you respond? It destroyed Brian Wilson, who broke his brain trying to craft his Beach Boys masterpiece. *Smile*, Wilson's lost record, was never deemed perfect enough for release. The Beatles had set the bar too high. Other bands simply pumped out knockoffs, complete with trippy lyrics, weird sounds, far-out covers. Psychedelia washed over the nation, a flood of floppy hats and little round glasses. Only Bob Dylan figured a way out of the trap. Once, years ago, I found myself stranded on skis atop an impossibly steep hill, wondering what to do, when my friend Jim Albrecht flew past, bombing down the slope in two turns. "Of course!" I told myself. "You go by going!" Which is what Dylan did with *John Wesley Harding*, released as his peers struggled with *Sgt. Pepper*. Instead of answering flutes with flutes, he went back to Woody Guthrie basics. Acoustic guitar, human voice. Not more—less. When you're lost, go to the place where you started and begin again.

Chris Barber told me that Brian Jones wanted to do the same. Skip psychedelia; return to the Delta blues. Jones had never liked pop music anyway. Jagger was more malleable. Though he posed as a true believer, he was in fact a realist. If the kids want timpani, give them timpani. According to Tony Sanchez, Jagger argued with Jones, saying, "Pretty soon everything is going to be psychedelic, and if we aren't in there on our next album, we will be left behind."

"Brian hated the new sound," Sanchez writes, "and he fought bitterly—and vainly—for the Stones to stay true to their roots."

Their Satanic Majesties Request was released in December 1967. It was the Stones' response to the Beatles' response to the Beach Boys. The name was lifted from the legend on the sleeve of every British passport: "Her Britannic Majesty's Secretary of State requests and requires . . ." The songs are a grab bag, a few winners, many dogs. "Sing This All Together.""The Lantern.""Gomper.""In Another Land," originally titled "Acid in the Grass." In 1995, Jagger told Jann Wenner that the record was a misfire, a result of too much time plus too many drugs.

When you sell out and succeed, that's one thing. But what about when you sell out and fail? *Satanic Majesties* was a dud. It climbed the charts, then faded, then vanished. Critics called it a disaster, possibly a dénouement for the Stones. Writing in *Rolling Stone*, Jon Landau said the record was bad enough to "put the status of the Rolling Stones in jeopardy." But I think it was a good thing. I think it was necessary. I think it was the Stones getting the hippie moment out of their system. On *Satanic Majesties*, you can hear the band sweating out the tie-dye like a cold.

Andrew Oldham was a flickering presence at the sessions. He was there, then gone, dressed like a dandy, riding his mania. He did not like the new music, or the clothes, or the pretense. He was a child of rock 'n' roll with a love for showbiz. He did not believe the world was on the threshold of a new age, nor did he think human nature had changed.

His internal weather was constant: cloudy with a chance of thunderstorms. He sensed the band moving away from him as they'd moved away from Giorgio Gomelsky. Jagger knew the first era was over: the youth wave. The Stones would have to reinvent themselves as something new with someone else. "All of a sudden, Mick and I figured that we had more of an idea what this band could do than Andrew," Richards said. "Andrew just wanted hit records; we wanted great ones."

"I think drugs had something to do with it, but I think the driving force was just the need to move on from Andrew," Gered Mankowitz told me. "The Stones needed to take over their own careers. I suppose it was like teenagers leaving a family. They'd reached a point where they felt that Andrew couldn't contribute anymore."

The final break came in September 1967, when Oldham walked out of a recording session at Olympic Studios. He got into his chauffeur-driven Rolls, said a few words to the driver, ghosted through the city. He told the driver to pull over, called Jagger from a pay phone.

"Mick, I'm not coming back."

"Well, Andrew, if that is how you feel."

Just like that, Andrew Oldham was so much older. He drifted in a deep blue funk. He went from London to New York to L.A. to South America. His life shifted tenses, from living to remembering. For a lot of people who've worked with the Stones, everything is dated from those few months or years when they stood in the center ring. Nothing compares. When you're out, you're out. Of energy, confidence, everything. They got so much from the association—a sense of importance, belonging, borrowed celebrity. More than they realized till it was over. They spend the rest of their lives telling the stories. When I exchanged emails with Andrew Oldham in 2015, he was in a hospital in Germany, suffering alone. He'd broken a hip in an airport on his way back from a talk he'd given about the early days at the Crawdaddy. So here he was, an old man, humping his luggage across Europe in search of a little audience, while the Stones were still out there, playing, night after night, to seventy thousand people.

22

THE DEATH OF BRIAN JONES, PART ONE

By 1968, Brian Jones was in what my high school guidance counselor would've called "a bad place." He'd always been the beautiful Rolling Stone, the only truly pretty member of the group. Not interesting or appealingly ugly but classically attractive, with golden hair and fine features. But it was gone—flushed down the toilet with the drugs when the police burst in. Alexis Korner said Brian was "starting to look hideous" by the summer of 1967. "Like a debauched vision of Louis XIV on acid, gone to seed. It was then that I suddenly realized there could be such a thing as an acid casualty."

According to the journalist Nick Kent, Jones began his day with speed and cocaine, a few tabs of acid, and some Mandrax or Tuinal to blunt the edge. Mandrax is a quaalude. As gentlemen prefer blondes, Brian preferred downers. Here's a tip: Before swallowing a Tuinal, pierce the capsule. It enters the bloodstream that much quicker.

"When I shot him [in 1968] he looked horrible," the photographer Ethan Russell told me. "It's a close-up. He's twenty-six but looks forty-eight. I didn't see it at the time. Maybe because I had a job to do. He went upstairs, put on his American flag shirt, and came down waving a gun. All I could think was, 'How cool!' I flat did not see this guy in front of me. He still had the beautiful hair. I guess all I saw was that beautiful hair."

It welled up inside Brian—the anger and fear, the indignation, *the*

gall of them!—punking his personality, rendering him unreliable, dysfunctional, nasty. "He wasn't showing up [at sessions]," Charlie said. "And you know what happens when people don't show up—you do without them. And then when you do without them, suddenly they're not needed."

"First they took my music, then they took my band, and now they've taken my love."

These words, spoken by Jones to his friend Dave Thomson in 1967, tell you everything.

First they took my music.

Brian started the Stones as a blues band. He wanted to cover Chicago classics, the Elmore James and Little Walter tunes that had given him solace when he was isolated in Cheltenham. In doing this, he hoped to serve the music, increasing its audience and paying back the men who'd inspired him. But as the Stones gained fame, they were seduced by the prospect of more fame, which meant playing music with a broader appeal. With this in mind, Brian helped repurpose the Stones. Over time, he came to feel like an apostate. He'd betrayed the mission, traded his musical soul for a velvet coat and Spanish heels.

"He just wanted to be in a blues band and didn't really think it was gonna be show business," Jagger said later. "Perhaps [his] biggest ambition . . . was playing the Marquee on Thursdays."

Then they took my band.

Brian played in several groups before he was twenty years old. He'd usually been the most talented musician, the prodigy in a pool of light. He started the Stones so he could lead. He booked the shows, did the interviews, spoke between the songs. His band meant his vision, his name, his set list. For a time, he was the star. But as the Stones toured the countryside far from clubs filled with aficionados, the crowds inevitably began to focus on the singer, who serves as the voice and face of any group. Jones resented it. When a studio engineer complained that Jagger's voice was lost in the mix, he snapped, "We're the Rolling Stones, not Mick Jagger and the Rolling Stones." It got worse when Jagger and Richards started writing. With the phenomenon of "Satisfaction," Jones lost the last vestige of control. Just like that, he was back where he'd started: a performer in someone else's band. Why did he stay? Because money and fame are as addictive as Mandrax.

Now they've taken my love.

Brian was a cheater and a cad. He sought approval from strangers, mostly women. He needed to see himself in their eyes: the rock star, the pop god. Only then did any of it seem real. He was searching, but what was he searching for? Approval, love, eternity? He was reckless in pursuit, cruel, monstrous. How many illegitimate children did he father? The current count is five. He did not seem to distinguish—he named two of them Julian. He might stick around a month or two but always took off in the end. He believed he'd finally reached the conclusion of his quest with Anita Pallenberg. He gave her his life and soul. Then what happened? Keith took her, just as Mick had taken the band. Imagine going back on the road, the great love of your life still on the tour, only now in the bed of the other guitar player.

• • •

By the end of the sixties, Jones began to lose his mind. LSD destroyed his ego, pulled him apart synapse by synapse. Anita said he never really recovered from that first acid trip. He turned jumpy in the aftermath. He was a paranoid with real enemies, his sanity challenged by the drug busts and police scrutiny that characterized the era. According to Richards, the London *Times* editorial had the right idea but the wrong Stone. Mick and Keith were strong. It was Brian. He was the butterfly being broken on the wheel. He was convinced that friends were talking about him. He was obsessed with the idea that he was being mocked. He believed himself the subject of the Bob Dylan lyric about the vagabond "with no direction home / like a rolling stone," as he believed himself the object of Dylan's query in "Ballad of a Thin Man": "Something is happening here, but you don't know what it is, do you, *Mr. Jones.*"

Brian's lawyer described him in court as "a very sick boy."

"A potential suicide?" asked the judge.

"Certainly."

23

SYMPATHY FOR THE DEVIL

In the spring of 1968, the French filmmaker Jean-Luc Godard went on a rock 'n' roll bender. Stopping by a store on his way home from a nightclub, he bought out the bins—the Beatles, the Stones, the Who. The idea came to him one track at a time. He would capture one of these bands at work, show a song being created, then interweave it with scenes from the political world. The result would be something greater than the sum of the parts, which is why he called it *One Plus One*. Godard eventually struck a deal with Jagger, filming the Stones at Olympic Studio over four nights in June 1968. The director stood behind a 35 mm camera equipped with special film to record extended shots, nine or ten minutes, forever in movie time, but exactly how long it takes the Stones to explore a groove. "That's the way it went in those years," Jagger said. "A director wants to film you, and it turns out to be Godard, and he happens to come by when you're working on 'Sympathy for the Devil.'"

The song was partly inspired by Mikhail Bulgakov's novel *The Master and Margarita*, which Marianne Faithfull lent to Jagger. Bulgakov had fallen afoul of Russian censors, who considered his work an attack on Stalin. Though written in the 1930s, it was not published in English until 1967, when it became a literary sensation. In it, the devil, described as a professor of black magic, turns up in Moscow to wreak havoc. His background is a chronicle of misery. Whenever evil ran free, he was in the shadows, pulling the strings. The story culminates at the Devil's Ball, a party to end all parties, where a billion damned souls dance to a band that plays something like rock 'n' roll. "In one row sat orangutans, blowing shiny trumpets. Perched on their shoulders were merry chimpanzees with accordions. Two baboons with leonine manes were playing grand pianos, and these pianos were drowned out by the thundering, squealing, and banging of saxophones, violins, and drums in the paws of gibbons, mandrills, and marmosets."

"Yes, I gave Mick the book, or perhaps he found it lying around the flat, which amounts to the same thing," Faithfull told me. "Point is, he devoured it. Stayed up all night reading and reading."

When I listen to "Sympathy for the Devil" I hear Mikhail Bulgakov in Jagger's descriptions of Pontius Pilate, the massacre of Russian royals, the German blitzkrieg. After each verse, Mick shouts, "Hope you guess my name." Singing as the devil gives him license to glorify some of the most shameful events in history. It's a brilliant homage— a pastiche of the oldest myths behind the blues. We're back at the crossroads, only now behind the eyes of the old man who gives back the guitar but hangs on to your soul.

I first heard the song when I was ten. My brother played it again and again, each time asking, "Who's singing?"

Me: Mick Jagger.
Him: Yes, but who's he singing as?
Me: Mick Jagger.
Him: Yes, but who is *he*?
Me: Mick Jagger.
Him: But who's he *supposed* to be?
Me: Mick Jagger.
Him: But who does he *think* he is?
Me: Yeah, who the hell does he *think* he is?

Godard captured the song at every stage. It's fascinating to watch this iconic piece of music, which started as a Dylan-like folk tune, assume the shape we know. It happened over days. In the first frames, the Stones sit in a circle, cross-legged on the floor at Olympic, playing acoustic. Keith speeds the rhythm to 6/8 time as the country groove gives way to samba. The tempo is quickened still more. Drums are added, bongos. The mood is free, everyone barefoot, jumping from instrument to instrument: Wyman on the cabasa, Richards on the bass guitar. We see the great sideman Nicky Hopkins playing piano, hammering out those beautiful crescendos. "The rhythm patterns were constantly changing," Olympic sound engineer Phill Brown said. "Charlie appeared to be struggling from time to time, while Brian sat for hours in his booth, strumming his acoustic guitar and chain-smoking."

We see listless moments, too, Brian passed out in a sound booth, Keith curled up on a couch. The backup vocals were recorded near the end, the singers gathered in a half circle under a hanging microphone, Brian *woo-wooing* beside Keith and Anita. Robert Kennedy was assassinated June 5, 1968—an event that can be inferred when Jagger's lyric suddenly changes from "I shouted out who killed Kennedy" to "I shouted out who killed the Kennedys."

It's how the Stones composed many of their best songs. In the end, the credit always went to Jagger/Richards, but the process was intensely collaborative. It would kick off with a riff. Then the band would start goofing, changing, adding. When I talked to Chris Kimsey, an Olympic engineer who went on to produce several Stones records, he used the verb "hunting." "There are bands who come in with a finished song, or close to it, then record," he said. "Not the Stones. They'd come in with a general idea, then go hunting for the thing in the studio. They did many versions of each song, went after it again and again. They did version after version of 'Brown Sugar' just to hear them. Even early songs like 'Ruby Tuesday' and 'Jumpin' Jack Flash' were pretty much conceived in the studio. That's how they wanted it. For musicians in that period, the studio was a sacred place."

One of Godard's shots stands out: Keith, shirtless, impossibly thin, seemingly too slight to contain his own internal organs, no shoes, faded jeans, in headphones, a guitar strap across his shoulders, a perfect silhouette of man and instrument. He's waiting, preparing in the way of a surfer who's caught sight of a wave. Two, three, and he's up, picking out the line, his body plugged into the current, riding the charge. Though you can't hear the music, you can see it passing through him, a groove refracted. You see his happiness, too, how all the drugs and heartaches and misery are just the price he pays to get to this place where he vanishes into his task, where he becomes music.

One Plus One premiered in late 1968. If not for the Stones, the film would be impossible to watch, a seemingly pointless collection of random scenes—a girl in a pornographic bookstore reading aloud from *Mein Kampf*; a character called Eve Democracy acting out Norman Mailer's *Playboy* interview—intercut with the Stones. Asked what it meant, Jagger said, "I have no idea." Richards described it as "a total load of crap." A producer recut the film without permission, ending it with the final version of the Stones song and renaming it *Sympathy for the Devil*. It turned the movie into a music video. The premier made headlines when, according to UPI, "The French film director Jean-Luc Godard punched the Canadian producer Iain Quarrier in the face and stomach on the stage of the National Film Theater Friday night before 600 startled movie fans. The fisticuffs broke out after Mr. Godard urged the audience to walk out rather than stay to see his latest film, 'One Plus One.' He charged that the addition of a song, 'Sympathy for the Devil,' had ruined the film."

Of course, the real issue was control. Whose film was it, Jagger's or Godard's? Jagger did not try to take over the movie, but the charisma of the band simply overwhelmed whatever political point the director had been trying to make. His supposed subject was upheaval and revolution. His actual subject was the Stones at the start of the golden run that would carry them through four records, from *Beggars Banquet* (1968) to *Exile on Main Street* (1972)—perhaps the greatest creative stretch in the history of rock 'n' roll.

24

THE GOLDEN RUN

It started in May 1968 with the release of "Jumpin' Jack Flash," which was seen as a comeback, a return to form following the feuding, drug busts, and prosecutions that few thought the band would survive. *Satanic Majesties* was the death rattle. "Jumpin' Jack Flash" was the resurrection. *Rolling Stone* described it as "Delta blues by way of Swinging London." The roots reinvented. Utterly old, completely new. Recorded at Olympic a few months before Godard arrived, here were the Stones as we still know them, out of the shadow of Chess Records, Andrew Oldham, and the Beatles. A band is lucky if it has a single moment. A hit song, a gold record, an unforgettable summer. When you hear them, you recall a specific time. Great bands rise and fall, then rise again. The Stones have lived and died so many times they might as well be immortal. Their first incarnation was as a blues cover band at the Crawdaddy; their second incarnation was as the pop sensation behind "Satisfaction." "Jumpin' Jack Flash" was the third incarnation, the postvelvet, postacid Stones. You feel the excitement from the first chords.

According to Bill Wyman, "Jumpin' Jack Flash" started as a riff he played early one evening on the piano at rehearsal.

Keith laughed.

What's so funny?

You recognize it, don't you?

Richards later said the famous "Jumpin' Jack Flash" riff was in fact the "Satisfaction" riff in reverse.

Text: While thinking he has invented something new, Wyman has merely played back a warped version of Richards's earlier work. Subtext: In this new era, the Stones were going to invert everything they'd done before.

"Jumpin' Jack Flash" opens with a strange-sounding lick. It's halfway between acoustic and electric. Keith, who, in those days, traveled with three things—clothes, guitar, and Philips recorder—cooked up the effect in cheap motels while the band crossed America. "Playing an acoustic, you'd overload the Philips cassette player to the point of distortion so that wham, when it played back it was effectively an electric guitar," he writes in *Life*. At Olympic, rather than try to replicate the sound with professional equipment, he merely plugged his tape recorder into the sound board. An acoustic guitar run through the Philips, then run through a top-of-the-line equalizer resulted in a new instrument altogether. Distortion was the message, that metallic wail. You hear it in several definitive songs: "Jumpin' Jack Flash," "Street Fighting Man," "Gimme Shelter." Keith gave it up because Philips stopped making that machine, and his old one broke.

"Jumpin' Jack Flash" was fattened up with instruments, fills. The track is commandingly rich, as thickly woven as Manila rope. Keith deployed musical knowledge he'd been acquiring since his first days at Regent Sound. "I used a Gibson Hummingbird acoustic tuned to open D, six-string," he explained. "Open D or open E [tuning], which is the same thing—same intervals—but it would be slackened down some for D. Then there was a capo on it, to get that really tight sound. And there was another guitar over the top of that, but tuned to Nashville tuning. I learned that from somebody in George Jones's band in San Antonio in 1964. The high-strung guitar was an acoustic, too. Both acoustics were put through a Philips cassette recorder. Just jam the mike right in the guitar and play it back through an extension speaker."

The lyric began with a quotidian exchange. If you're a writer, certain phrases, picked up by accident, will adhere to you like burrs; when you get home, you realize you're covered in them. Early one morning, Keith and Mick, crashed at Redlands, were awoken by a monstrous stomping.

> Mick: What's that?
> Keith: That'd be the gardener, Jack Dyer.
> Mick: He makes a racket.
> Keith: He's got size fourteen feet!
> Mick: It sounds like he's jumping.
> Keith: Yeah, well, that's him. Jumpin' Jack.

According to the scholar Robert Alter, a character in the Bible is defined by the first words he or she speaks. King David, for example, starts by saying: "How much would a person get for killing that man?" This works with the Stones, too. If you want to know the mood of the band at a particular moment, look at the first line of the song. "Connection" opens with "All I want to do is to get back to you." "Mother's Little Helper" opens with "What a drag it is getting old." "Jumpin' Jack Flash" opens with "I was born in a crossfire hurricane." The mood is near-death and glorious return: *Fuck you, we're still here, having fun. In fact, it's a gas.* It was a smash—number one on both sides of the Atlantic. "The Stones had laid off touring for the best part of two years," Norman Jopling told me. "They'd been a good working band when they stopped, but when they came back they were a legend. They'd changed their style. They'd changed everything. And they returned with such a bang."

What set off that golden run?

According to Marianne Faithfull, it began with that vision Mick and Keith shared during the acid trip at Redlands. They sketched a strategy in the weeks that followed, how the Stones might live beyond the first moment, which Jagger called the "youth wave." Interesting that the Beatles, as a band, did not outlive that moment. What started in bowl haircuts ended in beards. They'd stopped touring in 1966. By 1969, they were as good as done. It became official in 1970. The split had a tremendous impact on the Stones—another key ingredient of the golden run. The Stones had always been defined in opposition. They were the alternative, the opposite, the anti. Their fame grew in a negative space created by the Beatles. The Stones' first big hit was written by Lennon/McCartney, and many of those that followed were seen as responses to or copies of the Fab Four. "As Tears Go By" was said to be a response to "Yesterday." *Satanic Majesties* was said to be a copy of *Sgt. Pepper*. But after the Beatles broke up, there was no longer a model. The Stones were alone on top and finally free to find their own path. What resulted was a new sound that would make them, in my opinion, even greater than the Beatles.

What defined the golden run?

That string of perfect records that arrived, one after another, like summer afternoons: there's a unifying quality that leads you to consider them a single work. Attention to detail, layers of sound, texture—these are albums made for people with Nakamichi tape decks and KEF speakers, beanbag chairs and leisure time. You can even make a case that producer Jimmy Miller was a secret author of the run. He'd been a drummer, Brooklyn born, before taking his place behind the glass. Tall and bearded, with a weakness for excitement, he was working with Traffic in Studio B when Jagger ran into him. He'd produced "Gimme Some Lovin'" and "I'm a Man." Jagger asked him to come by and check out the Stones' new material. Within a week, he'd filled the vacuum left by Oldham's departure. The Stones finally had a proper producer, though he went at it casually, by instinct. "His main gift I think was his ability to get grooves. Which for a band like the Stones is very important," the engineer Glyn Johns told *Goldmine* in 2010. "Look at the difference between *Beggars Banquet* and *Satanic Majesties*. [Jimmy Miller] put them right back on the rail."

The golden run was characterized by ambition. You hear it in the intricacy of the arrangements, the quality of the sidemen, the breadth of the lyrics. Jagger wanted to compress the entire era into a three-minute single. And the sound! The playing! Keith's guitar had become sublime. Have you ever looked closely at his fingers, those arthritic, knobby digits? In 1961, he could play two, three songs. In 1971, he was Mozart on a six-string. He'd perfected a particular style, a twangy weave that resulted from innovations, adjustments, tricks. How do you get a guitar to mimic the noise in your head? He began goofing with open tuning.

Since time out of mind—the early Renaissance, probably—when the first Spanish and Italian guitars turned up, the six-string has been tuned the same way, each string tightened to a specific note. From the sixth string to the first, from low note to high: E, A, D, G, B, E. When you strum without pressing any strings, you get an E minor 11th chord. Not satisfied, Keith began experimenting. Open D. Open B. In such setups, the strings are retuned so that a fingerless strum gives you a D or a B chord. Keith did it for novelty, for fun. He'd been searching for a new sound as you might search for a new high. He found it with open G. It's easy: Put a guitar in your lap and start turning the tuning knobs. From sixth string to first, retune the strings to D, G, D, G, B, D. When you strum, you get a G major chord. As that bottom D does not really work with Keith's playing style, he removed the string. In this configuration, Keith uses hardly any fancy fingering. It's all barre chords, his index finger blocking entire frets as he trips down the neck of his Telecaster. Keith had modified his way to simplicity.

Keith's open G tuning was first heard on "Honky Tonky Women," a song written by Jagger and Richards on vacation in Brazil in December 1968. The cowbell that starts the song—that's Jimmy Miller—is followed by Charlie's drum, then Keith's riff. The best guitarists turn their instruments into a voice. Neil Young's classic solos, often played on a single string, are a mechanical iteration of his all too human whine. Ditto Eric Clapton and Jimi Hendrix. With open G, Keith found a voice that wheezes when it laughs, that's full of whiskey, late nights, and trouble. It proceeds like a man who only appears to be drunk: sloppy and slurry but never missing a step. Art that seems artless. It became a Stones trademark: that cranky, rusty, rangy, awkward rhythm guitar.

Where did he get that sound?

Richards credits Ry Cooder, a California prodigy who jammed with the Stones at Redlands. Everyone was sitting around playing "Sister Morphine" when Keith was taken by Cooder's distinct tone. "How do you do that?" By the end of the night, he'd fallen for open G as you might fall for a girl. Which brings up a common complaint: the Stones are vampires, feeding off other musicians. Jagger and Richards started as record collectors, searching music store bins, and in a sense that's what they've remained. Their gift is for recognizing sounds that can be appropriated. In other words, their brilliance is less in their playing than in their taste. Muddy Waters, the Beatles, Peter Tosh—whomever they admire, they absorb. When Byrds front man Roger McGuinn first heard Tom Petty's "American Girl," he said, "When did we record that?" When Ry Cooder first heard "Honky Tonk Women," he called the Stones bloodsuckers.

Of course, Roger McGuinn did not invent Roger McGuinn from scratch. He'd been imitating Bob Dylan, who'd been imitating Woody Guthrie. That's America. A mishmash, a stew. Nothing comes from nothing. Every river is fed by another river that vanishes at the sea. Ahmet Ertegun, the founder of Atlantic Records, told me about his own search for the originator, the great player who'd invented it all— but no matter how far back he went, he was sent back still further, to a lost master who can never be found. In short, while admiring Ry Cooder, I consider his beef with Keith Richards bullshit. Forget the fact that open G had been around for years—if Richards stole the sound from Ry Cooder, why don't Ry Cooder songs sound anything like the Stones? Why aren't they nearly as evocative, menacing? It gets at a deep unfairness: all the skill in the world does not add up to genius. Ry Cooder is a technically better player than Keith Richards, was goofing with open G first, and was after some of the same effects, but he did not have that same artistic soul. Spanish poets call it *duende*, that mysterious thing that can turn the work of even a semiliterate artist into a masterpiece. The songs don't come from the tuning; the tuning is a net woven to capture the song that was there from the beginning.

Beggars Banquet was the Stones' first true tour de force. It was recorded between February and June 1968 at Olympic Studios in Barnes, London. It's worth lingering on that studio, which was, in its way, just as important as any single musician. You can't listen to *Beggars Banquet* without imagining the smoky rooms, the people hanging out, sleeping it off, or rousing themselves for one more take. Olympic began as a vaudeville house early in the last century and was later fitted for recording. It was home base for the Stones by 1966, where they were most at ease, where nothing could touch them. One evening, as the band recorded "Dandelion," the cops burst in. "Mick was smokin' a big joint," Glyn Johns said. "Mick was so brilliant. He puts this joint behind his back and says, 'Andrew, what we need on this are two pieces of wood bein' hit together in unison. Like claves.' 'What about these,' offered the bobbies as they voluntarily pulled out their truncheons. So [Mick] escaped by puttin' 'em on the record."

Not long ago, I spent a day at Olympic with Chris Kimsey, who began working there when he was fifteen. The studio had been remade by the late 1990s. It's since been renovated into a movie theater and a private club. The hallways are lined with pictures of Mick and Keith—they hover over the place like benevolent deities. Kimsey, burly and kind, pointed out everything with the melancholy of a man who has watched the kingdom fall. He seemed slightly lost as he led me through the theater, which had been Studio A. He talked about the artists who recorded there, Mick and Keith jamming in the bathroom for the echo. "When you listen to the great records, it's this place you're hearing," he told me. "It's a unifying element. It gives everything that Olympic sound."

Most sessions began with the Stones sitting in a circle on the floor playing through a tune on acoustic instruments—this was the methodology of Glyn Johns, a famed producer and sound engineer who collaborated on many of the Stones classics. Charlie Watts pounded a kind of pillow drum. Like a read-through for a play, it established tempo, delineated groove, and gave each player time to absorb the mood and the message. In these years, the Stones achieved a seamless correlation between their music and their lives. As the vibe grew out of the studio, the songs grew out of the moment.

Take that signature tune "Street Fighting Man." In New York, London, and Paris, crowds were protesting the Vietnam War. Jagger joined a throng that marched on the American embassy in London. If you go there today, you will see high walls and narrow windows, barricades, wire, and statues of Eisenhower and Reagan, but on March 17, 1968, you would have seen thousands of people demanding change. For Mick, this flirtation with dissent was an anomaly, a moment of engagement punctuating an apolitical life. A rock star is a status quo figure. He does not want struggle, but its aura. "Street Fighting Man" is not about revolution—it's about limits. When it comes to protesting, celebrity just gets in the way. Wherever Jagger went that day, the message changed from "America out of Vietnam!" to "It's Mick!" The lyric registers this reality with a shrug: "What can a poor boy do, except to sing in a rock 'n' roll band?" Bruce Springsteen called it one of the greatest lines in rock history. When Jagger brought it in to the studio, Keith added his own signature. The lick that opens "Street Fighting Man" is among his most distinct. It leads to a maraca groove that's as sinewy as a girl dancing in the jukebox light at a biker bar.

Or "Stray Cat Blues," the album's eighth track, which is a rock star singing about a groupie. "I can see that you're fifteen years old. . . ." Or "Parachute Woman," the fourth track, which is about groupies, or record promoters, or possibly both. It's a slow blues, barnacled by influence—a Bob Dylan lyric, a Muddy Waters riff—remade by the vibe in Studio A, the Stones playing Ping-Pong between takes. On most nights, they did not start till two in the morning. The first takes were walk-throughs, at half speed, Evel Knievel running his bike to the top of the jump and letting it roll back. Then, all of a sudden, they find the extra gear. Phill Brown, who would become an admired sound man and record producer, worked the control board at those sessions. "On rare occasions, usually during an exceptional performance by a musician, a feeling would occur of being transported and becoming unaware of my surroundings," he wrote later. "This wonderful, detached feeling took over, for example, while I was listening to 'Parachute Woman' loud at 3 A.M. with 20 people in the control room. Then it was everything—romantic, happy, and all-powerful—a great rush."

"Sympathy for the Devil" was being recorded in the wee hours of June 10. Mick was in the studio in headphones, singing. Marianne caught his eye from the booth. With red lipstick, in reverse letters, she wrote on the glass: BURN BABY BURN. At some point, the studio actually did catch fire. Richards believes Jean-Luc Godard had taped tissue paper to hot lights on the ceiling, which, well, you know. "I think we have a fire," Glyn Johns said calmly. People headed for the exits as Jimmy Miller gathered up the masters. "Within fifteen minutes [he] was gone with the tapes," said Phill Brown. The fire department put out the blaze, but there was a hole in the roof. The Stones continued recording beneath the open sky. Now and then, you think you might hear a plane flying over.

Released in December 1968, *Beggars Banquet* was immediately recognized as a breakthrough. "The Rolling Stones' coming of age," said Glyn Johns. It has ten tracks, each a gem, but my favorite is "No Expectations," as that's the last song in which you have Brian Jones at his finest. He was a mess by then. Even when he did show up, he was usually too wasted to contribute. That's what made "No Expectations" so special. Keith recorded a crisp acoustic track and Mick's vocal is evocative, but it was Brian who made the tune with his slide guitar, the same sort of bottleneck work that first caught the attention of Mick and Keith at Alexis Korner's club a lifetime before. It was as if a fog had lifted, and for a moment, there was Brian. "[He] was emotionally very up one night," Phill Brown wrote, "and played a beautiful slide acoustic guitar." Haunting and forlorn, like no other sound in music. It makes my mind wander and my teeth itch. I picture shotgun shacks when I hear it, green fields and levees, thunderheads a moment before the rain comes down. The Buddhists talk of a flame so pure it consumes all its fuel. On "No Expectations," Brian Jones vanished into his playing.

25

THE DEATH OF BRIAN JONES, PART TWO

If you're overcome by a desire to live in a fairy tale, you might be in trouble.

Brian Jones, wasted, hurt, angry, needing to get away, was looking for a retreat. He found it two hours southeast of London at an estate called Cotchford Farm. To Americans, it resembles the millions of Tudor homes that dot our suburbs, but this was the original, the platonic ideal that stands behind all those crude copies. An English house in the countryside surrounded by gardens, arbors, and trees. It was built in the 1400s, knocked down and built again. Jones was taken by its provenance. For years, the house belonged to A. A. Milne, creator of Winnie-the-Pooh. The map on the title page of *The House at Pooh Corner* shows the mansion and its grounds, the ponds and streams where Pooh wanders in the ever-expanding now. The book's enchanted Hundred Acre Wood was a fantastical version of Ashdown Forest, which began at the foot of the lawn. The only human in *Pooh* was based on Milne's son, Christopher, affectionately known as Moon. Pooh was named for a Canadian black bear that Moon loved to visit at the London Zoo. Of course, there's the story, then there's the life, as there's Hundred Acre Wood, then there's Ashdown Forest, where your father's too busy being famous to be much of a father. "Some people are good with children," Christopher Milne wrote later.

"Others are not. It is a gift. You either have it or you don't. My father didn't—not with children."

A. A. Milne bought Cotchford Farm circa 1924. He referred to it as a cottage, but it was in fact a spread. Eleven acres of meadows and outbuildings, as well as a main house. Milne spent most of his time in the parlor, which, with its fireplace and French windows, he called "the most lovely room in the whole world." According to *A. A. Milne: The Man Behind Winnie-the-Pooh* by Ann Thwaite, Milne planted the trees and his wife designed the garden, and later, when *Pooh*, written in the study over the garage, became a sensation, she commissioned the statue of Christopher Robin and the sundial beside it. The relief that decorates that sundial—Pooh, Piglet, Eeyore, Rabbit, and Owl dancing—speaks of the fallen empire of childhood. Milne's manuscripts are said to be buried beneath the sundial. Now and then, when Brian was drunk, he'd threaten to dig them up.

The author died in 1956. Christopher Milne sold the house soon after—to an American, Stewart Taylor, and his Spanish wife, Margarita. They put in the heated pool that was such a novelty in gray Britain. I wonder if Brian lingered beside the pool on his first visit. Borges says we pass our grave every day without knowing it. The

Taylors fought and divorced. The house was back on the market in 1968. According to Bill Wyman, Jones was immediately enamored of the estate. Now and then, he quoted the words on the sundial: "This warm and sunny spot belongs to Pooh / And here he wonders what it's time to do."

"It's perfect," Jones explained. "It's exactly what I'm doing."

By then, the guitarist actually looked like Winnie-the-Pooh, a tubby towhead not much taller than a circus midget. Brian made the final payment in November 1968. He intended Cotchford Farm—it cost around £30,000—as a weekend retreat but ended up spending most of his time there. He began renovating before he moved in, bringing the house up to rock star code. This was important, as it meant that from the fall of 1968 until his death, Jones was almost never free of construction workers, crew chiefs, backhoe operators, and the like, most of whom resented the small, weak, needy, weird, and unaccountably wealthy celebrity.

Brian Jones retreated to Cotchford Farm as Prince Prospero in Edgar Allan Poe's "Masque of the Red Death" retreated behind bolted castle doors. Poe's story tells us there is no escape from history, which, for the prince, was the medieval England of the plague years. For Brian, history was the nightmare of the late sixties, riots, and assassinations. Martin Luther King, Jr., had been shot in April 1968. (Jones named his Australian wolfhound Luther in response; he called his cocker spaniel Emily—who knows why?) Then Robert Kennedy was killed a few weeks later. In May, the police raided Brian's flat on Kings Road, London. They found a fist of cannabis inside a ball of yarn. His defense? *An obvious frame-up. I don't even sew!* "They roughed him up," Richards said. "He wasn't a cat that could stand that kind of shit and they went for him like when hounds smell blood."

. . .

The Stones played the *New Musical Express* awards show in London on May 12, 1968. It was Brian's last public appearance with the band. Glassy-eyed and fading, he played the autoharp on "You Got the Silver," Keith's lament to Anita Pallenberg, which, considering that Anita Pallenberg was the cause of all the trouble, is ironic.

Morocco remained a haven, the last unspoiled place. Jones traveled there in the summer of 1968 with Suki Potier and the record producer George Chkiantz. Brion Gysin served as guide. They drove to a Rif mountain town two hours south of Tangiers, where local musicians had gathered for the Rites of Pan Festival. Joujouka, a desert crossroads where Paul Bowles ate cannabis jam beneath the sheltering sky. Probably because everyone was high, recollections vary. Brian loved the music and recorded it for two days. The locals called him Brahmin Jones. He took acid and reeled like a popped balloon. The festival culminated in an all-night ritual. Near dusk, Brian watched two men carry a goat down the road—a white goat with sad eyes, horns, and a tuft of beard. It would be slaughtered that night. Turning to Suki Potier, Brian said, "That's me."

On June 8, 1969, Mick, Keith, and Charlie drove to Cotchford Farm to fire Brian. He rarely turned up at sessions, and drug prosecutions made it impossible for him to tour. "They'd reached that point where they realized Brian was just a hopeless catatonic," Sam Cutler told me. "He was one of those people like Syd [Barrett] in Pink Floyd, and a few others in the music business, who thought the road of excess leads to the palace of wisdom. When you've got someone who's totally gone like that, it's cut 'em loose or die with 'em." Keith studied his fingernails as Mick explained the hard truths to the founder of their band. "We carried Brian for quite a long time," Jagger said later. "We put up with his tirades, and his not turning up for over a year. So it wasn't like suddenly we just said, 'Fuck you. You didn't turn up for a show. You're out.'"

Charlie sat quietly. He'd been brought along for mood, the sober ranch hand to keep the others from getting out of control. Brian stared through bloodshot eyes—*Don't you know God is Pooh Bear?* He reminded Mick and Keith that it was he—Brian—who had started the group and come up with the name. Mick nodded, *Yes, yes, we're aware of your contributions.* By way of a divorce settlement, Brian would be paid a lump sum of around £100,000 plus £20,000 a year as long as the Stones existed. According to Keith, Brian took it quietly, as if he'd been expecting it, as if, like Colonel Kurtz in *Apocalypse Now*, he'd been in the wilderness waiting for them to terminate his command. "I'm sure it nearly killed him," Charlie said. "He'd fought so hard to put it all together in the beginning."

You shouldn't be surprised. The Stones had been shedding people from the start. Use 'em up, toss 'em aside, move on. It's a machine that runs on bodies. Brian Jones was simply the grandest goat yet sacrificed to insatiable Pan—who has thick lips, and loose limbs, and slouches. There's something monstrous about Mick Jagger. Forget Keith; Keith is a trance-ridden melody. Forget Charlie; Charlie is a mercenary, having chosen success over jazz. Forget Bill; Bill is the back line. When you talk about the brain of the Stones, you're talking about Mick, who's always operated with a cruel edge that bleeds into the music. You see it in the remorseless way the Stones have continued decade after decade after decade. Everyone I ask to explain this longevity gave the same answer: Mick Jagger. His will, determination, and intelligence. Of course, Jones really forced the others to dump him. His behavior left little choice. But there was something cold in the way it was done. What is the quality that allows Mick to operate with such lack of sentiment? Is it ambition, or something more?

Once upon a time, Mick Jagger's drive and the effect it had on people were associated with evil, which is why songs like "Paint It Black" and "Sympathy for the Devil" went over so seamlessly. They confirmed what we already knew: Mick is Lucifer. But that's wrong. Mick is not Lucifer. He's showbiz, a pop version of the classic Hollywood diva, for whom the show must always go on, for whom obscurity is even more terrifying than death. It's a special kind of charisma that generates tremendous light but little heat. People crave that light but get no sustenance from it. It destroys them. Life with Mick is life astride a black hole. Time accelerates. Two years ages you immeasurably. Yet none of it touches him. Because no one else matters. He's the ego that became the world. He stands before the millions but the millions don't exist. At the center of the universe, Mick Jagger dances alone.

Brian reached into his pocket, pulled out a bomber. He wanted to get high. The joint at the end of the dream, the seal of rock 'n' roll death. After they smoked that last peace pipe, Mick said it was time to go. Keith followed, then Charlie. As you get older you'll notice that no matter what direction you walk, you're walking away. There were ceremonial hugs, the sort exchanged by mob bosses on Mulberry Street two hours before the hit. Brian stood in the door watching them leave, then went into his house, put his head in his hands, and cried.

The band released a statement a few hours later. Jones issued a statement of his own, saying he hadn't been fired but had quit because "I no longer see eye to eye with the others over the discs we are cutting." His mood is revealed in a telegram he sent to Janie Perrin, the wife of the Stones' publicist, Les Perrin: I'M VERY UNHAPPY. SO UNHAPPY. I'VE DONE THINGS. BUT I'VE SORTED OUT THINGS FINANCIALLY AND MORALLY. I'VE DONE THE BEST I CAN FOR THE PEOPLE I LOVE. I LOVE YOU AND LES VERY MUCH.

Jones spent the ensuing days wandering Cotchford Farm, taking drugs, drinking, and planning his funeral. He said he wanted to be buried beside the Christopher Robin statue in a casket lined with blue silk. He had a new girlfriend, Anna Wohlin, a Swede everyone agreed looked just like Anita. His infatuation with Creedence Clearwater Revival's second album, *Bayou Country*, a triumph of bluesy roots, suggests his desire to go back to first things. He'd been talking about starting a new band, possibly with Alexis Korner, Jeff Beck, or Jimi Hendrix. He'd met with John Lennon, who, like Brian, dreamed of breaking away and dedicating himself to the old music, freed from hippie pretense. There was even talk of joining the Beatles, or starting a supergroup. Some say he'd begun recording his own songs. "Brian had made a single," Janie Perrin said. "This was to be his first record since breaking with the Stones. He'd cut the demo and was really pleased." That lost side is a kind of holy grail. Never heard, never found, probably never existed.

The Stones had already brought in a new guitarist, Mick Taylor from Hatfield, an industrial town outside London. His father worked in an airplane factory. "When I was 14, I started listening to music like Elvis," Taylor told *Fusion* magazine. "I got hold of a guitar and taught myself to play."

In the oldest articles, Taylor is depicted as angelic, an adjective meant to characterize his playing as well as his appearance. Almost all the words used to describe him can also be used to describe figures in Renaissance paintings. Rosy and cherubic, doughy with innocent features and flowing blond hair. Whereas Keith Richards was rhythmic, Mick Taylor was melodic, a combination that, as much as anything, explains the brilliant sound the Stones achieved in the middle years.

Taylor was in several bands, including the Juniors and the Strangers, before he was old enough to do much of anything. When he was sixteen, he started a group called the Gods. Around this time, he went to see John Mayall and the Bluesbreakers, a band that served as a kind of finishing school for the scene. Because guitarist Eric Clapton had failed to show up for the concert, Taylor approached Mayall during an intermission and asked if he could sit in. He became a full-time member of the Bluesbreakers soon after.

Jagger has given various accounts of how Taylor came to join the Stones. He likely spotted him working at Olympic. Jagger once said he first heard him practicing in the bathroom at the studio—the beauty of his playing was something you noticed. Taylor made his Stones session debut on "Live with Me" and "Honky Tonk Women." You hear the difference immediately. His guitar has a clear, fresh, dreamy tone, as if someone's opened a window. He started as a contract player, making £120 a week. He was almost ten years younger than the others, a product of the next generation, one of those kids who'd grown up listening to the band. He was shocked by their lack of proficiency. "There was such a huge difference between the way the Stones sounded on record and the way we sounded down there," Taylor told Christopher Sandford in *The Rolling Stones: Fifty Years*. "Everything was out of tune, sloppy. . . . Most of the magic was down to the people who were producing. We had Jimmy Miller and great musicians like Nicky Hopkins and Billy Preston. Otherwise they could have sounded like any old Camden Town blues band."

July 3, 1969—most of the Stones were at Olympic, recording Stevie Wonder's "I Don't Know Why," when the call came. "[Mick], Keith and Charlie sat around, dazed and disbelieving," Bill Wyman writes. "Charlie called me at the Londonderry House Hotel at 3 A.M., half an hour after we had gone to bed. Astrid and I were stunned, in tears."

"It was dreadful, that next morning in the office," Shirley Arnold, who worked for the Stones in London, told *Mojo*. "Charlie was crying. Mick couldn't speak. I hadn't been to sleep. I got a mini-cab to work at seven o'clock. Driving through the West End and seeing the newspaper signs: 'Brian Jones drowns.'"

Stones publicist Les Perrin went with Keith's driver, Tom Keylock, to Cotchford Farm. They stood by the swimming pool "inspecting"— Perrin's word. Brian had been found near the drain.

· · ·

I have a copy of Brian Jones's *New York Times* obituary before me. It was reprinted from the AP. It was short, which suggests that the *Times* did not feel the guitarist warranted full-scale treatment. Despite the Stones' popularity, they did not count as official news. The Eisenhower elite were still in charge. The rock star deaths of the 1960s were covered in the way that hip-hop deaths were covered in the 1990s—a shame, but what do you expect? Jones is pictured in a dark coat and polka-dotted tie beneath the headline BRIAN JONES DIES; FOUND IN HIS POOL. The reporter does not seem certain of the identity or significance of the deceased. He gets the age wrong, his language is weird—"last month Mr. Jones left the quintet"—and the central dynamic goes unremarked upon: the Stones pushed, Jones died. "Mr. Jones, clad in swim trunks, was taken from the pool by three friends staying at his home, Cotchford Farm," the story reads. "An ambulance was called and attendants attempted mouth-to-mouth resuscitation but the entertainer was dead when a doctor arrived."

The particulars were later described in an official inquest. The narrative is confused, perhaps because of the stress of the events, the substances ingested, or the need to hide certain facts from the police. As far as I can make out, Brian was with three people when he died: his girlfriend, Anna Wohlin; his contractor, Frank Thorogood; and Thorogood's girlfriend, Janet Lawson. Brian had been drinking all afternoon. Took Tuinal, took Mandrax. He loved the way downers made him feel. That easy, ruinous, bottom-of-the sea mood. He'd had six or seven brandies. At around eleven that night, he decided to go for a swim. Janet Lawson declined, but Anna Wohlin and Frank Thorogood agreed to join him. It was a cold night, but the pool was quite warm—some say 80 degrees, some say 90 degrees. Steam drifted across the surface, like mist on the tar pits. Jones went off the diving board, lolled on his back, turned on his face. "Brian was staggering, but I was not too concerned because I had seen him in a worse condition and he was able to swim safely," Thorogood told police. "He had some difficulty in balancing on the diving board and I helped to steady him. But this was not unusual for him."

At around midnight, Thorogood went inside to take a call or have a smoke or get a towel. Here and there, witnesses disagree. At some point, Janet Lawson went out to check on Jones. Then she began to scream. (As in the Sherlock Holmes story, the dogs did not bark.) "After we had been in the pool for about twenty minutes I got out and went into the house for a cigarette, leaving Brian in the pool," Thorogood explained. "I honestly don't remember asking Janet for a towel. I know I got a cigarette and lit it, and when I went back to the pool Anna appeared from the house about the same time. She said to me, 'He is laying on the bottom.' Or something like that."

Jones was near the drain, hair waving. Thorogood hesitated, then jumped in. So did Wohlin. They had to dive again and again. They got Brian up on the third try, laid him on the pool deck. Efforts were made, but he was beyond saving. The conspiracy theories began as soon as the news broke. There was supposedly a two-hour delay between the drowning and the arrival of police. Why? What happened in the interim? There had supposedly been a party at the house that night but all the guests were gone by the time the cops arrived. Why? Where'd they go? Some said Frank Thorogood, having been fired that day, killed Brian Jones. Others said it was a group of workmen who, drinking and taunting the star, accidentally went too far. Brian's inhaler was found next to the pool. Maybe he'd had an asthma attack. Bill Wyman thinks Brian might've had an epileptic seizure—Anita Pallenberg is convinced this was the case. "Some very weird things happened [the night Brian died]," Richards told *Rolling Stone* in 1971. "There were people there that suddenly disappeared. . . . We were at a session that night and we weren't expecting Brian to come along. He'd officially left the band. . . . And someone called us up at midnight and said, 'Brian's dead.' Well, what the fuck's going on? We had these chauffeurs working for us and we tried to find out . . . some of them had a weird hold over Brian. There were a lot of chicks there and there was a whole thing going on, they were having a party. I don't know, man. I just don't know what happened to Brian that night. There was no one there that'd want to murder him. Someone didn't take care of him."

Over the decades, writers have come forward, in the way of Columbo, to track down, seek out, and solve this great rock 'n' roll mystery. *Brian Jones: Who Killed Christopher Robin?* by Terry Rawlings. *Paint It Black: The Murder of Brian Jones* by Geoffrey Giuliano. In 2008, the journalist Scott Jones turned up enough new evidence to cause police to reopen the investigation the following year. Of particular interest was an interview with Janet Lawson, who's convinced that Frank Thorogood murdered Jones. "Frank came in in a lather," Lawson said. "His hands were shaking. He was in a terrible state. I thought the worst almost straightaway and went to the pool to check. When I saw Brian at the bottom of the pool and was calling for help, Frank initially did nothing."

Keith's driver, Tom Keylock, later said Frank Thorogood made a deathbed confession. "I want to put my house in order," Thorogood told Keylock as they sat alone in a hospital room. "It will probably shock you but we've been friends for so many years. . . . It was me that did Brian. . . . I just finally snapped." Those who knew Jones and Keylock dismiss this confession: Too neat, too convenient. The main result has been to draw suspicion to Keylock himself.

Of course, the old axiom holds: If you want to find a killer, look for the person with motive. In fact, the only person with a reason to kill Brian Jones was Brian Jones. Sad, unhealthy, overweight, addicted, discarded, done. I'm not saying he committed suicide. I'm saying that he put himself in a position where he could easily die. "I think he took a load of downers," Watts said later, "which is what he used to like, drank, which he used to do and shouldn't have done, 'cause he wasn't strong enough to drink. And I think he went for a swim in a very hot bath."

In the days that followed, the Stones continued with their regular schedule of recording and performing, as if they did not care. Which was probably not the case. I don't think it's a lack of sentiment you see in their actions, but shock. How can a person just vanish from the world? It's ludicrous. It's insane. For most of the Stones, this was their first experience with mortality. According to Marianne Faithfull, each member of the circle was affected in his or her own way. Anita was ridden with survivor's guilt. She would cut pictures of Brian out of magazines, hang them on her walls, then throw them out in the morning. "Keith's way of reacting to Brian's death was to become Brian," Faithfull writes. "He became the very image of the falling-down, stoned junkie perpetually hovering on the edge of death."

26

DEATH FUGUE

The Stones were scheduled to play a free show in Hyde Park two days after Brian died. The concert had been organized by Sam Cutler, a rock promoter at the center of the scene. Lank, long-haired, and raffish, Cutler later became famous as the tour manager of the Grateful Dead. He described himself to me as "a control freak and a psychedelic fascist. I never believed in this unbridled consumption of drugs," he explained. "I've always been somebody that got people together. I've done some of the biggest shows in the fucking world. You don't do that when you're fucked up on drugs. Not possible. Not physically possible. Not mentally possible. Although I took many, many 'trips' with the Grateful Dead, I've always been careful about what I did and where I did it. I've also been fortunate that I'm in touch with myself. I'm not off in the woods with the fairies."

When the conversation turned to drugs, I made the mistake of referring to heroin's addictive properties as common knowledge, as in, "Everybody knew . . ."

"No, everybody did not know," Cutler snapped. "Did Janis know? No, Janis did not know. That's why she died. Did Jimi know? No, Jimi did not know. That's why he died. It's something I hope you stress in your article, or book, or whatever this is: what was not known about drugs was learned at great cost by my generation."

Cutler grew up outside London, a music fanatic from the start. By fifteen, he'd fallen in with teddy boys, greasers. He had a weakness for energetic characters. He excelled in school, was college bound, but went off with the circus instead. He worked for local bands, including Alexis Korner's Blues Incorporated. In the midsixties, he began putting on shows—arranged the venue, the sound system, everything. "I did all the free shows in Hyde Park, starting with Blind Faith," he told me. "We had a hundred fifty thousand people at that one, a groovy summer's day, no hassles. The English really know how to go to the park and behave. Everybody smoking joints, nice, mellow, kind of like 'wow.' Mick was there and digging it with everyone else. He and I had a few long talks about what was involved. And he decided, 'Let's do one of these with the Stones; let's make it the biggest free show this city has ever seen.'"

The show was meant to reintroduce the band to the public after a seemingly endless hiatus, and to unveil Mick Taylor as the newest Stone, but Brian's death put a wrench in the works. Killed the buzz, ruined the mood. For a moment, it seemed the show would be canceled. Because: *How can you!* But Jagger, who always finds a way, simply recast the gig as a memorial. Instead of being the first show post-Brian, it would be a celebration of his life. "Brian will be at the concert," Jagger told a reporter that morning. "I mean, he'll be there! But it all depends on what you believe in. If you're agnostic, he's just dead, and that's it. When we get there this afternoon, he's gonna be there. I don't believe in Western bereavement. You know, I can't suddenly put on a long black veil and walk the hills. But it is still very upsetting. I want to make it so that Brian's send-off from the world is filled with as much happiness as possible."

Fans began arriving the night before, carrying candles. There were some three hundred thousand of them in Hyde Park by the following afternoon. Jagger went onstage in soft white shoes, studded dog collar, and a white dress originally made by the British designer Michael Fish, for Sammy Davis, Jr. He asked the crowd to be quiet so he could read from *Adonaïs*, Shelley's eulogy to Keats. Like bad tequila, Jagger's poetic moment is impossible to take straight. In the long beat between the last stanza—"Life, like a dome of many-color'd glass / Stains the white radiance of Eternity / Until Death tramples it to fragments . . ."—and the first guitar lick, thirty-five hundred butterflies were released. Staggered by unseasonable heat, most of them expired onstage. Text: We're honoring our friend. Subtext: The Stones are surrounded by death.

When introducing the band, Sam Cutler spoke the phrase that became a trademark. "It was a spur-of-the-moment thing," he told me. "When I got to the mike, it just came out: 'The greatest rock 'n' roll band in the world.' Mick took me aside after the show. He said, 'Hey, man, that's too much, don't do that again.' But here's the thing—I was being sarcastic! I'd heard the Stones in rehearsal earlier and they were atrocious. I mean, terrible! So when it came time to bring 'em out, I did it with a roll of the eyes: 'The greatest rock 'n' roll band in the world . . .'"

That phrase took on a life of its own. For years, you couldn't go to a Stones concert without hearing it. It was effective because people are suggestible. If you tell them the Stones are the world's greatest rock band, then, later, when they hear the Stones, they'll think, "I heard somewhere they're the world's greatest rock band." Eventually, other bands had to respond. Which is why the Who became "the world's loudest rock band" and the Clash became "the only rock band that matters."

But people who agree on little else agree the Stones sounded terrible at Hyde Park. Because they'd laid off live performances for years; because they hadn't prepared; because the set list consisted largely of songs they'd never played in public, including "Street Fighting Man" and "Honky Tonk Women"; and mostly because Brian was gone and his demise gloomed over everything. In other words, he was missed. Jones's guitar and sensibility had always been crucial. You can believe the Mick Taylor Stones were the best version of the band and still acknowledge they lost something when Brian died. It was more than musicianship. It was soul. "Brian was . . . incredibly essential," Phil May, the lead singer of the Pretty Things, told Laura Jackson in *Golden Stone.* "You can see that by the fact that the Stones have never been the same without him. I'm not saying they aren't good. But they've never been the same without Brian. Anyone else up there, and I have nothing against either Micky Taylor or Ron Wood, is just another guitarist. It was something spiritual with Brian. He was a left wing—a spiritual element. I dunno, but it was vital. You could've cut off Brian's guitar arm and he'd still have it. Even the problems surrounding him within the band were central to the electricity of the Rolling Stones."

Brian Jones was buried on July 10, 1969, following a service at the church where he'd been a choirboy. Mick Jagger skipped the funeral, as did Keith Richards, Marianne Faithfull, Anita Pallenberg, and Andrew Oldham. Because they had meetings, appointments, previous engagements, whatever. Life is what you do but also what you miss. They left it to the strangers who lined the streets of Cheltenham to memorialize their friend. But Charlie was there with his wife, as were Bill Wyman and a handful of band employees. Because that's what you're supposed to do.

Accounts of the funeral have a gospel-like clarity. "We saw the coffin—it was bronze, really a lovely coffin," said Shirley Arnold, who worked for the Stones. "We all started to walk in behind the coffin to go into the church. [Charlie's wife] was walking with me, and she was crying and I was crying 'cause where we were walking, we could've touched the coffin, and Brian was in there." The priest read a telegram that Brian had sent his parents a few years before, which he suggested be taken as Brian's dying words: "Please don't judge me too harshly."

There is something sacred about Brian's death. It stands for so many others. Brian was the first dead rock star of that era, the charter member of the 27 Club. Brian Jones, Jimi Hendrix, Janis Joplin, Jim

Morrison, Kurt Cobain—they all died at twenty-seven. Why? What does it mean? You can get lost in the kabbalah of it, the witchcraft of numbers, but it feels like logic. Brian had been dancing on the edge of the abyss for three or four years. It was natural for him to fall in. His death also makes you think of those who survived: Mick, Charlie, Bill, and especially Keith. Like Jesus, Brian died so they did not have to. Brian paid the debt for everyone. Mick Jagger famously said, "I'd rather be dead than singing 'Satisfaction' when I'm forty-five." Roger Daltrey famously sang, "I hope I die before I get old." Well, Roger Daltrey is still alive, and Mick Jagger is rocking in his seventies, but Brian actually did it. Were he alive today, he'd be just another bloated British rock star trying to save the rain forest. As it stands, he'll always be twenty-seven, a cool-eyed, harp-wielding Elmo James. He died so we could love him again.

27

DOWN UNDER

Mick Jagger left England soon after the Hyde Park show. A day before Brian's funeral, he was seated on a plane beside Marianne Faithfull en route to Sydney, where he'd play Ned Kelly in Tony Richardson's film about the Australian folk hero. Jagger was attempting the tricky shift from stage to screen. Fearing rock music would fade, Jagger was on the lookout for a more stable, dignified way to earn a living. *Ned Kelly* was his Elvis moment: get clear as the King had done with *Love Me Tender*. That he'd do it with what was essentially a cowboy flick is perfect. Film producers, wanting to harness that pop energy, often cast rock stars in Westerns—Bob Dylan and Kris Kristofferson in *Pat Garrett and Billy the Kid*, Johnny Cash in *The Last Days of Frank and Jesse James*—because a rock star is an outlaw. That *Ned Kelly* is a weak film, certainly not worth missing Brian's funeral for, does not change the essential point: even then, Jagger was looking for a way out.

Marianne was supposed to play Ned Kelly's sister. She'd memorized the lines, prepared her take, but was in fact a mess. Because she was afraid of air travel, a doctor had prescribed her Tuinal, a barbiturate—a three-month supply—for the flight. She took a few before takeoff, a few during ascent, a few when the plane reached cruising altitude, a few more with drinks, a few more when the cabin lights dimmed, then kept going—fifteen in all. "Brian's death unnerved me terribly," she explained later. "I identified with him so strongly. He was the emblematic victim of the sixties, of rock, of drugs, of Mick and Keith. His fate could easily have been mine."

Having taken a hiatus from her own career, Faithfull had made herself the full-time public companion of Mick Jagger. It was like sinking all your money into a volatile stock. Up and down. Up and down. Then everything collapsed. By the end of 1969, Marianne knew Mick had been unfaithful, possibly more than once, possibly hundreds of times. "One night shortly after he got back [from America], Mick suggested that I start using ice-cream flavored douches," Faithfull writes. "I'm not stupid. I realized that this must be the sort of thing that American chicks did. But I didn't put two and two together till I read *I'm with the Band* [by the groupie Pamela Des Barres]. Pamela has a whole rap about strawberry- and peach-flavored douches."

Marianne was seated next to Mick, but a million miles away. She went through customs, then walked groggily from the airport to the car, from the car to the hotel, from the lobby to the bed. She was out for hours, white hotel sleep. When she woke, she was not sure where she was, or who. It was the middle of the night, or maybe day. She went into the bathroom and stared at herself in the mirror. It was not her face looking back. It was Brian's. Inside the glass, smiling. The room was on a high floor. Marianne tried to open the window—she imagined the fresh air, the pull of gravity, the ground rising to meet her. It was locked. She found the bottle in her bag. One hundred and fifty sleeping pills. She swallowed them. She got back into bed with Jagger and closed her eyes. "I thought it was the only way I could hurt Mick, killing myself," she told me. "I remember thinking 'I'll show him.' Looking back, it all seems so absurd. I don't even want to hurt him, the poor thing. He's been hurt enough."

Like a girl in a fairy tale, she slept for six days and six nights. In her sleep, she dreamed. In her dream, she saw Brian again. He looked as he had in the beginning, before drugs and disappointments. He told her he'd been alone for a long time. He put his hands on her shoulders and said, "Welcome to death!" They walked until they reached a precipice. Brian asked Marianne if she would be coming along, then slipped into the abyss. She woke up in a hospital, with her mother and Mick at her side.

Marianne recovered, but, as you probably know, you never recover completely. She'd gone to sleep in one world and woken up in another. Nothing could ever be the same or go back to the way it had been. The tragedy of life is to have Eden and lose it. For Marianne, it was the beginning of her wilderness years—the desperation, the tumble into heroin. Jagger broke up with her to save himself. That's how it is with addicts. If you don't cut yourself free, they will carry you with them to the bottom.

Marianne Faithfull's story is one of the great junkie epics. Billie Holiday. Etta James. She was number one on the charts, rich and beautiful, glamorous, breathtakingly young. In the course of months, she lost it all. By the end of the sixties, she was in the gutter, begging money for the next fix. An urchin, a freak.

By the time I spoke to Faithfull, she was old and still beautiful, but in the way of a dilapidated house. Good bones, falling down. She'd given up cigarettes for e-cigarettes. She'd busted a hip. Her laugh was pure mischief. Because of tremendous personal strength, she'd made her way back from the depths, returning in the late 1970s with a new voice. Her album *Broken English*—it sounds like it's about the language, but it's really the girl who was broken—is a jewel created under tremendous pressure. When I asked about the overdose in Australia, she said, "It was an awful thing to do to Mick, to Tony Richardson, to my mother, to my little tiny son who was in England, to myself. I remember having these feelings of 'I'll show them! They'll realize when I'm dead they shouldn't have done that!' Completely forgetting [that when they do realize it], you'll be dead!"

She said the Redlands bust had been the beginning of the end. "I simply couldn't stand it any longer, all the different women and all that stuff. And then my big thing in Australia where I took the hundred and fifty Tuinal, was unconscious for six days, during which time Mick wrote love letters to [his lover] Marsha Hunt, which I didn't know about, thank God. That only came out about six months ago."

I'd never heard about this. It shocked me. I asked how, after all these years, she'd found out. Marianne laughed—and it was a cynical and world-weary laugh—saying, "'Cuz she sold them."

"Ah, that's terrible."

"Well, I don't know, is it? Does it matter?"

I thought a moment, then said, "Well, I guess, in the grand scheme of things, nothing really matters."

"Now you're getting it," she told me, laughing again.

There was something I'd long wanted to ask, and this moment, in which we'd both accepted the imperfection of the world, seemed right. "In your book you talk about a dream you had, during the overdose, where you met Brian Jones . . ."

"Well, that was just a hallucination, a barbiturate hallucination," she said, quickly.

"I always wonder if there's some truth in those things, you never know," I said.

"I don't know," she said, hesitating. "I'm not saying it's true. I'm just saying I had that hallucination. And what I describe in my book is exactly what happened. Only now I know more about things like that, as you can see. Maybe it was just a drug hallucination. Or maybe it *was* true."

"Did you believe it was true at the time?"

"Yes, I did, of course."

"I mean, sometimes I think we shouldn't be so dismissive of what we felt at the time," I said.

"I'm really not," she said. "I'm not at all. And I'm also not just trying to please you, that is *not* my sort of thing."

I asked if she'd learned anything she could share with the rest of us. "You've had pretty much every experience a person can have."

"No one can really be told anything," she said. "Everyone has to go through it themselves. But, just to be kind, I'll give you my motto: 'Never let the buggers grind you down.'"

28

ROCK 'N' ROLL CIRCUS

In his book *The True Adventures of the Rolling Stones*, Stanley Booth tells an anecdote that can be dissected in the way of a homily. In it, you have Keith Richards in a drop of rain.

Keith, flying commercial, strikes up a conversation with his seatmate, an ad man who works for a big firm. Keith digs the guy as an example of another life, a road not taken. In explaining why his situation is superior, Keith says, "You're not free, man, you've got to do what they say."

"You have to play what people want," the ad man replies. "What's the difference?"

"We don't have to do anything we don't want to do," says Keith. "I threw my favorite guitar off the stage in San Francisco."

"You can't do that every night," says the ad man.

"I can do it as often as I feel like it," says Keith.

"Well, what I do isn't bad," says the ad man. "I've never hurt anybody."

"How can you be sure?" says Keith, thinking. He rambles a bit, then returns to his central point: "I really think it's true that you can't do what you want to do. So many people aren't doing what they want to do."

"Most of us do both," says the ad man. "We like what we do but we have to make money. It's a compromise."

"But that's so sort of sad," says Keith.

"But the world is not perfect," says the ad man.

"No," says Keith. "The world *is* perfect."

This took place in 1969, when the Stones were promoting *Let It Bleed*, the second album of their golden run. A lot of the tunes were recorded at Sunset Sound in L.A. During the sessions, which lasted for months, Jagger and Richards stayed at Stephen Stills's house near Laurel Canyon, which had become the unofficial capital of the music world. The West Coast scene at its stony peak, a commune of rock stars and hangers-on, the dusty hills jammed with houses that were in turn jammed with singer-songwriters, the distant strum of Spanish acoustic guitars, a party that did not end so much as shift from late night to early morning. At one point, the canyon was home to most of the Byrds as well as Crosby, Stills & Nash, Jim Morrison, Frank Zappa, and Joni Mitchell. It's a force behind Mitchell's record *Ladies of the Canyon* and stands behind Graham Nash's song "Our House." For the Stones, it offered a respite, a dream of another life. Hanging out, writing music, getting high. Each day the same: the same groupies, producers, musicians, dealers, actors, and models; the same sun on the same swimming pool; the same tennis court; the same cocaine cut into the same rails; the same muscle cars parked in the same driveway.

Gram Parsons spent day after day on the couch, crashed or glassy-eyed, strumming a guitar. He was a Gatsby boy, a long-haired scion of fruit barons, the richest family in Winter Haven, Florida. When he was nine, he went to see Elvis, which would make all the difference. If you're exposed to something that cool that young, you can be ruined. He began dressing like the King, performing for company. He fronted several bands in high school, including the Pacers and the Legends. He attended Harvard for one semester, but, having fallen in with folkies, he rarely went to class. He dropped out and moved to New

York, taking up residence in a huge house in the Bronx where, with friends, he rehearsed around the clock. They performed as the International Submarine Band, a name lifted from *The Little Rascals*. On a trip to L.A., he landed a job with the Byrds, one of the most popular bands in America. Hired to play keyboards, he hijacked the group—Roger McGuinn, who led the Byrds, called him "a monster in sheep's clothing."

Assuming he'd hired just another rock 'n' roll organist, McGuinn was surprised by Parsons's devotion to country music as well as country culture. "And he exploded out of his sheep's clothing," McGuinn explained, "[and] *God! It's George Jones! In a sequined suit!*"

Parsons trained the Byrds for a mission of his own, a mission akin to that of the Rolling Stones. Whereas Jagger and Richards mainstreamed the Delta blues, Parsons wanted to remake the sound of his childhood, the B-flat wail of Ernest Tubb and Hank Snow, as rock 'n' roll. He urged the Byrds to cut an album in a new style, which he called Cosmic American Music. It seems natural today—alt-country has been perfected by Steve Earle, the Jayhawks, and Wilco, among others—but it was nuts back then. To hippies, country music was reactionary, square. But Gram Parsons made the case. The result was *Sweetheart of the Rodeo.* Though a flop at the time, it's since been recognized as one of the greatest rock albums ever made.

Parsons met Jagger and Richards on tour. The Byrds were playing a London club called Middle Earth. Keith and Mick had gone to see McGuinn and his famous electric twelve-string guitar, but they were transfixed by the hippie kid on the organ. After the show, they all went to Stonehenge to get high and talk about aliens. Keith urged the Byrds to skip South Africa because "they're not being kind to the brothers." Gram would cite this admonition when he quit the tour a few days later, but even friends say he was really just jumping ship to hang out with the Stones. When the Byrds left for Johannesburg, Parsons moved into Redlands. In the weeks that followed, Parsons and Richards commingled, trading licks and trading clothes. It was a love affair absent only the sex—the epic jam continued when Mick and Keith moved into Laurel Canyon. "Gram taught me country music," Richards said. "How it worked, the difference between the Bakersfield style and the Nashville style. He played it all on the piano. Merle Haggard, 'Sing Me Back Home,' George Jones, Hank Williams. I learned the piano from Gram and started writing songs on it."

"It went on for weeks," Phil Kaufman, who served Parsons and the Stones as a kind of nanny, told me. "Gram would make a point, then say, 'Phil, play this George Jones or that Merle Haggard or Buck Owens.' The Stones were blues guys. Gram interjected the country lick into them. And there was none of that weirdness. Gram was a rich kid so he could hang without being a straphanger. He could carry his own weight."

The Stones toyed with country music from the start—Roy Rogers was Keith's first hero—but Parsons introduced a crucial element, the laid-back seventies twang that has faded as beautifully as a pair of jeans.

His influence was enormous.

How can you tell?

By the way Jagger denies it.

Years ago, I worked with Jann Wenner on a long Jagger Q&A. We prepared by reading all the books, listening to all the records. Jann brought his guitar to the office to play the riffs. I wrote perhaps a thousand questions. Later, I listened to the tapes and helped edit the transcripts. The interview appeared in the magazine on December 14, 1995.

In my questions, I'd given special attention to Gram Parsons and the country infusion that changed the Stones during *Let It Bleed*. I was surprised by the vehemence of Mick's response. I felt bad for putting Jann on the receiving end of it. When Jann asked if Gram had been an influence, Mick, who's usually happy to acknowledge sources, snapped *no, nada, nein*—zero influence. Mick said country music was nothing new for the Stones, had in fact been an element from the start. It came not from Parsons but from English folk ballads, the very soil of Britain. Then he changed the subject. But listen to Gram Parsons performing "Love Hurts" beside Mick Jagger performing "Wild Horses." Gram Parsons taught Mick Jagger how to sing American country.

One night, Keith sang "Honky Tonk Women" for Parsons, who picked up a guitar and played it back, remade as Cosmic American Music. The result is "Country Honk," the original tune reverse-engineered, turned back into its sources. The Stones recorded it a few days later; it's the third track on *Let It Bleed*. But when they listened to the playbacks, something was missing.

It's a fiddle, Gram said.

What?

You need a country fiddle.

Well, do you know one?

Parsons had met Byron Berline, the great country fiddle player, a short time before. Though he was not yet twenty-five, Berline was rank with pedigree, having recorded with the Dillards and with Bill Monroe, the man who invented bluegrass. His playing was whiskey straight from the cask, learned from his father in Appalachia. "I was in Oklahoma when I got that call," said Berline, whom I tracked down in his fiddle shop. "It was Keith Richards and Phil Kaufman. At first, I didn't understand who they were. Then I remembered: Oh yeah, my roommate in college played all that Rolling Stones. I'd say, 'Man, would you turn that off?' What would my roommate think if he knew these guys were calling me! They wanted me to come out to L.A. and record. Immediately. They picked me up at LAX the next day. Phil Kaufman was driving. We went up to Sunset and Doheny where they had rented that house. They were all hanging out. They said, all right, we're going to go to the studio. So we get in limousines and drive to Sunset Sound on [Sunset Boulevard at North Cherokee]. They were remodeling and there were bulldozers pushing dirt and all that kind of stuff. I went through the track. No way to tune back then unless you had a pitch fork, so it was tough. But I finally started laying it down. Then they called me in. I thought, 'Oh, hell, they don't like it, they're going to send me home.' It was Glyn Johns and Mick Jagger. They said, 'We got an idea; we want you to go out on the sidewalk and record your track out there. Just to create an ambience.' I said, 'Really?' People were experimenting with a lot of different things back then. Well, we go outside and ... I'll never forget this. I'll bet Mick Jagger doesn't remember it, but I do. There's a bulldozer about fifty yards away pushing dirt, pretty noisy. Jagger waves his arms and puts his finger across his throat to shut it down, kill it. Which the guy did, immediately, turned off the engine and walked away. Strange. So we set up a microphone right out in the street. That's how I played. On a little speaker. With all them guys standing around. At the start of the track, you can hear a car horn. That's Phil Kaufman leaning on the wheel of his Cadillac. The Doors had come down to visit—the group the Doors. Bonnie Bramlett was there to sing. Leon Russell was hanging around. It was a party atmosphere. I played it seven or eight times. The last time, my bow slipped 'cause it was getting damp in the evening. And that's the track they wanted. I said, 'Don't you hear that bow slip?' And they said, 'Oh, yeah, that's cool.'"

"Live with Me," "You Can't Always Get What You Want," "Monkey Man." Every song on *Let It Bleed* is built on biography. Keith Richards conceived the opening track, "Gimme Shelter," in Robert Fraser's flat—burned out, hungover, staring out a big window as a thunderstorm broke over London. It mirrored his internal weather. Mick Jagger and Anita Pallenberg had been cast as lovers in the movie Donald Cammell codirected with Nicolas Roeg, *Performance*. Though the sex scenes were tame, the leaked outtakes were graphic. Each day, Keith, who had offered Anita money to turn down the role, parked in front of the townhouse where the film was being shot and glowered. "Gimme Shelter" is that glower turned into music. Its feat is to transcend its subject, to turn the chaos of Keith's life into chaos in general. In 2012, Jagger, who filled in the lyrics and bridge, described the song as "a very moody piece about the world closing in on you a bit. When it was recorded, early '69 or something, it was a time of war and tension, so that's reflected in this tune." It was cut at Olympic Studio and recut in L.A., where a producer added the famous background track of the soul singer Merry Clayton moaning the penultimate lyric: "Rape! Murder! It's just a shot away . . ." "The use of the female voice was the producer's idea," Jagger says in *According to the Rolling Stones*, an oral history of the band published in 2003. "It would be one of those moments along the lines of 'I hear a girl on this track—get one on the phone.'"

. . .

Life in the studio had been remade. Once upon a time, it was quick and dirty, in and out, but it had became a lazy float down the river. Once upon a time, five songs meant five hours in a soundproof room. By the late sixties, weeks might be devoted to a single passage in the rock opera. Many of these songs are less about the world than about the recording process itself. That's why producers often included a few moments of the band at work in the studio, hanging out before the drummer counts four. In this era, the sideman became a storied figure, the ace player recruited like a mercenary to fix a track. One of the best—the most magical if not the most skilled—was Al Kooper of Queens, New York, who'd famously bluffed his way onto a Hammond organ at Bob Dylan's "Like a Rolling Stone" session. That organ is a trademark sound, distinct because Kooper didn't know what he was doing. "After the song became a hit, I went out and bought all the records that copied the 'Dylan sound,'" he told me. "I took them to Dylan's house and we listened to them laughing. The imitation 'Al Kooper organ' is my favorite, those great musicians copying my ignorance!"

Kooper, who went on to found Blood, Sweat & Tears and discover Lynyrd Skynyrd, among other bands, had a knack for turning up at key moments—a long, lean rock 'n' roll Zelig. He was backing Dylan when Dylan went electric. He was playing with George Harrison and Ringo Starr when they heard John Lennon was dead. On a trip to London in 1968, Kooper bumped into Brian Jones, who talked him into coming to a session. "I got there early," Kooper told me. "That's my thing. After a while, Mick and Keith showed up. Mick was wearing a gorilla coat. Keith had on a Tyrolean hat with a feather. Everyone sat on the floor with acoustic guitars so Mick could teach us the chords and changes on 'You Can't Always Get What You Want.' Jimmy Miller was the producer. And man, did he look ill! Basically, Jimmy was just rolling joints. Then he got into a situation with Charlie Watts, sweetest guy in the world. Jimmy comes over to Charlie and says, 'It would be great if you could play this fill.' Jimmy sings the fill.

ROCK 'N' ROLL CIRCUS

Charlie tries to play it and can't—not to Miller's satisfaction. Charlie finally says, 'Why don't you show me?' So Jimmy sits down and he's very, very comfortable. It's obvious he's a drummer. Charlie says, 'Why don't you play it instead of me having to play something I wouldn't.' Jimmy jumped at that. I saw it and thought, 'Disgraceful,'" said Kooper, who, in his own producing work, tries to remain invisible. "Charlie, without resentment, went into the control room and watched," Kooper continued. "So that's not Charlie on 'You Can't Always Get What You Want.' It's Jimmy Miller.

"The song took all night. It was really Mick who produced it. At some point I said to him, 'If you ever want to put horns on this, I know exactly what to do.' He called a year later. . . . 'Remember what you said?' He sent me the tapes in New York. I wanted to imitate the Memphis horns, Stax. I wrote an arrangement and hired players but they couldn't do it. It sounded terrible. I was devastated. I knew they'd never use it. But I thought, you know what? Let me play the intro. I played organ at the session but I'll erase that and do it on a French horn. I just really wanted to play horn on a Stones record. So that's what I did. And that's the only thing they kept."

"You Can't Always Get What You Want" is often compared to the Beatles' "Hey Jude." There's a similar end-of-the-era sentiment. In it, Jagger name-checks just about everything that was happening: the demonstration, the Chelsea drugstore, Mr. Jimmy. He hired the Bach Choir to sing a preamble. The melody is achingly simple, just two chords—A and D—with a B minor in the chorus for melancholy.

On a car trip in 1978, my brother Steven said the shift from the sixties to the seventies is perfectly captured in the differing sentiments between "You Can't Always Get What You Want" and the hit of the moment, "With a Little Luck" by Wings.

Steven: With a little luck? What kind of a loser depends on fuckin' luck?

Mom: Steven!

People say "You Can't Always Get What You Want" was inspired by Marianne Faithfull, less the lyric than its aching sadness. When I asked Marianne if "Wild Horses" had been written for her, she said, "I was told so, but that doesn't mean anything. Musicians do that all the time. 'This song's for you, darlin'.'" But when I asked if she was behind "You Can't Always Get What You Want," she said, "Absolutely. That's my song. Every time I hear it, I'm right back with Mick in the flat. Music can't tell time."

29

1969

In the autumn of 1969, the Rolling Stones set off on their biggest American tour yet. They opened at Colorado State University in November. They had not crossed the country in three years. In that time, everything had changed. Instead of municipal theaters and fairs, they were playing arenas. Instead of crowds of clean-cut college boys, the seats were filled with hippies. Everything was color, swarm, and scrum. In the past, it did not matter how precisely they played, as the kids screamed over everything, but this new generation was filled with aficionados. "The Stones were surprised by America in sixty-nine," Sam Cutler told me. "It was like, 'Wow, everybody's listening to us!' They were chuffed! You can hear it on the live record *Get Yer Ya-Ya's Out!* They'd risen to the demand and were playing to perfection."

Gone was the slapdash fun of the early years, the intimate encounters on the road. Whereas the musicians had once seemed like a part of the audience, me or you raised to a slightly higher power, they'd been amped up into pop stars, supersized, removed. Made of different stuff, another species. The rock star was no longer the kid screaming in the basement club. He'd become a deity. Just look at the outfits! Elvis, Hendrix, Jagger—they dressed like the sun god Helios, burned guitars, went on vision quests, became divine—which turned them into targets. It's no coincidence that the age of the celebrity is an age of assassins. JFK, MLK, RFK—killed because they got too famous. Jagger later admitted to being in fear throughout the '69 tour. Before each show he'd ask himself, *Is tonight the night?*

The '69 tour ended in December. The Stones had played twenty-four shows in four weeks. Instead of returning to England, they went into a studio. They'd been writing on the road and wanted to capture the sound while it was hot. The journalist Stanley Booth, traveling with the band, suggested they record in the bunkerlike facility at 3614 Jackson Highway in Sheffield, Alabama, owned by Booth's friend, the producer Jim Dickinson. Keith later said Muscle Shoals was, in its way, just as important to the Stones as Chess. The funk, the smell of whiskey and beer—the stale glory of a basement three days after an epic party. It was built around a rhythm section, the Swampers, who'd gained renown as the engine beneath Aretha Franklin, the Staple Singers, and Wilson Pickett. The Stones went to Alabama in search of a tone, that nasty Delta sound.

If you go to Muscle Shoals today, you can almost see the mark where the Stones reached flood tide, where, in the course of two days, they cut some of their most iconic sides. It started with "Brown Sugar," which Jagger goofed with in Australia but finished here, which is probably why it plays with so many taboos. It's a slave owner telling his story in the language of his chattel; the blues reflecting on its own antecedents. In it you hear the African Gold Coast, the middle passage, the auction block, the cotton fields. Once again, Jagger put himself in the place of the old blue-eyed devil, a "scarred old slaver [who] knows he's doing all right, [you] hear him whip the women just around midnight." Even Mick couldn't get away with that today. But the power of a song is to tell many stories at once. "Brown Sugar" also means interracial sex—the working title was "Black Pussy"—as well as heroin, which cooks to golden molasses. "I watched Mick write the lyrics," Dickinson said. "It took him maybe forty-five minutes. . . . He wrote it down as fast as he could move his hand. I'd never seen anything like it. He had one of those yellow legal pads . . . and when he had three pages filled, they started to cut it."

Jagger prepared the band in the way of Buddy Rich, bullying the musicians into shape. "No, no, the tempo's all wrong. It's not—not so bouncy. It should sound fuckin' *dirty*." The real drama is Keith finding the groove, the seam he can ride from can till can't. They started after it at noon and chased it till the next morning. Jagger threw away the outtakes, which can make it all seem like magic, as if the perfect take appeared from nowhere, with nothing behind it. At seven or eight in the morning, with the final cut in the can, they went to the Holiday Inn for breakfast, then sat around Keith's room listening to what they'd done.

My favorite Stones song is "Wild Horses," which the band recorded at the next session. Richards wrote the melody in England before the tour. He was at home with Anita and their baby, Marlon—named after Brando—who'd been born August 10, 1969. Keith had gotten over the bitter jealousy he'd experienced when Anita and Mick were shooting *Performance*, cast it off like a velour coat gone out of style. If you live like that, survival depends on willful amnesia. You forgive and forget or suffer and die. Marlon's birth came as a new beginning for the couple, and Richards experienced the days that followed as a fantasy of domestic life. The coming tour moved him toward melancholy—he did not want the moment to end. "Wild Horses" is that melancholy captured in a few chords, the ache and jaded enthusiasm of the Stones reduced to concentrate. Keith passed it on to Mick with a note appended: "Wild horses couldn't drag me away." Jagger rekeyed it to his own particulars: Marianne, overdose, breakup. "He changed it all around," Richards said later, "but it's still beautiful."

The Stones went through take after take after take, a process chronicled by the filmmakers David and Albert Maysles, who, in the fall of 1969, came on to make a documentary about the band.

Mick and Keith banter before the tape rolls.

Keith: Lights out.
Mick: Lights out, mouths shut.
Keith: Lights out in the boys' dorm. Two in a bed.

The song opens with the strum of an acoustic guitar, followed by a country slide, followed by Jagger's drawl. The drum doesn't come in till the chorus. The piano, played by Jim Dickinson, sounds like something you'd have heard in a bar in Deadwood during the Gold Rush. It's crushed velvet and indolence, a moment so sweet it's rotten. It's the sort of song you're careful not to listen to too often. You don't want to play it out. You go to it only when you need it. Best is if it catches you by surprise. I've been told every form of art wants to be music. For me, every form of music wants to be "Wild Horses."

After the session, the Stones listened to the song in the studio. Fagged out in the half light. Albert Maysles, who filmed the scene, told me he considers it a peak in his career, "when that intangible thing was captured." Art is not linear; it's circular. An artist does not improve, nor progress. He simply rides the wheel, waiting for the clouds to break and the sun to appear. Maysles captured one of those sunny moments. You see it on the faces of Mick, Charlie, and Bill. You especially see it on the face of Keith, who closes his eyes as he listens, deep in the cushions of a couch, smiling. He's managed to get the song in his head onto tape. He's managed to make something perfect. "I used to listen to classical music with my father," Maysles told me. "I'd look at him as he listened, and when the sound was right, he looked just like Mick and Keith do in those shots. It's the face of a person in the midst of satisfying a deep-down desire."

The songs recorded at Muscle Shoals, along with a handful of others—including "Sway," "Bitch," and "Dead Flowers"—would be released in 1971 as *Sticky Fingers*, the third album of the golden run.

Meanwhile, the gun was being loaded.

Meanwhile, the scenery was being rolled into place.

As the Stones worked in the studio, their representatives were putting together the show that would end the era. The band had been condemned for overcharging and cheapskating their fans. They decided to respond with a free concert, a festival as much as a show, a bookend to Woodstock, which had gone off successfully the previous summer. Because they wanted to exclude the police, the demon pigs of the free love generation, they decided the band would be guarded at the show not by state troopers, but by the Hell's Angels.

30

THANATOS IN STEEL

So here comes Sonny Barger, the primo president of the Hell's Angels, blazing onto the scene like a flame. He called his motorcycle—a customized Harley with extended handlebars and chopped-down axles—"Sweet Cocaine." In 1968, when some fool made the mistake of stealing Sonny's bike, word went out: "Nobody, and I mean nobody, rides a motorcycle in this town until I get 'Sweet Cocaine' back."

"We rounded up everybody who was responsible, tied them up, and took them over to my house," Barger writes in his autobiography. "Every half hour or so, the front door would open and another accomplice was tossed into the living room. When we found the last guy the punishment began. One at a time we bullwhipped them and beat them with spiked dog collars, broke their fingers with ball peen hammers. One of them screamed at us, 'Why don't you just kill us and get it over with?'"

Barger grew up in the fifties, a product of the same aimless postwar malaise that formed Mick and Keith, John and Paul, Marianne and Anita. Too much freedom, not enough freedom. Too much danger, not enough danger. No big war, no cause to give your life meaning. In high school, he was a greaser, just like the teddy boys of John Lennon's Liverpool. His father worked in the Central Valley, laying pavement for Highway 99. It's poetic: the old man building roads the young man will ride. Sonny's mother abandoned the family; everything fell apart. He never had a real home. It explains the anger, the edge. The fact that he was scrawny, all wire and bone, emphasized the point. Make the wrong sort of joke to Sonny, you'll end up swallowing your own teeth.

Sonny has a code: "If a cat don't want to fight with me, don't want to hassle with me, I want to be his friend. If he don't want to be my friend, then outta sight. Don't even talk to me. But if he don't want to be my friend and he's gonna get in my face, I'm gonna hurt him, or he's gonna hurt me."

Because he wanted to join a crew of knock-around guys and there wasn't one, Sonny formed a gang. Oakland, 1954. Delinquents in leather jackets, name stitched on back: "Earth Angels." When he was sixteen, he lied about his age and enlisted in the Army. He went through boot camp and was sent to Honolulu. He fell in love with cycles in the motor pool. But at some point, his real age was discovered. At seventeen, he was back home, a washed-out jarhead. He took work as a custodian: the night crew, pushing a mop and dreaming of Indo-China. He filled out, got strong. Big white teeth, sneer. Hair greased, clothes dirty. He tore the sleeves off his coat to show the guns, which did not scale with the body. He was built like a lobster: massive claws, modest shell. You'd see him at dawn, on his way home from work, riding north on Highway 1, the sedans and station wagons scattering like pigeons beneath a hawk.

In 1954, Barger went to see Stanley Kramer's film *The Wild One*, starring Marlon Brando and Lee Marvin as leaders of opposing motorcycle outfits. It's based on a true story, the takeover by bike gangs— the Pissed Off Bastards, the Boozefighters—of Hollister, California. It changed Barger's life. Lee Marvin became a hero; Barger went looking for a club.

The early motorcycle gangs had formed in California after the war by "thousands of veterans . . . who flatly rejected the idea of going back to their prewar pattern," Hunter S. Thompson writes in *Hell's Angels*. They rode in formation under names taken from old military units or coined while drunk. The Boozefighters operated by the credo "Jesus Died So We Could Ride." But by the mid-1950s, when Sonny went looking for them, most of those veterans had gotten over the hump, assimilated back into civilian life. Sonny started his own outfit instead. In this, he was part of a boom, the second flowering of motorcycle gangs: the Gypsy Jokers, the Nightriders, the Comancheros, the Presidents, Satan's Slaves.

Hell's Angels: the name had been bouncing around for years. Some traced it back to a World War II fighter wing. Others said the name came not from war but from a fantasy of war, specifically Howard Hughes's 1930 movie *Hell's Angels* starring Jean Harlow. There'd been a Sacramento gang called that in the late forties and early fifties, but it was defunct. A friend of Sonny's found one of their old patches in a secondhand store—a skull with wings, the flying death's-head. In the spring of 1957, Sonny had several made to order and started his club. It grew until it became many-headed and mean.

The life of a Hell's Angel was the most dangerous sort of fun. It consisted of fights, parties, and "runs"—multiday events in which thousands of bikers took possession of the highway, moving in a horde from liquor store to campsite en route to a predetermined location, a city or park or house on cinder blocks where the true debauch would begin. As with any society, there was a hierarchy. An elite known as the Filthy Few had a special patch that signified they were "the first to party and the last to leave." According to mythology, the patch was akin to a teardrop tattoo: worn only by killers. The ethos of the gang was most perfectly expressed in a brawl. There was no man-on-man. No traditional sense of honor. The Angels battled in a swarm—everyone in, kick 'em till they stop moving.

The Angels had dozens of chapters and many thousands of members by 1969. Like Caribbean pirates, they self-governed by written law, a constitution that was amended whenever the need arose. As you read each rule, you picture the necessitating episode:

+ No spiking the club's booze with dope
+ No throwing live ammunition into bonfires on runs
+ No messing with another member's wife
+ No using dope during a meeting
+ Weapons will be shot only between 0600 and 1600 hours

In their own way, the Hell's Angels lived like rock stars, footloose and free, an affront to the bourgeoisie. And oh, how they loved to get fucked up! In the late fifties, it had been Benzedrine and reds, the same sort of truck-driver drugs that Keith and Brian gobbled on their first tours. In the early sixties, the sprees were fueled by a cocktail of narcotics: Seconal (red devils), amyl nitrite (blue heaven), Nembutal (yellow jackets). By the midsixties they'd discovered hallucinogens.

Hunter Thompson began riding with the Angels in the early sixties, an association that led to a biker/hippie alliance that mixed outlaws with Beat poets and jam bands. Like the Stalin/Hitler pact, it couldn't last. It fell apart on October 16, 1965, when Barger and his boys beat up a bunch of antiwar protesters.

Even after the melee, the bikers occupied a romantic place in the rock star imagination. They were seen as rugged individualists who took a lot of acid and lived by a code. (Peter Fonda and Dennis Hopper hung around Barger while researching *Easy Rider*.) But this love was not reciprocated. Over time, the outlaw bikers came to hate actors and musicians who turned them into symbols. It was the ancient greaser/preppy thing—rich kids hanging out with the sons of forklift operators. Even Hunter Thompson came to be despised. "Hunter turned out to be a real weenie and a stone fucking coward," writes Barger. "You read about how he walks around his house now with his pistols, shooting them out of his windows to impress writers who show up to interview him. He's all show and no go. When he tried to act tough with us, no matter what happened, Hunter Thompson got scared. I ended up not liking him at all, a tall, skinny, typical hillbilly from Kentucky. He was a total fake." The Angels stomped Thompson at their last meeting, leaving the writer bruised but with a perfect ending for his book. "Peter Fonda went to the same school as Hunter Thompson," Barger added. "Chickenshit High."

It's a bad sign when the venue keeps changing. The Stones were going to hold their free concert at Golden Gate Park, but it didn't work out. Then it was Sears Point Raceway just outside the city, but there was an issue with the deposit. "It kept falling apart," Ronnie Schneider, a Stones road manager involved in the negotiations, told me. "Big deals are like that—they fall apart. But if there's enough money out there, they keep coming back together, even when they shouldn't."

The discussions, conducted in the way of a summit, with agents gathered over maps in San Francisco, eventually focused on the Altamont Speedway, a racing oval in a valley beyond Livermore. The grounds, consisting of a track, an infield, and a grandstand, had been offered free without conditions by its owner, Dick Carter, who wanted the publicity. It was not the worst place imaginable, but close. If you stand on the hill that overlooks the site, you'll see why. It's stark, exposed to the wind and weather, without proper facilities, miles from the nearest big town. Scarce parking, no shade, and only one road in, a concrete ribbon that snakes through the hills.

I have in front of me a book called *Altamont: Death of Innocence in the Woodstock Nation*. I read through it with embarrassment. It chronicles the era of festivals, gatherings of dancing hippies, each convinced they'd shed the old hatreds. My generation is hard-boiled in comparison. Too much sentiment makes us uncomfortable, as we heard so much of it from the big brothers and big sisters who smoked pot under the bridge. Edited and introduced by Jonathan Eisen, the book is a snapshot of the baby boomer in self-important youth: "What the hip community has done then is to create for itself . . . festivals, which are billed as tribal gatherings. . . . They are giant aggregations of people who come together to listen to music they can hear elsewhere perhaps in order to prove to themselves that there are thousands of others just like them into the same kind of trip, or perhaps to be among people who will not judge them for their hair or the freakiness, who will be kind to each other."

Ronnie Schneider told me he was opposed to the free concert from the start. "The entire premise was bullshit," he explained. "It started with the writer Ralph Gleason saying the Stones had been overcharging, taking advantage of fans. The Stones felt terrible about that, and wouldn't listen when I said, 'Hey, he's got the facts wrong—it's not true.' But they got caught up in the story. And there was this example of Woodstock. 'It's got to be like Woodstock.' But Woodstock wasn't free. It only became free when people began knocking down the fences."

"Ralph Gleason led the charge with the promoter Bill Graham," Sam Cutler said. "They had been criticizing the Stones over ticket prices. The Doors were charging $7 for top-price tickets in the United States, the Stones were charging $8.50. Gleason wrote a column about that. Then wrote another criticizing the Stones for playing, essentially, black music. Whatever the fuck that means. Gleason actually suggested the Stones pay royalties to black artists. Fucking idiot. Idiot. I mean, the Stones were the greatest supporters of black music. They had Chuck Berry and B. B. King and all kinds of wonderful artists on the bill. Nobody else would give those people work. It was such a low way of criticizing the Stones. So they felt sensitive and vulnerable, and the hippies, the Grateful Dead, they were all suggesting the Stones do a free concert."

When Altamont was finally settled on as the location, Cutler had just a few days to prepare. He recruited several acts to fill out the festival, including Santana, the Jefferson Airplane, the Grateful Dead, and Gram Parsons's new band, the Flying Burrito Brothers.

At some point, Cutler turned to the question of safety. Security guards had been a presence at Stones concerts from the start, at times so involved they seemed like a part of the show. In early footage you often see professional bouncer types protecting the band from its fans, intercepting girls who rush the stage, clearing space for the Stones to play. Someone suggested they hire off-duty cops at Altamont, but the police were hated in 1969. "The Chicago riots had happened recently," Charlie Watts explained, "and there had been a lot of images of cops beating people up, so you thought that if you had cops in charge, it was going to be worse."

If not the police, who would protect the Stones?

One day, Sam Cutler drove from San Francisco to Mickey Hart's ranch in Marin, where he met with a Hell's Angel named Terry the Tramp. Hart, who played drums in the Grateful Dead and served as a conduit between the hippies and the bikers, told Cutler to invite the Angels to the show—bring 'em in, give 'em beer, otherwise you'll have trouble. "Rock Scully and the Dead said the Hell's Angels should be taken care of so they're cool, 'cuz they always come to these concerts in San Francisco anyway," Cutler told me. "When they played in Golden Gate Park, the Dead used to give them five hundred dollars' worth of beer. The Angels would sit there, get drunk, have fun. No problem. That's what I went there to talk about. That was the whole deal. There was no 'The Rolling Stones have hired the Hell's Angels for security.' It's a canard."

Sonny Barger understood the arrangement differently. According to Barger, a San Francisco "hipster" named Emmett Grogan had the idea of hiring the Angels to work security at Altamont. In return, the Angels would receive five hundred dollars' worth of beer.

"I tried to fight the urban myth of the Angels and the five hundred dollars in beer," Ronnie Schneider told me. "It didn't happen, but everyone says it did, so it might as well have. Later, when the band was going on [a national TV show], they said, 'Ron, is there any one thing we can say?' I said, 'Yeah, do me a favor, please, kill that stupid story that we paid the Hell's Angels five hundred bucks.'"

The arrival of the bikers at Altamont, as shot by the Maysles, is one of the greatest tanks-through-the-tulips scenes ever put on film—the history of America retold in a moment. Here you have the hippies, those who'd claimed spots in front of the stage, in their beads and sandals, tents and yurts, gathered like homesteaders on the grasslands, each family with its plot of earth. There you have the Angels, nihilistic cowboys hired by the cattle boss, with their long hair and colors, beards and dirty jeans, the engines of their machines throbbing as they kicked and punched and idled their way through, thirsty for women and beer.

The road into Altamont was quickly overwhelmed, turned into a parking lot, VW buses and Oldsmobiles left behind as people streamed over the hills. It was windy and unseasonably cold, even for December. The sun sat on the lip of the earth, then faded. Darkness. Around three hundred thousand people turned up for the last party of the decade.

Jagger and Richards decided to check out the scene. They choppered in on the eve of the show, descending like deities. They walked across the hills where people made camp, tents and bonfires beneath a starry sky. They picked up followers, kids who trailed along in freaked-out silence. Ronnie Schneider, the Stones' road manager, was with them, as was the journalist Stanley Booth. It was a strange scene, a hippie Brigadoon: you find it only when you're fucked up.

Emerging from the crowd, a girl touched Jagger's arm and asked, "Are you real?"

As the Spanish conquistadors walked across the causeway into the fantastical Aztec capital of Tenochtitlán, Bernal Díaz del Castillo turned to the warrior beside him and asked, "Is this a dream?" It's not the city's existence you doubt, but your own.

"At one point, as we stood by a campfire, a guy handed us this big gallon jug of wine, the kind you put over your shoulder, and we drank," Ronnie Schneider told me. "Then he handed up a joint. Nobody said a word. Here's Mick and Keith, but nobody said anything. We smoked, stood around the fire for a few minutes, then started toward the stage. As we were walking, I turned and looked. There were about forty people following us. Just watching—not a word. When we were getting ready to leave, Keith said, 'It's beautiful, man, I'm going to stay.'" He spent the night wandering among the campfires, drinking with the peasants and reading the sky.

"Meanwhile" is a term you resort to when writing about Altamont, as the big event is composed of scores of simultaneous smaller events. Ideally, they'd be shown on a thousand screens in the biggest theater in hell. On this screen, Mick and Keith walk the grounds. On that one, Sonny Barger swallows a handful of reds and fires up Sweet Cocaine. On this one, the cars and vans jam the road over Livermore Pass. On that one, Meredith Hunter, a Stones fan who will be dead in a few hours, puts on his lime-green suit and packs his pistol. On this one, Sam Cutler, with his greasy hair and goatee, works through the night, assembling the sound system and stage. "It was obviously going to be a disaster for many reasons," Cutler told me, "but mainly because of that stage. It was like fucking two foot six high. Chip Monck had designed it for another site, and it was totally inappropriate for Altamont. Nowadays outdoor stages are eight or ten foot high. You have a set of stairs at the back so that one person can control access, who gets on and off. At Altamont, the stage was just above the knees. Anyone could just step up onto the stage. It was a fucking nightmare."

By morning, the beatific mood had turned ominous—blue sky riddled with black. Bad drugs were flooding the grounds, yellow acid tabs laced with chemicals, possibly strychnine. It was called a God dose—because if you take it, that's who you meet. They were being passed out like flyers, but nobody could determine the source. Conspiracists said it was undercover CIA agents who wanted to show that the whole hippie thing was a fraud—thousands of kids sent into a state of psychosis, racing up and down the hills, tearing out their hair. "As soon as I saw Altamont at dawn I knew in my gut it was going to be heavy," Cutler said later. "It was bitterly cold. There were a lot of drunk and stoned people stumbling about. Somebody came up and told me it was going to be the heaviest day of my life and then gave me a big chunk of opium, which I swallowed. You know, it went from there."

When I asked Albert Maysles, who, with his brother, David, chronicled Altamont in the film *Gimme Shelter*, when he first knew it was going bad, he said, "That morning. It was just the energy of the Raceway, the crowd. I'm not a mystical person, nor am I a young man, nor was I young then, but you could just feel it the way hippies said they could feel things. Hours before the first band started, I sat in the crowd, just to get a sense of it. And this guy comes over to me, and, well, he is not right in the eyes, ya know? And he says, 'If you don't leave this spot right away, I'll kill you.' Of course, I got out of there. But, funny thing, that was the exact spot where the killing took place."

When I asked Ronnie Schneider when he first knew it was going bad, he said, "Well, let's see ... I was on that first chopper in with Mick that afternoon. Two P.M. We got out and were walking to the trailers, and this guy comes up and punches Mick in the face. That's when I knew."

You see it in the film. The kid moves like an assassin. He hits Jagger and yells, "*I hate you, you're so fucked.*" "Mick was cool about it," Schneider told me. "Of course, I wanted to kill that kid, but Mick kept saying, 'Don't hurt him, don't hurt him.'"

Who was he? What did he want? When asked, people who were there shrug. Crazy kid, insane time, bad acid. But I wonder: Did the kid have a legitimate grievance? Even if the answer is no, I'm giving him one. That kid punched Mick Jagger because the Stones had put him and everyone else in an untenable position, squeezed between the landscape and the Angels.

The violence began before the first band took the stage. By noon, the ground in front of the speakers was in full-scale riot. It started with wannabes trying to impress the Angels. They stormed through the crowd, pushing, starting fights. In the film, you see them beat people with a swinging rhythm. The Angels claim they got involved only when their motorcycles, parked in front of the stage to form a barricade, were threatened. Barger writes about a particular incident— a guy leaning on the seat of a Harley, though he'd been warned not to, pushing the springs into the battery, which promptly shorted, sending up a plume of smoke. The Angels shoved people away; people shoved back. "Big mistake," writes Barger. "That's when we entered the crowd and grabbed some of the assholes vandalizing our bikes and beat the fuck out of them."

"I ain't no cop," Barger said later. "I ain't never gonna ever pretend to be a cop. And you know what? I didn't go there to police nothing, man. They told me if I could sit on the edge of the stage so nobody would climb over me you know I could drink beer until the show was over. And that's what I went there to do. But you know what? Some cat throws something and bangs my bike or some cat kicks over my bike he gotta fight."

Sam Cutler thought everything would calm down when the first band went on, but Sam Cutler was wrong. Carlos Santana opened the festival and his set was punctuated by violence. "The fights started because the Hell's Angels pushed people around," Santana later said. "It all happened so fast . . . we didn't know what was going on. There were lots of people just fucking freaked out."

"What was it like?" Cutler asked. "It was like watching the peace and love generation smash itself to bits."

The Jefferson Airplane went on next. That's when things got out of hand—it's also when Cutler probably should have called it a day and sent everyone home. The Angels were beating up a black kid in front of the stage. Marty Balin, one of the Jefferson Airplane's lead singers, jumped into the crowd to break it up. Then, just like that, Balin was out cold. You see confusion on the faces of the other musicians, disbelief, panic. When someone asked the biker, known as Animal, why he'd knocked out Balin, he said it was because "he spoke disrespectful to a brother Angel."

The Grateful Dead never made it to the stage. You see this in the film: Rock Scully and Jerry Garcia, who'd just arrived by helicopter, looking spooked as Bob Weir describes the scene.

Bob Weir: *They're beatin' up musicians!*
Jerry Garcia: Oh, bummer.

A moment later, the Dead are back on the chopper, heading over the hills.

The Stones were waiting in their trailer. They'd gotten reports on the violence but didn't seem too concerned. Mayhem had always been a necessary element of the Stones scene. If the front rows didn't give way to chaos, you didn't get the full experience. The Stones knew that, which is why, according to Ralph Gleason, they created the conditions that led to a breakdown. In this sense, Altamont was less aberration than culmination—the purest expression of the live show.

The band was introduced to Sonny that afternoon. "They came out of the trailer in their prissy clothes and makeup and we shook hands," Barger writes, "then they disappeared back inside."

The Stones went on hours late, leaving the crowd to stew in liquor and pills. ("Thunderbird and Ripple, the worst fucking rotgut wines there are, and bad acid," Richards said.) Barger claims Jagger was

waiting for darkness, as that's when his makeup would pop and he'd look most satanic. Jagger blamed Bill Wyman, who'd missed the first helicopter. He turned up at seven. The band took the stage a few minutes later, the Angels leading the way. Charlie Watts later spoke about the violence of the entrance, the brutal efficiency of the Angels, who cleared a path "like the Third Reich coming through."

Jagger was wearing a tight black shirt and pants, an elaborate Elvis-like belt and buckle, and a red scarf that trailed like a cape. The legs of his pants were studded with ornament, his shoes as soft as slippers. You can't see them without thinking of rusty nails and tetanus. The front of his shirt, which he'd worn throughout the tour, was decorated with the Greek letter omega. This was code, a message relayed in the euphemistic way of Kenneth Anger, Aleister Crowley, the Book of Revelation. In the Bible, omega, the last letter in the alphabet, stands for the end of time—the Four Horsemen, Judgment Day, the world on fire—as alpha stands for the beginning. By emblazoning it across his chest, Jagger was announcing himself, on a frequency received by lunatics, as God and Devil, Christ and Antichrist. "I am alpha and omega, the beginning and the ending, saith the Lord, which is, and which was, and which is to come, the Almighty."

It was a joke, of course, just some cool shit you might try while your parents are downtown, but now and then someone takes the joke seriously. Jagger must have known he was in trouble as soon as he got out there. He was surrounded by bikers who were supposed to protect him but were in fact holding him prisoner. You see it in the movie and the photos, you hear it in the stories: the Angels owned the night. They were at their leisure, in their jackets on the stage. Now and then, a biker glared at Mick. His hair was long and loose, his lips big and red; he moved like a woman or a cat. If you're a certain sort, something in you wants to crush the pretty things. A menacing German shepherd paced between the amps.

I tried to interview Sonny Barger. He's still around. Lives in Arizona. Quite old. Cancer left him without a voice box. His words are mechanical, communicated via a vibrating gizmo he presses to his throat. But he still rides. And he's still Sonny Barger. If anything, age has made him meaner. He said he'd talk to me but only about his movie. *What movie?* He sent me a copy. It's called *Dead in Five Heartbeats*, as that's how many you'll have left after Sonny cuts your jugular. Its aesthetics are those of snuff films and porn. It's about a biker whose code and persona are not unlike Sonny's, recast as a myth: the Angel as fabled creature, akin to the lost king of Germany who one day will ride down from the mountains to unify the warring tribes. I did not do the interview because I could not think of a connection between that film and what I wanted to know. Once I got to Arizona, I'd ask only about Altamont. Sonny would get pissed off and curse me through that mechanical voice box and then I'd have a pissed-off mechanized Sonny Barger on my ass. But later, which is always the way, the connection between the film and the concert occurred to me. It's about real versus fake, outlaw versus wannabe. Early in the movie, the biker sees a bully pushing his girlfriend around. The bully looks formidable but the biker throttles him without half trying, then says something like *Everyone thinks he's a tough guy, till he meets a real tough guy.*

Mick Jagger had long pretended to be the devil. Then one night he threw a party and the real devil showed up. The Stones have never recovered. In the campfire tale, the man sees a ghost and his hair turns white. What did the Stones see at Altamont? Their own demise, the fate of all those who held the grenade too long. I grew up after Altamont. I never believed in the satanic power of Mick Jagger, nor experienced the Stones when they were lit by messianic energy. When I watched them, I knew it was a fantasy.

The band played "Jumpin' Jack Flash" and "Carol" and started "Sympathy for the Devil." Jagger's way of winking at his fans. "I am Lucifer." Then the violence began. Everywhere at once. Angels beating hippies with fists and clubs, pool cues. Jagger paused to tell the crowd, "Something very funny happens when we start that number," then carried on.

I've interviewed many people who were either on the stage that night or in proximity to it. Each offered a slightly different recollection. Together they chronicle Altamont in the kaleidoscopic way of the Wallace Stevens poem "Thirteen Ways of Looking at a Blackbird."

The concert progressed in stops and starts. The band would play, the violence would erupt, the band would stop playing. Or play a mellow groove they described as "cool-out music." Jagger told the audience to calm down, take it easy. He had everyone sit on the grass. He was giving the crowd tips on how to survive a night with the Angels. In these attempts, as well as in his efforts to placate the bikers, the singer revealed more than he intended. This was not Mick Jagger, son of the devil, personification of flame. It was Michael Jagger, student of economics, scared shitless, too far from home. As the cameras rolled, he pleaded with the crowd in a hippy-dippy language he never believed in and was alien to the Stones: "Sisters—brothers and sisters—brothers and sisters—come on now. That means everybody just cool out—will ya cool out, everybody. . . . Who—who—I mean, like, people, who's fighting and what for? Hey, peo-ple—I mean, who's fighting and what for? Why are we fighting?"

Keith's reaction was more manly, truer to the vision. He stood up to the Angels, threatening to walk off—"We're not playing. Calm down or we ain't going to play no more"—leaving them to battle three hundred thousand pissed-off flower children.

"I . . . stuck my pistol into his side and told him to start playing his guitar or he was dead," writes Barger. "He played like a motherfucker."

Keith has neither confirmed nor denied this story. For years, he spoke of Altamont only in the most circumspect way. "Ah, it's obvious [who was to blame]," he told *Rolling Stone* in 1971. "Maybe they'll do me the next time I go there, but [the Angels] were out of control, man."

Maysles focused his camera on a Hell's Angel standing a few feet from Jagger. Big and beefy, gritting his teeth, fighting some inner madness. Maybe acid, maybe psychosis. Either way, he's insane. Nearly everyone I interviewed mentioned this man. "He was staring straight at Mick, hands clenching and unclenching, pulling his hair, face contorted," Ethan Russell, who was onstage taking pictures, told me. "He was stoned and violent, probably murderous, and standing not eight feet from Mick. I mean, how would you perform in such a circumstance?"

It demonstrates the line Jagger had to walk that night, how in truth he behaved more bravely than you might imagine. "It's one of the greatest shots I've ever gotten," Albert Maysles told me. "It fills the screen, and tells you everything you need to know. That's what Altamont felt like."

Meredith Hunter, a Stones fan in a lime-green suit, drove to Altamont with his girlfriend, Patty Bredehoft. He was from Berkeley, California, coffee-colored, tall and slim, distinguished by a vertiginous Afro. His friends called him Murdock. Bredehoft called him Murdock Supreme. He was flashy and wore the sort of candy-colored suits favored by wiseguys in old movies. As he was only eighteen, he was probably still figuring out what he wanted to be, but death freezes you. It turned Murdock into a totemic figure, the tragedy of Altamont, the corpse at the end of the trail.

Not to say he was a saint. Or a hippie. Meredith Hunter embraced violence with both fists. He was a badass motherfucker, a member of a street gang called the East Bay Executioners, known to traffic in amphetamines and carry a gun. His arms were covered with track marks, his temper could click from mellow to crazy just like that. When footage of Hunter at Altamont surfaced, drug users said he was clearly bombed on reds. They could tell by his eyes and the way he kept licking his lips. "One speed dealer got killed by another at a concert," Sam Cutler complained, "and somehow the Rolling Stones were responsible?"

Hunter worked his way close to the stage, which brought him to the attention of the Angels. According to witnesses, the bikers picked on him either because he was too close or because of the way he was dancing. He went to his car to get his girlfriend before the Stones came on and was back in front of the stage when they kicked off "Under My Thumb." What happened next happened fast. An Angel attacked Hunter. The crowd scattered. Hunter tried to run but the bikers swarmed, and then he drew his pistol.

> Sam Cutler: "I saw the long-barreled silver gun shining in the stage lights."
> Stanley Booth: "I looked away from Mick and saw, with that now familiar instant space around him, bordered with falling bodies, a Beale Street nigger in a black hat, black shirt, iridescent blue-green suit, arms and legs stuck out at crazy angles, a nickel-plated revolver in his hand."

"When we finally worked our way up to the front of the crowd and the Rolling Stones started playing, there was a lot of pushing and there were Angels on the stage," Patty Bredehoft told a grand jury. "Murdock kept trying to go further up toward the front. I couldn't keep up with him because I wasn't strong so I sort of waited back, didn't try to get as far as he did. He was as close as he could get, where there were some boxes with people standing on the boxes. I'd say there were about five people in between me and him. . . . I was getting pushed around, and as I glanced up there, I saw either [an Angel] had hit Murdock or pushed him or something, but this Hell's Angel who was standing, pushed him or knocked him back. It didn't knock him down, but knocked him back over the stage, and as he started to come back forward towards the Hell's Angel, another Hell's Angel who was on the stage grabbed him around the neck. They were scuffling around. I'm not sure which Hell's Angel it was, but I just remember he was scuffling around and there was a couple of people blocking my view of him because he was down on the ground. I couldn't really see him. As the people backed away, Murdock came around by my side and pulled a gun out. They came toward—well, a group of Hell's Angels . . . they came toward him and they reached for his arm and then they were all kicking and fighting and stuff, Murdock and the Hell's Angels . . ."

The Angels say Hunter knew just what he was doing—that he was

not running but setting up, aiming. According to Barger, he fired once. Others say he fired twice. People scattered. Some dived to the ground. Why did he pull the pistol? Was it hysterical fear? Was it drugs? Was he trying to warn the Angels, push them back? Or was he an assassin? In which case the Angels were heroes.

> Rock Scully: "There was no doubt in my mind that [Hunter] intended to do terrible harm to Mick or somebody in the Rolling Stones, or somebody on that stage."
>
> Sam Cutler: "Without the presence of the Angels, it might very well have been Mick's body laid out in the morgue."

As soon as Hunter drew that pistol, his life was over. A biker later identified as Alan Passaro appears in minute 83 of the Maysles film, a ghoul in leather, arrested in time. His mouth is a smear. His eyes are obsidian. His right arm is raised high. The blade flashes. According to later reports, Hunter was stabbed five times. In the neck, in the back, in the stomach. "Tell Mick he had a gun!" an Angel shouted to Cutler. "The guy had a gun! He got two shots off! He had a gun!"

In *Gimme Shelter*, Sam Cutler crosses the stage, then whispers, first in Mick's ear, then in Keith's. I asked if Cutler remembered what he'd said. "Of course I remember," he told me. "It was the most terrifying moment of my life. I told Mick there was a guy who'd been stabbed to death and he'd had a gun—that's what I'm saying in that movie: 'Mick, there's a guy with a gun. Get off the fucking stage. Now!' But Mick was very brave. He said, 'No, no, no. We can't stop now, we can't.' He was convinced that if they stopped and withdrew there would be a complete riot. He had the balls of a lion, Mick did."

"What about Keith? What did you tell him?"

"Same fucking thing."

"Same fucking thing?"

"Same fucking thing."

"How did he react?"

"Same fucking way."

"Same fucking way?"

"Same fucking way."

Meredith Hunter lay dying fifteen feet from the stage. The Angels stood in a circle around him, looking down. Several people later reported his last words.

"I wasn't going to shoot you," Hunter told his killer.

"Why did you have a gun?" asked Passaro.

In a crane shot, you'd see the crowd, the body at its center, the band in the distance. To some, it seemed almost inevitable, the tragedy that long awaited the Stones, the natural end point of all their invocations of anarchy and violence. Writing in *Creem* magazine in 1973, Patti Smith called it "the perfect moment. The miracle of Altamont. The death of the lime green spade. Not shocking. Necessary. The most graceful complete moment. Compare [Hunter's] dance of death with Mick's frenzied movement. Mick's spastic magic. Unlucky motor."

An Angel stood over Hunter for several minutes, not letting anyone near. "Don't touch him," he said. "He's going to die anyway, just let him die."

One afternoon not long ago, I talked to a sixty-eight-year-old emergency room doctor named Robert Hiatt who had served as a volunteer medic at Altamont. "It was very rudimentary," he told me. "We didn't have the basic tools you'd have in a hospital. Mostly we treated people on bad acid trips. We had Compazine, an antipsychotic drug that calmed them. But usually you'd just try to find a person willing to sit with somebody having a bad experience, talk 'em down. Sometimes they didn't need medication at all. People's reaction to drugs is influenced by the environment, and the environment at Altamont was bad.

"I was working in back of the stage when a guy came up with a frantic look on his face, shouting 'We need a doctor!' We went around front, under the scaffolding, and when we got into the bright lights the Stones were right there, playing. There were four people carrying a body. They were gonna put it on the stage, and I could see Keith looking at this body being brought to the stage with panic on his face. Then people were saying, 'Here's the doctor, here's the doctor.' The crowd parted like the Red Sea. They gave me the body. He was limp. I carried him back to the clinic area, the tents. And we examined him; he was unconscious already. I saw multiple stab wounds in his back. We didn't have any IV fluid or anything to do for him except get him out of there. As far as I saw, he never had a chance. By the time I had him in my arms he was pretty much dead, and there was no way to pull him back. We couldn't intubate him, couldn't put a thoracic tube in, any of the things I would do in an emergency room. They got him in an old station wagon and took him up to a hill where the helicopters landed. I think he died in transit."

If asked to list the most interesting concerts in the history of rock 'n' roll, I would include, along with Bob Dylan at Newport and Jimi Hendrix at the Monterey Pop Festival, the Rolling Stones at Altamont—after the stabbing. It's the same band and it's the same crowd, but the context has utterly changed. The Stones played eight songs *following* Meredith Hunter's death, including "Midnight Rambler," "Live with Me," "Gimme Shelter," "Honky Tonk Women," and "Brown Sugar"—its first public performance. People at the show say it was the best the Stones ever sounded. Terror had given their music a razor edge and apocalyptic power. It was the end of the project, the final appearance of the band as conceived by Brian, Mick, and Keith in 1962 and sharpened by Andrew Oldham in 1964. The Stones as bad boys: *We piss anywhere, man.* Just like that, the illusion shattered.

Four people died at Altamont. Hundreds were injured. There have been other rock 'n' roll disasters, of course. Eleven people were trampled to death at a Who concert in Cincinnati in 1979. But this was different. At Altamont, the spectators were beaten by the Stones' own security—the band had loosed the furies on its own fans. What's more, as the violence, which seemed to grow directly out of the music, took over, Mick Jagger was revealed as overmatched, powerless. "Menace is most effective when its limits are not known," George Trow wrote in *The New Yorker* in 1978. "Jagger's 'demonic' persona was not enhanced by the death at Altamont, as some people supposed; it was *destroyed*. In the face of one man's real death, Jagger's 'demonic' posture was shown to be merely perverse."

After the last number—"Street Fighting Man"—the Stones put down their instruments and ran. Through the crowd and up the path, the mob howling, the night closing in. If you stumbled, the demons would devour you. Two helicopters waited on top of the hill, the blades spinning into a void. Everyone jammed in, hysterical. "We had all five Rolling Stones in my helicopter," Ethan Russell said, "plus Ian Stewart, Jo Bergman, David Horowitz, Gram Parsons and [Michelle Phillips], Ronnie Schneider, and a bunch of others—seventeen people. It was certified for ten. We barely cleared the hills. That we didn't crash is incredible."

"I was toward the front," Ronnie Schneider told me. "The pilot said, 'We got a problem.' Not what you want to hear from a pilot. I said, 'What's wrong?' The guy says, 'We're way overweight. I can't land normally. I'm going to have to glide it in like an airplane.'"

At the Livermore airport, the Stones hopped a plane to San Francisco, where they scrambled into the limos and town cars that carried them back to their hotel.

. . .

The Angels stayed at the Speedway long enough to finish their beer and pop some reds, then took off, riding low and mean, the country-side blurred into a smear.

The Stones were at the Huntington Hotel on Nob Hill by nine that night. The band and their people met to discuss what had happened and what needed to be done. "It was the most intense room to be in on earth," Pamela Des Barres told Ben Fong-Torres. "Everyone was high; Gram [Parsons] was there, leaning against the wall, nodding out. There was a whole discussion about what to do. Mick was actually thinking about quitting [music], retiring. 'I didn't want it to be like this,' Mick said, very quietly."

The Stones decided to take the next flight home. "I talked to Mick about it just before he left," Sam Cutler—who, according to Ethan Russell, was still wearing a sweater stained with Hunter's blood—told me. "He wanted to leave immediately, get out of Dodge, know what I mean? I thought that was a completely coward-like thing to do. But Mick's attitude was: If we don't leave we're gonna be sued for this, sued for that, and God knows what else; there's gonna be all kinds of legal complications. So his attitude was: he's leaving, with the money. Which is what he did. But I said somebody should be there from the Rolling Stones, and he said, 'Okay, if you're gonna stay, we'll pay your hotel, we'll pay your legal bills, we'll get a lawyer to represent you.' And of course they didn't do any of that."

"What do you mean?" I asked. "They didn't pay the bills?"

"I never heard from them again," Cutler told me. "That was the end."

"They left you on the beach? Why would they do that?"

"Well, that's a question that maybe should be directed to the Rolling Stones rather than to me," said Cutler, bitterly. "I mean, it would be interesting to see what they have to say about it. But that's what they did. They didn't pay me and they abandoned me. Hey, thanks, guys. Nice guys."

"Did you ever see the Stones again?"

"Well, yeah, I saw them a few years ago, when they were playing in Australia."

"Did you ask them what happened?"

"Yeah, and Keith looked at me and said: 'Fuck me, Sam Cutler! Or should I say, fuck you!' To which I replied: 'Take your fucking choice. I don't give a fuck.' That was the beginning of our conversation. There's one gentleman in the Rolling Stones, Charlie, who I love. He's still a friend of mine. The rest of 'em, I don't know how much style they've got."

Most of the crowd drifted away from the Speedway as soon as the Stones had gone, but a few people stayed. Albert Maysles shows them leaving in the half-light in *Gimme Shelter*: the stragglers, hippie dead-enders carrying rucksacks to their cars. When I asked Maysles if he meant to make a larger point, he said, "It was not just the end of that concert but the end of the era. The people who left in the morning were the last people."

The backlash began immediately. It was as if all the aggression stirred up by the Stones over the years turned against them. They were denounced by the music press and denounced by the fans. They were denounced by other musicians—blamed not merely for poor planning but for puncturing the hippie bubble. Lyndon Johnson prolonged that senseless war. Charles Manson founded a death cult. But the Stones deep-sixed love. "I'm not downgrading the Angels, because it's not healthy and because they only did what they were expected to," David Crosby told *Rolling Stone*. "But I don't think that the Angels were the major mistake. I think they were just the most obvious mistake. I think the major mistakes were taking what was essentially a party and turning it into an ego game and star trip. An ego trip of 'look how many of us there are' and a star trip of the Rolling Stones, who are on a star trip and who qualify in my book as snobs....I think they have an exaggerated view of their own importance; I think they're on a grotesque ego trip."

The night after Altamont, as the San Francisco press were denouncing the Angels, Sonny Barger snorted as much cocaine as he could handle, then called KSAN-FM. "Flower people ain't a bit better than the worst of us," he said on the air. "It's about time everybody started realizing that. We were told if we showed up we could sit on the stage and drink some beer that the Stones' manager had bought us, you know. I didn't fucking like what happened there....I'm a violent cat when I got to be. But there ain't nobody gonna take anything I got and try to destroy it. And that Mick Jagger, he put it all on the Angels. He used us for dupes. As far as I'm concerned, we were the biggest suckers for that idiot I could ever see."

When Sam Cutler woke up Sunday morning in the hotel, everyone was gone. The lobby was filled with reporters. He snuck out without paying, then headed across the Golden Gate Bridge to Marin, where he hoped to take refuge at Mickey Hart's ranch. A few hours later, he was visited by a Hell's Angel called Sweet William, a longshoreman well known in Haight-Ashbury. Big and mean, Sweet William sat astride his bike, talking, talking. He told Cutler his presence was required at a meeting of a Hell's Angels court. Underworld jurisprudence, a star chamber of bad men. Cutler was being subpoenaed to answer for the sins of the Rolling Stones. He could have made a run for it, but he believed the band owed the Angels at least this much.

He thinks his appearance at that court probably saved Mick Jagger's life. "I was told they wanted to see me, and it was nonnegotiable, know what I mean?" Cutler said. "The next day, they took me to a house in San Francisco. Fucking scary. It was the presidents of all the clubs in California—Richmond, Oakland, San Bernardino—sitting on a kind of dais, like the fuckin' Supreme Court."

When Cutler went to shake hands, one of the Angels said, "I don't want to touch a piece of shit." Cutler asked if he could make a statement; he was told to shut up. Then the inquiry began. Most of the questions were about the cameras: who was filming and what for, where's that footage? The Angels were worried it might provide evidence against gang members. Cutler told the Angels about the documentary.

Albert Maysles had a graduate degree in psychology. After several years in the wrong field, he switched careers. His first film was about insane asylums in Russia. His first great film, made with his brother, David, chronicled the lives of door-to-door Bible salesmen. The Maysles brothers filmed the Beatles when they arrived in America—it's the footage you see whenever that story is told. They did not know they'd captured the murder of Meredith Hunter till ten days after the event. Most of the shots were a muddle. Like a dove in a snowstorm, you could look right at it and still not see it. It was David who picked it out. When he ran the film at normal speed—24 frames per second—he saw nothing, but when he went frame by frame the nightmare emerged: the lime-green suit, the pistol, the biker, the knife. With this footage—the entire episode is captured in forty frames—the filmmakers bookended their earlier work on the Beatles. John and Paul crossing the tarmac at JFK—that's dawn. Al Passaro plunging the blade into Meredith Hunter at Altamont—that's dusk.

Albert and David were contacted by the Alameda County Sheriff's Office. The cops wanted to see their footage. The brothers agreed to screen it if they could film the police as they watched. It was their technique. Make a movie, then film the stars of the movie watching it. Because the movie never ends. When the filmmakers were contacted by the Angels, they offered the same deal. You watch, we film. David Maysles went out to show it to the Angels a few days later. When Hunter was stabbed on screen, the Angels cheered. They did not let Maysles film them, though. They beat him up instead. "David ended up on the floor," Ronnie Schneider told me, "getting kicked in the nuts." If the film were released, they told Maysles, they expected to be paid. "Five percent," said Schneider, "plus a million dollars."

The Maysles brothers flew to England to show the footage to the Stones and film them watching it. Jagger played down Altamont from the start: just a bad night in a lifetime of good and bad. But the Maysleses' movie tells another story. In it, you see Hunter's murder register on Mick's face like a blow. He bites his nails, looks away. As he stands to leave the screening room, he stares directly into the camera. A wised-up, cynical stare: the look of a man who'd been in crisis but wasn't anymore; a man who's just decided, "Fuck it."

When I asked Stones photographer Ethan Russell about this, he said, "Yeah, that was the moment. I understood it a few years later when the Stones did that song 'It's Only Rock 'n' Roll.' But it had never been *only* rock 'n' roll. It had always been more. That's what Altamont took away. It's like one morning you wake up and realize, 'Oh, so it's not going to change the world after all. It's only rock 'n' roll.'"

Meredith Hunter's mother sued the Stones for half a million dollars. The band fought the case, eventually settling for a reported ten thousand dollars. Hunter is buried behind a church in East Vallejo, California. Lot 63, grave C. Not many visit, but some do, and those some regard Hunter as an embodiment: the last man, the fan who paid the ultimate price. His life was black and green, lit by reds, violent from start to finish—Murdock Supreme of the East Bay Executioners.

Alan Passaro was charged with the murder. Identified in the May-sleses' footage, he was described in the press as a "21-year-old Chicano." A Gypsy Joker from San Jose, he'd been an Angel only four months at the time of Altamont. New to the gang, he'd perhaps been overly eager to prove himself. In mug shots, he has the ducktailed hair of a fifties hoodlum. Dark hooded eyes. Soul patch. Small mouth twisted into a smirk—the sort of guy who'd call a policeman "copper."

The trial was held thirteen months after the killing. Passaro's attorney, George Walker, argued self-defense: the chaos of the night, the rock star, the gun. *What else can a poor boy do?* Passaro said he was not even sure he'd stabbed Hunter. He only knew he'd "stabbed at" him. The jury deliberated for just over twelve hours. *Rolling Stone* magazine reported the reading of the verdict: "Passaro, 22, threw back his head and let out a whoop...." He celebrated his acquittal by returning to prison, where he was serving a two-to-ten-year sentence for marijuana possession.

The Stones are a story that I've studied all my life. I've studied it as the ancients studied war. It's my Hemingway, Dickens, Homer. I've studied it in books, on vinyl, and up close. Yet it keeps surprising me. There's always something strange and new. Alan Passaro's fate is an example. He got out of prison in the late seventies. In 1985, he was found facedown in Anderson Lake, southeast of San Jose, California. In a waterproof bag strapped to his back, the police discovered ten thousand dollars in cash—the same amount the Stones had paid Meredith Hunter's family.

The Angels held a grudge against the Stones for years. For using them as dupes, patsies. In the underworld, it was rumored that the gang had issued a murder contract on Jagger and Richards. There's no way to prove this claim, but the fear it generated was real. You saw it in Jagger's unease, how anxious he seemed in a crowd. You heard it when Keith said, "Maybe they'll do me the next time I'm out there."

A few years ago, Mark Young, who'd been an FBI agent in the 1970s, told the BBC that the Hell's Angels had indeed plotted to assassinate the Stones. According to Young, there was a plan, actually put into motion in 1979, to ambush Jagger while he was vacationing in Montauk, where, according to reports, he'd rented Andy Warhol's estate. In the manner of the Navy Seals, the bikers would attack from the sea. Up the beach, past the hedgerows. Big house, outbuildings, pavilions. All of it would be wired and detonated. But the boats over-turned in a freakish swell. The Angels, dumped into the water, had to swim for their lives. In this way, God intervened. In this way, the song remains the same. This story is extremely dodgy. I've tried to nail it down, but it can't be done. Like everything with the Stones, history gives way to legend wherever the pavement meets the open fields.

The Altamont Speedway itself seems hexed. Considered a great track by experts, it's always given spectators the creeps. The *San Francisco Chronicle* described it as a "wind corridor" where the monstrous gusts never stop blowing. The bathrooms smell like sulfur, lingering evidence of the devil. In its forty-three years as a going concern, it was shut down six times. Its most recent owner, Mel Andrews, invested $1.8 million, but it didn't help. ("I probably was not aware of the history," he told a reporter.) The facility closed, likely for the last time, after the 2008 racing season. On Google Maps, it looks forsaken. The service roads are rutted. The grandstand is falling down. Tall grass grows in the infield.

31

SMACK

When did Keith Richards take his first hit of heroin?

Even he doesn't know.

He says it was probably an accident, that he mistook a line of smack for a line of blow at a party at the rag end of the decade. It was everywhere. Cheap, nearly impossible to avoid, an unintended consequence of the Vietnam War. When we opened a channel to Southeast Asia, soldiers flowed out and China white flowed in.

Heroin had been a passion of Keith's heroes—black blues players who'd chased the high until they lost everything. If you're of a certain temperament, you do things you know are bad for you because without the experience, you can't emulate the art. To make music with the depth of the masters, Keith had to experience what they experienced, had to touch the seafloor, where the pearl is buried in the muck. When he speaks about his junkie years—"I know the angle," he told *Zigzag* magazine in 1980, "waiting for the man, sitting in some goddamn basement waiting for some creep to come, with four other guys sniveling, puking and retching around"—it's not without a certain pride. Fame removed Keith from the kind of suffering that stands behind the Delta blues. He'd never know cotton shacks or rent parties. He sought that crucial authenticity in debauchery instead.

Heroin was in part Keith's response to Altamont. He reeled from riot to stupor. He loved how it made him feel—how it answered

every question, removed every obligation, annihilated every stare. ("I never liked being famous," he said. "I could face people a lot easier on the stuff.") Like prime rib with cabernet sauvignon or creeper weed with high school, junk went perfectly with that bleak, washed-out moment. Vietnam, the streets filled with psychotic vets, LSD cut with strychnine, Richard Nixon in the White House. The shift from the sixties to the seventies was the shift from LSD to heroin. LSD was aspirational. Heroin was nihilistic. The promise of hippie epiphany was gone; only the high remained. Keith came to personify that—the oldest young man in the world; stand him up and watch him play; shoot him up and watch him die.

The Stones were in the same condition as the culture, having come to realize, despite all their hit records and sold-out shows, that they were essentially broke. When they asked Allen Klein for more of what they assumed was their money, he sent it grudgingly, in dribs and drabs. Jagger finally reached out to his friend Christopher Gibbs, the art dealer, who put him in touch with the private London banker Prince Rupert Loewenstein. At first glance, Loewenstein, a prematurely middle-aged aristocrat who spoke with a slight German accent, seemed an unlikely partner for the Stones. "My tastes . . . leaned towards Bach, Mozart, Beethoven, Schubert and Brahms," Loewenstein writes in his memoir. "The name of the [Stones] meant virtually nothing to me at the time, but I asked my wife to tell me about them. She gave me a briefing and my curiosity was tickled.

"Mick slipped into the room, wearing a green tweed suit," Loewenstein goes on. "We sat and talked for an hour or so. It was a good, long chat. His manner was careful. The essence of what he told me was, 'I have no money. None of us have any money.' Given the success of the Stones, he could not understand why none of the money they were expecting was even trickling down to the band members."

It took Loewenstein eighteen months to untangle the contracts and deals. He explained the problem to the band in 1970: Klein advised you to incorporate in the United States for tax purposes; as this new company was given the same name as your British concern— Nanker Phelge (named after their old Edith Grove housemate)— you've assumed it's the same company; it's not. The American Nanker Phelge is owned by Allen Klein; you are his employees. Royalties, publishing fees—all of it belongs to Klein, who can pay you as he sees fit. This also gives Klein ownership of just about every one of your songs. "They were completely in the hands of a man who was like an old-fashioned Indian moneylender," Loewenstein writes, "who takes everything and only releases to others a tiny sliver of income, before tax."

Jagger was humiliated, ashamed. Here was the smartest rocker, the LSE student, being taken in a game of three-card monte. "There was one frightening incident in the Savoy Hotel when Mick started screaming at Klein who darted out of the room and ran down the corridor with Mick in hot pursuit," Loewenstein writes. "I had to stop him and say, 'You cannot risk laying a hand on Klein.'"

Loewenstein proposed a two-step course of action. One: the Stones immediately sever all ties with Klein. The second step had to do with Inland Revenue, as the British equivalent of the IRS was then called. As Klein had cashed checks from Decca, he never withheld or paid the band's taxes. The musicians had accrued a tremendous debt as a result. Not only were they broke, they were in danger of being sued. What's more, the Stones' earnings—on paper—put them in the top bracket, which in Britain at the time meant paying a marginal income tax rate of up to 98 percent. In other words, the government would take almost everything you made over a certain amount. This made it nearly impossible for the Stones to earn enough money to ever satisfy Inland Revenue. If they wanted to live safely in England, they'd have to move somewhere with a less punishing structure, then make enough money to square themselves. The term for this is "tax exile."

"My advice is contained in four words," Loewenstein told Jagger. 'Drop Klein and out.'"

The Stones broke with Klein in December 1970, then sued for $29.2 million. A settlement for $2 million was reached in 1972, though litigation carried on for years.

As for exile, Loewenstein suggested France. The prince, who had pull with Parisian officials, was able to arrange a deal: the Stones agreed to stay in the country for at least twelve months and spend at least £150,000 per year; in return, no additional taxes would be levied by the French government. Band members began leaving England in the spring of 1971.

Keith and Anita quit heroin before they went into exile. They did it to avoid certain hassles. Being addicted means having to carry drugs, hook up with local dealers—expose yourself in a million dangerous ways. Keith kicked first. Vomited and wept; wept and prayed. He was clear-eyed when he arrived at Gatwick Airport in April 1971, twenty-seven years old, the coolest person walking the planet other than Elvis and Brando, but Elvis and Brando were past their prime, slouching toward late afternoon, whereas Keith was at his apex. In photos taken that day, he has the look of a man used to being looked at. The sharp angles and rock star lines that would later characterize his face had not yet hardened. He carried his son, Marlon. Anita was in London, in the midst of withdrawal. She would join Keith and Marlon in France as soon as she was clean.

A house had been selected for the family in Villefranche-sur-Mer, a port on the Côte d'Azur. Fleetingly small, bathed in boredom and sunlight. Nothing is happening. Nothing has happened, or will ever happen. Exactly what Keith required. I visited the town shortly before my mother died—checked in to a hotel on the harbor, talked to strangers, walked. The ancient streets are steep and shaded by plane trees. There are alleys and storefronts and wine shops that reek of time. In the summer, the squares are picked clean by *le sirocco*, a wind that originates in the Sahara and covers the rooftops in fine red sand. What you feel in Villefranche is not the Stones but their absence. The world's most powerful rock 'n' roll energy had once concentrated here, but that was decades ago. The bars where the boys once drank as the sun went down are long gone. What remains is the silence that you hear as you sit alone in a hotel room after the last song has played.

I hailed a taxi in front of my hotel and asked the driver to take me to the house where Keith and Anita once lived. He had no idea what I was talking about, so I asked him to take me to the house where the Stones recorded *Exile on Main Street*. Still no idea. So I told him about the summer of '71, the mansion in the hills, the drugs and the songs. He said "Oui, oui" but still did not know, so I just gave him the address: no. 10, avenue Louise Bordes.

The road wound around the shore and began to climb. The trees made a canopy overhead, a tunnel of leaves. The driver hit the brakes and pointed. There was a steel gate and, hundreds of yards beyond it, a house. I got out and stood before the closed gate, hands on the bars, studying the lawn and fountain, the complicated roof and chimneys, the windows, the front steps, the door. I closed my eyes and could actually feel the warm air turning into a groove, the lyrics drifting across the sky in cartoon bubbles. Then, just as I was about to lose myself entirely, the driver honked. "My boo-boo, monsieur," he said. "I have you at the wrong address."

I burned with shame as we went a quarter mile up the road. I got out timidly, but this time certain that I was in the right place. There were the street number and the nameplate. Grand houses, like racehorses, have names. Mick's country estate was Stargroves. Elvis lived at Graceland. The house in Villefranche is Nellcôte, a mansion in the European style, with porticos, columns, and gardens. I stood with my face to the gate. It was no longer magic I felt, but yearning. I longed to go inside and poke around. As the driver shouted *"Non, non,"* I climbed the fence and dropped down hard on the other side. I stood there for a long time, listening for alarms and dogs. I'd read that Nellcôte had been purchased by a Russian oligarch. I pictured a goon named Boris, a cell in a provincial jail, the sheriff's wife serving me foie gras and Beaujolais.

I walked up the long drive, knocked on the door. Nothing. I looked around the gardens and gates, then lost courage. The driver cursed me when I got back, but in words I couldn't understand anyway. Besides, I was proud of my transgression. *That's rock 'n' roll, baby.* And I'd gotten a lovely unobstructed view of the house. So I didn't get inside. So what? I already had a good idea of the interior. The grand staircase, the living room, the balcony that overlooked Cap Ferrat. It had all been described to me in great detail by June Shelley, who, in those crucial months in the early seventies, served the Stones as a girl Friday. She'd been an actress and the wife of the folk legend Ramblin' Jack Elliott, but was beached on the coast when her (second) husband spotted the ad in the *International Herald Tribune.* "Wanted. For English organization in the South of France, bilingual, organized woman, salary plus expenses, 25–35 years of age."

Shelley was interviewed by Jo Bergman, the Stones' manager, then taken to the mansion. "I confessed on the way that I didn't know all their names," Shelley told me. "I knew Keith Richards and Mick Jagger. But I didn't know the others. So Jo ran them down. She said, 'Bill Wyman, bass player, Renaissance man; moody, doesn't speak much. Charlie Watts, drummer, blah-blah-blah.' She described them each in a few words. 'Mick Taylor, new kid; this will be his first album with the boys. He looks like an angel with blue eyes, round face, blond hair, and worships Keith.' When we pulled into the garden at Villa Nellcôte, I knew everyone immediately from her description. Bill, Charlie, and Mick Taylor were sitting on the steps. It was like the circus had come to town; there were people everywhere, dogs and kids, trucks, men moving things around. Jo says, 'Hi, guys, this is June, she's going to be your new assistant.' They nod, and we go inside.

"What a crazy wonderful house," Shelley went on. "You went into a long hallway and there were rooms right and left. An old-fashioned kitchen and an old-fashioned study, a partially finished basement that we later fixed up so they could record."

Nellcôte was built in the 1800s for a British admiral, who spent many melancholic years there studying the horizon through a telescope. The Germans took possession during the Second World War. According to Richards, it served as a Gestapo headquarters. The basement was the setting of unspeakable horrors, which gave the house an appropriate sheen of menace. Dominique Tarlé, a photographer who stayed in the house that summer, spoke of exploring the basement with a friend and finding "a box down there with a big swastika on it, full of injection phials. They all contained morphine. It was very old, of course, and our first reaction was, 'If Keith had found this box ...' So one night we carried it to the end of the garden and threw it into the sea."

Richards rented Nellcôte for $2,400 a week. He kept on the old staff, including an Austrian maid and a cook affectionately known as Fat Jacques, who was fired that summer for reasons too fraught and nefarious to get into. The first floor became a kind of salon, with musicians crashed in every corner. The second floor remained off-limits, the private preserve of Keith, Anita, and Marlon. Even Jagger didn't go up.

The other band members were scattered across France. Bill Wyman rented a house near the sea. Charlie Watts was in the countryside. Jagger had settled in Paris, where he took on the life of the jet-set party boy. Reeling from the breakup with Marianne Faithfull, he was seen in all the gossips, whispering in the corner of every party, confiding his pain to every beautiful woman. He'd had a torrid affair with Marsha Hunt, the devastatingly beautiful black singer and model who'd become famous in the London company of *Hair*. That's her, with towering Afro, on the playbill. The Stones had asked Hunt to pose for "Honky Tonk Women," but she refused, later telling *The Philadelphia Inquirer* that she "did not want to look like [she'd] just been had by all the Rolling Stones." Jagger followed with phone calls, which turned into illicit hotel meetings. In her autobiography, Hunt claims that she was the inspiration for "Brown Sugar." In November 1970, she gave birth to Jagger's first child, a daughter, Karis. As in a story from the Bible, this love child, at first rejected, would later become a great solace and balm for her father in his old age.

It was at a party in Paris in 1970 that Jagger met Bianca Pérez-Mora Macias, the daughter, depending on the conversation, of a plantation owner or a diplomat or a wealthy businessman from Nicaragua. She was young but refused to be fixed to an exact number. Here was a rich girl so dismissive of rock 'n' roll that Jagger could not help but be entranced. Friends claimed that they looked like doppelgangers, twins. That Mick's love for Bianca was a kind of self-love. Bianca got pregnant early in 1971, and just like that, Mick was sending out wedding invitations. The ceremony was in St. Tropez that spring, soon after the band arrived in France. It was the celebrity clusterfuck of the

season. Helicopters buzzed the beach as the paparazzi closed in. Mick
chartered a plane to fly his friends from London. "If that plane went
down, you would have lost twenty years of popular music," Anna
Menzies, who worked for the Stones and was on the plane, told me.
"Bobby Keys was on that flight, Jim Price, Paul McCartney with
Ringo. Keith Moon. Peter Frampton, Robert Fraser, Eric Clapton.
There was so much booze the plane could've flown without fuel!"

The theme from *Love Story* played as Mick and Bianca walked
down the aisle. A reception was held at Café des Arts. It was a rage.
Can till can't. As on the last day. Jagger had hired a reggae band called
the Rudies, but everyone got up and jammed. Jade Jagger was born a
few months later. Asked to explain the baby's name, Mick told a reporter, "Because she is very precious and quite, quite perfect." Mick
and Bianca divorced in 1979. I won't go into that relationship further,
because it just makes me sad. Suffice it to say, the marriage is credited
with inspiring the great Stones song "Beast of Burden."

. . .

Keith and Anita were soon back on heroin. It started with a male nurse who shot Keith up with morphine after a go-kart wreck in which Richards, racing his friend Tommy Weber at a nearby track, flipped his vehicle, chewing his back into hamburger. Appetite whetted, Keith began looking for still more relief—it's a story hauntingly told by Robert Greenfield in *Exile on Main Street: A Season in Hell with the Rolling Stones*. One afternoon, Jean de Breteuil, a notorious drug dealer known, because of his suspenders, as Johnny Braces, showed up at Nellcôte. He handed Keith a woman's compact filled with astonishingly pure heroin. Richards passed out as soon as he snorted it. When he came to, he said he wanted more—a lot more.

By June, life at the house had settled into a strange junkie rhythm. Most days began at two or three in the afternoon. Keith would wake up, yawn, stretch, hack up phlegm, swallow whiskey, reach for pills. He started with Mandrax, a downer that shoehorned him into consciousness. It was a hot summer, often above a hundred degrees. Anita was pregnant. Keith shot up before his afternoon breakfast and did not make his first appearance downstairs until five or six, a gray smack-filled ghost. He spent hours listening to music or playing. At nine, he would go to the basement to work. Like an Arab trader, he slept all morning and crossed the desert at night. He emerged at dawn. If the weather was good, everyone followed him down to the dock, where he kept a speedboat, the *Mandrax II*. He stood at the wheel as the coast unspooled, crossing the border into Italy, where he'd tie up at a pier and stumble up stone stairs to a bistro for eggs and kippered herring, or pancakes with strong black coffee.

Marlon was eighteen months old. Keith was far older, but a heroin addict is a baby. It's all about bodily functions and human needs. You cry when you're hungry. You sleep if you can. You live desperately from feeding to feeding. In this way, Keith and Marlon fell into lockstep, the addict and the kid playing on the beach.

. . .

Nellcôte in 1971 was like Paris in the twenties. The biggest stars and brightest lights of rock 'n' roll came to pay tribute, get loaded, and play. People felt compelled not merely to visit but to party, measuring themselves against Keith. Like dancing with the bear, or staying up with the adults, or drinking with the corner boys. Eric Clapton got lost in the house, only to be discovered hours later, passed out with a needle in his arm. John Lennon, visiting with Yoko Ono, vomited in the hall and had to be taken away.

Gram Parsons turned up with his girlfriend, Gretchen. He was out of sorts, experiencing a kind of interregnum between lives. His band had broken up; his music was in a state of transition. At Nellcôte, Richards and Parsons resumed the work they'd begun years before, playing their way deep into the roots of American music. It went on for days and days, Gram, twenty-four years old, long-limbed and fine-featured but not quite handsome, sitting beside Keith on the piano bench. Their relationship was intense, mysterious. They connected spiritually as well as musically, loved each other sober and loved each other high. "We'd come down off the stuff and sit at a piano for three days in agony, just trying to take our minds off it, arguing about whether the chord change on 'I Fall to Pieces' should be a minor or a major," Richards said later. If you have one friend like that in your entire life, you're lucky.

History has been kind to Gram Parsons—the importance of his legacy revealed only in the fullness of time. The tone he worked on at Nellcôte with Keith, the perfect B-minor twang that can be heard on *Exile on Main Street*, inspired some of the great pop artists of later eras. The Jayhawks, Wilco, Beck—I hear Gram whenever I turn on my stereo. The mood was contagious. Jagger caught it like a cold. "Mick and Gram never clicked, mainly because the Stones are such a tribal thing," Richards explained. "At the same time, Mick was listening to what Gram was doing. Mick's got ears. Sometimes, when we were making *Exile on Main Street*, the three of us would be plonk-ing away on Hank Williams songs while waiting for the rest of the band to arrive." The country tunes that distinguish the Stones—"Dead Flowers," "Sweet Virginia"—wouldn't exist as they do if not for Parsons, who, like any third man, is there even when he can't be seen.

The Stones, then in the process of signing a distribution deal with Ahmet Ertegun and Atlantic Records, needed to make a follow-up to *Sticky Fingers*. They'd gone into exile with several cuts in the can, left-overs from previous sessions—some recorded at Olympic, some re-corded at Stargroves, Mick's country house. France was scouted for studios, but in the end, unable to find a place that could accommo-date Keith's junkie needs, they decided to record at Nellcôte. Side-men, engineers, and producers began turning up in June 1971. Ian Stewart drove the Stones' mobile unit—a recording studio built in the back of a truck—over from England. Parked in the driveway, it was connected via snaking cables to the cellar, which had been insu-lated, amped, and otherwise made ready, though it was an awkward space. "[The cellar] had been a torture chamber during World War II," sound engineer Andy Johns told *Goldmine* magazine. "I didn't no-tice until we'd been there for a while that the floor heating vents in the hallway were shaped like swastikas. Gold swastikas. And I said to Keith, 'What the fuck is that?' 'Oh, I never told you? This was [Ge-stapo] headquarters.'"

The cellar was a honeycomb of enclosures. As the sessions pro-gressed, the musicians spread out in search of the best sound. In the end, each was like a monk in a cell, connected by technology. Richards and Wyman were in one room, but Watts was by himself and Taylor was under the stairs. Pianist Nicky Hopkins was at the end of one hall and the brass section was at the end of another. "It was a cata-comb," sax player Bobby Keys told me, "dark and creepy. Me and Jim Price—Jim played trumpet—set up far away from the other guys. We couldn't see anyone. It was fucked up, man."

Together and alone—the human condition.

The real work began in July. Historians mark it as July 6, but it was messier than that. There was no clean beginning to *Exile*, or end. It never stopped and never started, but simply emerged out of the everyday routine. It was punishingly hot in the cellar. The musicians played without shirts or shoes. Among the famous images of the sessions is Bobby Keys in a bathing suit, blasting away on his sax. The names of the songs—"Ventilator Blues," "Turd on the Run"—were inspired by the conditions, as was the album's working title: *Tropical Disease*. The Stones might hone a single song for several nights. Some of the best—"Let It Loose," "Soul Survivor"—emerged from a free-for-all, a seemingly pointless jam, out of which, after hours of nothing much, a melody would appear, shining and new. On outtakes, you can hear Jagger quieting everyone at the key moment: "All right, all right, here we go." As in life, the music came faster than the words. Now and then, Jagger stood before a microphone, grunting as the groove took shape—vowel sounds that slowly formed into phrases. On one occasion, they employed a modernist technique, the cutout method used by William S. Burroughs. Richards clipped bits of text from newspapers and dropped them into a hat. Selecting at random, Jagger and Richards assembled the lyric of "Casino Boogie":

Dietrich movies
close up boogies

The record came into focus the same way: slowly, over weeks, along a path determined by metaphysical forces, chaos, noise, and beauty netted via a never-to-be-repeated process. They called it *Exile on Main Street*—Main Street being a pet name for the French Riviera as well as an invocation of that small-town American nowhere that gave the world all this music.

. . .

Gram Parsons was coming undone. He'd been using heroin, but living at Nellcôte kicked it into another gear. He lost weight, went green,
passed out. His proximity to the Stones unmoored him. In this
way, a talented musician turned first into a nuisance, then into a bummer, finally into a problem. Jagger was tired of having this junkie always underfoot. But Richards says it was less about annoyance than
jealousy: Mick is threatened by anyone who challenges his place in
Keith's life.

Mick and Keith . . . Despite all the fights, the relationship is romantic. Mick regards Keith in the way of a lover. You see it in the lip
curl, the possessive flash. He's the angry wife chasing away the pretty
young thing. Keith calls it a marriage. Which is not to say it's ever
been consummated—there's no evidence of that, despite the sexual
tension that exists in so many bands between the lead singer, who
preens like a diva, and the guitar hero, who hangs back like the man
of the house, seeing to fundamentals. Mick and Keith. Plant and
Page. Tyler and Perry. Axl and Slash.

By the middle of the summer, a decision had been made: *Gram's
gotta go.* This needed to be handled carefully, as Gram was not just
another hanger-on. He was an artist with a delicate soul, easily
wounded, in love with Keith. Being booted from Nellcôte was being
exiled from exile. *How was it done?* According to Robert Greenfield,
in *A Season in Hell with the Rolling Stones,* Keith called Linda Lawrence, a friend and former girlfriend of Gram's who, at that time, was
married to the singer Donovan. Also having been a girlfriend of Brian
Jones, Lawrence had experience in dealing with drug casualties.
"Could you please take Gram?" Keith asked Linda. "He's out of his
head and he needs to be with somebody."

Parsons and his wife were put on a plane to Ireland, where they
spent weeks on Donovan's estate. Keith hardly ever saw him again. In
the way of a Viking funeral, Gram was simply loaded onto a raft with
his possessions and pushed out to sea.

Richards was battling his own addictions and demons, and yet . . .

He must have known how important the friendship was to Gram. Musically, personally, and spiritually. Keith has spent decades rhapsodizing Gram and their special connection, but when Gram was there in all his messy aliveness, Keith gave it a miss.

Gram lay around for weeks, staring at the ceiling. He was like an unplugged machine. Some say he tried to kill himself. "On the toilet one afternoon," writes Greenfield. It was not uncommon. For courtiers, the Stones are the center of the solar system, the star around which everything turns. When they kicked you out, you dropped into darkness. "Gram was beautiful," Bobby Keys told me, "but in the end, like a lot of us—and I'm talking about myself, too, because God knows I had my own trouble—he could not survive the intensity."

Nellcôte was a banana that went from ripe to rotten in a moment. Drug dealers lingered in the parlor, menacing figures involved in the French Connection. In October, the house was robbed. Many of Keith's guitars were stolen, along with much else. June Shelley told me it was an inside job, probably a drug dealer recovering money he'd not been paid. It pushed Anita, who was pregnant, into a paranoiac fit. Multiple locks on the doors, a pistol in the nightstand. Convinced there was a plot to kidnap Marlon, she had the beach strung with barbed wire. People who'd spent time at the house—French nationals, mostly—were being arrested and questioned. There were rumors of a coming bust. Friends told the Stones, *Ditch before it's too late.*

At the end of November 1971, after eight months in France, the Stones fled the country like high school kids fleeing a party when someone yells "Cops!" Keith, Anita, Marlon, and Charlie took a midnight flight from Nice. Two weeks later, French police broke down the doors of Nellcôte. Heroin and cocaine were found. Charged with narcotics possession, Keith and Anita were tried in absentia and found guilty. Each was given a one-year suspended sentence and fined five thousand francs. Keith was banned from France for two years.

The cops also found Keith's records, Anita's clothes, the speedboat, a Jaguar XKE, a parrot named Boots, and two dogs. "They were in perfect health," June Shelley assured me. "I went by to feed and play with them every day."

The Stones reconvened at Sunset Sound in Los Angeles to finish the record. Richards had been in charge at Nellcôte, but Jagger took over in L.A., dubbing, mixing, recording, and rerecording. *Exile* would be the band's first double album. The label frowned on it—double records usually don't sell—but there were too many good songs for a single LP. In the end, the tunes were as meticulously arranged as scenes in a play. The first side of each disc is rock 'n' roll. The flip sides are Cosmic American Music. The first sides are a party. The flip sides are a hangover. The first sides are cocaine. The flip sides are smack. Side A includes "Rocks Off," "Rip This Joint," and "Shake Your Hips." Side C includes "Happy," "Ventilator Blues," and "Let It Loose." Side B includes "Sweet Virginia," "Sweet Black Angel," and "Loving Cup." Side D includes "All Down the Line," "Shine a Light," and "Soul Survivor."

The Stones had a tough time picking a single. Jagger wanted "All Down the Line," but engineer Andy Johns disagreed. Jagger argued his case. Johns said something like *I'd have to hear it on the radio to know for sure. That's the shame. You don't know till it's on the air, and by then it's too late.* Jagger and Johns were having this conversation in a limo, driving up and down the Sunset Strip. Jagger said something to Ian Stewart, also in the car, who made a phone call—the uber class were in possession of car phones as early as 1950. A few minutes later, "All Down the Line" came on the radio. Johns laughed. Jagger turned to him: *Well?* Johns thought a moment, then said, *I'd like to hear it on the radio again.*

Exile on Main Street was released in May 1972. Though it went straight to the top of the charts, critics did not like the record—not at first. They called it baggy, overlong, disorganized, a mess. Hemingway said: When they attack, they attack precisely what is strong, unique.

What critics really want is a slightly different version of what they already love. If you give them something new, they will hate you. At first. But great work invents its own genre. *Exile* grew and grew in estimation. By the end of the 1970s, it was recognized as the last great album of the golden run. To many, it's the best of them all—the quintessential Stones record.

Because the band had been liberated by the breakup of the Beatles. Because Mick and Keith had been freed by the death of Brian Jones and the exit of Andrew Oldham. Because the world had given up on the hippie dream, leaving the music with no other purpose than itself. Because everything is in it—the sixties and the death of the sixties, Chicago, Chess Records, Muddy Waters and Howlin' Wolf, Altamont and the Angels, Sonny Barger and Sweet Cocaine, Meredith Hunter, Jimi Hendrix and Janis Joplin, the death funk of the seventies, Vietnam and junk, the summer days in France, Gram Parsons and the sad country wail, late nights and early mornings, opium sickness and guitars … *Exile* wants to be listened to in a single sitting. It wants to turn your day into a reverie. It wants to take you back to the basement of Nellcôte. Say what you want about the records that followed, but what more does a band owe us? If the later years have been a kind of pantomime, at least the Stones have *Exile* to mimic.

And so I've come to the place in this book I call "The Deep-Sixing of Gram Parsons," a sad story that stands for all the other sad stories surrounding the band. He wandered away from Nellcôte in a daze, strung out, shattered. He was a twenty-four-year-old longhair in a Nudie suit. He went back to L.A., picked up a guitar, pieced himself together. He told everyone he was finally clean. He married Gretchen and signed a new record contract. He'd finish two solo albums: *GP* (1973) and *Grievous Angel* (1974). There's a special sound on these records, a heartbreaking purity. It's the 1970s distilled, whiskey and neon in the daylight. He'd put together a band, the Fallen Angels, with Byron Berline on country fiddle. Phil Kaufman served as "executive nanny." Kaufman did not know Gram at the beginning, but he was all tangled up with him at the end. In 1973, at the funeral of Clarence White—killed by a drunk driver—Parsons and Kaufman, depressed by the religious ritual and lack of joy, made each other a promise: whoever dies first, the other will take his body and burn it at Joshua Tree, a desert about a hundred fifty miles east of L.A.

Joshua Tree has always been a favored spot for satori and mystical adventure, a moonscape of sage and scrub, fantastic rock formations and ancient yuccas, whose spindly arms turn into grasping fingers at night. Parsons learned about it from an actor named Ted Markland, who'd gone there for a UFO convention. "Gram and Mick and Keith and Anita and Marianne used to go up the mountain out there to watch the sunrise and take mushrooms," Kaufman told me. "To that crowd, it was a holy place."

On September 17, 1973, Gram booked two rooms at the Joshua Tree Inn, a funky motel. He started drinking in the afternoon, then went to town. After dinner, he got onstage with a local band. "Unchained Melody" is the last song Elvis Presley ever sang. At the piano beside his racquetball court in Graceland. Gram Parsons's last song was Merle Haggard's "Okie from Muskogee," but he changed the chorus from the negative to the affirmative: "We *will* smoke marijuana in Muskogee." He'd consumed a fifth of whiskey by the time he got back to the motel. Plus pills. It put him in the mood for heroin. Just a taste. To take the edge off. Addiction is like malaria. It goes into remission but never goes away. He was with two girls and a boy. According to David N. Meyer, writing in *Twenty Thousand Roads: The Ballad of Gram Parsons and His Cosmic American Music*, another hotel guest called a dealer. A few minutes later, she checked in to room 1 with a briefcase full of morphine. Gram preferred lady dealers. He had a rich kid's terror of getting beaten up by a prole. She'd brought along her baby. *Where is that kid today?* Fixing a syringe, she told Gram to roll up his sleeve. He put his head back when she stuck him, smiling. Liquid delirium. Chemical relief. He wanted more. The classic junkie mistake. At the peak of addiction, Gram had developed a powerful tolerance. It took a massive dose to get him high. He was now asking for his old fix, though his tolerance was gone. He would meet the drug as a neophyte, unarmed and vulnerable. As soon as that second hit entered his blood, he was in trouble. The dealer recognized it at once and was gone with her suitcase and baby before the others knew what was happening.

He looked like a corpse, but one of the girls knew a trick. She sent the others for ice, which she shoved up Gram's ass. His eyes opened, confused, cold in a place he did not know existed. *Who am I? Why am I here?* The friends then made an incomprehensible mistake—they let Gram go back to his room to lie down. Room 8. The bed, the bathroom with the sanitary strip across the toilet. By the time they checked on him, he was dead. Phil Kaufman got the call at midnight. He drove from L.A. to clean out the room and ditch the drugs in the desert. Parsons's body had been taken to the hospital, where a medical examiner determined the cause of death to be "drug toxicity, days, due to multiple drug use, weeks." "Gram thought he could do what Keith Richards did," Kaufman said. "He thought he had Keith's metabolism. He was wrong."

Richards got the news as the Stones were touring in Europe. "It was me that gave him the bad word," Bobby Keys remembered. "It was after a gig in some town and we were drinking and having a real time, when I found out from someone. It was not unexpected but it was still completely devastating. I mean, fucking hell! I tried to break it to Keith carefully, 'cause he needed to know but I knew it would crush him. Keith and Gram had a special thing, man. I said, 'Keith, I got some bad news. GP is dead.' Keith couldn't believe it. Last we heard, Gram was clean, doing good. But you know how it is with junkies. They can fall through the floor any minute of any day. Keith and I sat in there drinking all night—drowning it like a couple of drovers in a cowboy movie when they get word that the Ringo Kid was killed in a shoot-out."

Why does the death of Gram Parsons strike such a poignant note? After all, many others had already died. Janis and Jimi, and especially Brian. I think it had to do with the sweetness of Gram—the way he seemed to want only to make music and be loved. When a person like that dies young, it's bad luck for everyone.

Some blame Keith. They say Keith corrupted Gram, led him into deep water where he could not swim. They say it was Keith's example that killed Gram. The rock star way of life was simply too attractive, too cool. "I'm aware of those rumblings—'Oh, Gram would still be around if it wasn't for Keith Richards'—I've heard it put as boldly as that," Keith has said. "And there is a possibility, to be totally honest, that yes, maybe hanging around the Rolling Stones didn't *help* him in his attitude toward drugs. But I would honestly say that his attitude toward those things reminded me of what was going on everywhere."

By the time Phil Kaufman went for Gram's body, it was at LAX, where it was to be shipped to New Orleans for the funeral. Kaufman drove a borrowed hearse into the hangar. Posing as an undertaker, he filled out a form—he signed it "Jeremy Nobody"—and left with the coffin. He was accompanied by a roadie named Michael Martin, who'd been at the Joshua Tree Inn with Gram. They drove through the night drinking and weeping and reached Joshua Tree before dawn, in the spooky wee hours of cactus shadows and coyotes. They pulled the coffin from the car, opened it just to make sure—"There was Gram lying naked," Kaufman writes in his memoir; "all he had was surgical tape on his chest where they had done the autopsy"— dragged it into the park, and set it beside the geologic formation known as Cap Rock, which has become a kind of shrine. People stand before it and pray to country music, or think about Gram Parsons, or study the guitar picks and the cowboy hats and messages fans have left behind. It's the Western Wall of Cosmic American Music, wa-

tered with many bitter tears. But at the time, there was nothing special about the spot. "Everybody thinks Cap Rock is a sacred meeting
place of spirits or what have you," Kaufman explained. "That's not
true. We were just two piss-heads who had gone as far as we could
take the body."

Kaufman soaked the coffin with fuel, threw a match, and retreated.
"When high-octane gasoline ignites, it grabs a lot of oxygen from the
air," he writes. "It went whoosh and a big ball of flame went up. We
watched the body burn. It was bubbling. You could see it was Gram
and the body burned very quickly, you could see it melting. We looked
up and the flames were actually going up into the air, into the desert
night. The moon was shining, the stars were shining and Gram's wish
was coming true. His ashes were going into the desert."

Kaufman was arrested and charged with grand theft—for stealing
the coffin. He pleaded to a misdemeanor and was fined three hundred dollars. By then, the story had made the papers: ROCK STAR'S
BODY CREMATED IN RITUALISTIC BURNING IN DESERT. The death of
Gram Parsons has become a legend complete with good guys and bad
guys, music and mischief, the last supper, the last bed, the last room.
The Joshua Tree Inn advertises it. You can stay in the Parsons suite
for $109 a night. The room is haunted by rock 'n' roll.

32

"WHERE'S MICK?"

In the mid-1970s, Keith Richards was included in a newspaper list of celebrities most likely to die in the coming year. When told about it by a reporter, he seemed shaken. Taking chances was one thing, but strangers calculating and printing the odds like a betting line in the *Daily Racing Form* is another. Keith hemmed and hawed but then, being Keith, found his footing, turned defiant, and wore it like a cape: *String me up and I still won't die*. Appearing on the death watch entered the repertoire, became part of the madman routine. No one knows just how close he came in the seventies, but he did seem, at times, to touch the hem of His garment. A prolonged near-death experience: amazing how endless it seemed and yet how short it really was. In 1964, Keith was fresh and sharp, with the twinkle of a kid who knows how well he can play. Five years later, he was blurred and diminished, rank with chemical experience. He'd been remade by the abyss. Even in pictures taken decades later, he looks as if he just stepped from a burning building. Even sober, he looks drunk. If you are a Keith Richards fan, every day is a good day because you're continually surprised to discover that he's still alive.

Keith decided to get clean after the band finished *Exile* for the usual reasons: there would be a tour, which meant borders and small towns filled with cops. Who wants to get busted or go cold turkey in some Podunk nowhere? Marshall Chess, who was then working for the Stones, arranged for Keith and Anita to take a cure in Nyon, Switzerland, outside Geneva. It was on this trip that Keith supposedly had all the smack-rich blood in his body exchanged for blood that was clean—a playground legend that turns Keith into a rock 'n' roll vampire, suckling on innocents. We need his licks; he needs our blood. Keith says it never happened, dismisses the whole thing as a rumor that grew from a toss-off remark he made to some reporters at an airport. ("I just wanted them off my back," he told a CBS reporter in 2010.) If we choose to believe the legend, it's because we need Keith to be immortal, a deathless guitar gun switching blood as you switch oil after a thousand hard miles.

I visited the clinic where Keith and Anita took the cure, the hospital where Anita gave birth to her second child, the towns and hotels where they convalesced for many months. Cobblestone streets and medieval buildings, steeples framed by mountains, the lake at the end of every sad street. I stayed at the Trois Couronnes, the storied behemoth of a hotel in Vevey where Keith and Anita ended up. It's one thing to read about a place, another to walk the alleys, talk to the people, breathe the air. By going there, you get the mood, which can then be recognized on the records. I was especially interested in Switzerland because Switzerland is the flip side of Nellcôte—it's where the bill was paid, the pain endured. On Side A, the rocker. On Side B, the ballad.

"One day, in March of seventy-two, I get a call from Marshall Chess that was unusual," June Shelley told me. "He said, 'June, I need you to get to Geneva as quickly as possible, fly if you can. I'm sending Keith and Anita to you with Marlon and the nanny. They're going to have a drug cure in Switzerland. I need you to meet them and organize the whole thing. We've arranged for a high-powered lawyer in Switzerland, a fancy guy who does big jobs. He's going to help. We've made reservations for you at a hotel outside Geneva, a little town. We have

Keith registered as Mr.'—you know, the reverse, instead of Keith Richard, Richard Keith. I go to the airport in Geneva and meet this fancy lawyer who takes care of this one and that one, and ... they missed the plane! We get paged. It's Marshall Chess: 'Keith didn't feel well enough today. We'll try again tomorrow.'"

A few days later, June had everyone settled in Nyon, but when Anita was told that Marlon could not stay with her at the clinic, she refused to go. Meanwhile, Keith, not having had his regular fix, began withdrawal. First a little sick, then very sick. Pale, sweat-covered. By the time June found a new physician and a new clinic—Dr. Denber, Vevey—Keith couldn't stand. June called an ambulance. The medics wanted to take him on a stretcher but Keith didn't want to scare Marlon. They carried him out on a chair instead, sitting up and helpless, like the last emperor of China.

June rode with him in the back of the ambulance, blue and red lights flashing through the dark mountains. He was white as a ghost, cold as a blizzard, eyes closed—this is the moment he probably came closest to fulfilling the predictions. "It was a drive from hell," June told me. "Keith was almost unconscious. He looked dead. We were hurtling through narrow roads, because the freeway didn't go all the way to Vevey. I was holding his hand, talking to him and thinking, 'Oh my God, I'm going to lose a Rolling Stone! Everybody in the world is going to blame me! I'll never be forgiven!' I know it's a stupid egoistical thing to think about, but that *is* what I was thinking about.

"The ambulance pulled up to the hospital and I ran inside," June continued. "This big Nurse Ratchet comes over to me. I'm yelling, 'Dr. Denber, Dr. Denber!' She said, 'He left.' She then asks, very coolly, 'Name of patient, address of patient,' blah-blah-blah.

"'Now where is the patient?' she asks.

"I am shocked: 'Don't you have the patient?'

"I assumed that when we pulled up, someone ran out and got the patient. But Keith was still out there in the ambulance, dying as the driver stood around smoking. In a moment, Nurse Ratchet turns into

Florence Nightingale. She runs around saying, 'My God, my God, my God.'"

Keith spent two weeks in the clinic in Vevey. After three days, he was strong enough to sit up. After five days, he could walk. He met a kid in the hospital, maybe fifteen, suffering from some terrible disease. The first thing the kid asked when he recognized Keith says everything: "Where's Mick?"

After seven days or so, Keith could play guitar. The kid played, too, so there they stayed, side by side, hour after hour, the sick kid and the rock star, strumming.

Sitting in bed one afternoon, Keith wrote "Angie" on acoustic guitar. A melancholy ballad, it might be about Anita, or Mick, or Marlon, or simply the mood: afterward, postscript, survival; death fugue and junk sickness; a moment captured in one of the saddest melodies of the decade.

A few days later, Keith moved into the Trois Couronnes with Marlon while Anita went in for the cure. She was in the third term of her second pregnancy. "But when Anita got to the clinic, they gave her something that brought on contractions," June told me. "She wasn't due for a couple more weeks, so it was a crisis. Dr. Denber couldn't deliver the baby at the clinic so he called the regular hospital and got hold of the top guy and said, 'You're going to have to deliver a baby and the baby may be heroin addicted.' You can imagine the reaction! The birth went okay. The baby was not addicted, which was a miracle. I visited Anita in the hospital. She went around to everybody asking, in a little plaintive voice, 'Is Switzerland a good place to raise children?'"

Anita named the baby Dandelion, but, for obvious reasons, Keith's mother, who ended up raising the child, used her middle name instead. As of this writing, Angela Richards is in her midforties and lives in Chichester, England, where she works with horses.

33

THE LAST GREAT RECORD

A few years after I went on the road with the Rolling Stones in 1994, I was put up for a screenwriting job. This led to several interviews with Martin Scorsese and Mick Jagger, who had long talked about collaborating on a movie about rock 'n' roll. Amazingly, I was hired. Or, as Ahmet Ertegun told me at the time, "You've scored a ridiculous gig!" It was as unlikely as Dandelion Richards being born clean. The assignment was powerfully vague: "a script about the music business." It was left to me to dream up characters, story lines, narrative arcs. I'd never written a screenplay, or serious fiction. I was a journalist, dedicated to facts. I later learned that my lack of experience was seen as a plus. Scorsese would not have to rid me of the bad habits of the Hollywood hack. He could instead start from scratch, teaching me not how to write a movie but how to write a Martin Scorsese movie. I was working on my first book at the time, *Tough Jews*, which also helped. Scorsese was taken with the subject matter and the sensibility: the Brooklyn gangsters of the 1930s, narrated in the manner of *Goodfellas*. The fact that I'd already worked with Jagger and the Stones, traveled with and interviewed them, was another plus. In any collaboration, Mick has to worry about his effect on people. His presence can throw even the most jaded pro into a tailspin.

The screenplay would tell the story of a Jerry Wexler–like music producer who'd gotten into the business at the dawn of rock 'n' roll and persisted through it all. I named my protagonist Herbie after my own father, then put him through adventures based on actual events. Jagger, Scorsese, and I were listed as co-writers, and we worked on it for years. We'd meet at Scorsese's townhouse on the Upper East Side of Manhattan, have a three-course dinner in the grand dining room, then get down to it. I talked over plots and characters as Jagger and Scorsese tossed out ideas of their own, spitballing the thing into shape. Mick and Marty told stories from their own lives. The director talked about Hollywood in the 1970s, living with Robbie Robertson and filming *The Last Waltz*. The rock star talked about being a pop idol in the 1960s, the girls on the road, the rivalry and friendship with the Beatles, the first trip to America, the scene as it was and the scene as it became, hangers-on, studio bosses, drugs—all of it. We might work for five or six hours without a break, but I never got bored or tired and never had enough.

Jagger made a list of people I should talk to, then helped arrange the meetings. I interviewed dozens of musicians, producers, and studio executives, each of whom had another story, another piece of the puzzle. Ahmet Ertegun, Jerry Wexler, Bob Krasnow, Peter Asher, Mario Medious . . . it was like learning about the movie business from Orson Welles or Irving Thalberg.

I spoke with Joe Smith, who'd run Warner Bros. Records, by the pool at the Mondrian in L.A. He told me about buying Van Morrison's contract from the mob. "I flew to New York with a briefcase full of cash," he said. "We made the exchange in a warehouse near the river. 'You got the dough?' 'Yeah, you got the contract?'" I spoke to Ahmet Ertegun at Atlantic Records. He told me about his search for investors in the 1950s. "Lionel Hampton wanted to become my partner and put up the money," he explained. "We were going to call it Hamptone Records, but his finances were ruled by his wife, Gladys, and when we went to see her, she said, 'Are you kidding? You're going to give our money to this little jerk?' Last year, Lionel came to see me in my office, looked around, and said, 'Oh my God, all this could've been mine. Damn you, Gladys!'" I spoke to Bob Krasnow, who ran Elektra Records, in his apartment in Manhattan. He made me take off my shoes and put on slippers, then talked about who invented what. "All this music came from black people," he said. "The Stones didn't invent it. It came from Chuck Berry, Bo Diddley, Muddy Waters, Howlin' Wolf. Leonard Chess and his brother only recorded black music. Syd Nathan [mostly] recorded black music. Ahmet Ertegun only recorded black music. So what was the outcome, what was the morality? Was a Cadillac given instead of what should've been given? These are questions you've got to ask. The answers will be funny and sad. Why did Mick Jagger want to make his first record in Chicago at the Chess Recording Studio? What's the story behind that?"

Jerry Wexler, who ran Atlantic with Ertegun, called me from his nursing home. We argued about the word "macher," a Yiddish term that means something like "bigshot." I'd used it to describe the first generation of rock executives in my book *Machers and Rockers*. He agreed that Leonard Chess had been a macher, but refused to accept the label himself. "Do you know what a macher is?" he asked me. "A macher is a man who goes up to the *bima* and reads from the holy book on the holy day and has no right! This man has no right to read from that book!"

Scorsese and I went over my pages again and again. He'd often refer me to specific scenes in favorite films. Now and then, he showed me movies in his screening room—movies he thought would be helpful, or were just fun to see. *The Big Knife. Death in Venice. Executive Suite.* Sometimes, it was the two of us in the screening room—he'd throw his head back as he laughed *Ha! Ha! Ha!*—and sometimes it was just me and the projectionist.

I took my pages to Jagger on the road. On one occasion, when the band was touring behind their 1997 record *Bridges to Babylon*, we worked in Mick's suite at the Four Seasons in Seattle as humidifiers churned our surroundings into a painting by Monet. "Sorry about the mist," he said, "but I have to sing tonight." He joked about the shows and the travel, life on a road trip that never ends. It was a different Mick than I'd met while reporting for *Rolling Stone* magazine. In those days, he was charming but careful, holding back. As we'd now become partners, I felt I was getting closer to the person behind the façade. He was chatty, story-filled, intimate, amusing. He went into greater depth about the early days, the first shows, the riots, the A&R men, Los Angeles back in the day, the hustlers and deejays, the American South, Villefranche, and the end of the hippie dream. His suggestions for the screenplay were mostly about mood. "You have to remember that a lot of these things were funny," he told me. "It only seemed serious and important later, in books and such, but at the time, we were having fun and laughing all the time and a lot of it was silly."

One night, when the Stones were not performing, we went out to dinner, then to see Taj Mahal in a little club. We came in late, after the lights were down, dashing in through a side door so no one would recognize Jagger. Of course, there was no way to miss him once the music began. He sang along and danced in his seat, plugged in to the groove. He said he loved Taj Mahal because Taj Mahal approaches the blues like a white kid—less by feeling than by intellect, thus just as inauthentically as the Stones. We ordered martinis. When the show ended, the crowd was left sitting in the dark as we were rushed back out through the side door.

Now and then, Jagger took me to a restaurant or a club. On occasion, he'd stay late into the night, soaking up whatever licks or melodies were popular on the dance floor. Or he'd drop me back at the hotel and go out with his bodyguard, which is as alone as he gets. The next day, I'd hear stories about Mick at the disco, how he'd danced all night or brought all the kids back to his room. But he was always sharp and clear when we got back to work in the morning. When making a point, he'd bang his knee. When making a big point, he'd bang *my* knee.

On some nights, I'd travel with the entourage to the arena, arriving hours before the show. I loved standing in the wings, watching the seats fill. I was fascinated by the crowds. When I went to see the Stones in the 1980s, everyone was footloose and young. Now everyone was old, clean, prosperous. The transaction was obvious: they paid for a ticket and got nostalgia in return. Everything had been tamed, corralled, controlled. No more general seating, with its crush in front of the stage; no more barely surviving the mosh pit. Affluence had replaced urgency. This was rock 'n' roll behind a velvet rope.

It was even more orderly backstage, where once upon a time drug dealers and groupies had roamed among the stars as freely as animals crossing the savanna. After Altamont, all that was shut down and order was imposed. It was about business as much as safety. Five-hundred-dollar tickets, the best seats filled by bankers, the tour itself sponsored by Pepsi or Coca-Cola—in the age of corporate rock, every encounter is tagged with a price gun. "We very soon formalized this policy of the 'meet and greet,'" Prince Loewenstein writes in his memoir, *A Prince Among Stones*. "At a specific time, just before they went onstage, the Stones would be on hand to meet—and greet— some of the people who were important for their career. It was quite often the only time that these businessmen would ever have the opportunity to come into direct, personal contact with the band. They could go back and tell their colleagues and their wives and girlfriends that they had met Mick Jagger."

I spent nights drinking with the entourage at the hotel bar. If one of the Stones turned up, it was usually Ron Wood, who'd replaced Mick Taylor on guitar in the midseventies. Taylor had quit because he knew life as a Stone would kill him. At one point, during the ensuing auditions, Eric Clapton, who was also in the running, dismissed Wood, saying, "I'm a much better guitar player than you."

"I know that," Wood agreed, "but you gotta live with these guys as well as play with them."

Which was the point—after the difficulty with Brian Jones and Mick Taylor, the Stones wanted someone who would last. Wood was perfect. Not only was he an excellent guitarist, hard and rhythmic like Richards, but he was a knock-around, up-for-anything sort of guy, who, with his beak nose and black-eyed grin, looks more like a Stone than anyone but Keith. Wood would stay at the bar till they shut down, talking about everything. He was affectionate and warm in a way rare on those later tours, which felt less like rock 'n' roll than like money—a Stones show has become a Broadway revival, the millionth iteration of *Annie*, where it's all about hitting the marks and selling the T-shirts.

That coolness comes from the top: Jagger and Richards. Their feud chills everything. The Stones broke up in the 1980s and reunited in 1988, but it's never been the same. It was not love that brought them back together, but calculation. Mick and Keith had realized they could never earn as much alone as they could together. They're like a bitter married couple who stay together for the kids. Only the kids are grown. Or maybe the money is the kids. Either way, men who once loved each other now do nothing but snipe at each other. It culminated in 2010 with the publication of Keith's memoir, *Life*. Keith ranted against his front man for selling out, acting like a baby, being a prima donna. He mocked Mick's solo work, questioned his character, even belittled his *Schwanzstucker*, "the tiny todger."

I spoke to Jagger about Keith's book soon after it was published. He seemed hurt, angry. He told me about driving to Connecticut to read the galleys at Keith's house. He told me about asking Keith to remove passages. When I asked about specific gripes, Mick urged me to consider the big picture. Here I paraphrase: *Imagine that everything Keith says is true. Now imagine those things being said by a business partner, a man you've joined in a multi-million-dollar enterprise. Now imagine that partner is drug addicted. Sometimes, you have a big meeting and he doesn't show. Sometimes, as you're about to make a big deal, he gets busted. Or maybe he gets busted on the eve of a world tour. What, in such a case, would you make of his complaints?*

Jagger laughed about some of the most salacious material—a cold, cynical laugh—then said he doubted Keith even read the book. It's so saturated with Keith's voice that it's hard to believe he was not closely involved, but I understand why Mick would choose to believe Keith had checked out. After reading it, your first thought is, *That's the end of the Stones, there's no way they can work together again.* But of course they have. On tour after tour. In the end, there is sentiment, then there is money. In other words, when you see Mick and Keith onstage, leaning together like Butch and Sundance, you're seeing actors. It's heartbreaking. Many of us fell in love with the band because they were a gang. At the center of that gang were the blood brothers, Mick and Keith. Their friendship was rock 'n' roll. The songs being written together amplified that point, for what is more intimate than co-writing? What happens when that friendship dies? What does it do to the music?

Like a lot of shitty things, it happened in the seventies. For years, Keith had been lost in a haze. Mick naturally took control. Without him, the Stones would have fallen apart. When Keith emerged from his stupor, he sought to reassert himself. Mick resisted. They clashed at rehearsals and at meetings—about stage sets, songs, disco, punk. In the end, it was really about dominance. The recording sessions became intolerable. "When we got to making [the record] *Undercover,* that was the worst time I'd ever experienced with them," Chris Kimsey, who produced the album between 1982 and 1983, told me. "We recorded a lot of it in Nassau [Bahamas], then mixed it in New York, at the Hit Factory. I would get Mick in the studio from like midday until seven o'clock, then Keith from like nine o'clock till five in the morning. They would not be together. They specifically avoided each other. Mick would say, 'When's he coming in? I'll be there later.' After about a week, it was killing me. And it was such silly things, like one would say, 'What did he do?' And I'd play a bit, and the other would say, 'Get rid of it.'"

Jagger was looking for a way out of the Stones. Can you imagine being trapped on a stage night after night with your high school friends? He wanted to be famous while being alone in the way of Michael Jackson or David Bowie. The breaking point came in the mid-1980s, when the Stones signed a new record contract. Only when the deal was done did the others learn that Jagger had promised not only several Stones albums, but two solo albums as well—there have been four Jagger solo records, including *Primitive Cool* and *Goddess in the Doorway*, which Richards called "Dogshit in the Doorway." Though Jagger promised to put the band first, he skipped a Stones tour to promote his solo album instead, backed by a supergroup. In doing this, the other band members believed Jagger had broken an unwritten rule: The Stones always come first.

At that point, the band basically broke up. Keith, who refused to talk to Mick, went out and made *his* own record. It was revelatory, for, whereas Mick's solo record sounded tepid, untethered, and weak, Keith's record sounded like the Stones. It made you reevaluate everything and wonder just who'd been responsible for what. In other words, Jagger's dash for freedom backfired. Instead of increasing his earning power and fame, it diminished both. Mick's solo records tanked. In *Mick: The Wild Life and Mad Genius of Jagger*, Christopher Andersen reports that *Goddess in the Doorway* sold just 954 copies on the day of its release. "Mick's two solo albums—he also released *Primitive Cool* in 1987—did not set the world on fire in the way he would have hoped," Prince Loewenstein writes. "I was [now] able to reinforce the important message, which I now had the figures to back up: 'The way you make money is as a band. You have to do group work. That is what the world wants from you.'"

The Stones reconciled at the Savoy Hotel in London in 1988, but the truth is evident to every serious fan: Jagger is still fronting the band because he came up short as a solo act.

When I asked Sam Cutler why the Stones keep going, he said, "They've outlived everyone. That's something, I guess. But, I mean, you have to look at their music and wonder about it, don't you? It's been a long time since they've produced anything that sets the world alight. They're going through the motions, making millions. But it depends what you want. You can just be a great rock 'n' roll band, and there's no question about the fact that they're a great rock 'n' roll band. They might not be the greatest rock 'n' roll band in the world anymore, but they still attract lots of people to their shows. So what can you say? I don't knock 'em. I love their music. As people I think they leave something to be desired, but so what? That's part of their charm."

In truth, the Stones began deteriorating long before Mick Jagger went out on his own. As I've said, the golden run ended with *Exile on Main Street*. So what went wrong? Why did the greatest rock band in the world lose the groove? Some believe they'd simply done what they'd set out to do—mission accomplished. Some believe they lost that all-important ability to reinvent themselves, which Andrew Oldham said a band must do every five years if it wants to remain relevant. Some believe they burned through their fuel, used up the inspiration and energy that carried them out of the Crawdaddy Club. But I think the death of the friendship explains the death of the band. By the late 1970s, Jagger and Richards had drifted into separate camps. Their songs, the best of which had always taken shape in the studio, formed in all those empty hours of hanging out, lost distinction. Without the friendship, there was no band. Nor love, nor music. It died the way every friendship that once meant the world to me died—little by little, then all at once, in a great big blowout, as the extras and half-formed characters looked on. Even after it ended they continued to churn out records, but they had yielded their place in the culture. No one depends on the Rolling Stones anymore.

When was the beginning of the end for the Stones and for rock 'n' roll itself?

In *Awopbopaloobop Alopbamboom* Nik Cohn dates it to 1966 and the introduction of LSD, which turned London's toughest blues band into a bunch of flower-sniffing hippies. Ethan Russell told me that the decline started after Altamont, when the Stones pulled back from the abyss. "America had been completely about music, politics, and the war," Russell explained. "That's the air everybody was breathing. Then the publicists arrived. After that, all the excess was choreographed, for show. On the seventy-two tour, instead of people like Chuck Berry or B. B. King or Abbie Hoffman hanging out backstage, you'd have the celebrities, Truman Capote and Princess Lee Radziwill. For the first time, your level of fame was used to gauge your importance. The birth of *People* magazine was the end of rock 'n' roll."

I can't define the difference between a record that is real and alive and a record that is phony and dead, but I know it when I hear it. *Sticky Fingers* is alive. No matter when you play it, it's new. *Steel Wheels* was old even when it was new. It's less an album than a product. At some point, the Stones went from writing new songs to writing cover versions of their own material. I always assumed *Tattoo You*, released in 1981, was the last true Stones album, whereas *Some Girls* was the last great Stones album. *Tattoo You* has great songs, perfect licks, a classic riff-driven single—"Start Me Up"—and a coherent sound. But I later learned that the record was really the creation of its producer, Chris Kimsey. "Mick and Keith were not talking at that point, and they needed an album," Kimsey told me. "I said to their manager, listen, I know of at least six good songs I recorded during previous sessions that were never used. So I went looking for them. It was a labor of love. If I hadn't been there, that album never would've come out. Only I remembered every cut from all the old sessions. 'Waiting

On a Friend' was from *Goats Head Soup*. 'Start Me Up' was from *Some Girls*. It was recorded the same day as 'Miss You.' It almost ended up in the bin again. It was a reggae riff originally, that's how Keith considered it. So when he first heard the version you hear today, he said, 'Get rid of it, sounds like something I heard on the radio.' Of course, I didn't get rid of it."

The fact that the most famous song on *Tattoo You* is an outtake from *Some Girls* only strengthens the case for *Some Girls* as the last great Stones album. It was released in the summer of 1978, when I was at camp in Eagle River, Wisconsin. I remember studying the cover in the senior cabin, listening to it again and again. That record is pure New York City in the late seventies. Fantasy Gotham. Cocaine and rats, the mean streets at dawn. The licks are as great as any Keith ever dreamed up. They made me feel like I could take anyone, even the kid with the nunchucks and Bruce Lee posters, but who wants to? *Some Girls* was a classic case of a gunslinger putting on his pistols for a final trip to town—the Stones' attempt to prove, once more, that they were the greatest. It was recorded at the peak of punk rock, when the Sex Pistols were attacking the Stones as sellouts and old men. If you want to be the king, kill the king—as the Beatles killed Elvis, as Elvis killed everyone who came before. Richards, not ready to be killed, was stirred back to peak form instead. When told that a member of the Sex Pistols had declared the Stones old and done—*someone's gonna push you off the stage*—Keith snapped: "Just let them try. We're the Rolling Stones. No one tells us what to do. We'll stop when we feel like it."

Some Girls was the last iteration of the band before it settled into complacency. The Stones in the age of punk and disco—the record actually sounds like a resolution of those opposites, in which Keith is punk and Mick is disco. "Miss You," "Beast of Burden." It's an argument caught on vinyl, Studio 54 and Andy Warhol slapped back to their senses by Keith and his four-note riff.

34

ON AND OFF THE ROAD

Some Girls was the bestselling album in the United States. It went platinum six times and spawned several hit singles, including "Miss You," the band's last American number one. Looking back, it's the obvious capper, the final marker before the wilderness begins. From there, it's nothing but dead letters and short days. As in a film, the ensuing decades slip by in montage, each band member going from early middle age to late middle age to frankly old.

Mick Jagger has devoted much of his time in recent years to the business of making movies, a second career that grew from his collaborations with filmmakers and photographers. Scorsese told me about the first time he met Jagger: Scorsese wanted to use "Jumpin' Jack Flash" in a crucial scene in *Mean Streets*. Jagger insisted on seeing the entire film first—he's become somewhat less cautious, as can be seen in dozens of flicks with directors who, at a crucial moment, turn the hard work of mood and tempo over to the Stones. Jagger has been interested in film since at least as far back as his work with Tony Richardson and Donald Cammell. Though he's been involved as a producer on several features—the James Brown biopic *Get On Up*, most recently—big success has eluded him. Mick Jagger in Hollywood is like a late-career story written by F. Scott Fitzgerald. It's all about the near miss and the almost and the key lesson that remains the same: to Louis B. Mayer, even Satan is just another schmuck on the line. The script I wrote with Jagger and Scorsese was a work of love. It kicked around for years, but remained stubbornly alive. In February 2016, after many iterations, it made its debut on HBO as a series called *Vinyl*.

Jagger's persistence in Hollywood strikes me as just another escape attempt, another run at adulthood, another search for a life free of Keith Richards—a quest that culminated in 2003, when Mick was knighted by Prince Charles. Asked what he felt when he heard about it, Richards said, "Cold, cold rage at his blind stupidity. . . . I threatened to pull out of the tour, went berserk, bananas! But, quite honestly, Mick's fucked up so many times, what's another fuckup?" By accepting the knighthood, Keith believed, Mick had sold out to the very forces of reaction that busted them at Redlands. Richards is the friend who won't let you forget the promise you made under the bridge.

Jagger's longest romantic relationship was with Jerry Hall, a leggy blond model from Texas. They started dating in 1977, before Mick's divorce from Bianca. Jagger and Hall were wed in a Balinese ceremony that the pop star later claimed wasn't really official and didn't really count. They split in 1999 after having four children, Elizabeth, James, Georgia, and Gabriel. That same year, Jagger had a son with the Brazilian fashion model Luciana Gimenez Morad. His name is Lucas. Jagger has seven children and five grandchildren. He recently became a great-grandfather. In 2001 he started dating L'Wren Scott, a fashion designer even taller than Jerry Hall. Scott was born in 1964, the year the Stones charted with "Not Fade Away." In 2014, while the Stones were touring in Australia, she hanged herself with a scarf.

The Stones canceled several concert dates. Mick flew back to America. The pictures of him taken in these hours—on a tarmac, on a hotel balcony—were shocking. His face looked gutted, his body fragile and small. Grief had emptied him, weakened him like a disease. He was suddenly so much older. The famous features—lips and hair—had rearranged themselves into the countenance of an elderly man. I've always admired Mick; for the first time, I sympathized with him. He's always been defined by sex and satisfaction—youth. He's now reached the far shore of that country. An old man defined by sex is a strange thing.

If Mick Jagger teaches you how to stay young, Charlie Watts teaches you how to be old, how to remain elegant while being completely still. He was ancient when he was twenty, which has made his passage to actual dotage as smooth as the transition from evening to night. He is the still point at the center of the storm, calmly pursuing his interests, which include the U.S. Civil War, the Stones, and jazz. When not playing with Mick and Keith, he has toured with his own band, the Charlie Watts Quintet, a jazz combo in the Chris Barber style. But Charlie did suffer a single season of dangerous curiosity. He remained sober in the drug years. He drank, but that's it. He was a metronome, smiling as he kept the beat. Then, in his middle age, at a time many others were switching to cornbread and iced tea, Charlie flirted with heroin, as if he suddenly decided, *Since I'm gonna die anyway, I might as well know what they knew*—"they" being the black jazz musicians who remain his heroes. "I don't know what made me do it that late in life, although in retrospect, I think I must have been going through some kind of a midlife crisis," Watts said. "I had never done any serious drugs when I was younger, but at this point in my life, I went, 'Sod it. I'll do it now.'"

Bill Wyman had his own midlife crisis—a spectacular one. It was signaled by an interview he gave to *The Sun* of London. "Two weeks ago I went to bed with nine different girls in a week but nobody knows about that," he told a reporter, "newspapers don't follow me around. No one worries about what Bill Wyman is up to, and that's fine by me. Just three or four months ago I went to bed with four different girls in one day. I promise you that's the truth, but everything is done very discreetly. I find it interesting to go with different girls.

They say variety is the spice of life—and it certainly is for me. . . . I don't know if I'm good in bed or not, but I've never had any complaints. And I've had more girls than any of the other Stones—more than all of them put together, probably. It's not something I ever talk about because I hate men who brag like that, but I remember sitting down with the band once when we were touring America years and years ago. We were in a hotel room and we spent four hours working out how many girls we'd been to bed with in the previous couple of years. I was running at just under three hundred at that time. Brian Jones was about one thirty-five. Mick Jagger was about thirty-two. Keith Richards was six. And Charlie Watts was zero."

Oh, Bill Perks, you poor, downtrodden man, lost in the back row with your bass guitar, small hands, high heels, and fear of oblivion!

Bill Wyman took up with a thirteen-year-old girl, a predilection as old as rock 'n' roll. Jerry Lee Lewis and his child bride. Chuck Berry and Sweet Little Sixteen. It's in the DNA: fast cars and nymphets. "I love young ladies of eighteen . . . or twenty-two . . . or twenty-three," Wyman told *The Sun,* "and they seem to enjoy me. I think sex is the healthiest thing of all. After I've been to bed with some twenty-two-year-old chick, I get up after a three-hour session with so much energy I feel I can do anything."

Wyman first spotted Mandy Smith at an awards banquet in 1984. "I saw two stunning girls leaving the dance floor and my heart just jumped," he writes. "She took my breath away. I felt like I'd been whacked over the head with a hammer."

Wyman talked to the older sister first, Nicola Smith.

"Well, you must be twenty," he told her.

"No," she said, "I'm fifteen. And Mandy's thirteen."

Mandy Smith wanted to be a model. Wyman got her a meeting with an agency—they told her to come back in a year—then asked to meet her mom. He went to the house with flowers and chocolate. He kissed Mandy in the hallway, then asked the mom if he could take the daughter out. Bill and Mandy began dating on the sly, though word eventually got out.

Teenage girl plus fifty-year-old man equals tabloid sensation. There was talk of statutory rape charges. "It was a nightmare," Wyman writes. "I didn't think I'd done her any harm, whatever her age. Quite the reverse. I was deeply upset at being in the limelight like this, because I'd looked after Mandy and treated her honorably: I'd tried to encourage her to continue her education when she'd flunked out; I'd tried to help her career; I hadn't introduced her to alcohol or drugs. I simply wanted to be with her."

The scandal might or might not have contributed to Wyman's decision to quit the Stones before the *Voodoo Lounge* tour. He told Ron Wood he'd simply grown tired of the slog, especially the air travel. "Bill hated to fly, and said he'd never get on another plane," Wood told me. When I asked Richards about it, he said, "When I first got word he was leaving, I wanted to cut Bill's throat. Nobody quits the Stones—nobody!"

Wyman was replaced by Darryl Jones, a Chicago bassist who'd played with Miles Davis. Wyman has spent the subsequent years working with his own band, the Rhythm Kings. He's the only living member of the Stones I've never interviewed. I tried to talk to him in London. At first he agreed, then said maybe, then said he had the flu. Which is fine. Bill Wyman's always been like a head on Easter Island, silently towering. Plus there are his books. Wyman has appointed himself the official Stones historian. A selection of his mementos—*Bill Wyman's Scrapbook*—was published in a limited edition. Leafing through the pages is dizzying. He's seemingly hung on to every stage bill, flyer, and receipt. You can piece together the entire age from his artifacts.

Anita Pallenberg had the bleakest second and third acts of any member of the Stones circle. In 1976, she was living in Switzerland with

Keith, Marlon, Dandelion, and their newborn baby boy, Tara, named for the Guinness heir Tara Browne. One morning, when Keith and Marlon were in Paris with the Stones, Anita found Tara dead in his crib. He was two months old.

Anita met Keith in Paris that night. She stood backstage as he performed. Parts of the show are included on *Love You Live*. Knowing the background changes the record. Listening to Keith sing "Happy"—"I never kept a dollar past sunset / it always burned a hole in my pants"—is electrifyingly sad when you know what was really on his mind. Anita and Keith left as soon as the concert was over. "Anita was crying and seemed to be having difficulty moving," Nick Kent writes in *The Dark Stuff*. "Keith was shepherding her along but he was crying too and looked all of a sudden to be impossibly fragile, like a stiff breeze could send him spinning to the ground. No longer the Scott and Zelda of the rock 'n' roll age, they looked like some tragic shell-shocked couple leading each other out of a concentration camp. I honestly never thought I'd see them alive again."

Pallenberg never fully recovered, nor did her relationship with Richards. Her daughter, Dandelion, was sent to live with Keith's mother in England soon after the baby died. In the summer of 1979, Anita was living with Marlon in South Salem, New York, a few miles from where I write these sentences. The house was a pit and she was a ruin, a weird hippie lady that locals regarded as a witch. Neighbors reported night chanting. Dead cats turned up in the yard. "She's a sick person," a local kid named Steve Levoie reportedly said. "She should be put away. The house was filthy, really dirty, and Anita was dirty herself. She even asked my sister if she wanted some coke. . . . She had a lot of young boys who would come to the house all the time. She would ask for sex and talk of sex quite often. She never asked me, but who'd want a dirty old woman like that?"

Anita, then in her midthirties, took up with a seventeen-year-old named Scott Cantrell. He'd come to do errands, then stayed. His mother had killed herself and he'd dropped out of school—just another wayward soul who fell into the diorama. Sex, drugs, and rock 'n' roll. None of it was very glamorous. On July 20, 1979, Cantrell shot himself in Anita's bed with Anita's gun—possibly playing Russian roulette.

While examining the crime scene, Detective Douglas Lamanna of the South Salem police noticed a newspaper with Anita's picture beneath the headline WHAT ANITA DID TO BIANCA.

"Is that you?"

"Yes."

"What'd you do to Bianca?"

Pallenberg was charged with possession of stolen property and illegal possession of weapons and ultimately paid a fine. Asked how she felt when the boy died, she told *The Sunday Correspondent*: "I didn't feel anything. That's one of the wonders of drugs and drink. You don't feel anything."

Anita returned to England, went back to school, and got a degree. She has since appeared in movies and TV shows. She rides her bike near Redlands. She's had a hip replaced and walks with a limp. She's old but looks even older. She's consumed more than her share of life, misery, heroin, and cocaine. Asked about Keith, she told a reporter, "He's aged the best—he was always the best."

Keith's life turned in 1977, while the Stones rehearsed for an upcoming tour. It started with Anita, who, because of either her flamboyant manner or her flamboyant appearance, attracted an unhealthy amount of attention on a flight from London to Toronto. Her luggage—twenty-eight pieces, according to Chet Flippo—was searched at customs. Hashish was found, along with a spoon and a needle with traces of heroin, giving Canadian police cause to search her local residence—three adjoining suites shared at the Harbour Castle hotel with Keith. Five Mounties went through drawers and shelves, the pockets of spangled coats, the toes of Western boots, the bodies of acoustic guitars. They found heroin, a razor blade, a knife, a brass lighter, a silver bowl, a teaspoon, foil, three red pills, and a hypodermic needle—all the fixin's.

Keith slept through the whole thing, which seems impossible until you consider the chemical nature of his slumber. He had to be slapped back to consciousness before he could be arrested. Bail was set and paid. He was back at the hotel that night, but in big trouble. Enough product had been recovered to charge him with not merely possession but trafficking. If convicted, he could spend decades in prison, just the way Captain Kidd went out: a cell in the colonies, a green island floating in the cold water beyond barred windows. What's more, he was sick. The cops had taken all his shit and he was going into withdrawal, swarmed by meanies, seeing the rat.

"I'll never forget going to [Keith's] room with Woody to find him writhing on the floor, vomiting," Bill Wyman writes. "We tried to give him pills but he threw them up. Woody said to me: 'What can we *do*?' I said, 'Well, we've obviously got to get him some heroin, haven't we?' I feared he would otherwise have died. Nobody seemed to be looking after him. And so Woody and I went out of the hotel, which was riddled with plain-clothes detectives, and scored some heroin to get him by. I've never done that for anybody before or since, but he simply had to have it at that point."

The case was resolved in a manner too drawn-out and bureaucratic to go into, but suffice it to say that the Canadian raid, which seemed like the end of Keith, proved to be a good thing. In forcing Keith to finally get clean, it probably saved his life. Keith and Anita apparently broke up because she refused to get off junk. Given a choice—love or obliteration—she chose obliteration. Keith went on. At first, his treatment consisted of wires connecting him to a mechanical box. This sent a pulse into his brain, shocking him with electricity and blunting the symptoms of withdrawal. He was still using the device a short time later when the band was rehearsing in Woodstock, New York. When I spoke to Ian McLagan, who played keyboards on that tour, he remembered the box with a shiver and spoke of how, in the middle of a sentence, Keith would get hit by a jolt and stabs of pain would register on his face. "He carried it around like it was a guitar," McLagan told me. "He hated it, but he was determined."

Keith met Patti Hansen at the Roxy roller rink in Manhattan in December 1979. It was his thirty-sixth birthday, and he was celebrating. She was a twenty-three-year-old *Vogue* model from Staten Island. It was a match made in blue-collar heaven. The train from Dartford; the ferry from St. George Terminal. Keith is a serial monogamist. No matter what happened on the road, he's been loyal to his partner. In every case I know, it was the woman who, in one way or another, left him. Linda Keith went off with Jimi Hendrix. Anita chose junk. And Keith is still with Patti Hansen. I remember flying beside him to New York after a show. When the plane banked over Long Island Sound, he looked out the window and smiled. "That's my home down there," he said. "When I see those lights, I know I'm close to everything I love."

Keith lives in a big house that backs up to a nature preserve in Weston, Connecticut. He lingers on his estate in the way of an aristocrat lingering on ancestral grounds, a sage old man fading toward gossamer. He's suffered various mishaps: stumbles, falls, fractures. *Lord, your sea is so big and my ship is so small.* In 2006, he fell out of a tree in Fiji, which, according to press reports, was a palm tree, but according to Keith was somewhat less picturesque. Two days later, while riding on a boat, he was knocked backward by a swell, banging his head a second time. That's when the pain began. He had a clot in his brain. He was taken in for emergency surgery. I've been told by people close to the band that it was far more serious than fans realize. Keith recovered but has never been the same. It was a near-death experience, and he emerged weakened and somewhat frail. He has to be extremely careful. Even after quitting heroin, he still sought derangement. The doctors said that had to stop. Backstage one night, a musician handed Keith a pill, which he swallowed without consideration. He did not even know what it was. A few minutes into the show, he stumbled and fell. Jagger simply stepped over his friend and kept performing.

Yet Keith still carries on in the old spirit, with the old joy. Once, when I asked a rapper what Lyor Cohen, one of the first executives of Def Jam Records, was like, he said, "Lyor is old and white but he's so fucking gangster—doing it like it needs doing, doing it like it's got to be done." To me, that's Keith. No matter how old, beat up, or infirm, he's still so fucking gangster, doing it like it needs doing, doing it like it's got to be done.

Keith and Patti raised two daughters in Weston, not far from where I now live. I first heard of this bucolic pocket of rolling hills on the Stones' plane as Keith mumbled his way home after a show. He blessed the place, and I've aged from early middle age to middle middle age myself here, raising my own children a bike ride from the Richards estate. Now and then, when I go to Luc's, a bistro in Ridgefield, Keith is at the bar with a glass of vodka in front of him and a big hat on his head. On such occasions, the owner of the restaurant, who's related to Keith, puts on a playlist consisting almost entirely of reggae. Keith drinks, listens, smiles, and laughs. He wears sunglasses and soft shoes with buckles. I nod to him and say hello and he acknowledges me and says hello back but it's impossible to say whether he remembers or has gotten into the famous man's habit of seeming to remember everyone.

On certain days, he lingers. When he lingers, I linger, soaking up the Zen-like rock 'n' roll of his presence. It means being in the exact right place at the exact right time; it means that Keith's road, which was Crawdaddy and Chess and Villefranche, and my road, which was SATs and college and rules, have led to the same place, emptied into the same song. It justifies every decision I've ever made.

35

THE HALL OF FAME

Last summer, I traveled to the Rock and Roll Hall of Fame in Cleveland—a place I'd long avoided—with my son Aaron. To me, such an institution seemed to violate the spirit of rock 'n' roll, which is all about right fuckin' here, right fuckin' now. A museum is nostalgia, used-to-be, the opposite of everything the Stones, Who, and Beatles stood for. The moment you build a shrine, you're saying the past is more important than the present.

It turned out to be less about music than clothes. I stood before the jacket Keith Richards wore at Altamont—head bowed. I stood before the flamboyant suit Jimi Hendrix wore at Monterey—head bowed. I stood before the Western tie Elvis wore in one of his movies—head bowed. Janis Joplin's scarf, John Lennon's glasses—it's an immense lost and found, an accretion of miscellany, the baby boomers telling us that since they've grown old, the music has grown old, too.

But maybe they're right: maybe the Hall of Fame simply acknowledges the truth. Rock 'n' roll died at Altamont and died again on the Internet. The music craves vinyl and mosh pits and dark clubs where smoke collects along the ceiling—it's too dirty and rank for a gluten-free world. But I keep coming back to the songs—not the lyrics, or the chords, but how they make me feel when they come on the radio on a summer night and the top is down and the moon is up and the sea is shining and every door is open and every girl is my girl and every hill is a grass stain and an epic adventure waiting to happen. "Honky Tonk Women." "Jumpin' Jack Flash." "Satisfaction." "Wild Horses." "Tumbling Dice." "Sweet Virginia." It's not just music. It's my nation. It's my country. It's where I've spent my life.

AFTERWORD

In an attempt to understand the music, I've learned to play guitar, though my use of the past tense is vainglorious. In fact, when it comes to the guitar, as with everything else, I'm in a perpetual state of becoming. I'd always wanted to explore the instrument beyond the four chords I'd picked up for the talent show. My failure to do so when I was young is all my parents' fault. I'm the baby of the family, the youngest of three. By the time I came around, everything had been attempted and ditched, my parents chewed up like gum. When I told them I wanted to take lessons, they said, "You'll just quit after we spend hundreds of dollars, like your sister." When I insisted, they told me to look in the attic for the old guitar, the hippie thing with the peace sticker on the back. Too big for me, no case. I'd walk to my lesson in the snow, holding that giant as teenagers shouted from passing cars: "Nice giant guitar, you dirty hippie kid!"

I told my instructor I wanted to learn "Wild Horses" and "Happy." He listened to the songs on tape but could not sufficiently puzzle them out. I now know why: Keith's open G tuning. My instructor taught me classical instead, the result being that my parents were proved right. I quit like my sister, thus becoming a spectator, content to dwell in the bleachers of life.

I thought I was too old to start—what's the point of learning these things if you're just gonna expire?—until my wife, Jessica, bought me a guitar for my forty-sixth birthday. My mother had just died, and the instrument and lessons became a way to reconnect with the axial lines. My teacher is named Brendan. He's ten years younger than I am. He taught me how to play my favorite Stones songs. It's become an obsession. I have not experienced anything like it since I first started writing stories. I sit on the porch and play till my fingers burn. I make my sons sing along with me. I look up the tablature of particular tunes on the Internet and fill the house with noise. I sneak off to the guitar store to touch the Fenders and Martins when I'm supposed to be at the bank. It's a good thing I did not learn when I was young. The college-age combination of marijuana and guitar would have frozen me like a bug in amber. My love for the instrument has grown along with this book. It's given me a new way to appreciate the music—the simplicity of a song like "Dead Flowers" is akin to the simplicity of a perfect algebraic equation. I've come to regard my teacher as a guru. I unburden myself in his little acoustic room at the store in town. He gives lessons and plays in bands but has not been outrageously successful. It's confusing. To me, Brendan seems like one of the best guitar players in the world. His commitment is certainly no different from that of Brian or Keith. It's all he cares about, the only thing he does. But he fills me with hope and admiration, too. As I tell my sons, pick one thing to be good at. In the end, it's only the playing that matters.

ACKNOWLEDGMENTS

A handful of people have been of crucial help in reporting and writing this book. My agent, Jennifer Rudolph Walsh, and my editor, Julie Grau, are at the top. Ditto my friend Mark Varouxakis, who accompanied me on a Rolling Stones grand tour. When Mark asked where we'd be going, I said, "Everywhere the Stones rehearsed and recorded, were wounded and healed, lived and died, shot up and got clean and made music." We did not make it to all those places, but we did hit a bunch. Cynthia Cotts did most of the fact-checking on the book—at a marathon pace and with equal parts passion and rigor. Additional checking was done by Julie Tate. I'd like to thank my parents, Herb and Ellen Cohen, too, if only to keep my streak of dutifulness intact. Also my sister, Sharon Levin, and my brother-in-law, Bill Levin, and of course my brother, Steven, for what he gave me and what he withheld, and my sister-in-law, Lisa Melmed. My kids—at the moment, I've got four: Aaron, Nate, Micah, Elia. And mostly I'd like to thank Jessica Medoff—when we were engaged, I'd introduce her as "Jessica Medoff, the future Jessica Medoff"—first reader, first medic, first with sutures, and first with tonic. She said I couldn't quit Diet Coke. And I did. And of course Francis Albert Sinatra.

NOTES

1 · ROCK STARS TELLING JOKES

The stories in this chapter come from my memory as well as notebooks and interviews from my days with the Stones, preserved, all these years, in a box that I've dragged from apartment to apartment, life to life. Special thanks to my wife, Jessica, who gathered all the tapes I made, on a now somewhat obsolete microrecorder, of Mick, Keith, Charlie, Woody, and those on the tour and in their orbit. I had these tapes newly transcribed by Jean Brown, who also transcribed them the first time, twenty years ago. I have found great satisfaction in going back over old interviews, which date from the mid-1990s, and seeing that my obsessions and the general drift of my curiosity has remained the same. A treasured memory is walking back and forth between the offices of *Rolling Stone* magazine and the dressing rooms of Rockefeller Center, where, in 1994, the Stones hung out for hours before the MTV Video Music Awards. Jann Wenner came by to say hello to his young reporter and his old friends. At one point, as Jann and I spoke, Charlie Watts interrupted us, poking his finger at me playfully, telling Jann, "You have to watch this one. He's a rascal, he is. Always takes the best seat on the plane." Jann looked horrified, then pleased. Back at the office, he took me into his office and said, "You're the sixth Stone!" My childhood encounter with Joe DiMaggio was at the Cracker Jack Old Timers game in Washington, D.C., in the mid-1980s. In the end, I did get a picture and a handshake from the Yankee Clipper, my father's hero, as well as pictures with Bob Feller, Ernie Banks, and Harmon Killebrew. MTV awarded the Rolling Stones a lifetime achievement award that night. This caused Keith Richards to say, "Lifetime award? I've still got a hundred eighty-seven years in me." For my first accounting of the Stones' afterparty at the Four Seasons, see my *RS* story, "Tour de Force: The Rolling Stones Rake It In and Rock the House," which ran November 3, 1994. It can be read on the magazine's website. When David Fricke, *Rolling Stone*'s music editor, and I went backstage at one of the concerts, a Stones PR person complimented me on my cover story, "The Rolling Stones: It's Show Time," which ran August 25, 1994. Fricke, in his sheepish way, said, "Hey, man, I wrote the headline!" "Oh, really?" said the flack. "You coined 'It's Show Time'? Bloody brilliant!"

2 · THE COWBELL AND THE POSTER

The cowbell in this chapter was played by Stones producer Jimmy Miller, leading the band into the groove that kicked off with "Honky Tonk Women" and continued through my childhood. The poster, the one that hung on my brother's attic room wall, was a blowup of a photo taken during a video promo shoot for the single "Respectable," the seventh track on *Some Girls*, which was released in June 1978. The original picture shows all five Stones, with Bill Wyman in back in a red shirt under a kind of long-sleeved denim deal, his face tucked between Mick's and Keith's. In 2005, when that image was used as a cover for the Stones release *Rarities: 1971–2003*, Wyman was gone. Having left the band over a decade before, he had been disappeared in the way of a Soviet functionary. That void—it's where so much Stones history takes the long nap. The Kansas album with the waterfall: *Point of Know Return*, released in 1977, when I was nine. In addition to "Dust in the Wind," it includes such classics as "Sparks of the Tempest" and "Hopelessly Human." The Slim Whitman album, *Love Song of the Waterfall*, was released a decade earlier, in 1965. It was just the sort of pop country collection—"In the Misty Moonlight," "Silver Threads Among the Gold," "On the Sunny Side of the Rockies"—you could imagine Wally King listening to in his downtime. For the Stones discography and studio notes, I referred to *The Rolling Stones: Complete Recording Sessions 1962–2012, 50th Anniversary Edition* by Martin Elliott with a foreword by Chris Kimsey, as well as the dozens of other Stones bios and books listed in the bibliography, as well as iTunes, Sonos, and my own record collection. Just about every record store I frequented in my adolescent years is gone, replaced by nail salons and banks, with the happy exception of Vintage Vinyl, which is still plugging away in Evanston, Illinois.

3 · THE 8:28 TO LONDON

While reconstructing the early life of the Stones, I've drawn on many sources, including interviews, books, and reporting trips. Of special interest were the memoirs and biographies and autobiographies of the principals: *Life* by Keith Richards, *Stone Alone* by Bill Wyman, and *According to the Rolling Stones*, a kind of oral history, as well as Andrew Loog Oldham's memoirs, *Stoned* and *2Stoned*. See also a handful of classic books on the band, including *The True Adventures of the Rolling Stones* by Stanley Booth and *S.T.P.: A Journey Through America with the Rolling Stones* by Robert Greenfield. Especially helpful were my discussions with Jagger and Richards back in the day, as well as a handful of documentary films, including *Charlie Is My Darling* (1966), directed by Peter Whitehead. In addition, I visited as many of the important places as my budget and family life would allow, including Dartford and London—because there is life in a book, then there is life on the ground. For the early history of rock 'n' roll, I relied on Nik Cohn's *Awopbopaloobop Alopbambboom: The Golden Age of Rock*; Glenn C. Altschuler's *All Shook Up: How Rock 'n' Roll Changed America*; Nick Tosches's *Country: The Twisted Roots of Rock 'n' Roll*; Robert Palmer's *Rock & Roll: An Unruly History*; and Peter Guralnick's masterful *Last Train to Memphis: The Rise of Elvis Presley*, as well as his book on Sam Phillips. Ditto everything by Greil Marcus, especially *Mystery Train: Images of America in Rock 'n' Roll Music*. I filled out my sense of the gray postwar British era, and how things changed, by talking to some of the stars of that moment, including Neil Sedaka and Lloyd Price. Linda Keith (the real Ruby Tuesday) gave me a more personal read on the Stones and the moment, as did Paul Jones, Acker Bilk, and Marianne Faithfull. See Tony Judt's *Postwar: A History of Europe Since 1945* and Philip Norman's *John Lennon: The Life* as well as the biographies of Jagger, including *Mick: The Wild Life and Mad Genius of Jagger* by Christopher Andersen. In several conversations, the way the mood changed between 1954 and 1956 was described to me as a shift from black-and-white to Technicolor.

4 · COLLECTORS

I relied on interviews for this chapter, some with the band members, others with bit players and fellow travelers, witnesses to the early years who either crapped out, left to start their own bands, returned to school, or went into advertising. Of special help were Paul Jones, later of Manfred Mann fame, who'd been offered the front-man gig by Brian Jones before Jagger took it. Dick Taylor, too. The Stones' first bassist went on to fame with the Pretty Things. He gave me a visceral sense of the art school days, the first rehearsals, the first clubs, the first temptations of fame. Keith Richards's book *Life*, which I reviewed for *Rolling Stone* (the review can be read on the magazine's website), was an invaluable resource on his early years, as were various books, including *The Rolling Stones: Fifty Years* by Christopher Sandford, *Jagger: Rebel, Rock Star, Rambler, Rogue* by Marc Spitz, and *Keith: Standing in the Shadows* by Stanley Booth. On the story of how Keith got his first guitar, check out the rocker's charming picture book for little kids called *Gus & Me: The Story of My Granddad and My First Guitar*, with illustrations by Keith's daughter Theodora Richards.

5 · UNBROKEN

A special pleasure of working on this book was the chance to research those crucial moments when a door swung open into a new era, a new room. I'm thinking particularly of reporting that allowed me to piece together this chapter, which concerns the early sixties in Great Britain, the years of the so-called Youthquake. Particularly helpful was Robin Morgan, formerly the editor of London's *Sunday Times* magazine, who not only shared research and conclusions from his book *1963: The Year of the Revolution; How Youth Changed the World with Music, Art, and Fashion* (co-written by Ariel Leve), but also introduced me to key figures of the era, including the *New Musical Express* journalist Norman Jopling, and the writer Mick Brown, author of *Tearing Down the Wall of Sound: The Rise of Phil Spector*, among others. Also helpful were my interviews with Paul Jones, Linda Keith, Marianne Faithfull, Charlie Watts, Ron Wood, David Bailey, and Tony King, who for many years worked as Jagger's personal assistant and everything guy. Tony was working at Decca Records when the Stones signed with that label in 1963. Ian McLagan, the keyboardist for the Faces who later toured with the Stones, was also invaluable, as was Peter Asher of Peter and Gordon, who seemed to be in the middle ground of every important scene. Asher was in the first wave of the British invasion, and later was the first employee of Apple Records. He was also the first fired—given the ax when his sister broke up with Paul McCartney. On the early history of Jagger, I relied on the books mentioned above, as well as interviews with Dick Taylor, Norman Jopling, and Paul Jones. On skiffle, I relied on lengthy interviews with Chris Barber, the father of skiffle and arguably the father of the entire British blues scene. Ditto Chas Hodges, a star of that first strange florescence of British music crossbred with black American folk. Several books were invaluable, especially *Skiffle: The Definitive Inside Story* by Chas McDevitt. Charlie Watts was good on skiffle, as was Ron Wood, as were certain passages in Bill Wyman's book, *Stone Alone: The Story of a Rock 'n' Roll Band*. On Alexis Korner and the Ealing Club, see Keith Richards's *Life*, as well as Stanley Booth's *Keith: Standing in the Shadows*, the compilation *According to the Rolling Stones*, and Robert Greenfield's Q&A with Richards that ran in *Rolling Stone* in 1971. There are great passages on the era in Pete Townshend's memoir, *Who I Am*, and in Robert Sandall's May 1994 Charlie Watts interview in *Mojo*, "Charlie Watts: The Rock."

6 · "VICAR APPALLED"

On my tour through landmarks of the Stones' London: I engaged the services of Richard Porter, an obsessive, snap-brim-hat-wearing music scholar who, for a handful of days, walked me around the city, showing me key spots. I had my friend Mark with me, my best friend since boyhood, who accompanies me on many trips and has the habit, after meeting famous people, of saying, "You know what? He's just a regular guy, like us." Mark and I then hit all the spots that Richard Porter and I had missed, including the London nightclubs, apartments, and saloons as well as the more distant shrines, such as Keith's house, Redlands, and Mick's house, Stargroves. As for Brian Jones and his early biography, the backbone of the chapter, I relied on interviews with several of the people mentioned above, especially Paul Jones, who was playing with Brian before Brian knew Mick and Keith, and Dick Taylor, who was a keen observer at the center of the scene.

I also mined several books—all those on the Stones in general, as well as a few in what I call the Brian Jones library, tomes centered on his life, his death, and the mystery surrounding his death. See, for example, *Golden Stone: The Untold Life and Tragic Death of Brian Jones* by Laura Jackson; *Brian Jones: Who Killed Christopher Robin? The Murder of a Rolling Stone* by Terry Rawlings; *Up and Down with the Rolling Stones: My Rollercoaster Ride with Keith Richards* by Tony Sanchez; *Stone Alone: The Story of a Rock 'n' Roll Band* by Bill Wyman; and *The Mammoth Book of the Rolling Stones: An Anthology of* the *Best Writing About the Greatest Rock 'n' Roll Band in the World*, edited by Sean Egan. A new volume was added to the Brian Jones library while I was busily writing this book: *Brian Jones: The Making of the Rolling Stones* by Paul Trynka. On the naming of the band and that first live performance, I relied on Dick Taylor, who considers it a signal moment of his life. It's fascinating to read the early set list—it was just the beginning, but the taste and obsession were already there. In these dread later days of rock 'n' roll, when the Stones can't seem to muster up the spark to write new songs or come up with a new record, I offer them a suggestion: go into a studio and cut the set list of that first gig. It would make a wonderful bookend to the storied career of the band. As my mother used to say, If you start in blues, you should end in blues.

7 · CHARLIE AND BILL

Maybe the most illuminating conversation I had while working on this book was the ten minutes spent on the phone with Acker Bilk, a trad jazz clarinetist who was topping the charts when the Stones broke. It was all vitriol and sarcasm, the disgust a monarch feels for the rabble who forced him into exile. Bilk, whom you might liken to Chuck Mangione or Kenny G, was in fact a great player and the author of one of my all-time favorite tunes, "Stranger on the Shore." His time had run its course, that's all. For the nuts and bolts of the moment—when trad jazz gave way to blues in the UK—I relied on interviews with Chris Barber, Paul Jones, and Chas Hodges, as well as articles that appeared, at the time, in *Jazz News* and *New Musical Express*. On Bill Wyman's background, I relied on the bassist's own book, *Stone Alone: The Story of a Rock 'n' Roll Band*. Ditto the scrapbooks, *Rolling with the Stones*, which he had published in 2002 and rereleased as an expensive collectors' edition in 2013. That book, which was kindly sent to me as a PDF by Wyman's publicist, Charlotte Hayes-Jones, seemingly includes every early set list, flyer, poster, and note, as well as wonderful photos. From this source alone you could reconstruct the first ten years of the band's existence. Charlie Watts is the only member of the band with no memoir and no major bio. For his story, I relied on newspaper and magazine stories and interviews, as well as a sort of quickie bio, *Charlie Watts* by Alan Clayson. Most important were my own interviews and discussions with Watts, held back in the 1990s. His background is covered in several books about the Stones in general: *The Rolling Stones: Fifty Years* by Christopher Sandford; *Rocks Off: 50 Tracks That Tell the Story of the*

Rolling Stones by Bill Janovitz; *S.T.P.: A Journey Through America with the Rolling Stones* by Robert Greenfield; the compilation *According to the Rolling Stones;* and *The Mammoth Book of the Rolling Stones: An Anthology of the Best Writing About the Greatest Rock 'n' Roll Band in the World,* edited by Sean Egan. See also the very good interview Watts gave for *Mojo* in May 1994. As for seeing the Stones rehearse, I learned about this by seeing the Stones rehearse. The best way to understand the songs and the style, though, is to pick up a guitar and try to play one of the songs, especially those from the early years, before Keith vanished into the funhouse of exotic tunings.

8 · EDITH GROVE

For researchers, aficionados, and other madmen, the crucial text on life at Edith Grove is the book written by Mick, Keith, and Brian's civilian roommate, *Nankering with the Rolling Stones: The Untold Story of the Early Days* by James Phelge. More than a firsthand document, it's a good book. It captures what it's like to have a friend and watch that friend go from regular guy to teen idol just like that. It's as if Elvis had a roommate in 1956 and that roommate could write. Phelge is still around. He's worked, on and off, in record stores and the music business, and can be followed on Twitter @JamesPhelge. Other sources on Edith Grove include *The Rolling Stones: Fifty Years* by Christopher Sandford; *Stone Alone: The Story of a Rock 'n' Roll Band* by Bill Wyman; *Brian Jones: Who Killed Christopher Robin? The Murder of a Rolling Stone* by Terry Rawlings; *Keith Richards on Keith Richards: Interviews and Encounters,* edited by Sean Egan; and *1963: The Year of the Revolution; How Youth Changed the World with Music, Art, and Fashion* by Robin Morgan and Ariel Leve. On first hearing the Beatles: James Phelge is good here, as is Keith Richards in *Life.* See also Mick Jagger's 1988 speech inducting the Beatles into the Rock and Roll Hall of Fame. It's on YouTube. The relationship between the Beatles and the Stones, particularly between Jagger and Lennon, remained rivalrous. It seemed as if Jagger wanted Lennon's approval and Lennon, knowing that, did not want to give it. Two quotes very much amused me, though I could not find room for them in this book. The first is Lennon speaking to *Rolling Stone:* "I think Mick is a joke, with all that fag dancing." (See "John Lennon, the *Rolling Stone* Interview," 1971.) The second is Lennon speaking to *Playboy* magazine in 1980: "In the eighties, they'll be asking, 'Why are those guys still together? Can't they hack it on their own? Why do they have to be surrounded by a gang? Is the little leader scared somebody's gonna knife him in the back?' That's gonna be the question. That's-a-gonna be the question! . . . They will be showing pictures of the guy with lipstick wriggling his ass and the four guys with the evil black make-up on their eyes trying to look raunchy. That's gonna be the joke in the future."

9 · GIORGIO!

Giorgio Gomelsky died in January 2016. Into his later years, when he returned to Europe, he ran a recording studio and loft space in Manhattan called the Red Door Collective. You could meet him if you were invited to— or felt like crashing—one of his parties. After the heartbreak of losing the Stones, Giorgio went on to a successful music career, most notably as the manager of the Yardbirds, which featured Eric Clapton, Jimmy Page, and Jeff Beck. I learned about him and his club, the Crawdaddy, from several people, most of them old-time rockers, including Paul Jones, Dick Taylor, and Ian McLagan. Also Norman Jopling, who covered the British blues scene for *New Musical Express*. You can read about Gomelsky, briefly, in dozens of books— he's one of those colorful types that attract journalists. I relied on several of the books and articles already listed above, with special attention to *Stoned* by Andrew Loog Oldham; *Rocks Off: 50 Tracks That Tell the Story of the Rolling Stones* by Bill Janovitz; *Up and Down with the Rolling Stones: My Rollercoaster Ride with Keith Richards* by Tony Sanchez; *Stone Alone: The Story of a Rock 'n' Roll Band* by Bill Wyman; *Nankering with the Rolling Stones: The Untold Story of the Early Days* by James Phelge; and *1963: The Year of the Revolution; How Youth Changed the World with Music, Art, and Fashion* by Robin Morgan and Ariel Leve. Gomelsky closed the New York chapter of his life with a final blowout on May 15, 2015. It was billed as "Last Days of Red Door & Homage to Giorgio Gomelsky." Everyone was there—except the Stones.

10 · MEET THE BEATLES

The Beatles turning up at the Crawdaddy: It's one of the great pop culture moments, like Eisenhower and Churchill playing poker on the moon. It would be great if there were film footage. As there isn't, I had to reconstruct the scene through various sources. Most important are the memories of the

Stones themselves, collected in books and interviews, notably the scene as recorded by Bill Wyman in *Stone Alone*. James Phelge was there, and his reminiscence is fascinating. See also *Rocks Off: 50 Tracks That Tell the Story of the Rolling Stones* by Bill Janovitz.

11 · TEENAGE TYCOON SHIT

Norman Jopling's original piece on the Stones can be read in several collections, including *The Mammoth Book of the Rolling Stones: An Anthology of the Best Writing About the Greatest Rock 'n' Roll Band in the World*, edited by Sean Egan. My copy of the article came from Jopling himself. It is now considered less a piece of journalism than a historical document, the Magna Carta of the Stones, but Jopling is a fine writer. Last year, he published some of his stories under the title *Shake It Up Baby! Notes from a Pop Music Reporter 1961–1972*. My interview with him was invaluable on the early years of the Stones and the era in general. Jopling told me about his own falling-out with the band, which resulted from his criticism of the song "19th Nervous Breakdown." Jopling's girlfriend had a drug problem and he told Jagger he considered the treatment of the topic too cavalier. For several years after, Jopling was persona non grata. On Andrew Oldham: I exchanged emails with Oldham for many months, courting him and trying to persuade him to sit for interviews. He was an integral player in the early years, probably as important as any member of the band. He dithered and considered before finally agreeing to answer questions by email. Which he did. But far more helpful were Oldham's memoirs, good books both of them: *Stoned* and *2Stoned*. Further info on Oldham, his background, his story, his importance, and so on was gleaned from interviews with his associates and friends, especially Al Kooper, Marianne Faithfull, Robin Morgan, Linda Keith, and Norman Jopling. Oldham's story is also told in books by and about the band, and these, too, were sources for this book: *Life* by Keith Richards; *Golden Stone: The Untold Life and Tragic Death of Brian Jones* by Laura Jackson; *Faithfull: An Autobiography* by Marianne Faithfull with David Dalton; *John Lennon: The Life* by Philip Norman; *Stone Alone: The Story of a Rock 'n' Roll Band* by Bill Wyman; *The True Adventures of the Rolling Stones* by Stanley Booth; *Nankering with the Rolling Stones: The Untold Story of the Early Days* by James Phelge; and *Mick: The Wild Life and Mad Genius of Jagger* by Christopher Andersen. See also *Tune In: The Beatles; All These Years* by Mark Lewisohn; *The Beatles: The Biography* by Bob Spitz;

and *Shout! The Beatles in Their Generation* by Philip Norman. On the Youth-quake, I'm indebted to Robin Morgan and the book he wrote with Ariel Leve, *1963: The Year of the Revolution*. On Dick Rowe and the Stones' first contract at Decca, see *The Rolling Stones: Fifty Years* by Christopher Sandford; *Stoned* by Andrew Loog Oldham; and *Beatles vs. Stones* by John McMillian. Ian Stewart and the way he was handled by Oldham is one of the trickiest and saddest situations of the entire story. Since Stewart is dead, I had to rely on secondhand sources, that is, the recollections of key players, especially the books *Life* by Keith Richards, *Stone Alone* by Bill Wyman, and *According to the Rolling Stones*. While researching, I happily came across *Boogie 4 Stu*, a recording of a tribute concert made shortly after Stewart's death in 1985. It's available on Sonos and iTunes. Many great musicians play on it, including Jagger, Richards, Watts, and Wood, as well as Ben Waters, PJ Harvey, and Jools Holland. My favorite is Jagger's vocal on a cover of Bob Dylan's "Watching the River Flow." It reminds you, all over again, of Jagger's vocal genius and power. Several people told me that it was the death of Stewart, beloved by every member of the band, that allowed the Stones to rally just enough to get back together in the late 1980s. In other words, Stewart served the band in life, and saved the band in death.

12 · PICTURES FROM THE ROAD

On the Stones' first tour of Great Britain, their first trip outside the familiar circuit of London clubs and bars, see the books mentioned above. Of particular interest are the memoirs of Wyman, Richards, and Oldham. The best material, not the nuts and bolts so much as the expressionistic sense of how it felt to become a star, came from Richards himself, in conversations we had in the 1990s. Ditto Watts, who, it seems to me, has never gotten over the oddity of being a rock star. His body rejects it like a mismatched kidney. See also the columns band members wrote from the road during that first tour—a classic Andrew Oldham PR scheme. On the early rock 'n' roll riots, see *John Lennon: The Life* by Philip Norman; *Awopbopaloobop Alopbamboom: The Golden Age of Rock* by Nik Cohn; *Ronnie: The Autobiography* by Ron Wood; *All Shook Up: How Rock 'n' Roll Changed America* by Glenn C. Altschuler; *Rock & Roll: An Unruly History* by Robert Palmer; *Keith Richards on Keith Richards: Interviews and Encounters*, edited by Sean Egan; *Who I Am* by Pete Townshend; and *1963: The Year of the Revolution* by Robin Morgan and Ariel

Leve. Some additional information comes from interviews with Ian McLagan and the late great Hy Weiss. On the Beatles and the Stones' second single,
see the memoirs of Oldham as well as the Beatles books mentioned above.
More information came from interviews with Peter Asher, Paul Jones, Dick
Taylor, and others. On the JFK assassination and how it affected America,
rock 'n' roll, the Beatles, and the Stones, I relied mostly on interviews. Especially enlightening was my conversation with Lloyd Price, one of the first rock
stars, who was washed away by the mood change that followed Kennedy's
death.

13 · NO LOVE IN A DOME

This chapter is memoir. My own. The stuff about my college experience and
seeing the Stones in New Orleans in the fall of 1989 comes from memory,
though it's been fact-checked. I am proud to say that I had most of the details
right. The account of my early writing career at *The New Yorker* and *Rolling
Stone* is the story of my life. I've written about some of it before, most point-
edly in my memoir *Lake Effect* (Knopf, 2002). As for my time with the Stones
in Toronto, some of the details come from my memory, though I was able to
refer to old notebooks as well as interviews I did at the time with the Stones
and people in their world. Anyone interested can read the pieces I wrote back
then for *Rolling Stone* on the magazine's website. I wrote about the experience
again in my review of Keith Richards's book *Life*, which ran in *Rolling Stone*
on November 11, 2010. Though I'm drawing here on the same experience, the
pages in this book are different and new—twenty years has a way of changing
every perception. I imagine I'll still be writing about it twenty years from now.
If you're a writer, your life and what happened to you are basically all that you
have. My time with the Stones was a signal event. I never get tired of thinking
about it.

14 · FIRST LICKS

Andrew Oldham locks Mick Jagger and Keith Richards in the Chelsea flat,
telling them not to come out without a song: it's one of the great pop legends.
I've chased it down through dozens of books and interviews. The story has
changed slightly over the years, and it's unclear whether the principals, when

they tell it, are recalling what happened or recalling an earlier version of the story. Yet the key facts remain: Mick and Keith were confined and forced to produce. They were not natural-born songwriters, but original composition was the order of the day—they came to it by necessity and hard work. The chapter is built on interviews conducted over more than twenty years, in conversations with Jagger and Richards as well as with Tony King, Peter Asher, Paul Jones, Bobby Keys, and others. Books, too: *The Rolling Stones: Fifty Years* by Christopher Sandford; *Stoned* and *2Stoned* by Andrew Loog Oldham; *Rocks Off: 50 Tracks That Tell the Story of the Rolling Stones* by Bill Janovitz; *Golden Stone: The Untold Life and Tragic Death of Brian Jones* by Laura Jackson; *Keith: Standing in the Shadows* by Stanley Booth; and *Life* by Keith Richards. On the Jagger/Richards songwriting method more generally, I relied on the books listed above, as well as interviews with producers and technicians who were on the scene and watched the band compose, including producer Chris Kimsey and sound engineer Phill Brown. Ahmet Ertegun, whom I interviewed in the 1990s, was of special help. Ditto Clive Davis, who never worked with the Stones but understands how a song gets written. See also Jann Wenner's Q&A with Jagger, which ran in *Rolling Stone* December 1995. (I worked on that interview with Wenner, writing questions and editing transcripts.) For specifics on the writing process regarding that first true single, "The Last Time," see *Life* by Keith Richards; *Keith: Standing in the Shadows* by Stanley Booth; and *According to the Rolling Stones*. See also Keith Richards's 1992 interview with Jas Obrecht in *Guitar Player*, in which Keith characterized "The Last Time" as the first true Stones song.

15 · AMERICA

The story of the Stones in that van outside Harrisburg, PA, on the first U.S. tour when the lightning—which seemed to me both real and symbolic—hit comes from Stanley Booth's *The True Adventures of the Rolling Stones*. In addition to my own interviews, information on that first American tour comes from contemporaneous articles as well as the books mentioned above, especially the memoirs by Richards and Wyman. See also *Bill Wyman's Scrapbook*, in which everything that could be clipped or folded is stored and preserved. I also made use of magazine stories written at the time, some of them classics such as Tom Wolfe's profile of Phil Spector, "The First Tycoon of Teen," which is included in Wolfe's collection *The Kandy-Kolored Tangerine-Flake*

Streamline Baby. See also "Teenage Crowd at Airport to Greet the Rolling Stones," *New York Times*, June 2, 1964. On Murray the K, see Wolfe's profile, as well as Nik Cohn's *Awopbopaloobop*. On the American scene at the time, and how "race" music was regarded, I relied on interviews, especially with Lloyd Price, Buddy Guy, Bob Krasnow, Ahmet Ertegun, Clive Davis, Berry Gordy, and Ethan Russell. Especially brilliant on this subject is *New Yorker* writer George W. S. Trow; see his book, *My Pilgrim's Progress*. See also *Main Lines, Blood Feasts, and Bad Taste: A Lester Bangs Reader*, edited by John Morthland; *Escaping the Delta: Robert Johnson and the Invention of the Blues* by Elijah Wald; and Trow's two-part profile of Ahmet Ertegun, "Eclectic, Reminiscent, Amused, Fickle, Perverse," which ran in *The New Yorker* in 1978. On the Stones' other early tours of America I relied on the recollections of firsthand witnesses, especially Gered Mankowitz, the Stones' first official photographer, and Ronnie Schneider, a Stones road manager. On Jagger's sex appeal, see Patti Smith's essay "Jag-arr of the Jungle" (*Creem*, 1973). See also Charlie Watts's 1994 interview with *Mojo*. "All I can remember about that era was being in America somewhere and just seeing the whole balcony moving up and down with girls screaming over it," Watts told the magazine. If you want to know what it all looked like, see *The Lost Rolling Stones Photographs: The Bob Bonis Archive, 1964–1966* by Larry Marion. On Chicago in the early sixties, see everything by Studs Terkel as well as *Chicago: A Biography* by Dominic A. Pacyga and my book *Monsters*. On the history of the blues, I made use of many books (see bibliography), with special attention to *Blues Fell This Morning: Meaning in the Blues* by Paul Oliver; *Deep Blues: A Musical and Cultural History of the Mississippi Delta* by Robert Palmer; *Searching for Robert Johnson: The Life and Legend of the "King of the Delta Blues Singers"* by Peter Guralnick; *Blues People: Negro Music in White America* by LeRoi Jones; *The Blues: A Very Short Introduction* by Elijah Wald; *The Land Where the Blues Began* by Alan Lomax; and *The Devil's Music: A History of the Blues* by Giles Oakley. Also helpful were the essays in David Hajdu's collection, *Heroes and Villains: Essays on Music, Movies, Comics, and Culture*. Ditto David Evans's *Big Road Blues: Tradition and Creativity in the Folk Blues*. Evans is a "Doctor of the Blues," a professor of ethnomusicology at the University of Memphis as well as a serious guitar player. My interview with him was especially enlightening. On Muddy Waters in Chicago, I got much from my interview with Buddy Guy, who took me on a tour of the South and West Sides of Chicago, ending at Muddy's house. This resulted in a *Rolling Stone* story that ran in 2006 ("The Kingpin") and can be visited on the magazine's archive. I also made use of books, including *Can't Be Satisfied: The Life and Times of Muddy Waters* by Robert Gordon. On the great migration, I was helped by old articles from the *Chicago Defender*. See, for example, "When You Come North" (May 30, 1925), which includes the advice to migrants: "When you come North, attire yourself properly before going on the streets. Don't allow people to see you put in bedroom clothes or kitchen aprons." On October 16, 1965, Muddy Waters addressed the Stones directly in the *Defender*. "The Rolling Stones, sure I dig them, they're a part of me, you know they're named after one of my records. Those boys jam." On Leonard Chess and Chess Records, see *Spinning Blues into Gold: The Chess Brothers and the Legendary Chess Records* by Nadine Cohodas; *The Story of Chess Records* by John Collis; and *I Am the Blues: The Willie Dixon Story* by Willie Dixon and Don Snowden, as well as my own book *The Record Men: Chess Records and the Birth of Rock & Roll*. See my interviews with Marshall Chess, who worked at the label with his father and his uncle Phil and later ran a record label for the Stones. Also helpful on Chess were notes written about the Stones for the Rock and Roll Hall of Fame by Chess producer Don Snowden in 1987. Ditto an email exchange I had with Andrew Oldham in 2014. "I guess Chess Records, Vee Jay and Atlantic were the musical Donald Sterlings of their day," Oldham explained. "I had two days. I was not interested in meeting anyone except [Chess engineer] Ron Malo. We cut 13 things in two days. The Stones were in heaven. It was wonderful."

16 · SATISFACTION

The quote that opens this chapter comes from a conversation with Jagger. It was a casual remark, an aside shared while we were working together on a screenplay. It resonated because I was then working up my own general philosophy of the hit. Simply put, I believed that nothing can get going without a hit. In this way, the career of the Stones was made possible only by "Satisfaction," as the career of the United States was made possible only by the U.S. Constitution, which was one of the greatest hits of all time. On the early American tours, see the books mentioned above and below, especially *According to the Rolling Stones*; *The Rolling Stones: Fifty Years* by Christopher Sandford; *The True Adventures of the Rolling Stones* by Stanley Booth; and *Brian Jones: Who Killed Christopher Robin? The Murder of a Rolling Stone* by Terry Rawlings. The backbone of these pages comes from interviews with Richards and Watts, as well as more recent interviews with Stones photographers Gered Mankowitz and Ethan Russell, and Stones manager Ronnie Schneider. The details on the Sinatra/Richards encounter come from Oldham's memoir 2Stoned. The story of "Satisfaction," inception to single, starts with Keith's slumber and the mysterious arrival, as if from heaven, of the riff. A rock 'n' roll legend of Prometheus and the fire, it's well chronicled. The best source is probably Richards's book *Life*, but, as Bob Dylan said, "My father said so many things." On Jack Nitzsche and his role with the Stones, see "Turning the Key of the Universe: Jack Nitzsche Remembered," David Dalton, *Gadfly*. As for the rest of the "Satisfaction" story—finishing the song in Clearwater, Florida, the first recordings, the vote, and the rest—the key sources are primary, including interviews with Jagger and Richards and the memoirs of Richards, Wyman, and Oldham. Almost every stage in the process was captured in photographs. See, for example, the photos collected in *The Rolling Stones: On Camera, Off Guard 1963–69* by Mark Hayward; *The Rolling Stones 1972* by Jim Marshall and Keith Richards; and *The Rolling Stones: A Life on the Road* by the Rolling Stones and Jools Holland. You can see just about any single moment described in this book with a specific well-crafted Google search, such as "Rolling Stones hotel swimming pool Florida." Jagger's comments on songwriting come from my interviews with the band in the 1990s. On the songwriting process, see also the books listed above as well as Jagger's 1995 interview with *Esquire* magazine, "Self Satisfaction." On Allen Klein, see 2Stoned by Andrew Loog Oldham; *Rocks Off: 50 Tracks That Tell the Story of the Rolling Stones* by Bill Janovitz; *John Lennon: The Life* by Philip Norman; *Tune In: The Beatles; All These Years* by Mark Lewisohn; *The Beatles: The Biography* by Bob Spitz; and *Shout! The Beatles in Their Generation* by Philip Norman. See also Fred Goodman's recent book on Klein, *Allen Klein: The Man Who Bailed Out the Beatles, Made the Stones, and Transformed Rock & Roll*, which came out in the course of my own reporting. My brother worked for Klein before law school, which helped me hardly at all. More helpful were my interviews with Klein's nephew Ronnie Schneider, who worked in the law office before setting out on the road with the Stones. Later, when the Stones and Klein broke, Schneider stuck with the stars. When I asked Schneider if this had ruined his relationship with his uncle, he told me a story that I've been turning over in my head ever since. "Yeah, he was mad as hell," Schneider told me, "but my father sat me down in the middle of all that and said, 'Look, Allen's got to live his life, but you've got to live yours.'"

17 · REPORTING

On my own time with the Stones in Canada and on the road, I referred to my memory as well as my notebooks and interviews. Whenever possible, I confirmed my recollection in public sources, newspaper articles and magazine interviews, as well as via interviews given by the principals that can be seen on YouTube. The Internet has remade certain aspects of reporting. You used to have to hustle for the smallest scrap of information. I'm talking press conferences, microfiche. It would now be possible to research an entire book without leaving your room. The split between Jagger and Richards, chronicled here, continues. Recently, when I was asked by *Billboard* magazine to interview Richards about his new record at his house in Connecticut, I was given only one direction: Don't ask about his relationship with Mick. If there was any one person responsible for the special access I got to the Stones in those years—and it was special—it was not Mick or Keith so much as it was Mick's personal assistant Tony King, who championed me all the way. So: Thank you, Tony King. As for Keith's medical kit, that is, the doctor's bag, I included the detail in my first *Rolling Stone* stories about the band, but it was cut. Why? Because this was not so many years after Keith's famous drug bust in Toronto and some editors feared that the mention of that medical bag would attract some overly ambitious FBI agent or cop. No one wants to be the writer or editor responsible for shutting down the Stones. I've felt safe including it here because Richards himself has since chronicled all this and more in his own memoir, *Life*.

18 · ACID

The information on the history of drugs comes from a handful of books, especially *Acid Dreams: The Complete Social History of LSD; The CIA, the Sixties, and Beyond* by Martin A. Lee and Bruce Shlain and *LSD: My Problem Child; Reflections on Sacred Drugs, Mysticism and Science* by Albert Hofmann. Also helpful was *Rolling Stone Magazine: The Uncensored History* by Robert Draper. I relied on interviews as well: with Keith Richards, Charlie Watts, and Ron Wood, but also with Linda Keith, Ahmet Ertegun, Ronnie Schneider, Gered Mankowitz, the keyboardist Ian McLagan, and the sax player Bobby Keys. Especially enlightening was my long interview with Marianne Faithfull. On acid rock, see *1968: The Year That Rocked the World* by Mark

Kurlansky; Nik Cohn's *Awopbopaloobop*; *John Lennon: The Life* by Philip Norman; *The Dark Stuff: Selected Writings on Rock Music* by Nick Kent; *Rock & Roll: An Unruly History* by Robert Palmer; and *Who I Am* by Pete Townshend. See also *Charlie Watts* by Alan Clayson; *Every Night's a Saturday Night: The Rock 'n' Roll Life of Legendary Sax Man Bobby Keys* by Bobby Keys with Bill Ditenhafer; *Faithfull: An Autobiography* by Marianne Faithfull with David Dalton; *Golden Stone: The Untold Life and Tragic Death of Brian Jones* by Laura Jackson; *Keith: Standing in the Shadows* by Stanley Booth; *Keith Richards on Keith Richards: Interviews and Encounters*, edited by Sean Egan; *Life* by Keith Richards; *Naked Lunch* by William S. Burroughs; *Ronnie* by Ron Wood; and *Stone Alone: The Story of a Rock 'n' Roll Band* by Bill Wyman. For Charlie Watts's thoughts on LSD see *S.T.P.: A Journey Through America with the Rolling Stones* by Robert Greenfield and also Keith's 1980 interview with *Zigzag* magazine. But the bible on the Stones and drugs is the book written by their drug dealer, *Up and Down with the Rolling Stones: My Rollercoaster Ride with Keith Richards* by Tony Sanchez, aka Spanish Tony.

19 · THE BUST

While reporting this book, my friend Mark and I drove to Redlands from London. We kicked around, studying the landmarks and comparing them to photos taken on the day of the bust, meanwhile hoping to catch site of Anita Pallenberg, who, we'd been told, still spends time at the house. Pallenberg is the one interview I really wanted for this book and did not get. But I did speak to Marianne Faithfull. She took me through the events leading up to the bust, the bust itself, and its aftermath. Material for these sections comes from this interview—portions of which were included in a story I wrote for *The Wall Street Journal Magazine* ("Marianne Faithfull's Gloriously Reckless Rock 'n' Roll Life," September 4, 2014)—as well as passages from Faithfull's memoir, Richards's memoir, and other books that delve into the subject, including *The Rolling Stones: Fifty Years* by Christopher Sandford; *Up and Down with the Rolling Stones: My Rollercoaster Ride with Keith Richards* by Tony Sanchez; *Jagger: Rebel, Rock Star, Rambler, Rogue* by Marc Spitz; and *According to the Rolling Stones*. I relied on contemporaneous accounts as well, mostly from British broadsheets and tabloids that, more than just reporting, participated in these events. For Marianne Faithfull's background, I turned to several books, most importantly the memoirs of Faithfull and Oldham, as

well as interviews with Faithfull, Peter Asher, Linda Keith, and others. As for
the trippy day at Redlands before the bust, see the iconic photos by Michael
Copper, as well as the books of several journalists and bystanders, including
2Stoned by Andrew Loog Oldham and Keith: Standing in the Shadows by
Stanley Booth. In Keith Richards on Keith Richards: Interviews and Encounters,
edited by Sean Egan, the guitarist muses on the motivation of the authorities
behind the bust: "First, they don't like young kids with a lot of money. But as
long as you don't bother them, that's cool. But we bothered them. We bothered 'em because of the way we looked, the way we'd act. Because we never
showed any reverence for them whatsoever. Whereas the Beatles had."

20 · MOROCCO

I planned to go to Morocco and Tangier and stay in the same hotels, visit the
same restaurants, walk the same streets and bazaars, and take the same drugs
as the Stones in '67, but didn't. Because I ran out of money, then my mom died.
The information in these passages was woven from various sources, including
my interview with Faithfull, the books mentioned above, and a handful of others, especially Self-Portrait with Friends: The Selected Diaries of Cecil Beaton,
1922–1974 by Cecil Beaton and Richard Buckle and Cecil Beaton: Photographs
1920–1970 by Philippe Garner, David Mellor, and Cecil Beaton. On Anita Pallenberg's background and relationship with Brian Jones, see Golden Stone: the
Untold Life and Tragic Death of Brian Jones by Laura Jackson; The True Adventures of the Rolling Stones by Stanley Booth; Up and Down with the Rolling
Stones: My Rollercoaster Ride with Keith Richards by Tony Sanchez; Keith Rich-
ards: A Rock 'n' Roll Life by Bill Milkowski, edited by Valeria Manferto de
Fabianis; The Dark Stuff: Selected Writings on Rock Music by Nick Kent; and
Brian Jones: Who Killed Christopher Robin? The Murder of a Rolling Stone by
Terry Rawlings. On Kenneth Anger and the dark arts, I relied on a lot of
books, some of them nuts: Book of the Law and The Book of Lies by Aleister
Crowley; Do What Thou Wilt: A Life of Aleister Crowley by Lawrence Sutin;
Kenneth Anger by Alice L. Hutchison; and Anger: The Unauthorized Biography
of Kenneth Anger by Bill Landis. See also Blown Away: The Rolling Stones and
the Death of the Sixties by A. E. Hotchner and Mick: The Wild Life and Mad
Genius of Jagger by Christopher Andersen. The best source on the Keith/
Anita affair is Keith himself. Certain passages of his memoir are a rock 'n' roll
Madame Bovary. Flaubert plus Elvis equals Life. In writing about Morocco

and Tangier, I was inspired by a handful of novels, including *The Sheltering Sky* by Paul Bowles and *Naked Lunch* by William S. Burroughs, which includes my favorite description of Tangier: "Cooking smells of all countries hang over the City, a haze of opium, hashish, the resinous red smoke of *yagé*, smell of the jungle and salt water and the rotting river and dried excrement and sweat and genitals. High mountain flutes, jazz and bebop, one-stringed Mongol instruments, gypsy xylophones, African drums, Arab bagpipes . . ."

21 · THE TRIAL

Personal interviews, court records, contemporaneous newspaper accounts, and a handful of books supplied most of the information presented in this chapter. Of special importance were discussions with Marianne Faithfull. Equally important were the memoirs of Faithfull and Richards, as well as several books: *Jagger: Rebel, Rock Star, Rambler, Rogue* by Marc Spitz; *And on Piano . . . Nicky Hopkins: The Extraordinary Life of Rock's Greatest Session Man* by Julian Dawson; *The Rolling Stones: Fifty Years* by Christopher Sandford; and *Who I Am* by Pete Townshend. On *Sgt. Pepper, Satanic Majesties,* and other artifacts of the psychedelic era, see Cohn's *Awopbopaloobop; John Lennon: The Life* by Philip Norman; *The Mammoth Book of the Rolling Stones: An Anthology of the Best Writing About the Greatest Rock 'n' Roll Band in the World,* edited by Sean Egan; *Stone Alone: The Story of a Rock 'n' Roll Band* by Bill Wyman; *Rock & Roll: An Unruly History* by Robert Palmer; and *Up and Down with the Rolling Stones: My Rollercoaster Ride with Keith Richards* by Tony Sanchez. On Andrew Oldham's departure from the band, see *2Stoned*; see also *Rocks Off: 50 Tracks That Tell the Story of the Rolling Stones* by Bill Janovitz. The exchange that ends the chapter comes from my email correspondence with Oldham. I've paraphrased. Robert Fraser died in 1986, nineteen years after he was released from prison; see "Art Dealer Robert Fraser's Swinging London," Liesl Schillinger, *Wall Street Journal,* February 23, 2015. On the cover of *Sgt. Pepper*: in the final pressing, Hitler's face was obscured.

22 · THE DEATH OF BRIAN JONES, PART ONE

In chronicling stage one of Brian Jones's decline, I relied on several sources, the first being books, including *Are We Still Rolling? Studios, Drugs and*

Rock 'n' Roll—One Man's Journey Recording Classic Albums by Phill Brown; Cohn's *Awopbopaloobop*; *The Rolling Stones: Fifty Years* by Christopher Sandford; *Golden Stone: The Untold Life and Tragic Death of Brian Jones* by Laura Jackson; *Life* by Keith Richards; *Let It Bleed: The Rolling Stones, Altamont, and the End of the Sixties* by Ethan A. Russell with Gerard Van der Leun; *Up and Down with the Rolling Stones: My Rollercoaster Ride with Keith Richards* by Tony Sanchez; *Faithfull: An Autobiography* by Marianne Faithfull with David Dalton; *Stone Alone: The Story of a Rock 'n' Roll Band* by Bill Wyman; and *Brian Jones: Who Killed Christopher Robin? The Murder of a Rolling Stone* by Terry Rawlings. Andrew Oldham writes terrifically on Brian Jones in the bad time in *Stoned.* See also Nick Kent's brilliant writing on those waning days in *The Dark Stuff: Selected Writings on Rock Music.* Ditto Lou Reed's 1971 essay "Fallen Knights and Fallen Ladies." "After the Beatles came the Stones and of the Stones one could never have ignored Brian Jones with his puffed up Pisces, all-knowing, all-suffering fish eyes, his incredible clothes, those magnificent scarves, Brian always ahead of style, perfect Brian," writes Reed. "How could Brian have asthma, a psychological disease (we're told) and certainly something strange for a member of a rock and roll group." I learned still more from interviews, especially those with people who spent time with Jones at the end: Phill Brown, Chris Kimsey, Paul Jones, Gered Mankowitz, Marianne Faithfull, Ronnie Schneider, and Ethan Russell, who took those famous sad pictures. See also: "Brian Jones: The Bittersweet Symphony" by Rob Chapman, *Mojo,* July 1999; Keith Richards Q&A, Robert Greenfield, *Rolling Stone,* 1971. The quotes that end the chapter—"A potential suicide?" and "Certainly"—appear in several places, including *The Rolling Stones: Fifty Years* by Christopher Sandford. Here's how Pete Townshend describes Jones at the end in *Who I Am:* "I hadn't seen him for a year or more. His eyes were bloodshot and he was in tears, wilting under the effect of an elaborate cocktail of uppers and downers."

23 · SYMPATHY FOR THE DEVIL

This chapter is a magpie creation, put together from a handful of sources. You start with the movie itself, Jean-Luc Godard's *One Plus One.* The making of the song has been chronicled in many of the books already mentioned. For background on the filmmaker, I relied on *Everything Is Cinema: The Working Life of Jean-Luc Godard* by Richard Brody as well as Pauline Kael's *New Yorker* essay on Godard collected in *The Age of Movies: Selected Writings of Pauline Kael*. Kael's description of Godard's first feature-length work, *Breathless*, can stand for the Stones as portrayed in the early articles: "What sneaks up on you in *Breathless* is that the engagingly coy young hood with his loose, random grace and the impervious, passively butch American girl are as shallow and empty as the shiny young faces you see in sports cars and in suburban supermarkets, and in newspapers after unmotivated, pointless crimes. And you're left with the horrible suspicion that this is a new race, bred in chaos, accepting chaos as natural, and not caring one way or another about it or anything else." I reread *The Master and Margarita* by Mikhail Bulgakov. What a great book, filled with echoes and portents. I began to see hints of it all over the Stones. Good books have a way of bleeding into the rest of life. For example, I could not read Bulgakov's description of the devil without thinking of Jagger: "Two eyes bored into Margarita's face. The right eye had a gold spark deep in its center and could pierce a soul to its depths; the left eye was vacant and black, like the narrow eye of a needle, like the entrance to a bottomless well of darkness and shadow."

24 · THE GOLDEN RUN

On the creation of "Jumpin' Jack Flash" and the start of the golden run, see *Life* by Keith Richards; *And on Piano . . . Nicky Hopkins: The Extraordinary Life of Rock's Greatest Session Man* by Julian Dawson; and *The Rolling Stones: Fifty Years* by Christopher Sandford. I relied on Marianne Faithfull's recollection of this time and these events, in my interview with her as well as in her memoirs *Faithfull: An Autobiography* with David Dalton and *Memories, Dreams and Reflections*. Open G tuning is described in Keith's book *Life*, but I still remained fuzzy on it even after several readings. I don't think you can fully understand it if you don't play guitar—you need to goof and experiment to get what's going on and understand how liberating the alternative guitar tunings can be. Special help came from my guitar teacher, Brendan Sadat. Ditto Dennis Ambrose at Random House. See also *Escaping the Delta: Robert Johnson and the Invention of the Blues* by Elijah Wald and *Rocks Off: 50*

Tracks That Tell the Story of the Rolling Stones by Bill Janovitz, who, helpfully, plays guitar and sings in the band Buffalo Tom. Cynthia Cotts, who worked with me on this book and remained dogged on the topic of getting G tuning just right, tracked down the secretary of the Lute Society in England and a history assembled by the Lute Society of America. Both sources agreed that the standard tuning evolved as a switch from the standard tuning of the five-string medieval lute. In other words, the early six-string players were running away from tradition in the same way Keith would four centuries later. On "Honky Tonk Women" and Ry Cooder's beef with Richards, see *Rocks Off* by Bill Janovitz; *Stone Alone* by Bill Wyman; and Robert Greenfield's 1971 *Rolling Stone* interview with Richards. I tried to talk to Cooder for this book, but nope. For a fascinating take on this, see "Ry Cooder's Elegant Indignation" by my friend Alec Wilkinson, which ran on the *New Yorker* website on August 29, 2011:

> If you wonder what [Cooder's] sensibility sounds like when applied to rock 'n' roll—one version of it anyway—the most widely known example I can think of comes from the period when Cooder had been hired to augment the Rolling Stones during the recording of "Let It Bleed." He was playing by himself in the studio, goofing around with some changes, when Mick Jagger danced over and said, How do you do that? You tune the E string down to D, place your fingers there, and pull them off quickly, that's very good. Keith, perhaps you should see this. And before long, the Rolling Stones were collecting royalties for "Honky Tonk Women," which sounds precisely like a Ry Cooder song and absolutely nothing like any other song ever produced by the Rolling Stones in more than forty years.

On *Beggars Banquet*, Jimmy Miller, and the Olympic studio routine, see *Backstage Passes & Backstabbing Bastards: Memoirs of a Rock 'n' Roll Survivor* by Al Kooper; *Stone Alone* by Bill Wyman; and *Are We Still Rolling?* by Phill Brown. I relied on interviews, too—with Chris Kimsey, Phill Brown, Al Kooper, and Anna Menzies. The Glyn Johns anecdote—"Mick was smokin' a big joint"— comes from "Engineer Andy Johns Discusses the Making of the Rolling Stones' 'Exile on Main Street'" by Harvey Kubernik, *Goldmine*, May 2010. The Marianne Faithfull incident—BURN BABY BURN—comes from *Are We Still Rolling?* by Phill Brown. The story of the fire comes from Chris Kimsey, who spent a day with me at Olympic, then sent me off to see other members of the old crew.

25 · THE DEATH OF BRIAN JONES, PART TWO

Information on Cotchford Farm comes from several sources, including *Golden Stone: The Untold Life and Tragic Death of Brian Jones* by Laura Jackson; *Stone Alone* by Bill Wyman; *Brian Jones: Who Killed Christopher Robin?* by Terry Rawlings; and *A. A. Milne: The Man Behind Winnie-the-Pooh* by Ann Thwaite. Especially helpful was my visit to the house, made with my friend Mark in the winter of 2014. On Brian's continued decline, I relied on the interviews and books cited for "The Death of Brian Jones, Part One" as well as Nick Kent's *The Dark Stuff*. For the sad scene in which the Stones fire Brian, I relied on various sources, including Laura Jackson's *Golden Stone*, Marc Spitz's Jagger bio, and *Up and Down with the Rolling Stones* by Tony Sanchez. Charlie Watts's quote—"I'm sure it nearly killed him"—appears in "Brian Jones: The Bittersweet Symphony" by Rob Chapman, *Mojo*, July 1999. Brian's telegram—I'M VERY UNHAPPY. SO UNHAPPY—appears in *Golden Stone* by Laura Jackson. On Brian's post-Stones plans, see *The Rolling Stones* by Robert Palmer and *Brian Jones: Who Killed Christopher Robin?* by Terry Rawlings. On Brian's songs, see *The Rolling Stones* by Robert Palmer; *Stone Alone* by Bill Wyman; and *Stoned* by Andrew Oldham. The details regarding Mick Taylor and his background come from *The Rolling Stones: Fifty Years* by Christopher Sandford and *Ronnie* by Ron Wood. See also the articles "Mick Taylor Interviewed" by Tony Norman, *Fusion*, November 14, 1969, and "Rolling Stone in Exile," Robin Eggar's interview with Mick Taylor in *The Sunday Express Magazine*, May 2002. I interviewed Taylor's onetime boss, John Mayall. Details regarding Brian's death, that mysterious fade-out at the center of rock 'n' roll, have been covered extensively. My best sources were *Life* by Keith Richards and *Stone Alone* by Bill Wyman. Jones's obit can be read on the *New York Times* online archive. Frank Thorogood and Tom Keylock: this long history of he said/she said shenanigans can be read about in half a dozen books, including *The Rolling Stones: Fifty Years* by Christopher Sandford; *Golden Stone* by Laura Jackson; and *Brian Jones: Who Killed Christopher Robin?* by Terry Rawlings. The mystery of Brian's death will probably never be solved. As my father says, it depends less on what happened than on who you are.

26 · DEATH FUGUE

An amazing aspect of working on this book is that almost everything I researched and wrote about has been photographed and filmed and can be viewed. I relied on several books and interviews while writing about the Stones' famous Hyde Park concert, performed shortly after the death of Brian Jones. As for interviews, Sam Cutler was especially helpful. As for books, in addition to the many mentioned above, I am indebted to *Let It Bleed: The Rolling Stones, Altamont, and the End of the Sixties* by Ethan A. Russell with Gerard Van der Leun; *Nankering with the Rolling Stones: The Untold Story of the Early Days* by James Phelge; *And on Piano . . . Nicky Hopkins: The Extraordinary Life of Rock's Greatest Session Man* by Julian Dawson; and *You Can't Always Get What You Want: My Life with the Rolling Stones, the Grateful Dead, and Other Wonderful Reprobates* by Sam Cutler. (See also Tony Norman's interview with Mick Taylor, which ran in *Fusion* magazine on November 14, 1969.) But just as important was the footage of the show itself—film and pictures that capture each moment, each detail of the greater scene. A DVD of the concert, which had been made for TV, was released in 2006. You can watch it, as you can watch the film about the Stones' return to Hyde Park in 2013—part of the band's celebration of its fiftieth anniversary. They actually played two concerts in Hyde Park in the summer of 2013. Before the first show, Jagger joked, "I'll try and keep the poetry to a minimum." (See *The Hollywood Reporter*, "The Rolling Stones Returning to Hyde Park After 44 Years, Set North American Tour," by Stuart Kemp, April 3, 2013.) Jagger's quote given to a TV reporter before the '69 show—"Brian will be at the concert"—appears in *Up and Down with the Rolling Stones* by Tony Sanchez. See also *A Prince Among Stones: That Business with the Rolling Stones and Other Adventures* by Prince Rupert Loewenstein, who would take over the band's finances. Hyde Park was his first Stones concert, and in his book he writes about a strange exchange he had with Jagger that day: "I asked him whether he thought that he could move the crowd into action by his voice in the way Hitler had done. He thought carefully and replied, Yes. To get the crowd to pull something down would probably take twenty minutes, but to get them to build something could be done but would take much longer, say an hour." On Brian's funeral, see the books mentioned above, especially the Brian Jones bios *Golden Stone* by Laura Jackson and *Brian Jones: Who Killed Christopher Robin?* by Terry Rawlings. The quote by Shirley Arnold—"We saw the coffin"—appears in *The True Adventures of the Rolling Stones* by Stanley Booth.

27 · DOWN UNDER

The story of Jagger and Faithfull's trip to Australia, which is pretty much the sole subject of this chapter, comes from Faithfull. Some from a phone interview I did with her in the summer of 2014, some from her memoirs, especially that first gem *Faithfull: An Autobiography* with David Dalton. It's worth going back and watching the film Jagger was in Australia to shoot, *Ned Kelly*, directed by Tony Richardson. It's a goofball, would-be, not good though not terrible, utterly forgettable film except for Jagger.

28 · ROCK 'N' ROLL CIRCUS

On Laurel Canyon, see *Laurel Canyon: The Inside Story of Rock-and-Roll's Legendary Neighborhood* by Michael Walker and *Canyon of Dreams: The Magic and the Music of Laurel Canyon* by Harvey Kubernik. On Gram Parsons, I relied on interviews as well as books. Phil Kaufman, who was Gram's road manager and friend, told me about the musician, as did Marianne Faithfull and Sid Griffin. Griffin never knew Parsons but has made a fetish of his legacy; see Griffin's *Gram Parsons: A Music Biography*. Griffin's band, the Long Ryders, has carried the cosmic country tradition into my generation. For me, most helpful were *Hickory Wind: The Life and Times of Gram Parsons* by Ben Fong-Torres; *Twenty Thousand Roads: The Ballad of Gram Parsons and His Cosmic American Music* by David N. Meyer; *Gram Parsons: God's Own Singer* by Jason Walker; *Calling Me Home: Gram Parsons and the Roots of Country Rock* by Bob Kealing; and *Road Mangler Deluxe* by Phil Kaufman with Colin White. See also *Country: The Twisted Roots of Rock 'n' Roll* by Nick Tosches. Keith's quote—"Gram taught me country music"—is from *Life* by Keith Richards. The story of "Honky Tonk Women" and how it was reverse engineered into "Country Honk" appears in several places, including *Hickory Wind* by Ben Fong-Torres. I am thankful to Byron Berline, who spent hours on the phone with me from his fiddle store in Guthrie, Oklahoma, telling stories about the Stones as well as stories about the fiddle, Appalachia, and the cool wind that blows through the coal country in November. *Let It Bleed:* The story of the record and the songs that make it up come from many sources, first and foremost being the memoirs of Richards and Wyman as well as *Are We Still Rolling?* by Phill Brown. On the movie *Performance*, see *The Rolling Stones: Fifty Years* by Christopher Sandford; Marc Spitz's *Jagger*;

Up and Down with the Rolling Stones by Tony Sanchez; *Faithfull* by Marianne Faithfull with David Dalton; *Keith: Standing in the Shadows* by Stanley Booth; and *Life*, in which Richards writes of Pallenberg's affair with Jagger. In addition to the books mentioned above, the stuff on Olympic and the recording of "You Can't Always Get What You Want" comes from interviews with Chris Kimsey, Phill Brown, and Anna Menzies. See also *Backstage Passes & Backstabbing Bastards: Memoirs of a Rock 'n' Roll Survivor* by Al Kooper. Most important were my interviews with Al Kooper, especially the day I spent with him at his house in Massachusetts. Al Kooper is among the coolest men alive. He does not know everything, but what he does know he knows really well.

29 · 1969

For historical background on 1969, I relied on the archive of *Time* magazine and *The New York Times* and a handful of books, including *Postwar* by Tony Judt and *1969: The Year Everything Changed* by Rob Kirkpatrick. On the Stones tour that began at the end of that year, I relied on my interview with Sam Cutler, as well as the recollections of Jagger and Richards in interviews and books. On the Stones at Muscle Shoals, the best source, and the source of many of the incidents described, is Stanley Booth, who set up the session, which he describes in *True Adventures of the Rolling Stones*. Much in this chapter comes from my interviews with the filmmaker Albert Maysles, who was with the Stones from the end of the tour until they left America that winter. The back-and-forth in the studio was written up in the books of Stanley Booth and Bill Wyman. Much of it was filmed by Albert Maysles and his brother David and can be seen in *Gimme Shelter*, their Altamont documentary. See also Greg Camalier's documentary on the studio, *Muscle Shoals*, which includes interviews with Jagger and Richards. I drew on several books, too: *Muscle Shoals Sound Studio: How the Swampers Changed American Music* by Carla Jean Whitley; *The Muscle Shoals Legacy of Fame* by Blake Ells; and *The Wrecking Crew: The Inside Story of Rock and Roll's Best-Kept Secret* by Kent Hartman. An interesting note about Jagger's "Brown Sugar" lyric "scarred old slaver": in *Life*, Richards claims Jagger was actually singing "Skydog slaver," a tribute to Muscle Shoals standout Duane Allman. On "Wild Horses": Jagger later claimed the song was not about Faithfull, but I don't believe him. Alternate versions of songs the Stones cut at Muscle Shoals were released in the summer of 2015, included on a deluxe edition of the album

Sticky Fingers. I emailed Al Kooper soon after—he'd played on a famous lost version of "Brown Sugar," recorded at Olympic Studios on the occasion of Keith's and Bobby Keys's birthdays in December 1970. Eric Clapton plays guitar on this version, Al Kooper plays piano. "They pushed back the tables of food and booze, got out the instruments, and started to go at it," Kooper said. On the biographical background of "Wild Horses" and how Jagger changed it, see *Life* by Keith Richards, as well as interviews with Richards and Marianne Faithfull. Keith's quote, "He changed it all around," appears in Christopher Sandford's *The Rolling Stones: Fifty Years.*

30 · THANATOS IN STEEL

The Altamont chapter is inside the belly of the whale. Its sources include interviews new and old, reporting trips, newspaper articles, memoirs, history books, photographs, film. I interviewed so many people involved with the show I felt as if I was getting thirteen views of the same blackbird. The list included at least nine people who were on the stage that night: the Stones themselves, and also Albert Maysles, who made the film; Sam Cutler, who was running the show; and Ronnie Schneider, who was looking after the musicians. But the chapter is broken into sections and each section is distinct, composed of a unique set of sources and opinions.

On Sonny Barger, the Hell's Angels, and the history of the motorcycle gangs, those great steely hordes, I relied on several books, including: *Hell's Angel: The Life and Times of Sonny Barger and the Hell's Angels Motorcycle Club* by Ralph "Sonny" Barger with Keith and Kent Zimmerman; *Hell's Angels: A Strange and Terrible Saga* by Hunter S. Thompson; *No Angel: My Harrowing Undercover Journey to the Inner Circle of the Hell's Angels* by Jay Dobyns; and *Hell's Angels: Three Can Keep a Secret If Two Are Dead* (best subtitle ever) by Y. Lavigne. See also that founding document, the magazine story that led to the movie, that inspired a thousand hard cases: "Cyclists' Raid: A Story" by Frank Rooney, which appeared in *Harper's Magazine* in January 1951.

On the negotiations that led to the Altamont concert, I drew on my interviews with Albert Maysles and Ronnie Schneider, a Stones employee who was party to the talks. The talks themselves, held in San Francisco, can be glimpsed in the Maysles film *Gimme Shelter.* Especially important was my interview with Sam Cutler, who stage-managed the Stones and can be seen

throughout the film. I also drew on my interview with Grateful Dead manager Rock Scully, who supposedly first broached the idea of the free concert
in the Bay Area.

On Mick and Keith and their visit to Altamont on the eve of the concert,
I drew on my interviews with Cutler and Schneider; see also the books of
Keith Richards and Stanley Booth.

On drugs and violence at the show, and the importance of the show in
general, I relied on interviews with Sam Cutler, Ronnie Schneider, Ethan
Russell, and Albert Maysles, all of whom were onstage that night. See also
the recollections in books, including *On the Road with the Rolling Stones:
Twenty Years of Lipstick, Handcuffs, and Chemicals* by Chet Flippo; Marc
Spitz's *Jagger*; *Up and Down with the Rolling Stones* by Tony Sanchez; *Hickory
Wind* by Ben Fong-Torres; *Stone Alone* by Bill Wyman; and *Keith Richards on
Keith Richards: Interviews and Encounters*, edited by Sean Egan. I also con-
sulted "Charlie Watts: The Rock" by Robert Sandall, *Mojo*, May 1994.

Sonny Barger on KSAN-FM. The interview, including the passages I've
quoted—"I ain't no cop"—can be heard on YouTube.

On Mick and how he behaved, see the documentary *Gimme Shelter*, as
well as my interviews with Sam Cutler and Ethan Russell. See also *Psychotic
Reactions and Carburetor Dung: The Work of a Legendary Critic; Rock 'n' Roll
as Literature and Literature as Rock 'n' Roll* by Lester Bangs, edited by Greil
Marcus. On November 16, 1969, Ralph Gleason wrote a column about a
Stones show earlier in the tour that seems to presage his criticism of Altamont, suggesting the violence was a case of showmanship run amok: "The
Rolling Stones show last Sunday deserves some comment. . . . A huge man,
looking like Theodore Bikel, went along the seats and told everybody to go
down and crowd the stage. I saw him do it. There was an onstage fight between Bill Graham and one of Jagger's management, which ended with Graham throwing the cat off the stage. What Jagger and his management want,
really, is controlled riot. Apparently, Mick is so insecure he cannot believe
people dig him unless he is threatened by a mob at the lip of the stage. It is
really a shame. The withdrawal of the ushers and guards over Graham's ob-
jections was quite obvious. I witnessed too that it created a situation that was
quite dangerous." As for Jagger trying to talk down the crowd: this version
comes from Stanley Booth's book *The True Adventures of the Rolling Stones*
and has been checked against the film by Cynthia Cotts. On the Angels and
their behavior before and after the concert, see Barger's biography, as well as
my interviews with Cutler, Russell, and Schneider. Keith's quote about Thun-

derbird and Ripple comes from his memoir, *Life*. On Meredith Hunter, see *The True Adventures of the Rolling Stones* by Stanley Booth; *Hell's Angels* by Ralph "Sonny" Barger; *Life* by Keith Richards; and *Let It Bleed: The Rolling Stones, Altamont, and the End of the Sixties* by Ethan A. Russell with Gerard Van der Leun. On the last minutes of Hunter's life, I relied on my interview with Robert Hiatt, the doctor who attended him.

Here's Greil Marcus, quoted in *Salon*, on the Stones' post-stabbing performance at Altamont: "It was almost as if the only way they could get out alive was to play so well that people would step back from them in awe. I'm not talking about calculation, but an instinct."

The backlash against the Stones at Altamont was led, surprisingly, by *Rolling Stone* magazine. Ralph Gleason, who founded the magazine with Jann Wenner, described the motivation this way: "We either go out of business right now or else cover Altamont like it was World War II." Sources on this include *Rolling Stone Magazine: The Uncensored History* by Robert Draper; *1969: The Year Everything Changed* by Rob Kirkpatrick; *Altamont: Death of Innocence in the Woodstock Nation*, edited by Jonathan Eisen; and *My Pilgrim's Progress* by George W. S. Trow. See also "Eclectic, Reminiscent, Amused, Fickle, Perverse," George W. S. Trow, *The New Yorker*, May 29 and June 5, 1978; "Jag-arr of the Jungle" by Patti Smith, *Creem*, January 1973. For pictures of Altamont, see *Altamont* by Keith C. Lee and the Honorable John J. McEneny. The backlash touched everyone involved with this disaster, including the filmmakers. In a wrongheaded review of the movie that ran in *The New Yorker*, the otherwise spot-on Pauline Kael took the Maysles brothers to task, suggesting that by setting up the cameras and lights and establishing the filming conditions, they were at least partly responsible for the violence. They did not just film, in other words—they incited, even staged. The Maysleses responded to the critique in a brilliant letter—Kael was attacking not just the movie, but the very notion of cinema verité—that *The New Yorker* never published. The entire contretemps can be read at thedocumentaryblog .com/2007/09/10/pauline-kael-vs-gimme-shelter. Michael Sragow investigated Kael's charges for *Salon*; his article can be read at salon.com/2000/08/10/ gimme_shelter_2.

On the saga of Sam Cutler, what happened to him at the show, after the show, and in the days that followed, I relied primarily on Cutler's version of events. See also Cutler's book, *You Can't Always Get What You Want*. On the Maysles brothers' reckoning with the Angels, I relied on my interview with Albert Maysles as well as interviews with Ronnie Schneider, who was a producer on *Gimme Shelter*, and Ethan Russell. On the Angels' grudge against the Stones and rumors of their attempts to assassinate Jagger, see "Hells Angels Plotted to Kill Mick Jagger, Agent Says" by Mike Nizza, *The New York Times*, March 3, 2008. See also *Mick: The Wild Life and Mad Genius of Jagger* by Christopher Andersen. On Meredith Hunter's grave and the aftermath of Altamont in general, see "Altamont Death; Angel Not Guilty," *Rolling Stone*, February 18, 1971; and *Let It Bleed* by Ethan A. Russell with Gerard Van der Leun. On the fate of the Altamont site, see "R.I.P. Altamont Raceway" by David White, *San Francisco Chronicle*, May 25, 2009. In 1995, Jann Wenner asked Jagger how he felt about Altamont and the killing, all these years later. "Well, awful. I mean, just awful," Jagger said. "You feel a responsibility. How could it all have been so silly and wrong? . . . How awful it was to have had this experience and how awful it was for someone to get killed and how sad it was for his family and how dreadfully the Hell's Angels behaved."

31 · SMACK

On Keith Richards and heroin, see Richards's memoir, *Life*. ("I have no clear recollection of the first time I tried heroin," he writes. "It was probably slipped in with a line of coke, in a speedball—a mixture of coke and smack.") Also helpful were my interviews with Stones lawyer and fixer Bill Carter. Ditto Marshall Chess—son of Leonard—who worked for the Stones in the 1970s and was himself smack-addicted. See also Keith's 1980 interview with *Zigzag* magazine, in which he discussed addiction. On heroin in general—what it was like, why they loved it—I was informed by interviews with Marianne Faithfull and Chris Kimsey and by several books mentioned above, including *Acid Dreams* by Martin A. Lee and Bruce Shlain; *Every Night's a Saturday Night* by Bobby Keys; *Faithfull: An Autobiography* by Marianne Faithfull with David Dalton; *Keith: Standing in the Shadows* by Stanley Booth; *Naked Lunch* by William S. Burroughs; *Ronnie* by Ron Wood; *Stone Alone* by Bill Wyman; *Up and Down with the Rolling Stones* by Tony Sanchez; and *Who I Am* by Pete Townshend. And of course *Fear and Loathing in Las Vegas* by Hunter S. Thompson.

On the tremendous fisting of the Stones by Allen Klein and Mick's efforts to set the band back on a sound financial footing, I relied on discussions with Ronnie Schneider and on newspaper articles and books, including Fred Goodman's *Allen Klein*; Marc Spitz's *Jagger*; and Bill Janovitz's *Rocks Off*. A definitive source is the book written by the Stones' financial guru, *A Prince Among Stones: That Business with the Rolling Stones and Other Adventures* by Prince Rupert Loewenstein. When the book was published in 2013, Jagger commented: "Call me old-fashioned, but I don't think your ex–bank manager should be discussing your financial dealings and personal information in public." (*The Mail on Sunday*, February 9, 2013.)

My crucial source on the Villa Nellcôte and the making of the album *Exile on Main Street* was June Shelley, who worked as a kind of girl Friday for the Stones in the South of France. I supplemented my interviews with Shelley with a visit to the house and with a handful of books: *Exile on Main Street: A Season in Hell with the Rolling Stones* by Robert Greenfield; *John Lennon: The Life* by Philip Norman; and *Stone Alone* by Bill Wyman. And of course *Life* by Keith Richards—that's the best. The scene at Nellcôte was perfectly captured by the French photographer Dominique Tarlé in a book titled *Exile*, which is hard to find and (if you do) incredibly expensive.

On the making of *Exile on Main Street* and the music itself, I was guided by Bobby Keys, who was the guy playing sax in the nook at the end of the hall. We spoke for the last time shortly before he died in 2014. (See "Rolling Stones Saxophonist Bobby Keys Dead at 70," *Rolling Stone*, December 2, 2014.) Also helpful were Bobby Keys's *Every Night's a Saturday Night*; Julian Dawson's *And on Piano . . . Nicky Hopkins*; John Morthland's *Main Lines, Blood Feasts, and Bad Taste*; and Bill Janovitz's *Exile on Main Street*.

On Gram Parsons, Joshua Tree, and his death, I relied on my interview with Parsons's friend and road manager, Phil Kaufman, as well as books: *According to the Rolling Stones*; *Hickory Wind: The Life and Times of Gram Parsons* by Ben Fong-Torres; *Road Mangler Deluxe* by Phil Kaufman with Colin White; and *Twenty Thousand Roads* by David N. Meyer. For a heartbreaking depiction of those last days, see Nick Kent's article "Twilight in Babylon: The Rolling Stones After the Sixties," collected in *The Dark Stuff: Selected Writings on Rock Music*. On fleeing France and finishing the record in Los Angeles, see *Life* by Keith Richards.

32 · "WHERE'S MICK?"

In the winter of 2014, for reasons I don't fully understand, I was overwhelmed by a desire to go to the places where Keith Richards shot up and kicked heroin, went cold turkey, suffered the horrors of withdrawal, cried and was carried to heaven and hell, got clean and relapsed. I wanted to see where his blood had been junked up and transfused, according to what Richards calls a media myth. I drove from Villefranche to Lake Geneva, from exile to hospital, paradise to purgatory. Along the way, I read the books and articles that inform this chapter—there is nothing like reading an epic in the land where that epic was made. These include *Exile on Main Street* by Robert Greenfield; *Every Night's a Saturday Night* by Bobby Keys; *Life* by Keith Richards; *Rocks Off* by Bill Janovitz; *The Rolling Stones: Fifty Years* by Christopher Sandford; *S.T.P.: A Journey Through America with the Rolling Stones* by Robert Greenfield; *Stone Alone* by Bill Wyman; and *Up and Down with the Rolling Stones* by Tony Sanchez. See also Keith Richards's 1980 interview with *Zigzag* magazine, in which, speaking of smack addiction, he said, "I know the angle—waiting for the man, sitting in some goddamn basement waiting for some creep to come, with four other guys sniveling, puking and retching around, and you're waiting for something to happen, and it's already been 24 hours and you're going into the worst. How does it feel, baby?" But the most important source for these pages was June Shelley, who vividly described her trip with Keith from the hotel outside Geneva to Dr. Denber's clinic in Vevey—from life to death and back to life. See also Nick Kent's essay "Twilight in Babylon: The Rolling Stones After the Sixties." On Dandelion Richards, her birth and life, see *Exile on Main Street* by Robert Greenfield, *The Rolling Stones: Fifty Years* by Christopher Sandford, *Up and Down with the Rolling Stones* by Tony Sanchez. See also the article "Pictured: The Daughter of Rolling Stones Hellraiser Keith Richards Whose Birth Nearly Tore the Band Apart," by Richard Simpson, *The Daily Mail*, May 18, 2010.

33 · THE LAST GREAT RECORD

While traveling with the Stones in the 1990s, I interviewed each member of the band several times. I also interviewed many of the people putting together and running the show, the engineers, musicians, and techs, including Michael Cohl, the promoter; Chuck Leavell, the keyboardist; Darryl Jones, the bassist who replaced Bill Wyman; Fiona Williams, the band's stylist; and Jim Callaghan, Mick Jagger's bodyguard. "I think they're still rebels," Callaghan told me as we sat in a car outside the arena as the Stones played. "Keith should have been a gypsy. Woody, always laughing and joking. Mick's always been serious. While he's doing this. But then you get him in another place and he'll be laughing. Charlie's always been the same. Never changes."

Even when not cited, these interviews and the knowledge that came from them form the backdrop. On my time working with Mick Jagger on the screenplay, I referred to my notebooks as well as my memory. The older I get, the more aware I become that a person is little more than a memory machine. You just keep vacuuming them up. What do you do with all this detritus, all these fading hotel rooms? You write a book. The project I was working on with Mick Jagger and Martin Scorsese—I toiled at it for eight years, from 1997 till 2005—has morphed and changed and been reborn over the years. It finally made its debut in the winter of 2016 on HBO as the weekly series *Vinyl*, a show I co-created with Jagger, Scorsese, and Terence Winter.

On Mick Taylor's exit from the band, see *According to the Rolling Stones* as well as Mick Taylor's interview with Tony Norman, *Fusion* magazine, November 14, 1969, and his interview with Robin Eggar, "Rolling Stone in Exile," *The Sunday Express Magazine*, May 2002. On Ron Wood, his background and work with the Stones, I relied on *Ronnie* by Ron Wood and *Stone Alone* by Bill Wyman as well as on my own interviews.

My conversation with Jagger about Richards's book was on a phone call arranged by Jann Wenner. Jann tapped me to review Keith's book for *Rolling Stone*. The magazine had run an excerpt of the book, and Jann wanted me to get Mick's side of the story before I sat down to write the review. Jagger asked me not to "run tape on" him, and I did not. He did not say the conversation was off the record, so I took notes. And those are what I've referred to here. I believe this is the only time Jagger has ever commented on Keith's book. He's usually mum about all the controversy that swirls around the band. I did not think the Stones would survive the publication of Keith's book. I was wrong.

On Jagger's solo career, see *Life* by Keith Richards; *Mick: The Wild Life and Mad Genius of Jagger* by Christopher Andersen; *A Prince Among Stones* by Prince Rupert Loewenstein; and *Stone Alone* by Bill Wyman. On Jagger's anatomy, see Marc Spitz's biography, *Jagger: Rebel, Rock Star, Rambler, Rogue*, in which Jerry Hall comes (sort of) to her ex-husband's defense: "Mick is very well endowed. Keith is just jealous."

On *Some Girls*, *Tattoo You*, and the question of the Stones' last great record, I relied on my own ears and horse sense, as well as on discussions with Chris Kimsey, a producer on those albums, and the opinions of some of the great record men I've interviewed over the years.

34 · ON AND OFF THE ROAD

In my mind, this chapter is a kind of "Where are they now?"—though pretty much everyone knows exactly where the Stones are now. I wanted to telescope the lives led by the members of the band in the years that came after their peak, years that, from a distance, look like a hangover. In this sense, the Stones song that best sums up their post-moment history is "Coming Down Again," released in 1973 on *Goats Head Soup*. The biographical information on each Stone comes from books, articles, and interviews. On Jagger, see *Mick Jagger* by Philip Norman; *Mick: The Wild Life and Mad Genius of Jagger* by Christopher Andersen; *A Prince Among Stones* by Prince Rupert Loewenstein; and *The Rolling Stones: Fifty Years* by Christopher Sandford. Also invaluable were my conversations with Jagger and other band members, as well as innumerable newspaper articles and magazine stories. See, for example, "Mick Jagger: Rock Memoirs a 'Glutted Market,'" Kevin Rutherford, January 22, 2014, *The Hollywood Reporter*, and "Self Satisfaction," a Jagger interview, *Esquire*, 1995.

On Charlie Watts, see my own interviews as well as "Brian Jones: The Bittersweet Symphony" by Rob Chapman, *Mojo*, July 1999; *Charlie Watts* by Alan Clayson; "Charlie Watts: The Rock" by Robert Sandall, *Mojo*, May 1994; *According to the Rolling Stones*. On Bill Wyman, see *According to the Rolling Stones*; *Stone Alone* by Bill Wyman; *Up and Down with the Rolling Stones* by Tony Sanchez. On Anita Pallenberg, see *Faithfull: An Autobiography* by Marianne Faithfull with David Dalton and *Life* by Keith Richards, as well as "Lady Rolling Stone," by Lynn Barber, *The Guardian*, February 23, 2008. On Scott Cantrell, see "The Death in South Salem," by Chet Flippo, *Rolling Stone*, September 6, 1979; *Keith Richards: A Rock 'n' Roll Life*, text by Bill Milkowski, edited by Valeria Manferto de Fabianis; *Life* by Keith Richards; "A Young Boy's Crush on Keith Richards' Mate Anita Ends in a Tragic Suicide," Cheryl McCall, *People*, August 13, 1979; and *Exile on Main Street* by Robert Greenfield. On Keith Richards, see *Keith: Standing in the Shadows* by Stanley Booth; *Life* by Keith Richards; "Raw, Raunchy and Middle-Aged; Rolling Stone Keith Richards at 45," Bob Spitz, *The New York Times Magazine*, June 4, 1989; *Ronnie* by Ron Wood; and *A Season in Hell with the Rolling Stones* by Robert Greenfield. On Richards's 1977 Toronto drug bust, see *On the Road with the Rolling Stones* by Chet Flippo and *Stone Alone* by Bill Wyman. On Richards in Connecticut and his life today, see "Keith Richards: A Pirate Looks at 70," by Stephen Rodrick, *Men's Journal*, July 2013, and "The Dish:

Keith Richards Seen in Ridgefield," *Greenwich Time*, October 26, 2013 ("Rolling Stones guitarist Keith Richards, who lives in Weston, was seen having lunch at Luc's Cafe & Restaurant in Ridgefield . . ."). In a Q&A on the *Esquire* magazine website ("Keith Richards Explains Why Sgt. Pepper Was Rubbish") he reacts to the news that José Feliciano lives in the same town:

Q: Do you know that José Feliciano lives in the same town as you in Connecticut?
A: I do know that, but I've never met him. We've never crossed paths, even though Weston is a very small town—there's a gas station and a market.
Q: So you're actually the second-best guitar player in Weston, Connecticut.
A: I'd go for that. He's a far better guitar player than me.

35 · THE HALL OF FAME *AND* AFTERWORD

Jann Wenner set me up at the Rock and Roll Hall of Fame, which meant free entry plus a kind of backstage tour, in which a guide in rubber gloves held certain holy relics before us. A shirt worn by Johnny Cash—it looked to be XXL—glasses worn by John Lennon, and the red baseball hat stuffed into the back pocket of Bruce Springsteen's Levi's on the cover of *Born in the USA*. As for the guitar lessons, they continue. I'm bad, but not as bad as I used to be.

INTERVIEW LIST

Though I've been working on this book in earnest for only the last few years, I consider it the product of a lifetime of study—the culmination of my love for and interest in the Rolling Stones that began when I was banned from my brother's room, reached a crescendo when, miraculously, I fell inside the speaker, turning up on the bus and plane and stage and wings and guitar rooms and hangouts and bars with the boys, and has continued through this long cool-down that has been my life. More than the Stones, it's been about rock 'n' roll, which is everything. I've listed the interviews that have formed the background and bedrock of this project—not just the people I have interviewed recently, though there were dozens, but those that I met in the course of my journalism and life who have filled me in and told me how things work. There are three questions a writer has to answer. What happened? That's the first, and the easiest. A lot of people can give you that. The others are more precious, strange. What did it feel like? What did it mean?

- Sam Cutler
- Clive Davis
- Mike "Eppy" Epstein
- Ahmet Ertegun
- David Evans, blues historian
- Marianne Faithfull
- David Geffen
- Gary Gersh
- Berry Gordy
- Sid Griffin
- Buddy Guy
- Robert Hiatt, Altamont medic
- Chas Hodges
- Mick Jagger
- Darryl Jones
- Paul Jones
- Norman Jopling
- Phil Kaufman
- Linda Keith
- Bobby Keys
- Chris Kimsey
- Tony King
- Al Kooper
- Bob Krasnow
- Chuck Leavell
- Gered Mankowitz
- John Mayall
- Albert Maysles
- Ian McLagan
- Mario Medious, A&R man

- Anna Menzies
- Robin Morgan
- Jerry Moss
- John Pasche
- Richard Perry
- Lloyd Price
- Sylvia Rhone
- Keith Richards
- Marlon Richards
- Julie Rifkind
- Ed Rosenblatt
- Ethan Russell
- Ronnie Schneider
- Rock Scully
- Neil Sedaka
- June Shelley
- Joe Smith
- Seymour Stein
- Gary Stromberg, rock 'n' roll PR man
- John Sykes
- Dick Taylor
- Art Teller
- Phil Walden
- Charlie Watts
- Jerry Weintraub
- Hy Weiss
- Jerry Wexler
- Fiona Williams, Stones stylist
- Ron Wood

BIBLIOGRAPHY

BOOKS

Altschuler, Glenn C. *All Shook Up: How Rock 'n' Roll Changed America.* Oxford, England: Oxford University Press, 2004.

Andersen, Christopher. *Mick: The Wild Life and Mad Genius of Jagger.* New York: Gallery, 2013.

Bangs, Lester. Edited by John Morthland. *Main Lines, Blood Feasts, and Bad Taste.* New York: Anchor, 2003.

———. Edited by Greil Marcus. *Psychotic Reactions and Carburetor Dung: The Work of a Legendary Critic; Rock 'n' Roll as Literature and Literature as Rock 'n' Roll.* New York: Anchor, 1998.

Barger, Ralph "Sonny," with Keith and Kent Zimmerman. *Hell's Angel: The Life and Times of Sonny Barger and the Hell's Angels Motorcycle Club.* New York: HarperCollins, 2001.

Beaton, Cecil. Edited by Richard Buckle. *Self-Portrait with Friends: The Selected Diaries of Cecil Beaton, 1922–1974.* New York: New York Times, 1982.

———. Philippe Garner, and David Mellor. *Cecil Beaton: Photographs 1920–1970.* Stewart Tabori & Chang, 1996.

Booth, Stanley. *Keith: Standing in the Shadows.* New York: St. Martin's, 1996.

———. *The True Adventures of the Rolling Stones.* Chicago: A Cappella, 2000.

Brody, Richard. *Everything Is Cinema: The Working Life of Jean-Luc Godard.* New York: Picador, 2009.

Brown, Phill. *Are We Still Rolling? Studios, Drugs and Rock 'n' Roll—One Man's Journey Recording Classic Albums.* Portland, OR: Tape Op Books, 2010.

Bulgakov, Mikhail. *The Master and Margarita.* New York: Penguin, 1997.

Burroughs, William S. *Naked Lunch.* New York: Grove, 2013.

Clayson, Alan. *Charlie Watts*. London: Sanctuary, 2004.

Cohen, Rich. *Monsters: The 1985 Chicago Bears and the Wild Heart of Football*. New York: Farrar, Straus and Giroux, 2013.

———. *The Record Men: Chess Records and the Birth of Rock & Roll*. New York: WW Norton, 2004.

Cohn, Nik. *Awopbopaloobop Alopbamboom: The Golden Age of Rock*. New York: Grove, 2001.

Cohodas, Nadine. *Spinning Blues into Gold: The Chess Brothers and the Legendary Chess Records*. New York: St. Martin's Press, 2000.

Cooper, Michael, with Terry Southern and Keith Richards. *The Early Stones*. New York: Hyperion, 1992.

Crowley, Aleister. *The Book of Lies*. New York: Samuel Weiser, 1987.

Cutler, Sam. *You Can't Always Get What You Want: My Life with the Rolling Stones, the Grateful Dead, and Other Wonderful Reprobates*. Toronto, ON: ECW, 2010.

Dawson, Julian, and Klaus Voormann. *And on Piano . . . Nicky Hopkins: The Extraordinary Life of Rock's Greatest Session Man*. Backstage Books/Plus One Press, 2011.

DeLillo, Don. *Great Jones Street*. New York: Penguin, 1994.

Dixon, Willie, with Don Snowden. *I Am the Blues: The Willie Dixon Story*. Cambridge, MA: Da Capo Press, 1990.

Draper, Robert. *Rolling Stone Magazine: The Uncensored History*. New York: HarperCollins, 1991.

Egan, Sean, ed. *Keith Richards on Keith Richards: Interviews and Encounters*. Chicago: A Cappella, 2013.

———. *The Mammoth Book of the Rolling Stones: An Anthology of the Best Writing About the Greatest Rock 'n' Roll Band in the World*. Philadelphia: Running Press, 2013.

Eisen, Jonathan, ed. *Altamont: Death of Innocence in the Woodstock Nation*. New York: Avon, 1970.

Elliott, Martin. *The Rolling Stones: Complete Recording Sessions 1962–2012, 50th Anniversary Edition*. London: Cherry Red Books, 2012.

Ells, Blake. *The Muscle Shoals Legacy of Fame*. Mount Pleasant, SC: Arcadia, 2015.

Faithfull, Marianne, with David Dalton. *Faithfull: An Autobiography*. New York: Cooper Square, 2000.

Flippo, Chet. *On the Road with the Rolling Stones: Twenty Years of Lipstick, Handcuffs, and Chemicals*. New York: Dolphin, 1985.

Fong-Torres, Ben. *Hickory Wind: The Life and Times of Gram Parsons*. New York: St. Martin's Griffin, 1998.

Fornatale, Peter, with Bernard M. Corbett. *50 Licks: Myths and Stories from Half a Century of the Rolling Stones.* London: Bloomsbury, 2013.

Goodman, Fred. *Allen Klein: The Man Who Bailed Out the Beatles, Made the Stones, and Transformed Rock & Roll.* New York: Houghton Mifflin, 2015.

Graham, Bill, with Robert Greenfield. *Bill Graham Presents: My Life Inside Rock and Out.* Boston: Da Capo, 2004.

Greenfield, Robert. *Exile on Main Street: A Season in Hell with the Rolling Stones.* Boston: Da Capo, 2006.

———. *S.T.P.: A Journey Through America with the Rolling Stones.* Boston: Da Capo, 2002.

———. *The Last Sultan: The Life and Times of Ahmet Ertegun.* New York: Simon & Schuster, 2010.

Guralnick, Peter. *Searching for Robert Johnson: The Life and Legend of the "King of the Delta Blues Singers."* New York: Plume, 1998.

Hajdu, David. *Heroes and Villains: Essays on Music, Movies, Comics, and Culture.* Boston: Da Capo, 2009.

Hartman, Kent. *The Wrecking Crew: The Inside Story of Rock and Roll's Best-Kept Secret.* New York: Thomas Dunne Books, 2012.

Heylin, Clinton. *The Penguin Book of Rock & Roll Writing.* London: Viking, 1992.

Hofmann, Albert. *LSD: My Problem Child; Reflections on Sacred Drugs, Mysticism and Science.* New York: McGraw-Hill, 1980.

Hotchner, A. E. *Blown Away: The Rolling Stones and the Death of the Sixties.* New York: Simon & Schuster, 1990.

Hutchison, Alice L. *Kenneth Anger.* London: Black Dog, 2011.

Jackson, Laura. *Golden Stone: The Untold Life and Tragic Death of Brian Jones.* New York: St. Martin's, 1992.

Jagger, Mick, with Keith Richards, Charlie Watts, and Ronnie Wood. Edited by Dora Loewenstein and Philip Dodd. *According to the Rolling Stones.* Boston: Chronicle, 2003.

Janovitz, Bill. *Exile on Main Street.* London: Bloomsbury, 2005.

———. *Rocks Off: 50 Tracks That Tell the Story of the Rolling Stones.* New York: St. Martin's, 2013.

Johns, Glyn. *Sound Man: A Life Recording Hits with the Rolling Stones, the Who, Led Zeppelin, the Eagles, Eric Clapton, the Faces. . . .* New York: Blue Rider, 2014.

Jopling, Norman. *Shake It Up Baby! Notes from a Pop Music Reporter 1961–1972.* London: Rock History, 2015.

Kael, Pauline. Edited by Sanford Schwartz. *The Age of Movies: Selected Writings of Pauline Kael.* New York: Library of America, 2011.

Kaiser, Charles. *1968 in America: Music, Politics, Chaos, Counterculture, and the Shaping of a Generation*. New York: Grove, 1997.

Kaufman, Phil, with Colin White. *Road Mangler Deluxe*. Glendale, CA: White-Boucke, 2001.

Kent, Nick. *The Dark Stuff: Selected Writings on Rock Music*. Boston: Da Capo, 1995.

Keys, Bobby, with Bill Ditenhafer. *Every Night's a Saturday Night: The Rock 'n' Roll Life of Legendary Sax Man Bobby Keys*. Berkeley, CA: Counterpoint, 2013.

Kirkpatrick, Rob. *1969: The Year Everything Changed*. New York: Skyhorse, 2011.

Kooper, Al. *Backstage Passes & Backstabbing Bastards: Memoirs of a Rock 'n' Roll Survivor*. Milwaukee: Hal Leonard, 2008.

Kubernik, Harvey. *Canyon of Dreams: The Magic and the Music of Laurel Canyon*. New York: Sterling, 2009.

Kurlansky, Mark. *1968: The Year That Rocked the World*. New York: Random House, 2005.

Landis, Bill. *Anger: The Unauthorized Biography of Kenneth Anger*. New York: HarperCollins, 1995.

Lee, Martin A., and Bruce Shlain. *Acid Dreams: The Complete Social History of LSD; The CIA, the Sixties, and Beyond*. New York: Grove, 1994.

Lewisohn, Mark. *Tune In: The Beatles; All These Years*. New York: Crown, 2013.

Loewenstein, Prince Rupert. *A Prince Among Stones: That Business with the Rolling Stones and Other Adventures*. New York: Bloomsbury, 2013.

Mankowitz, Gered. *The Stones: 65–67*. London: Vision On, 2002.

Marion, Larry. *The Lost Rolling Stones Photographs: The Bob Bonis Archive, 1964–1966*. London: It, 2010.

Marshall, Jim, with Keith Richards. *The Rolling Stones 1972: Photographs*. San Francisco: Chronicle Books, 2012.

Masouri, John. *Steppin' Razor: The Life of Peter Tosh*. London: Omnibus, 2013.

McDevitt, Chas. *Skiffle: The Definitive Inside Story*. London: Robson, 1997.

McMillian, John. *Beatles vs. Stones*. New York: Simon & Schuster, 2014.

Meyer, David N. *Twenty Thousand Roads: The Ballad of Gram Parsons and His Cosmic American Music*. New York: Villard, 2008.

Milkowski, Bill. Edited by Valeria Manferto de Fabianis. *Keith Richards: A Rock 'n' Roll Life*. New York: White Star, 2012.

Millard, André, ed. *The Electric Guitar: A History of an American Icon*. Baltimore: Johns Hopkins University Press, 2004.

Morgan, Robin, and Ariel Leve. *1963: The Year of the Revolution; How Youth Changed the World with Music, Art, and Fashion*. New York: Dey Street, 2014.

Norman, Philip. *John Lennon: The Life*. New York: Ecco, 2009.

———. *Mick Jagger*. New York: Ecco, 2012.

———. *Shout! The Beatles in Their Generation*. New York: Touchstone, 2005.

Oldham, Andrew Loog. *Stoned: A Memoir of London in the 1960s*. New York: Vintage, 2001.

———. *2Stoned*. New York: Vintage, 2003.

Oliver, Paul. *Blues Fell This Morning: Meaning in the Blues*. Cambridge, England: Cambridge University Press, 1990.

Pacyga, Dominic A. *Chicago: A Biography*. Chicago: University of Chicago Press, 2009.

Palmer, Robert. *Deep Blues: A Musical and Cultural History of the Mississippi Delta*. New York: Penguin, 1982.

———. *Rock & Roll: An Unruly History*. New York: Harmony, 1995.

———. *The Rolling Stones*. New York: Doubleday, 1984.

Phelge, James. *Nankering with the Rolling Stones: The Untold Story of the Early Days*. Chicago: A Cappella, 1998.

Rawlings, Terry. *Brian Jones: Who Killed Christopher Robin? The Murder of a Rolling Stone*. London: Helter Skelter, 2004.

Richards, Keith. *Life*. New York: Little, Brown, 2010.

Russell, Ethan A., with Gerard Van der Leun. *Let It Bleed: The Rolling Stones, Altamont, and the End of the Sixties*. New York: Grand Central Publishing, 2009.

Sanchez, Tony. *Up and Down with the Rolling Stones: My Rollercoaster Ride with Keith Richards*. London: John Blake, 2010.

Sandford, Christopher. *The Rolling Stones: Fifty Years*. London: Simon & Schuster, 2012.

Shelley, June. *Even When It Was Bad It Was Good*. Bloomington, IN: Xlibris, 2001 (self-published).

Spitz, Bob. *The Beatles: The Biography*. New York: Back Bay, 2006.

Spitz, Marc. *Jagger: Rebel, Rock Star, Rambler, Rogue*. New York: Gotham, 2012.

Sullivan, John Jeremiah. *Pulphead: Essays*. New York: Farrar, Straus & Giroux, 2011.

Sutin, Lawrence. *Do What Thou Wilt: A Life of Aleister Crowley*. New York: St. Martin's, 2002.

Thompson, Hunter S. *Fear and Loathing in Las Vegas: A Savage Journey to the Heart of the American Dream*. New York: Vintage, 1998.

———. *Hell's Angels: A Strange and Terrible Saga*. New York: Ballantine, 1996.

Tosches, Nick. *Country: The Twisted Roots of Rock 'n' Roll*. Boston: Da Capo, 1996.

Townshend, Pete. *Who I Am: A Memoir*. New York: Harper Perennial, 2013.

Trow, George W. S. *My Pilgrim's Progress: Media Studies, 1950–1998*. New York: Vintage, 2000.

———. *Within the Context of No Context*. New York: Atlantic Monthly, 1997.

Trynka, Paul. *Brian Jones: The Making of the Rolling Stones*. New York: Viking, 2014.

Waksman, Steve. *Instruments of Desire: The Electric Guitar and the Shaping of Musical Experience*. Boston: Harvard University Press, 2001.

Wald, Elijah. *The Blues: A Very Short Introduction*. Oxford, England: Oxford University Press, 2010.

———. *Escaping the Delta: Robert Johnson and the Invention of the Blues*. New York: HarperCollins, 2004.

Walker, Michael. *Laurel Canyon: The Inside Story of Rock-and-Roll's Legendary Neighborhood*. London: Faber & Faber, 2006.

West, Jessica Pallington. *What Would Keith Richards Do? Daily Affirmations from a Rock and Roll Survivor*. New York: Bloomsbury, 2009.

White, Timothy. *Catch a Fire: The Life of Bob Marley*. New York: Henry Holt, 2006.

Whitley, Carla Jean. *Muscle Shoals Sound Studio: How the Swampers Changed American Music*. Charleston, SC: History Press, 2014.

Wolfe, Tom. *The Kandy-Kolored Tangerine-Flake Streamline Baby*. New York: Picador, 2009.

Wood, Jo. *It's Only Rock 'n' Roll: Thirty Years Married to a Rolling Stone*. London: It, 2013.

Wood, Ron. *Ronnie: The Autobiography*. New York: St. Martin's, 2007.

Wyman, Bill. *Bill Wyman's Scrapbook*. London: Concert Live, 2013.

———. *Stone Alone: The Story of a Rock 'n' Roll Band*. Boston: Da Capo, 1997.

SELECTED NEWS ACCOUNTS

Associated Press. "Brian Jones Dies; Found in His Pool." *New York Times*, July 3, 1969.

Barber, Lynn. "Lady Rolling Stone." *The Guardian*, February 23, 2008.

Black, Johnny. "The Greatest (Pop TV) Show on Earth: The T.A.M.I. Show, October 1964." *Rock's Backpages*, March 2010.

Chapman, Rob. "Brian Jones: The Bittersweet Symphony." *Mojo*, July 1999.

Chicago Defender. "The Low Down." October 16, 1965. (Muddy Waters on the Rolling Stones.)

Chicago Defender. "Rock 'n' Roll and Crime." June 25, 1958.

Chicago Defender. "When You Come North." May 30, 1925. (Advice for the Great Migration.)

Cohen, Rich. "Keith Richards Delivers a Classic Rock Memoir." *Rolling Stone*, October 25, 2010.

———. "Marianne Faithfull's Gloriously Reckless Rock 'n' Roll Life." *The Wall Street Journal Magazine*, September 4, 2014.

———. "The Rolling Stones: It's Show Time." *Rolling Stone*, August 25, 1994.

———. "Tour de Force: The Rolling Stones Rake It In and Rock the House." *Rolling Stone*, November 3, 1994.

Eggar, Robin. "Rolling Stone in Exile." *The Sunday Express Magazine*, May 2002. (Interview with Mick Taylor.)

Flippo, Chet. "The Death in South Salem." *Rolling Stone*, September 6, 1979.

Greenwich Time. "The Dish: Keith Richards Seen in Ridgefield." October 26, 2013.

McCall, Cheryl. "A Young Boy's Crush on Keith Richards' Mate Anita Ends in a Tragic Suicide." *People*, August 13, 1979.

Needs, Kris. "No One Shot KR: Keith Richards 1980." *Zigzag*, November 1980.

Nizza, Mike. "Hell's Angels Plotted to Kill Mick Jagger, Agent Says." *New York Times*, March 3, 2008.

Norman, Tony. "Mick Taylor Interviewed." *Fusion*, November 14, 1969.

Obrecht, Jas. "The Keith Richards Interview." *Guitar Player*, 1992.

Robbins, Ira. "Stone Wino Rhythm Guitar God Keith Richards Can Still Rip It Up!" *Pulse!* November 1992.

Rooney, Frank. "Cyclists' Raid: A Story." *Harper's*, January 1951.

Sandall, Robert. "Charlie Watts: The Rock," *Mojo*, May 1994.

Schoemer, Karen. "Keith Richards: Stones Icon, Rock Survivor." *New York Times*, October 18, 1992.

Sheff, David. "John Lennon and Yoko Ono: The *Playboy* Interview." *Playboy*, September 1980.

Smith, Patti. "Jag-arr of the Jungle." *Creem*, January 1973.

Snowden, Don. "Chess Studios: Notes for the Rock & Roll Hall of Fame." Cleveland: Rock and Roll Hall of Fame, 1987.

Spitz, Bob. "Raw, Raunchy and Middle-Aged; Rolling Stone Keith Richards at 45." *The New York Times Magazine*, June 4, 1989.

Susman, Gary. "Beggars Banquet." *EW.com*, December 12, 2003.

Trow, George W. S. "Eclectic, Reminiscent, Amused, Fickle, Perverse." *The New Yorker*, May 29 and June 5, 1978.

Wenner, Jann. "John Lennon, the Rolling Stone Interview." *Rolling Stone*, January 21, 1971.

Wild, David. "Blood Brothers." *Rolling Stone*, May 21, 2007.

FILMS

Charlie Is My Darling. Directed by Peter Whitehead, 1966.

From the Vault: Hyde Park 1969. Directed by Leslie Woodhead, 1969.

From the Vault: The Marquee Club Live in 1971. Directed by the Rolling Stones, 1971.

Gimme Shelter: The Rolling Stones. Directed by Albert Maysles, David Maysles, and Charlotte Zwerin, 1970.

Ladies & Gentlemen: The Rolling Stones. Directed by Rollin Binzer, 1974.

Let's Spend the Night Together: The Stones in Concert. Directed by Hal Ashby, 1983.

Muddy Waters and the Rolling Stones: Live at the Checkerboard Lounge, Chicago 1981. Directed by Muddy Waters and the Rolling Stones, 2012.

Ned Kelly. Directed by Tony Richardson, 1970.

One Plus One. Directed by Jean-Luc Godard, 1969.

Performance. Directed by Donald Cammell and Nicolas Roeg, 1970.

The Rolling Stones: All 6 Ed Sullivan Shows. 2011.

The Rolling Stones: Crossfire Hurricane. Directed by Brett Morgen, 2013.

The Rolling Stones—Rock and Roll Circus. Directed by Michael Lindsay-Hogg, 1996.

Rolling Stones—1969–1974: The Mick Taylor Years. Directed by Tom O'Dell, 2010.

Shine a Light: The Rolling Stones in Concert. Directed by Martin Scorsese, 2008.

Some Girls: The Rolling Stones Live in Texas. Directed by the Rolling Stones, 2011.

Stones In Exile. Directed by Stephen Kijak, 2013.

Sweet Summer Sun: Hyde Park Live. Directed by the Rolling Stones, 2013.

The T.A.M.I. Show, 1964. Directed by Steve Binder, 2010.

LIST OF ILLUSTRATIONS

INDEX

ABOUT THE AUTHOR

RICH COHEN is the author of the *New York Times* bestsellers *Tough Jews, The Avengers, Monsters,* and (with Jerry Weintraub) *When I Stop Talking, You'll Know I'm Dead.* He is the co-creator of the HBO series *Vinyl* and a contributing editor at *Vanity Fair* and *Rolling Stone,* and has written for *The New Yorker, The Atlantic,* and *Harper's Magazine,* among others. Cohen has won the Great Lakes Book Award, the Chicago Public Library's 21st Century Award, and the ASCAP Deems Taylor Award for outstanding coverage of music. His stories have been included in *The Best American Essays* and *The Best American Travel Writing.* He lives in Connecticut.

ABOUT THE TYPE

This book was set in Jenson, one of the earliest print type-
faces. After hearing of the invention of printing in 1458,
Charles VII of France sent coin engraver Nicolas Jenson
(c. 1420–80) to study this new art. Not long afterward, Jenson started a new career in Venice in letter-founding and
printing. In 1471, Jenson was the first to present the form
and proportion of this roman font that bears his name.

More than five centuries later, Robert Slimbach, devel-
oping fonts for the Adobe Originals program, created
Adobe Jenson based on Nicolas Jenson's Venetian Renaissance typeface. It is a dignified font with graceful and bal-
anced strokes.